MICRO-THEORY
AND
ECONOMIC CHOICES

The Irwin Series in Economics

Consulting Editor   **Lloyd G. Reynolds**   Yale University

MICRO-THEORY AND ECONOMIC CHOICES

R. Stephen Polkinghorn
California State University, Sacramento

1979

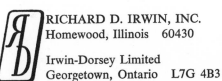

RICHARD D. IRWIN, INC.
Homewood, Illinois   60430

Irwin-Dorsey Limited
Georgetown, Ontario   L7G 4B3

© RICHARD D. IRWIN, INC., 1979

ISBN 0-256-02143-0
Library of Congress Catalog Card No. 78–70950
Printed in the United States of America

1 2 3 4 5 6 7 8 9 0 K 6 5 4 3 2 1 0 9

Preface

This is an economic theory book. It describes theory as a way of looking at events that permits an economist to predict some of those events before they happen. Thus theory is a way of looking at reality but it is not a description of reality. It is an abstract, simple, and sometimes unrealistic picture of reality. Its simplicity and logical elegance give it a charm of its own. I am convinced that undergraduate students can see and appreciate that charm. They need only see theory for what it is; a carefully designed, insidiously clever, pair of glasses through which economists look at a complex, confusing world.

However, abstract, unrealistic, or charming economic theory may get, it never escapes from reality. Its function is to predict real events and it must succeed to survive. This book contains a number of examples of the application of theory to the prediction of events. That number could be readily expanded at the expense of a longer book. I hope that in the end students will understand that the test of this theory is in its application to real problems. The proof of this pudding is in the eating even when the pudding appears to be half baked.

In describing the economic theory of choice, this book stresses the axioms and the deductive techniques that lead to prediction. A modern and rigorous presentation would use mathematics. This book sticks to simple geometry. The student will discover that geometry can be used to reveal the implications of most of the concepts that are important at this level. Moreover, I have tried to make the analysis as logical and precise as words and diagrams permit.

Economic predictions are deduced from a model of the way in which individuals choose among the alternatives open to them. Thus, economic theory as presented in this book is a theory of choice. This emphasis makes economics a theory of human behavior, a social science. Using this framework we can discuss production, firms, prices, and all of the usual topics of an intermediate microtheory course. We can also analyze a number of problems that involve choice but would not otherwise be seen as "economic." Though this book does not discuss the economics of marriage, or divorce, or suicide, or crime, for example, it is important for students to realize that much can be added to our understanding of these topics once the particular perspective of the economist is well understood.

Like anyone else who has ever written a book of this type I owe thanks to many people. I shall not be able to list them all, but my biggest debt is to the shockingly blank faces of the students who did not understand my early attempts to explain theory. They forced upon me a process of continuous revision over many years. I am also especially indebted to the University of Cape Coast in Ghana where I taught for two years and found time to complete the first draft. While there I had the opportunity to go through that first draft with V. K. Bhasin, a very competent young Indian economist whose comments occasioned a number of appropriate revisions. Thanks are also due to a graduate student, Madeline Ransom, who devoted much of her time to pointing out my mistakes. My family has been very patient with my endless talk about "the book" and this is specially true of my wife Bette, who is an economist in her own right and will probably write a better book. Finally I sincerely give my thanks to the two literary critics who typed my manuscript and its continuous revisions, Julia Ghormley and Paulette Gray.

January 1979   **R. Stephen Polkinghorn**

Contents

Contents

PART III
PRODUCTION

PART V
WELFARE

PART I

INTRODUCTION

Chapter 1

Economic theory

A THEORY OF HUMAN BEHAVIOR

To be alive is to be doing things. The things we do seem to each of us to be done for a reason. We usually think we have a plan that makes our actions seem reasonable. The plan is usually so obvious to us that we are bewildered when friends seem uncertain about what we will do next.

On the other hand, the things other people do are much harder to understand and anticipate. We often say in exasperation that other people are irrational or lack common sense or are too emotional. The exasperation arises because they do things we did not expect. "For reasons too obvious to need elaboration," we want to know what to expect of other people's behavior. We want to be able to predict human behavior. Economics is a science of human behavior, and economic theory, a technique for making predictions about it.

You may feel the last sentence is doubtful. Is economics really a study of human behavior? The answer must clearly be yes, and the tone and direction of current theory place particular emphasis on behavior. In an article with the improbable title, "A Theory of Marriage," the economist Gary Becker notes that,

> In recent years economists have used economic theory more boldly to explain behavior outside the monetary market sector. . . . As a result, racial discrimination, fertility, politics, crime, education, statistical decision making, adversary situations, labor force participation, the uses of leisure time and other behavior are much better understood. Indeed, eco-

3

nomic theory may be well on its way to providing a unified framework for all behavior involving scarce resources.[1]

If one needs an example, one can look at a recent economic study of suicide.[2] This study does not suggest that psychological and social factors are unimportant, but it does reveal some interesting things about economic factors. For instance, the data suggest that suicide rates fluctuate with the business cycle, rising as unemployment rises. Not surprisingly, the suicide rate is more sensitive to the unemployment rate among older people. Less obviously, the suicide rate does not seem to be sensitive to the seriousness of a recession. Mild postwar recessions seem to have produced increases in the suicide rate that are similar in size to those produced by the big depressions of the prewar period. Finally, it appears that suicide rates decline as income rises (for all but the youngest age groups). This conclusion applies to a comparison of rich and poor at a particular point in time, and it also appears that suicide rates decline as a whole society becomes richer over time.

Work that is being done with problems like suicide, and others mentioned above, make older definitions of economics seem dated. Definitions that describe economics as a theory of price or value, or as a theory of the firm or as an analysis of the creation and distribution of wealth suggest topics that are still very important in economics. They are nevertheless too narrow. In this book we will stress choosing among alternatives as the particular human behavior that ties the new and diverse areas of study together with the usual subject matters of microeconomic theory.

DO ECONOMISTS REALLY KNOW ANYTHING?

What does it mean when an economist says, "We know a lot about behavior"? It means, as we have implied above, that he can predict what people will do in certain circumstances. "Knowing" is sometimes defined in other ways, but to define it as the power to predict is to define it in a scientific way. This is the kind of definition we want to use when talking about economic theory. It also suggests the kind of test we will use when we want to answer the question, "Do economists really know anything?" We will look to see if their predictions come true.

Economic predictions about human behavior are called laws, or generalizations, or propositions. Each one states what will happen under a particular set of circumstances. The law must specify the circumstances and set forth the event that will follow. A whole set of related

---

[1] Gary S. Becker, "A Theory of Marriage, Part I" *Journal of Political Economy,* vol. 81 (1973), pp. 813–14.

[2] Daniel S. Hamermesh and Neal M. Soss, "An Economic Theory of Suicide," *Journal of Political Economy,* vol. 82, no. 1 (January–February 1974), p. 83.

laws or generalizations can be called a theory or a model. Thus economic theory is an elaborate model of human behavior that includes many specific propositions. It is only one among a number of scientific models of behavior, and these coexist with many nonscientific models. It is worth noting that wherever several scientific models deal with the *same* events, the existence of several models means that our explanations are not very successful; not yet so successful that we have *an* explanation of those events.

How good *is* economic theory? The answer is not likely to appear in the first chapter, but you will discover that it is common even among economists to "poor-mouth" economic theory. It is said to be a set of relatively useless propositions; propositions that are too abstract and unrealistic; propositions that were only true during some historical period now past, and so on. These views are also very common among college sophomores, reluctantly beginning their first serious course in economic theory. Strangely enough, it is not uncommon to hear economics also described as the most advanced of the social sciences. If both these judgments are correct, other social sciences are surely in trouble. I personally reject the first. It seems to me that we need not judge economics so harshly. Perhaps the basis of this opinion will become clear by the end of this book.

THEORY AND REALITY

Instead of now answering the question, "How good is our theory?" we might ask: "If it is not good enough, what can one do about it?" Can we just set it aside and look at reality afresh, dealing with it directly, finding out what it is really like? The answer is unequivocally NO! We must "see" reality as the pictures our brain creates out of the information it gets through our senses. We are always one step removed from reality by our mental processes.

Furthermore, the brain is not a passive recorder of sense data. It cannot be passive even if we should want it to be. It is bombarded by an overwhelming number of observations. The moment we awake (and even as we dream) a torrent of sense impressions flow into the brain. Look around the room you are now in and see how much your brain could record if it took account of everything your eye can see. Obviously your brain will have to sort and organize very quickly or it will drown in the stream of impressions and you will feel dizzy and confused.

"Organize" is probably not the right word. "Evaluate" is better. Each of us has a model of reality that enables the brain to evaluate what the eye sees. The process is so quick and automatic that we do not "see" some things, presumably unimportant things, even when our eye rests on them. The model also tells us what is important and concentrates our attention there. Someone else with a different model will see what we do not and tell us we are insensitive clods. One thing is clear. We never operate without a model. We cannot operate without a model. We cannot start all over and build a new model freshly from raw data. There is too much raw data for us to comprehend. We must direct our attention only to those events we believe to be most important. What we believe is important determines the character of our model.

That means, of course, that in this book we will ask, "Is the economic model, the economic way, a good way to look at reality?" Peter Newman has said, "We can only hope to observe phenomena *systematically* if we have a set of instructions that tell us what to look for. Different sets are different theories; some ways of looking at reality are useful and fruitful, others are not."[3]

WHAT IS A MODEL?

Model builders make certain assumptions and then, by deduction, reach the conclusions that are the laws or generalizations of the science. For instance, an economist may assume that individuals can always tell which of two alternatives they prefer. Such an assumption, like the postulates of geometry, is often very unrealistic. It cannot usually be derived in a simple direct way from experience. It is not clear how assumptions are discovered (or invented, perhaps?). We are tempted to describe a very useful assumption as a brilliant insight, with the intent to imply that a mind with some superior sensitivity was involved; that it is somewhat beyond the ken of most of us to have such insights. One thing is clear. There is no set of rules for making observations and then setting forth the assumptions that will be useful in explaining them.

No matter how unrealistic the assumption, if it works well we are likely to *think* of it as realistic. Thus we warp our observations of reality to fit our model of it. So it was that at one time we had little trouble thinking of the world as if it was really like Euclid's geometry: all lines and points and circles and triangles. On the other hand, if the assumption is not so useful, we have the feeling it would work better if it could be replaced by one that was more realistic. Actually we should recognize that realism is not a necessary attribute of useful assumptions and that useful assumptions are not likely to give us realistic pictures of the world, no matter how well they work.

We get from assumptions to the laws and propositions of economic theory by using deductive logic. Logic is an elaborate set of rules for making inferences. They have evolved as an essential part of our way of thinking. It is invidious in our society to be called illogical. Science is

---

[3] Peter Newman, *The Theory of Exchange* (Englewood Cliffs, N.J.: Prentice-Hall, 1965), p. 1.

logical, and a significant part of the exposition of economic theory is concerned with logic. In fact, most economists spend their time finding logical error or extending theory logically to new conclusions and, of course, testing the laws against reality). Only occasionally is someone clever enough to suggest a new assumption that turns out to be useful.

The propositions that are logically deduced from the assumptions have two parts. They set forth certain circumstances and then predict the event that will occur under those circumstances. The circumstances are supposed to be only those that are necessary and sufficient to the event that follows. The propositions are implied by the assumptions; they are imbedded in the assumptions and are drawn out by deductive logic. The assumptions can be unrealistic, but there is a sense in which the propositions may not be. It *must* be possible for reality to refute them. In economic science as in any other, the proof of the pudding is in the eating, no matter that it may appear to be only half baked. If propositions are formed in such a way that they cannot be refuted by some empirical test, they have no place in science. If they are tested and refuted, they will be dropped from science. Thus a science will consist only of those propositions that have been tested and have not yet been refuted.

EXPERIMENTS

Faced with a new proposition, the scientist will try to design the "crucial experiment," the experiment in which variables are controlled in such a way that all of the necessary circumstances are met and the predicted event observed. Sometimes this is fairly easy to do in a laboratory. There, the variables may be so obviously under control that most scientists will quickly agree to accept the outcome of the experiment. Sometimes even in a physics laboratory control is very, very difficult. Scientists will be slow to accept the results. The experiment may have to be repeated many times by many people before the result is accepted.

Experiments in economics and other social sciences cannot usually be made in the laboratory at all. Our experiments are "tossed up" by the flow of events. We can treat the 1929 depression as an experimental test of a macroeconomic theory. We take one of our propositions and ask whether, and to what extent, the necessary circumstances were met during that depression and whether the predicted event occurred. The crucial variables are usually not so obviously controlled that agreement about the outcome of the experiment is quick and easy. Thus experiments in social science are less effective at refuting false propositions. Falsehoods linger; they die only after repeated experimental assault.

Now if all this makes economic theory seem to be a high-risk field, recall that we cannot live without theory even if we want to. We can only try to be conscious of our theory; to ask what assumptions it makes, how well its propositions have been tested, whether its logic is valid. Much of the study of economic theory is the development of this consciousness.

MODERN ECONOMIC MODELS

Perhaps it will help to begin the discussion of microeconomic theory with a description of some of its general characteristics. Later we will ensure that the theory has these characteristics by making certain explicit assumptions.

Scarcity. "Economic" implies scarce. It is scarcity that forces us to economize. The scarcity assumption in our theory really seems to involve ". . . in some way, simple and indisputable facts from experience."[4] In spite of affluence, scarcity of goods is still very real in our lives. If one thinks only of goods, one may begin to dream of satiation and an end to the spectre of scarcity, but both scarcity and economics extend beyond material goods. As long as death must come, and as certainly as "desire is the opposite of death," we must deal with scarcity. The economist Frank Knight argued years ago that goods tend to confuse us about our motives.[5] We think of ourselves as wanting things and directing our actions toward getting them. What we really want, however, is experience—the experience of wanting and getting and using something and then of learning to want something else. Thus, as long as life is finite, time at least will always be scarce and must certainly be economized.

Time and things are scarce only in relation to their uses. It is obvious that most of us have a multitude of things to do with our time each day. When we choose to do one thing, we are choosing not to do something else. The value of that something else is the cost of the thing we chose to do. Something that is scarce will always have a cost. Fresh eggs are scarce every day and we must pay a price if we want them. Rotten eggs, which exist in much smaller quantities, are nevertheless plentiful rather than scarce because they have no uses.

Choice. Things that have many uses (including things like time) force us to make choices. To face scarcity is to face the necessity for choice. Economists have always recognized that they were concerned with choice, but in the last few years we have become very conscious of this aspect of theory. We now describe micro-theory as a branch of the theory of choice, and we make less use of the old titles like "The

---

[4] Lionel Robbins, *An Essay on the Nature and Significance of Economic Science* (New York: Macmillan, 1935), pp. 78–79.

[5] Frank H. Knight, *Risk, Uncertainty and Profit* (Boston: Houghton-Mifflin, 1921; reprinted by the London School of Economics, 1948), chapter 3, pp. 53–54.

Theory of Price," or "The Theory of the Firm." In fact, there is some tendency to see economics as *the* theory of choice and to apply its models to areas well outside the usual domain of economics. The important thing here is the emphasis this places on behavior and economic theory as a theory of behavior. It is a shift from production and resources and material well-being to human actions and decision processes and schemes of organization.

Optimizing. The most powerful notion the economist has ever had is the notion that he should treat behavior as if choosing meant optimizing.[6] Optimizing behavior can be observed in the real world. We sometimes try "to get the most for the money" or the most profit from a business. We try to maximize, subject to some constraint like income or input prices, but this model is more general than these examples suggest.

Even criminal activities may be better understood if it is assumed that criminals are trying to maximize. A recent study suggests for instance that the incidence of specific crimes is positively related to estimated relative gains and negatively related to estimates of relative costs.[7] Thus the incidence of a crime like robbery may be expected to rise if the average take increases or if the probability of arrest and/or conviction falls. This study also suggests that the characteristics of individual offenders may be partly explained by reference to their legitimate and illigitimate employment opportunities. Thus young males with little schooling may turn to crime simply because it promises a higher standard of living even when the prospects for arrest and conviction are included as costs. Finally, it seems likely that effective law enforcement pays, if for no other reason, simply because it increases the cost of crime and thus makes it less profitable.

It is probably a mistake to see the optimizing notion as rising out of "simple and indisputable facts from experience." The optimizing assumption is too sweeping and observable phenomena provide too many exceptions. It nevertheless characterizes the economic approach to reality and any situation in which optimizing models seem to work is likely to be called economic. The notion tends to define the boundary of the discipline.

Preferences. Optimizing choice implies the existence of preference patterns. "Preference pattern" is a name for the set of tastes and value

---

[6] In economics the terms "optimize" and "maximize" are both used. Their meanings are virtually the same. It is conventional, however, to use maximize when the behavior of an individual unit is being considered. We say the firm maximizes profits. On the other hand, if the problem is being considered from a social point of view, then optimize is likely to be used. For instance, we may analyze the conditions for an optimum allocation of resources.

[7] Isaac Ehrlich, "Participation in Illegitimate Activities: A Theoretical and Empirical Investigation," *Journal of Political Economy,* vol. 81, no. 3 (May–June 1973), pp. 521–65.

judgments that are used to compare alternatives and rank them from most preferred to least preferred. Optimizing choices clearly require such a ranking. Western economists generally impose a special condition on preference patterns. They insist that *individual* preference patterns "ought" to be primary in our theory.[8] In other words, we believe that we ought to have an economic system that permits individual people to make choices in the light of their own tastes and preferences.

We can postpone until later the study of the nature of private preference patterns. However, we can observe at this point that the "ought" in the sentence above makes that sentence a statement about values. It is not a "fact from experience" nor an economic law. It is, instead, a statement about what we think ought to be considered important.

Once having accepted that value statement, western economists have spent much of their time in the analysis of the way in which markets reconcile the preferences of many individuals. They have not, on the other hand, spent as much time analyzing the way in which a central planning commission can get production and consumption to conform to its *own* goals or preferences. This value judgment is very old in economics, but still very important. It has a major impact on the selection of topics in a micro-economic theory course and, hence, in this book.

Money.   Money is a "measuring rod." Economists could not have gone so far had they not had money to use. Prices and incomes measured in money make our propositions about reality testable. We, more than any other social science, are enabled to reject false propositions by reference to empirical observations, observations of money prices and money incomes. The political scientist may find the concept of power is as potentially useful as optimization is to the economist, but he has never been able to measure its effects as successfully.

The awareness of scarcity, the assumption of optimizing choice, the use of money to measure and the primacy of individual preference; these seem to characterize modern microeconomic theory. Perhaps the list should be longer, but these items at least should be on it.

THE ECONOMIC SYSTEM

The economic system is not economic theory. Theory purports to explain the working of the system. We may say that the system is a complex of institutions, laws, customs, and habits that constrain in one way or another human behavior. But then one must ask, "Which institutions, which laws, which habits and customs are economic?" The system can-

---

[8] This is not to say that preferences arising out of political processes are excluded. We have a navy, though battleships probably do not rank very high in an individual preference pattern. The question is one of emphasis, and in a western economy the emphasis on private preferences is very great.

not answer. Real events do not come with labels; men must attach them. It is thus most likely that the economic system will include those areas of human behavior that economic theory can explain. Theory draws boundaries around the system. This is not an especially attractive conclusion. We want the economic system to be a structure that economic theory tries to explain. Instead, the system threatens to become only those structures that theory *can* explain.

A more satisfactory approach suggests that we ought not to be very precise in our definition of the system. We certainly ought not to let a definition inhibit us from looking at some phenomenon not currently defined as important by our theory. Instead we ought to see the economic system as a rather large range of phenomena that might conceivably be explained by theory now or later. This attitude will enable us to explore the boundaries easily for ways to extend or make more powerful the predictions of theory.

In dealing with the economic system, economic theory has always taken the position that the system is "machinelike." Our explanations assume that its parts are related to each other in mechanical ways. Predictions can be made in the same way that one could, in physics, analyze the work done by a series of levers. There is a considerable hazard in taking this view. Perhaps the system is more like an organism than a machine. Maybe it flows and adapts over time so that outcomes are not mechanically related to beginnings. This was one of the major criticisms of economic theory made by Thorstein Veblen before 1900 and followed by many later critics.[9] The criticism is undoubtedly legitimate. It is not hard to find examples of growth, change, and adaptation. Certainly the shift in the structure of the dominant firm from the small single proprietorship to the large corporation suggests that mechanical theories would have to be continually revised. What we need is a model that includes laws of growth and adaptation as internal parts of theory.

We do not have one, however, because organic models are so very much more complex. Ironically, even biologists have found it overwhelmingly difficult to develop organic instead of mechanical models of the phenomena they study. Add to this the fact that the mathematics, meaning the logic of mechanical models, has been well developed for a very long time because of its application in physics. These provide two good reasons for our backwardness. Lest we feel too depressed by ignorance, we can remember that organic change is not usually an important factor in short-run problems. Most economic problems are short-run in this sense.

---

[9] Thorstein Veblen, "Why is Economics Not an Evolutionary Science?" *Quarterly Journal of Economics* (July 1898), pp. 373–91; reprinted in Thorstein Veblen, *The Place of Science in Modern Civilization* (New York: B. W. Huebsch, 1919).

POSITIVE AND NORMATIVE ECONOMICS

When we refer to the propositions of economic theory we sometimes use the term "positive economics." Positive economics suggests immediately the possibility of its opposite, normative economics. The distinction is worth making because any proposition of positive economics is open to normative interpretation. For instance, the positive statement —that under competition everyone pays the same price for the same good in a single market—easily becomes the normative statement— that everyone ought to pay the same price. This in turn implies the value judgment, that competition is a good thing because it ensures a single price.

It may help in making the distinction to define normative economics as the analysis of the implications of some specific value judgment. For instance, we might analyze the effect on welfare of a policy of having a minimum wage. A value judgment is made that no one "ought" to be paid less than $2.65 per hour. The analysis would also require some additional value judgments about welfare—for instance, about the relative merits of different distributions of income. Quite obviously this analysis will lean very heavily on positive economics; that is, on a model of the way things work. For instance, we will have to predict the effect of a minimum wage on employment. Normative economics is not possible without positive economics.

Thus we might say that positive economics is concerned with *what is* and how it works, and normative economics with *what ought to be*. This is not a bad way to put the matter. It does not, however, imply that positive economics itself is completely value-free. Such is not the case. In the first place, positive economics tries to be a science and it is, therefore, committed to all of those value judgments that are a part of the scientific view of reality. This is not the place for a discussion of the philosophy of science, but there are many good discussions available and one of them ought to be explored.[10]

Another kind of value judgment is built into positive economics simply because we cannot study everything. Reality is so complex that we cannot make a blueprint. All of our positive economic theories leave some things out. We try to include what we think is important, but deciding what is important requires a value judgment. We could add many more examples of value judgments imbedded in economic theory. Perhaps these are enough to make the point.

It is thus wise to encourage in oneself a growing consciousness of the role of values in theory. This consciousness will make the difference be-

---

[10] Michael Polanyi, *The Tacit Dimension* (New York: Doubleday, 1967); Thomas Kuhm, *The Structure of Scientific Revolutions* (Chicago: The University of Chicago Press, 1970).

tween a careful technical analysis of a problem and a wise judgment about policy for dealing with it.

SUMMARY

Economic theory is like a special pair of glasses. These glasses are used to look at human behavior. They distort what we see in certain very specific ways. Most importantly, they lead economists to assume that maximizing is the motive for much human behavior. This distortion accounts for the success of economics but it also limits the perspective of economists.

The test of this or any other scientific view of reality lies in the success of its predictions. The predictions of economic theory are much more successful than they are generally thought to be and much less successful than we generally want them to be.

It is now time to have a look at a part of this theory, the theory of consumer behavior, to see what kind of predictions it makes. At least we all have been consumers, though most of us may feel we have had too little experience.

SELECTED READINGS

Friedman, Milton. "The Methodology of Positive Economics" in *Essays in Positive Economics* (Chicago: The University of Chicago Press, 1953), pp. 1–43.

Knight, F. H. *Social and Economic Organization.* Reprinted in Breit and Hochman, *Readings in Microeconomics* (New York: Holt, Rinehart & Winston, 1968), chapter 1.

Koopmans, T. C. "Measurement Without Theory," *Review of Economics and Statistics,* vol. 29 (1947), pp. 161–72.

Machlup, Fritz. "The Problem of Verification in Economics," *Southern Economic Journal,* vol. 22 (1955), pp. 1–25.

Chapter 2

Supply and demand

INTRODUCTION

Economists divide their theories about reality and their observations of reality into two categories: supply and demand. This is a clever move, but it is not an obvious one. Our observations of the real world do not come to us with supply or demand labels. There is nothing "natural" about this division. It is man-made. It is, however, very useful in that the most important theorems of economics have come from the analysis of the interaction of demand with supply. The rest of this book will be concerned with the character of supply and of demand and with the way they interact. It may, however, be helpful to start with a simplified description of that analysis.

DEMAND

It is possible for us to observe an exchange of some commodity between a buyer and a seller. Some quantity will be exchanged at some price. Economists see the observed exchange as providing evidence of the demand by the buyer for the commodity. That demand seems clearly related to the price at which the exchange takes place. The same observed exchange can also provide evidence of supply, but more about that later.

We may be able to observe the same individual engaged in other exchanges of the same commodity at other times. In that way it may be possible to build up a substantial amount of information about quantity demanded by this individual at different prices. From these observations, we can construct what is called a demand schedule. It might look like the one shown in Table 2–1.

Often it is easier for the economists to find out the total number of pounds of hamburger purchased each week by all buyers. We may have access to weekly or monthly supermarkets sales in a particular market area. We can then construct a *market* demand schedule. It will look very much like the individual schedule shown in Table 2–1 but of course the demanded quantities will be larger.

This general approach makes demand seem to be an empirical measurement, a matter of picking an individual or a group of individuals and observing their behavior in the face of different prices. We do in-

TABLE 2–1
Individual demand schedule for hamburger

Price per pound	Quantity demanded (pounds per month)
1.00	1.0
0.90	1.5
0.80	1.75
0.70	2.0
0.60	2.5
0.50	3.0
0.40	3.75

deed proceed this way to obtain what are called statistical demand curves. The procedure involves a group of accepted econometric techniques that have been used repeatedly. It is, however, a more difficult thing to do than most students might expect. The techniques are complex and the resulting curves are not completely free of ambiguities. Not the least of the difficulties arises simply because every observation is an observation of an exchange, and an exchange reflects both demand and supply conditions. It is very difficult to separate statistically the information about demand from the information about supply. We will not take time in this book to explain these techniques and difficulties, but it should be stressed that in spite of difficulties, the empirical estimation of demand is a widely used and accepted technique.

THE DEMAND CURVE

Partly because of the statistical difficulties mentioned above and partly for historical reasons, economists approach demand in another way as well. They *define* a demand curve that reflects only the most general and important characteristics of statistical curves. It is an idealization of statistical curves and consistent with what we know about them. This idealized curve is used in economic analysis. It is more widely used in generating the theorems and predictions of economic theory than statistical curves. It is the curve we will make the most use of in the rest of this book. Important as it is, the student should not lose sight of the fact that empirical information about demand remains the ultimate test of its usefulness. Whatever we can predict from theory must be tested against the events, like exchanges, that we can actually observe.

THE LAW OF DEMAND

The basic characteristic of demand is that the quantity demanded is inversely related to price. Thus, the demand curve we use in economic analysis has been given a negative slope. We have found little convincing empirical evidence of a statistical demand curve that has positive slope. The inverse relationship between price and quantity demanded seems to be consistent with casual observation of the response each of us makes to price changes. It is called the law of demand and it makes price the most important factor in the determination of quantity demanded. An individual demand curve can look like the one for tea shown in Figure 2–1.[1] This curve indicates, for instance, that when price is three dollars (P_1), quantity of tea demanded by this individual will be about 1.0 pounds per month (Q_1). On the other hand, when price is \$1.50 (P_2), then the curve indicates that a quantity demanded will be about 2.8 pounds per month (Q_2).

Price, however, is not the only factor that has an impact on demand. Most of us recognize that our income will affect the quantity we will want to buy at any particular price. Thus, as indicated on Figure 2–2, if our income is larger we may want to buy 1.9 pounds (Q_1') when the price is P_1 instead of 1.0 pounds (Q_1). In fact, empirical evidence indicates that quantity demanded will be larger when income is larger for most commodities at every price. We indicate this by shifting the whole curve to the right $(DD$ to $D'D')$ as shown on Figure 2–2. We will thus assume that all points on a single curve reflect the effects of a particular individual income and that any change in that income will shift the whole curve.

The prices of some other goods also seem likely to affect the quantity demanded.[2] Simply because butter is a substitute for margarine, a rise in

---

[1] This demand curve is presented as a straight line, but it will become clear later that this is a convenient but not necessary shape.

[2] Actually the prices of all other goods have some effect on the quantity demanded, but the influence is quite small unless the other good is a close substitute or complement.

the price of butter may induce people to shift to margarine and to buy more at each price. Again, we will assume that the price of any closely related good is the same at every point on a particular demand curve and that the whole curve must shift if that price changes.

Finally, we recognize that individual tastes will affect quantity demanded. The person who really likes tea will buy a larger quantity at any given price than someone who prefers coffee. We will therefore assume that tastes are constant all along any one individual demand

FIGURE 2–1

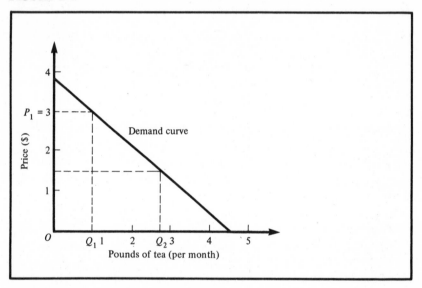

curve, and if tastes should change we will indicate this by shifting the entire curve.

Individual demand can therefore be pictured as a negatively sloped line along which income, prices of closely related goods, and tastes are held constant and along which price and quantity demanded vary inversely to each other. We can shift from this individual curve to a market demand curve simply by adding the quantities demanded by all individuals at each price to get market quantity demanded at that price. The argument up to this point has, however, been much simplified. Behind this demand curve lies an elaborate model of the way in which individuals make economic choices. This model, developed in Chapters 3, 4, and 5, will support the demand curve described above and increase our capacity to predict human behavior with it. However, even this simplified curve can be used to answer some questions.

FIGURE 2–2

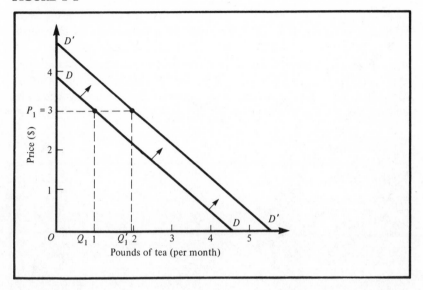

FOR INSTANCE

In the 1950s, passenger travel on U.S. railroads was coming to an end and Amtrak had not yet appeared. Many railroads found that they were required by the Interstate Commerce Commission to run certain trains whether they had passengers or not. In this circumstance the cost of providing passenger service is mostly a fixed cost. The train has to be run and its crew paid even if it runs empty and there are a few additional costs if it runs full.

How then should the railroad set the fare on this train? Since we take costs to be fixed, the railroad will want to maximize the total revenue (TR) from the sales of tickets. This means that it will want to set the price of a ticket (P) in such a way that

$$P \cdot Q = TR$$

will be as large as possible. When total revenues from ticket sales are as large as possible, then the amount that remains after the fixed costs are paid will also be as large as possible. And if this largest revenue is smaller than the fixed costs, the resulting losses will be as small as possible.

Notice that we are not suggesting that the *number* of tickets sold (Q) be made as large as possible. Setting the price at zero will lead to the largest number of tickets sold but it will also lead to total revenues

$(P \cdot Q)$ that are zero. Obviously a price of zero is too low. There will be a price that is too high as well. In fact the railroad can put the price so high that no one rides the train and total revenues are again zero. If you look at the demand curve on Figure 2–3 you can see that at A, price is so high as to reduce ticket sales to zero. The point where price is zero and number of tickets sold is maximized is at the other end of this curve (B). Total revenue from selling tickets is thus zero at both ends of the demand curve.

FIGURE 2–3

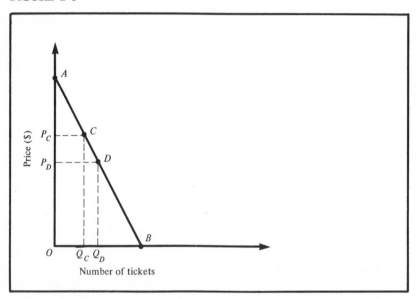

Look however at the point C on this demand curve. Here the price is P_C and the number of tickets sold is Q_C. Since both P_C and Q_C are greater than zero, total revenue ($P_C \cdot Q_C$) will be positive. Total revenue will be greater than zero everywhere along the curve except at the end points. Where will it be a maximum? Since

$$TR_C = P_C \cdot Q_C,$$

we can see that TR is the area of the rectangle $OP_C CQ_C$. This geometric relationship can be used at any point on the curve. At D, for instance, total revenue is equal to the area of the rectangle $OP_D DQ_D$.

Maximizing total revenue therefore means setting the price of a ticket in such a way that the resulting rectangle under the demand curve is as large as possible. In a later chapter we will use the concept of elasticity of the demand curve in a systematic way to find this price. We will then discover that D which lies halfway between A and B is the maximum point. Hence when a firm finds the costs of production of some good to be a fixed cost, the demand curve for that good will indicate which price maximizes total revenues and hence profits.

SUPPLY

As noted earlier, our observations of exchange provide supply information as well as demand information. We can and do make mea-

FIGURE 2–4

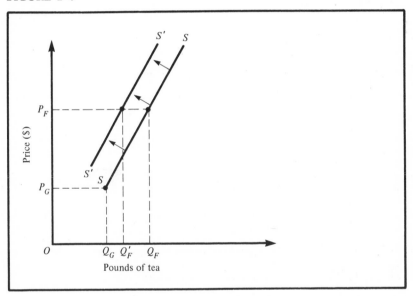

surements of quantity supplied at different prices by individual firms and by whole industries. The techniques are well developed and widely used, but they are encumbered with the same kinds of complexities and difficulties that surround the derivation of statistical demand curves.

We therefore make much use of an idealized supply curve as well. Its key characteristic is that quantity supplied is directly related to price. Because of our assumptions about the conditions under which production takes place, the supply curve indicates that firms and industries will supply larger quantities at higher prices.

The supply curve of an individual firm is shown on Figure 2–4 as the line SS. This curve indicates that when the price is P_G the firm will be willing to supply the quantity Q_G. The curve also indicates that at any price below P_G the firm will not produce at all. Once we get into the analysis of production and costs in Chapters 7–10, the reasons for this will be easy to see.

Thus the basic characteristic of supply is that quantity supplied is larger when the price is higher, but it also seems likely that the quantity supplied at every price will be smaller if the price of inputs is higher. Thus the quantity supplied at the price P_F may be Q_F' instead of Q_F if the price of labor is $3.00 per hour rather than $2.50. We will therefore assume that the prices of inputs are the same everywhere along a single supply curve and that the curve will shift (SS to $S'S'$) as indicated on Figure 2–4 if input prices rise.

We must also recognize that a change in technology is likely to change the quantity supplied at each price. Hence, a single supply curve will be assumed to depend on the use of a particular technology. A change in technology will shift the whole curve. Finally we must recognize that two goods may be produced together so that changes in the output of one shift the supply curve of the other. If war disrupts the production of wheat somewhere in the world its price may rise. Midwestern farmers may then respond by growing more wheat and less corn so that the supply curve for corn is shifted to the left because of a rise in the price of wheat. We will therefore assume that the prices of related goods (in production) are constant all along a supply curve and that any change in the price of a related good will shift the whole supply curve.

Therefore, the supply curve that we are going to use reveals the quantity that will be supplied at every possible price for a given technology and given prices of the inputs and given prices of closely related goods. This is a simplified statement of the conditions of supply, and it will be expanded when we get to a full discussion of production and costs. It is consistent with our observations of supply and the statistical supply curves we can construct.

EQUILIBRIUM

Now that we have simple versions of both demand and supply we can introduce the notion of equilibrium. Equilibrium is the end result of a process. We imagine buyers and sellers in a market adjusting to the demand and supply conditions discussed above until none of them wishes to make any further adjustment. They will then exchange a particular quantity Q_e, shown on Figure 2–5, at the price P_e. This price will "clear the market" meaning that the quantity supplied at this price will be equal to the quantity demanded at this price. No further adjustments will be contemplated simply because every seller can sell precisely the amount that he wants to sell *at this price* and every buyer can buy exactly as much as he wants to buy *at this price*. Because no further adjustments are contemplated we say this market is in equilibrium.

At any price above or below P_e, the market pictured in Figure 2–5 will not be in equilibrium. Consider the price P' for instance. The quantity supplied at that price (Q_S') is larger than the quantity demanded (Q_D'). Firms will find that they are unable to sell as much as they want to at that price. Consumers will not buy more than the quantity Q_D' and we presume that sellers will cut the price below P' in

FIGURE 2–5

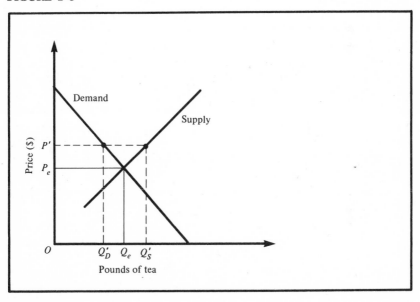

an effort to increase sales. This adjustment will bring the market closer to the equilibrium price P_e. It will increase the quantity demanded and decrease the quantity supplied, bringing them closer to the same value. If certain conditions are met we can predict that price will continue to be adjusted downward until the equilibrium price P_e is reached. We will discuss these conditions in some detail in a later chapter, but will assume here that markets do adjust to equilibrium.

If the price happened to be below P_e in Figure 2–5, we would make a similar argument about the upward adjustment of price until P_e is reached. In this case, however, we depend on the behavior of buyers, who cannot buy all they want at the lower price, to bid it up to P_e.

We thus see equilibrium as a kind of summary statement of the effects of all the conditions that determine both supply and demand. We can therefore use equilibrium to analyze the importance of those conditions. We can also use it to analyze the effect of any outside factor that changes one of those conditions. We will now consider a number of examples.

A FALL IN THE PRICE OF BUTTER

We think of butter and margarine as substitutes for each other. A change in the price of butter is likely to have an effect on the demand for

FIGURE 2–6

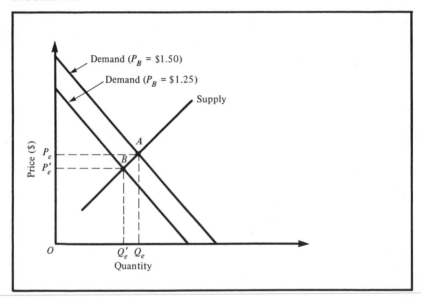

margarine. If butter falls in price we can expect people to buy less margarine simply because they will now buy more butter and use it in some situations where they would previously have used margarine. This means that the quantity of margarine demanded will be smaller at each margarine price. We indicate this by shifting the whole demand curve to the left on Figure 2–6. The curve on the left describes the demand for margarine when the price of butter (P_B) is $1.25 rather than $1.50.

We refer to this shift as a "change in demand." One of the conditions of demand, in this case the price of a closely related good, has changed and the whole curve is therefore shifted. We reserve the term "change in demand" for situations like this. The same is true of supply, where a change in supply means a shift in the whole curve. On the other hand, if we want to compare two points on the same curve, for instance A and B

on the supply curve of Figure 2–6, we use the phrase "a change in quantity supplied."

Thus in Figure 2–6 we have indicated a *change in demand* that shifted the demand curve to the left and resulted in a *change (reduction) in quantity supplied* from Q_e to Q_e'. The price has also been reduced so that our analysis leads to the prediction that:

> If two goods are substitutes then a fall in the price of one of them will lead to a fall in the equilibrium price and quantity of the other.

This is clearly a testable prediction using our observations of the price behavior of real commodities.

This prediction can be applied to the current proposal to permit increased imports of beef. It is, of course, expected that these will keep the price of beef from rising and may in fact produce some reduction. If the price of beef falls we can also predict that the price of pork is likely to fall as well, since it is probably correct to view beef and pork as substitutes.

It should be added that predicting the effect of some change in conditions will often require that we examine the possibility that there will be both a "change in demand" and "a change in quantity demanded." The recent taxpayers' revolt in California will require that state government give large sums to local governments to replace at least part of their lost property tax revenues. It seems quite possible that one result will be a rise in tuition for students attending state universities. This can be viewed as a rise in the price of higher education, other things equal, and will result in a fall in the quantity demanded. We might therefore predict that fewer professors will be needed and the state will be able to reduce some of the costs of education. The state will therefore benefit from higher revenues from tuition[3] and somewhat lower costs simply because a change in the price of education, other things equal, brought about a change in the quantity demanded.

"Other things," however, may not remain equal. It has been observed in the past that one of the determinants of the demand for education is the availability of alternative employment opportunities. The changes brought about by the taxpayers' revolt may result in an increase in unemployment, particularly among the young, who have little seniority in their present jobs. Many of these people will decide to go to school while they wait for job opportunities to get better. This will appear in our analysis as a change in demand. It will appear as a shift in the whole curve to the right, as an increase in the amount of

---

[3] We are assuming that a rise of, say, 10 percent in tuition will reduce the number of students by less than 10 percent, so that total expenditure on education by students will increase. This assumption involves a concept called the elasticity of demand. It will be fully discussed in a later chapter.

education that people want at every price. Since only a small part of the cost of educating a student is covered by his tuition and fee payments and the rest is paid by the state, this could mean that the costs of higher education actually increase. The change in demand and the change in quantity demanded have opposite effects on the cost of higher education to the state.

INDEPENDENCE

In the previous example we were able to predict the effect of a change in the price of butter because its only effect was on the demand for margarine. In the margarine market only the demand curve shifted and the supply curve held its position. This is not an uncommon situation. The impact of the real changes that we as economists want to analyze, is usually felt on only one side of the market. This is very fortunate and it goes a long way toward explaining why the choice of "demand" and "supply" as our major categories is so important.

Take a look at what happens if we consider a change that might shift both supply and demand curves simultaneously. Suppose the firms in some industry make the cost of their advertising a function of output. This would have the effect of shifting their supply curves upward as in Figure 2–7. If they were previously willing to supply the quantity Q_e at the price P_e they will now have to get a higher price. This price will have to be sufficiently higher to cover the added advertising costs. Consequently, the quantity Q_e will only be supplied if the price is P_A and since this is true of every quantity, we shift the whole supply curve from SS to $S'S'$.

However, the purpose of the advertising expenditure is to shift the demand curve. The firms want people to be persuaded that their product is a better product so that they will buy larger quantities at each price. Suppose the advertising has some success and the demand curve is shifted to the dashed line $D'D'$. The new equilibrium at P_e' will involve a higher price and a smaller output. The effect of the advertising is to make the good more expensive and reduce sales. On the other hand, if the advertising is very successful and the demand curve shifts to $D''D''$, then the new equilibrium will involve a higher price and *larger* sales as well.

In this example it is not at all clear how the change (in advertising expenditures) will affect the quantity sold because both supply and demand curves shift at the same time. In order to predict the behavior of quantity demanded we would need much more information than was needed in the butter and margarine case and indeed much more than we can usually obtain. We would need to know just how much the change in advertising shifts each curve whereas in the earlier example we

FIGURE 2–7

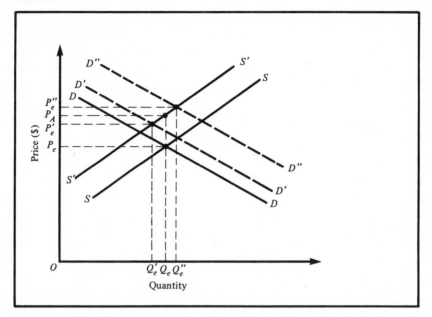

needed to know only the direction of the shift in the demand for margarine. Fortunately the factors that affect demand do not usually have any important impact on supply and vice versa. We can usually handle the problems we want to handle by shifting only one curve at a time. As a result, we can usually make fairly simple statements about the effects of a particular change. This is perhaps the main reason that we still divide our theories and our observations into the two categories, supply *or* demand, 200-plus years after Adam Smith.

COMPARATIVE STATICS

The whole discussion above that begins with a change in the price of butter makes use of a standard technique of economists. The price P_e on Figure 2–6 is the equilibrium price of margarine when the price of butter $P_B = \$1.50$. P_e' is the equilibrium price of margarine when $P_B = \$1.25$. We are thus comparing two equilibriums, one before a change and one after that change, in order to discover the affect of that change. Each equilibrium is a "static" situation, meaning that all adjustments have been made and no further changes in price or quantity will occur unless the basic conditions of either supply or demand are changed again. This is why the procedure is called "comparative statics."

Historically, this procedure has been the most common one used by economists. It is still the most common, though great effort is being made to develop dynamic techniques. The weakness of comparative statics is that it says nothing about the path along which a market adjusts from one equilibrium to another. In any real market, adjustment to equilibrium takes time. Thus, the market may spend much, maybe most, of its time out of equilibrium. If we live in an economy in which most markets are out of equilibrium most of the time, then the study of equilibrium can tell us which way we are moving, but not where we are. Moreover, the adjustment process itself may be erratic. If the price of some good is above equilibrium, then sellers are called upon to reduce it. They may overdo it. They may reduce it so much that it is below the equilibrium price and another adjustment is called for. It is entirely possible that adjustments to equilibrium are clumsy and prolonged and that life is therefore quite uncomfortable most of the time even when the equilibrium toward which we are moving appears to be very attractive. These possibilities account for our concern with the adjustment process, that is, with dynamics. It is probably also clear that equilibrium is a topic that we will want to discuss in greater detail in a later chapter. It ought to be added, however, that we will continue to use comparative statics in these pages because the technique is so well developed and understood, and because it is very useful in spite of these problems.

A SHORTAGE OF CARS

During World War II very few automobiles were made. When the war was over the manufacture and consumption of automobiles began again with great enthusiasm. After years with no production, it seemed that a shortage would be inevitable. Not so. This market undoubtedly had an equilibrium price at which quantity demanded would be equal to the quantity that producers were able to deliver. Production expanded quite rapidly after the war but even if it had not, there was still likely to be a point where supply and demand curves intersect.

In Figure 2–8 the steep supply curve suggests that output is relatively fixed because of the problems of converting from war production to automobiles. Manufacturers were probably quite willing and eager to produce many more cars at higher prices but the problems of conversion prevented that result. Nevertheless, there was almost certainly a price like P_e in Figure 2–8, that was an equilibrium price, meaning that there were neither too few nor too many cars at that price.

Such a price did not appear, however. The automobile manufacturers in fact kept the price well below P_e. They did this partly as a matter of public relations. The auto companies did not want to make it appear that they would keep Americans from getting the new cars they had waited for so long by making them too expensive. They also realized that as their conversion to peacetime production neared completion, the supply curve would shift to the right and become less steep. The equilibrium price could then be expected to be below P_e. Let P' represent the retail price actually maintained by the producers. The result is clear. This price produced a shortage. The quantity demanded (Q_D) clearly exceeded the quantity supplied (Q_S), and the shortage was created by setting this price, not by the war.

The price P' is an example of a ceiling price. It was enforced in this case by the manufacturers of automobiles rather than the government,

FIGURE 2–8

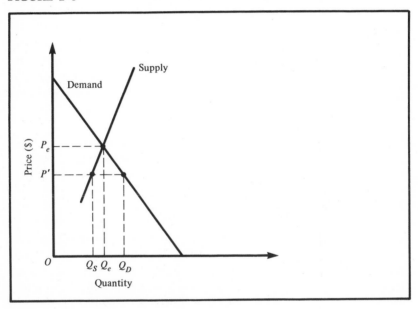

but a shortage results no matter who sets the price. The ceiling price in no way shuts off the demand, and people begin to look around for ways to make their demands effective. In 1946 and 1947 auto dealers tried to ration the available supply on a first-come, first-served basis. They kept lists of all people who had ordered cars, and presumably offered each car as it came in to the next person on the list.

This was not a particularly successful rationing scheme since the lists were not public knowledge, and favoritism and bribery were often used to get to the top of the list. Thus, favoritism and bribery became ways of satisfying the unsatisfied demand. Bribery, of course, had the effect of raising the actual price of the car. The need to pay a bribe in addition to the retail price thus reduced the quantity demanded and moved the market toward equilibrium. Moreover, while the retail price of the car was fixed by the manufacturer, there was no limit to the number of accessories that could be attached, and so most of the cars that came to dealers were deluxe models with radios and whitewall tires and all the other special features of that day. If you got offered a car with accessories you did not want, you had to take it anyway because it might be a long time before your name would come to the top of the list again. The accessories also raised the actual price of a car above P', bringing it closer to the equilibrium price P_e.

This discussion of the effect of a ceiling price suggests two important predictions. The first is that an effective ceiling price will cause a shortage, and the second is that the unsatisfied demanders will engage in a variety of activities designed to evade the ceiling. Experience with price ceilings during World War II suggests that many of these behaviors are quite undesirable and many are illegal. Favoritism, bribery, and black markets are common and familiar responses to unsatisfied demand. A look at another example will reveal some less familiar responses.

THE MINIMUM WAGE

The minimum wage is a floor price, not a ceiling price, but otherwise the analysis is quite similar. No employer is permitted to pay an hourly wage below the government-determined minimum amount. Suppose this minimum is represented by W' on Figure 2–9. Notice that this wage (W') is above the equilibrium wage rate (W_e). If it were below W_e it would be of no importance since the market would adjust to equilibrium at W_e and would not touch the floor. When the minimum wage is above the equilibrium wage, however, it becomes important. The quantity of labor supplied at this wage exceeds the quantity demanded. There is a surplus of labor (a shortage of jobs). A floor price always produces a surplus just as a ceiling price always produces a shortage.

We have had a minimum wage in this country since the end of World War II, and it has been extensively studied by economists. We can say a number of things about the effect of the surplus it creates by looking at those studies.

It is one of the purposes of the minimum wage to provide a larger income to those workers whose lack of skills, training, and experience puts them in the lowest wage brackets, a group that includes large numbers of teenagers. However, it is possible that the size of income is not changed. Instead, the timing of wage increases may be all that is affected. With each increase in the minimum wage, low-wage groups get a raise that they would have gotten anyway two to five years later. In other words, the minimum wage may not permanently improve the position of low-wage groups relative to other wage earners.

Not all workers are covered by the minimum wage, and so it is pos-

sible to discover its effect by comparing covered with uncovered workers. The study mentioned above indicates that covered workers experience a general rise in wages somewhat sooner than uncovered workers.
This in itself is not a bad thing, but there are unemployment costs as
well, and these bear very heavily on a particular group, teenagers. In
another study, it was found that when the minimum wage is raised
there is a marked reduction in the employment of teenagers in covered
occupations.[4] Moreover, it will be some time after the rise before the

FIGURE 2–9

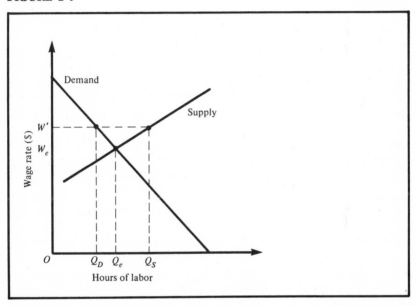

proportion of teenagers in those occupations is restored. In general the
employment of teenagers in covered employments will remain low until
inflation raises the whole wage structure to match the earlier rise in the
minimum wage.

In addition, the minimum wage makes unskilled labor temporarily
more expensive every time it is raised, and this seems to lead to some
more or less permanent changes that depress teenage employment.
Firms tend to revise their production techniques so as to reduce their
dependence on teenage labor. They find machinery and procedures that
can be substituted for teenagers.

What happens to the teenagers who cannot find jobs in occupations
covered by the minimum wage? No doubt, some of them succeed in

---

[4] Yale Brozen, "The Effects of Statutory Minimum Wage Increases on Teenage
Employment," *Journal of Law and Economics,* vol. 12 (April 1969), p. 109.

finding employment anyway by introducing bribery to the hiring process, but it has also been shown that the minimum wage will drive many teenagers completely out of the labor force.[5] It is thus likely to keep them in school and living at home longer than they might otherwise choose. Teenagers will also shift to uncovered employments, particularly as household workers.[6] Finally, small employers will shift from hired labor to family members and many a teenager will find himself working part time at the family store or on the family farm instead of working at McDonalds.[7]

PRICE RATIONING

Ceiling and floor prices prevent what economists sometimes call "price rationing" by preventing the achievement of equilibrium. When price is free to adjust, it will ration the available supply among demanders or the available demand among suppliers. The market for Christmas trees provides a good example of price rationing. We can suppose a very simple situation on the supply side that is not far from the actual situation, namely that the supply of trees is fixed when they go on sale in late November. This assumption is pretty realistic because the trees are usually cut at some distance from the place of sale and must therefore be cut in September and October. The decision about how many to cut is thus made long before anything is known about the demand and additional trees cannot be readily obtained before Christmas if the demand should warrant. We can thus describe the supply by the curve shown on Figure 2–10.

Each supplier knows how many trees he has to sell but it is doubtful that anyone knows the total number available from all suppliers. Thus, no one knows the market supply curve shown on Figure 2–10. It is also clear that no one knows precisely what the market demand will be this year though it may be possible to make some estimates based on experience in previous years. Let us suppose that we actually know the demand and supply and hence that we can draw the curves as shown on Figure 2–10. We therefore know that there is an equilibrium price at P_e but buyers and sellers do not know that. The first prices that sellers post and the first offers that buyers make would be equal to P_e only by accident. Suppose that the first price posted is P'. Then the quantity demanded (Q_D) will exceed the available supply (Q_e) at that price. This

[5] Thomas Gale Moore, "The Effect of Minimum Wages on Teenage Employment Rates," *Journal of Political Economy,* vol. 79 (July–August 1971), p. 897.

[6] Yale Brozen, "Minimum Wage Rates and Household Workers," *Journal of Law and Economics,* vol. 5 (October 1962), p. 103.

[7] Bruce Gardner, "Minimum Wages and the Farm Labor Market," *American Journal of Agricultural Economics* (August 1972), p. 473.

will come to the attention of sellers as they notice that the rate of sales is high, so high that they will be out of trees before Christmas. They will therefore raise the price above P'.

This is the point at which price begins to ration the available supply among demanders. As the price rises above P', some demanders will drop out of the market and others will buy smaller trees. Price is doing exactly what ration coupons will do, namely limiting the demand until it is no greater than the available supply. There is a price (P_e) that will

FIGURE 2–10

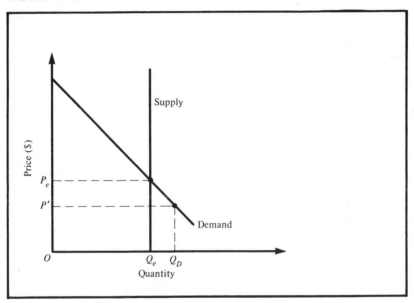

limit quantity demanded until it is precisely equal to the quantity supplied. At that price the Christmas trees have all been rationed among all potential demanders. They go only to these people who are willing to pay at least P_e.[8]

Notice that price rationing provides trees to those who are willing to pay. This is not the same as saying they will go to those who ought to

---

[8] The adjustment process is a little more complicated than this simple example suggests. We are treating both supply and demand as discrete amounts in a single Christmas season. Neither demand nor supply are rates per unit of time. Thus a fixed number of trees are available for sale on the first day. Some of them will be sold at the first price P' and then when the price is raised above P', the remaining supply of trees to be sold at this new price will be smaller. In other words, as time passes between late November and Christmas Day the supply curve is slowly moving to the left. So is the demand curve for the same reason. Some demanders have already bought their trees at the price P'. This need not, however, prevent the market from approximating the equilibrium price before Christmas.

get them. Many of us would feel that some trees *should* go to those who are unwilling to pay because their income is low. We might, therefore, decide to ration the trees on the basis of "deservedness" rather than price. In any real situation, however, deservedness will be very hard to determine. We will have to agree on some process for measuring the just deserts of each of us. If we really face this task, we will find it very complex and difficult.

Income is, of course, a major determinant of willingness to pay, and if we think that the distribution of income is quite fair in the first place, we will be well advised to leave the rationing to the price mechanism. That is, of course, a big "if," and yet the economy of time and energy inherent in price rationing makes it extremely attractive as a rationing technique. We are led, therefore, to the discussion of the distribution of income. This raises the question of deservedness in a somewhat different context. We cannot avoid the question if and when we want to talk about economic policy. It is probably easier, however, to talk about deservedness in relation to the distribution of money income rather than to consider it with regard to each of a multitude of separate commodities. As economists, we can say to policy makers that price rationing is cheap and efficient when compared to any other type of rationing, but we must then add that it will not answer the question of who *ought* to get what.

A FINAL EXAMPLE

What can we say, using comparative statics, about the effects of a tax? Suppose that the curves shown on Figure 2–11 represent the supply and demand conditions before any tax is imposed. There will be an equilibrium at the price P_e. How will this equilibrium change once an excise tax is imposed?

We will assume that the tax amounts to T cents for every item sold by the producers and that it is collected from the producers. Figure 2–11 indicates that a price P_e is high enough to induce producers to supply the quantity Q_e. If we still want the quantity Q_e to be forthcoming after the tax is imposed, producers will have to have at least P_e left after they have paid the tax. In other words, buyers will have to pay P_e plus the tax in order to get the quantity Q_e.

Thus the quantity Q_e will only be supplied at a price equal to $P_e + T$, and this is true of every possible quantity. The supply curve is effectively shifted upward by the amount of the tax. The market will adjust to a new equilibrium at the price P_T. It is now fairly easy to describe the effects of the tax by comparing this new equilibrium to the old one.

First, it is clear that imposing the tax will raise the market price of the good from P_e to P_T in this example.

Second, it is also clear that the equilibrium quantity produced and sold will be smaller: Q_T instead of Q_e.

Even more interesting is the fact that while consumers will pay more for the good, they will not pay enough more to cover the whole tax. One can see on Figure 2–11 that the difference between P_e and P_T is less than T, the full amount of the tax. We can say as economists that only part of the tax is passed along to the consumer through higher prices.

FIGURE 2–11

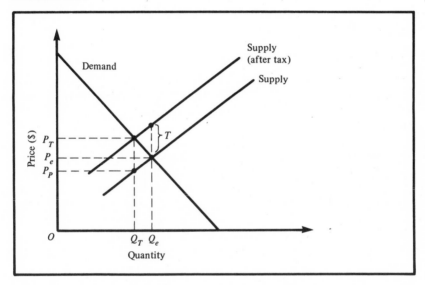

What has happened to the rest of the tax? It is being paid by the producer since the amount that he has left after paying the tax is P_P, which is less than P_e. How the tax is divided between consumers and producers depends on the actual shapes of the supply and demand curves. This can be seen easily in Figure 2–12 where the demand curve is much less steep. Then P_T will be only slightly higher than P_e, and the consumer will pay little of the tax. Most of it will be paid by the producer.

Notice that the division of the tax does not depend on the intent of the government, but instead depends on the shape of the curves. If the government wanted the tax paid by producers, and therefore specified that the tax be collected from the producers, then its will can frustrated by the market. In fact, the government can collect the tax from either party without affecting its division between them.

FIGURE 2–12

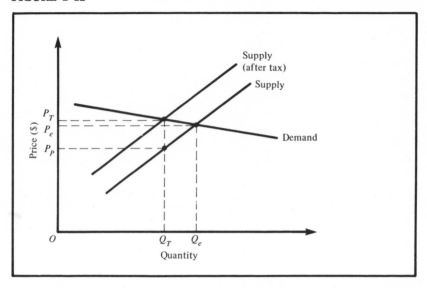

Suppose it is collected from the buyer. Each time he buys one item he pays a price and a tax. In other words, the total payment he makes includes the tax. Look at the demand curve on Figure 2–13. The consumer will be willing to buy the quantity Q_e if he has to pay P_e for each

FIGURE 2–13

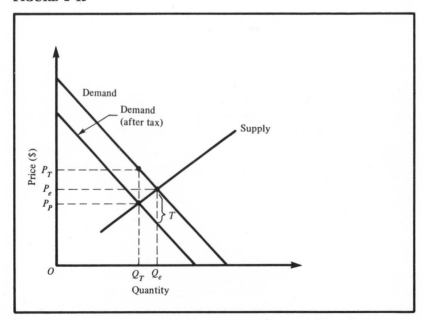

item. However, the producer will no longer get P_e when he sells this quantity. He will get P_e minus the tax. From his point of view the demand curve has shifted down by the amount of the tax. The new equilibrium will be the same as in Figure 2–11 with price at P_P. P_P goes to the producer and T is paid to the government. The sum of $P_P + T$ is equal to P_T, the same total that consumers had to pay when the tax was collected from the producers. Moreover, the division of the tax between consumers and producers is the same as before as well.

CONCLUSION

This chapter has presented an introduction to the use of supply and demand analysis with numerous examples. Behind this simple introduction lies a fascinating and precise theory of the way in which individuals make choices. We will consider two particular groups of individuals in detail. We consider consumers choosing among the different combinations of goods and services that they can afford. And we will consider producers choosing which goods to produce and among different combinations of inputs that can be used to produce those goods. The study of consumers will lead to the demand curve and the study of producers to the supply curve.

We will then ask in some detail, "What can we predict about the interaction of supply and demand under competition, under monopoly, and under certain forms of imperfect competition?" This will involve the concept of equilibrium and the technique of comparative statics. Finally, we will end this book with a discussion of some of the characteristics of an economy in which all markets are in equilibrium at the same time.

SELECTED READINGS

Boulding, K. E. *Economic Analysis: vol. 1, Microeconomics* (New York: Harper and Row, 1966), Chapters 11 and 12.

Brozen, Yale. "The Effects of Statutory Minimum Wage Increases on Teenage Employment," *Journal of Law and Economics,* vol. 12 (April 1969), p. 109.

Marshall, Alfred. *Principles of Economics,* 8th ed. (London: Macmillan, 1920), Book III, Chapters 1–3.

Radford, R. A. "Economic Organization of a P.O.W. Camp," *Economica,* vol. 12 (November 1945), p. 189.

PART II

CONSUMPTION

Chapter 3

Choice

INTRODUCTION

Economic theory is a model of the way individuals make choices among alternatives. This model starts with a precise set of assumptions about the nature of the alternatives and the way in which individuals will express their preferences among them. These assumptions are abstract and simple when compared to reality. This means that they do not exactly describe the behavior of any real person. Economists have adopted the term "economic man" to describe a chooser whose choices are always determined by these assumptions.

Abstract as this theory is, it must always lead to something real if it is to be useful. We can, by deduction from assumptions, describe the demand curve of an economic man, but this is not enough. We must then be prepared to interpret that curve as belonging to real men and women. We must see whether they actually behave in ways that could be predicted from the shape of that curve. If they do not, then the curve and hence the assumptions from which it was deduced are not very useful. If real men and women fail to do what a theory predicts, then the theory will be abandoned and replaced by other theories.

Thus, in spite of the obvious abstractness of economic theory and its assumptions, economics can never get very far from reality. It is always brought back by the ingenuity of the economist who uses the theory to predict what people will do in particular circumstances, and then finds a way to observe what they actually do in those circumstances. This process goes on continuously. It constitutes a continuous test of the usefulness of economic theory and its various parts. The body of theory presented in the rest of this book has repeatedly passed such tests. Economic man is alive and well in 1978 simply because he has not failed most of those tests.

WHO IS THIS ECONOMIC MAN?

Ever since Jeremy Bentham, economists have talked about happiness, utility, and satisfaction. In describing the basic assumption of economics they often say:

> Men try to maximize the satisfaction of their wants.

This is clearly an unrealistic statement. Real people are curious, capricious, and bound by habit and tradition. They are often led to do things that they cannot expect to maximize their satisfaction. These things may be done for perfectly good reasons, but maximizing satisfaction may not be among those reasons.

Fortunately, we can rephrase this statement. The most important part of the statement is the idea of maximizing, but it is unnecessary to be specific about what is maximized. Economic theory can be used to analyze the maximization of many different variables. When we discuss business firms, we will talk about maximizing profits, of course, but we will also consider maximizing sales and we could, if there were time, consider a number of other variables as possible maximands. In discussing consumers, we will talk about choosing the most preferred alternative without attributing that preference to satisfaction or any other particular human motive.

Even more important is the realization that economic theory is not a description of processes that go on in the minds of real people. We see maximizing as a device we can use to predict what people will do in certain circumstances, not how they will think about those circumstances. Maximization is like a pair of glasses through which the economist looks at reality. It leads to testable predictions that have so often been right that its usefulness should not be doubted. It should not be doubted even though it appears naively simple in comparison with the complexity of real human emotions and thought processes.

We will, therefore, talk as if we have an economic man who always chooses among alternatives in such a way as to maximize something. If we want to use the word "rational," we will use it only to refer to such choices and not to mean sensible or reasonable or any of its other everyday meanings. It is now time to look in some detail at the way economic man chooses.

CHOICE

Everything that we attribute to economic man is the result of definitions and assumptions. These definitions and assumptions determine what we mean by a maximizing choice. If we look first at consumption choices, we will find that they have the following characteristics:

1. The alternatives open to economic man as consumer are seen as baskets of commodities that can be *compared* in such a way as to make choices possible.
2. The preferences of economic man will result in a *ranking* of all these baskets from those he prefers most to those he prefers least.
3. Finally, it is assumed that among these baskets there are some that are *attainable* by economic man and that he will always choose among the attainable baskets the one he most prefers. This is the postulate that assures maximizing or optimizing behavior.

Behavior consistent with these statements is what economists mean by rational behavior. They cover what economists have in mind when they say, "Economic men are maximizers." One can deduce from them all of the usual economic propositions that can be tested by reference to the behavior of real people, but they contain no reference at all to satisfaction or any other subjective state of mind that might be held by a real person. In fact, we have not opened the skulls and looked into the brains of real consumers at all.

RANKING

We can begin the analysis of optimizing behavior by asking how an economically rational ranking of alternatives is made. We will think of the alternatives open to consumers as baskets of consumer goods, each basket holding a different combination of goods. Thus, it is combinations of goods that are to be ranked, not individual commodities. All baskets might be lined up along a sidewalk so that economic man can walk along comparing pairs of baskets and choosing the one he wants most.[1] By considering all possible pairs, he can ultimately arrange them in order from most preferred to least preferred. Any real man or woman with finite income would find some baskets he or she could not afford, but we will ask economic man to go ahead and rank these expensive ones anyway without as yet raising questions about which baskets are "attainable."

---

[1] This statement depends on a crucial assumption, namely, that all alternatives are comparable. Many of our most difficult problems arise from the necessity to choose between alternatives that are not readily comparable.

To be explicit, we are assuming that all baskets can be ranked solely on the basis of their contents in the form of goods and services.[2] In assuming this, we avoid a subtle problem that appears as soon as we remember that goods have prices. Real people tend to feel that things that cost more are worth more and perhaps should be ranked higher. This notion is often foolish, but it is a persistent part of our experience. If, however, we were to try to include it in our model, the matter would get very much more complicated. Choice would then depend (in part) on price, and price, we are soon to make clear, depends very much on choice. Our logic would run in a circle.

This is not the only hazard we can avoid by assuming that only the contents of each basket are important for choice. Many goods derive part of their attractiveness for one person from the consumption pattern chosen by someone else. For instance, the attractiveness of my house to me is greatly influenced by whether my neighbors keep their lawns mowed and neat. But again, if we try to take account of these kinds of factors, called externalities in consumption,[3] our model becomes too complicated. The best procedure is to keep the model simple at first. We can take account of these and other problems like them as special cases when the circumstances of the particular situation being analyzed suggest that they are very important.

Now, exactly what is in these baskets? Goods, of course, but not a particular quantity. Instead, each basket contains a rate of consumption of each good. For instance, there may be twelve quarts of milk *per week* in one basket and perhaps eight quarts per week in another. We can express the preference for a particular basket in mathematical form as:

$$U_C = F(x_1, x_2, \ldots x_m),$$

where $(x_1, x_2, \ldots, x_m)$ stand for the rates of consumption of each of the commodities, and U_C is used to represent the strength of preference of consumer C.[4]

U_C is used in this way because at one time economists conceived of preference as depending on utility, a quality of things that could be measured and added. This concept allowed the total utility of a given basket to be discovered and compared to total utility of other baskets.

---

[2] Preference for a particular basket depends on the proportion among goods as well. A tennis racquet is of little use without tennis balls, for they are complements. Beer may add little to the attractiveness of a basket that includes plenty of wine, since for most people, these are substitutes.

[3] Externalities are discussed at some length in Chapter 15.

[4] Some textbooks describe preference as if individual commodities are involved. They ask whether a suit of clothes is preferred to a new rug. This is not the view that economists want to use. Instead we want to compare whole baskets of goods. Different baskets really represent different styles and standards of living.

Now the concept has changed. Utility is no longer thought to be measurable or even to be identifiable in the real world as a quality of things. U and "utility" remain only as a part of our vocabulary. Thus the mathematical expression above should be read as follows: The preference of consumer C is a function of the rates of consumption of the m possible commodities in each basket. One more note: As a result of the earlier history of economics, in which utility played a more important role, economists still refer to the whole model of consumer choice as Utility Analysis.

FIGURE 3–1

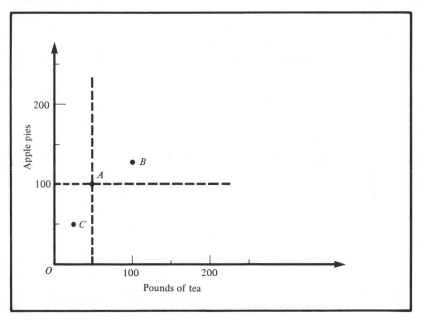

Preference for a given basket of commodities is a function of the commodities in the basket, but when the number of commodities, m, is greater than two, we cannot use geometry to describe the choice process. Mathematicians can do very well when m is greater than two. The necessary mathematics is becoming much more important in economics, especially in the analysis of general equilibrium. Students who are young enough to have the option should study mathematics along with economics. Nevertheless, economists have historically used geometry with great effectiveness. If we are careful, we can reduce the number of commodities to two without changing the conclusions of the analysis.

Suppose we use apple pie and tea as the two commodities. Then we can represent any basket of these two goods by a point on a diagram like Figure 3–1. With one of the goods, pie, measured on the vertical axis and tea measured on the horizontal axis, the point A represents a basket of 100 pies per month and 50 pounds of tea per month. Moreover, since the two axes extend to infinity, any basket that contains quantities zero or larger can be represented by a point, and every point represents a basket. The axes are the boundaries of the "consumption set," the set of all possible baskets of consumer goods and services. We specifically exclude any points that lie in the other three quadrants because we do not attach any economic meaning to negative rates of consumption. All x's in the mathematical function introduced just above are thus greater than or equal to zero.

We can now ask, "How would an economic man rank the baskets in the consumption set from most to least preferred?" We have implied above that he will consider them in pairs. Suppose we look at basket B in relation to A. Should B be ranked higher than A or should it be the other way around, or does it even matter? One thing is clear; B contains more of both goods than A. We will thus be tempted to say it ought to rank higher than A. That is a way of saying that we believe we are talking about "goods," not "ills." It is best to make this notion, which seems so sensible, into a specific assumption. We will assume that more of each good is always preferred to less of that good. This is the first of the assumptions that shape the model of consumer behavior.

We are by this method taking account of one all-pervasive aspect of our real experience; namely, scarcity—the scarcity of most goods relative to our wants. If we were easily satiated, then basket A might contain enough of both pie and tea to satisfy our appetites and B would not be preferred to A at all. Pie and tea would not be scarce relative to their uses in the quadrant above and to the right of A. Since real human beings seldom have the experience of satiety, we make the assumption that all "goods" are scarce relative to their uses.[5] Thus B is preferred to A and to C as well because it contains more of both goods and A is preferred to C for the same reason. In fact, any point in the quadrant above and to the right of A is preferred to A and the reverse is true of any point in the quadrant below and to the left of A. We have ranked two large chunks of the consumption set relative to basket A.

INDIFFERENCE CURVES

The status of baskets below and to the right of A is not so clear. It seems likely that some people would prefer a basket D to basket A on Figure 3–2 since it contains almost as much pie and much more tea.

---

[5] Some other assumptions about the possibility of satiety will be discussed later in this chapter.

And it would not be surprising if others found some baskets to the left of *E* to be less desirable than *A* since they contain much less pie and only a little more tea. In fact, there is no reason not to let economic man draw a line down through this quadrant (*AE*, for instance) that separates all those baskets preferred to *A* from all those that are not as desirable as *A*. The existence of such a line is, in fact, certain since a complete ranking of all baskets is assumed to be possible.

Line *AE* is one example and line *AF* another possibility. None of our

FIGURE 3–2

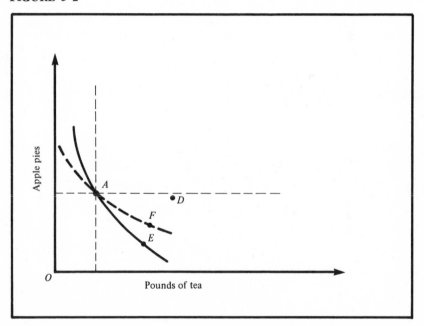

assumptions will tell us exactly where the line would be except that it will pass from the northwest quadrant (relative to point *A*, of course) to the southeast going through point *A* itself. This line or curve (*AE*, for example) thus divides or "partitions" the set of all baskets of commodities into three subsets as shown in Figure 3–3:

a.   Set *B*: the "better-than-*A*" set, which contains all points above and to the right of line *AE*.
b.   Set *W*: the "worse-than-*A*" set, which contains all points below and to the left of *AE*.
c.   Set *I*: the "indifferent-to-*A*" set, which contains all points like *A* and *E*, which happen to lie on the line itself.

This line is called an indifference curve. The name is meant to indi-

FIGURE 3–3

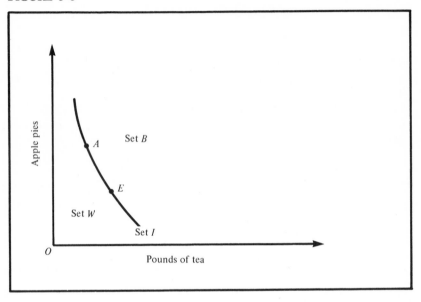

cate that baskets *A* and *E* are tied in the ranking of all baskets from most preferred to least preferred. Economic man might indicate that he is willing to choose between *A* and *E* by flipping an unbiased coin. We will write indifference thus: *AiE,* and preference thus: *BpA.* Since we developed line *AE* merely by figuring out the relationship of other points to *A,* we could do the same for *B* or *C* or any other point. Every point will therefore lie on some indifference curve, the space above and to the right of the axes is full of them, and the whole set or family of indifference curves is called an indifference map.[6]

THE BUDGET LINE

The indifference curve is one of the two fundamental curves used in the analysis of consumer choice. Since we will make use of the other curve, called the budget line, in explaining the shape of indifference curves, it is convenient to introduce it now. As we mentioned once before, the consumption set includes many baskets of goods that any

---

[6] It is tempting at this point to show the consumption set in three dimensions as a utility hill with the indifference curves as contour lines around the hill. Each curve would represent a particular level of preference or utility indicated by its vertical distance up the hill. This is not done because it leads inevitably, but not necessarily, to thinking of utility as a quantity measured along the vertical axis. We do not usually try to quantify utility. The reasons for this will be discussed at some length later in this chapter.

person with finite income cannot afford, though he may know how to rank them. Income and prices will determine which baskets he can afford. If we pick some particular prices and a particular income, we can divide the consumption set in a new way into two subsets, one of which is attainable and the other not. The concept of income to be used is a rate of flow of money income through time. It might be $500 per month. We usually ignore the possibility of credit buying, though it could be introduced at some cost in complicating the argument.

FIGURE 3–4

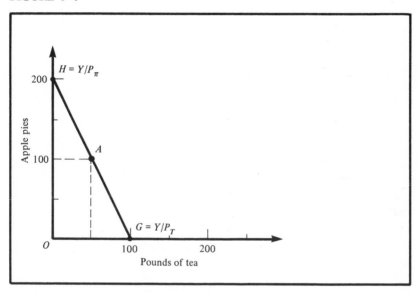

We can now find an attainable set as follows: Suppose the price of tea, $P_T = \$5.00$ per pound and the price of pie, $P_\pi = \$2.50$ per pie, and income $Y = \$500$ per month. If one were to buy nothing but pie, one could buy basket H in Figure 3–4 with 200 pies in it. On the other hand, if one bought nothing but tea, one could buy basket G with 100 pounds of tea. Thus H is found by dividing income by the price of pie $(H = Y/P_\pi)$ and similarly, $G = Y/P_T$. One could also buy basket A, which clearly holds 100 pies and 50 pounds of tea, for it too would not cost more than the $500 per month income.[7] In fact, this income is large enough to buy any basket on the line HAG and, of course, any

---

[7] It seems foolish to think about consuming 100 apple pies and 50 pounds of tea per month, but this is only because we have limited our discussion to two goods as if the world contained no others.

basket to the left of it. All points on the perimeter of the triangle *OHAG,* plus all of the points within it, constitute the attainable set[8] of baskets when:

$$Y = \$500 \text{ per month}$$
$$P_\pi = \$2.50 \text{ per pie}$$
$$P_T = \$5.00 \text{ per pound.}$$

HAG is the boundary of the attainable set. It is called the budget line, and it is useful here to derive its slope. In geometric terms, its slope is the tangent of the angle it makes with the horizontal axis at *G.* Using geometry we can find this tangent as the ratio of the "opposite side" *(OH)* to the "adjacent side" *(OG).* The opposite side *OH* is equal to Y/P_π and *OG* is equal to Y/P_T. Therefore, the slope of *HAG* is:

$$\frac{OH}{OG} = \frac{Y/P_\pi}{Y/P_T} = \frac{Y}{P_\pi} \cdot \frac{P_T}{Y} = \frac{P_T}{P_\pi}.$$

Thus, the slope of the budget line is equal to the ratio of the two commodity prices, and any change in one price relative to the other will change the slope. Income, the other constraint, has nothing to do with slope. It determines the location of the budget line. A rise in income will shift *HAG* to the right, parallel to itself.

The budget line describes the limits on consumption possibilities and, therefore, it is said to represent the budget constraint. Since we have assumed only two commodities, all income must be spent on one or the other and the equation of the budget constraint has the following form:

$$TP_T + \pi P_\pi = Y,$$

where T is the quantity of tea purchased and π the quantity of pie purchased. If all income is not spent, we can treat the resulting savings as purchase of another commodity such as security or protection against a rainy day, but then we will have three commodities instead of two. Rather than introduce a third commodity, we have chosen not to allow saving at all. This minor problem would disappear entirely if we were willing to deal with an m-commodity world in which savings could be one of the commodities.

One more note: Fixing the price of pie and tea is a temporary ex-

---

[8] The concept of an attainable subset with a boundary or frontier has many other applications in economic theory. This set need not have the neat triangular shape that results from the budget constraint used in this chapter. Attainable sets with other shapes appear in Chapter 8, where we discuss production possibilities, and in Chapter 18, on general equilibrium.

pedient. We are building a model of the way a consumer might choose among goods when he takes their prices as given. This is quite realistic since real consumers seldom find themselves in situations where their decision to buy seems likely to have any effect on price. Nevertheless, prices are themselves determined in part by consumer purchases; that is, by demand, so this assumption of fixed prices must ultimately be dropped.

Now that we have the budget line to work with, we will go back to the consideration of indifference curves. These curves have a number of very important characteristics that we will now discuss, one at a time.

NEGATIVE SLOPE

It was suggested above that an indifference curve cannot, for example, pass through A and B as the dashed line does in Figure 3–5. If it did, both A and B would be in the "indifferent-to-A" set, even though B contains more of both goods. B cannot belong to Set I, for we have assumed more of each good is always preferred to less. Thus, we can rule out positive slope for indifference curves. Neither can an indifference curve be horizontal like AJ, for this would put J, with the same amount of pie and more tea, in the "indifferent-to-A" set and confound our assumption once again. It cannot be vertical for the same reason, and so it must have a negative slope.

FIGURE 3–5

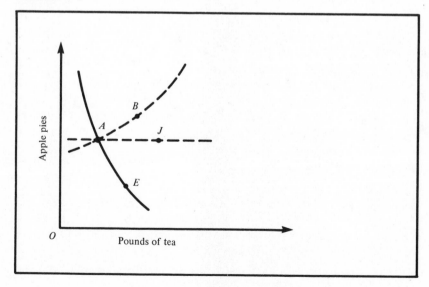

CONTINUITY

The indifference curve AE is drawn smooth and continuous in Figure 3–5. There are some technical mathematical reasons for doing it this way. They arise from the historically important use of calculus as a structure for economic reasoning. Other mathematical techniques are now in common use and the importance of continuity and smoothness is much reduced. Nevertheless, the geometry we are using is made easier by assuming continuity and smoothness, so it is worth discussing one further aspect of the question.

Continuity implies that goods are divisible into infinitely small units so that we can compare basket A with a basket, very close to A, that has just a little more tea and just a little less pie. This can be made to seem reasonable, even if one good is a golf ball, by recognizing that what we are putting into these baskets (and measuring along the axis) are rates of consumption over time, not individual units of the good. While one obviously cannot consume one half of a golf ball, one can consume one half of a golf ball per week by buying a new one every other week. In most cases the unrealism of infinite divisibility disappears as soon as it is recognized that we are concerned with a rate of consumption over time. Even a Cadillac can be consumed at one thirty-sixth of an automobile per month by buying a new one every three years; and the rate can be reduced to one forty-eighth per month by making the purchase every four years.

This argument means that there are baskets of goods all along the curve AE in Figure 3–5. We have made the goods themselves infinitely divisible. Once the curve is drawn, however, an additional idea is introduced. Preferences must also be continuous. It must be possible to compare a basket on the curve with another very close to it and know which is preferred. Real people probably have a threshold beneath which differences between baskets are not detected. Any one good in a basket must increase by at least some minimum amount before a person becomes aware of a change. The nice smooth continuous curves that we use simply abstract from this problem.

NONINTERSECTION

It is purely a matter of logic that indifference curves cannot intersect as AF and AE do in Figure 3–6. Intersection would imply that F and E are both in the "indifferent-to-A" set as follows: F is indifferent to A (FiA) because it is on the same indifference curve, and A is indifferent to E (AiE) for the same reason. We are tempted to conclude from these two statements that FiE. This conclusion involves transitive reasoning. Transitive reasoning is very common in our thought patterns. It establishes the order of three different things when they are compared two at a time. We will insist that the choices of economic theory be transitive.

Basket F, however, cannot be indifferent to basket E because F contains more of both goods than E, and so one of our other assumptions requires that F belong to the "better-than-E" set (FpE). We can remove the contradiction and preserve transitive reasoning only by forbidding indifference curves to intersect.

Surprisingly we are probably making a choice among values when

FIGURE 3–6

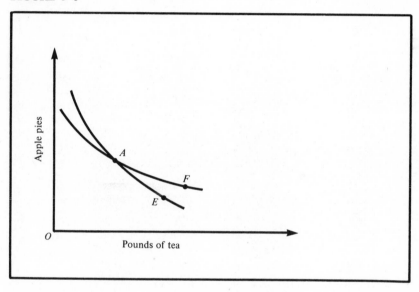

we enforce transitive reasoning. We get into the habit of transitive reasoning in our daily life because observations of any variable that can be measured will be transitive. If Mary is taller than Sue and Sue is taller than Bill, then Mary is clearly taller than Bill. In experiments that do not involve measurable quantities, however, people sometimes make intransitive choices. For instance, some person may indicate that he prefers tea to coffee and coffee to cola, and then also indicate a preference for cola over tea. There seems to be no reason not to accept these kinds of choices in everyday life. Experimenters have discovered, however, that if intransitive reasoning is pointed out to a subject, he will often react as if he has made a mistake. People seem to feel that their choices *ought* to be transitive, and if they become aware of intransitivity, feel they ought to revise their choice pattern. We apparently have normative convictions about the logic of our choices.

MAXIMIZING

Indifference curves must be convex when viewed from the origin. All of the examples used so far have had that shape. The easiest way to see why convexity is necessary requires that we know what it means to maximize using indifference curves and budget lines. This is therefore a good place to discuss maximizing.

Maximizing means only that economic man chooses from the attainable set of baskets the one (or ones, in case of a tie) that he most

FIGURE 3–7

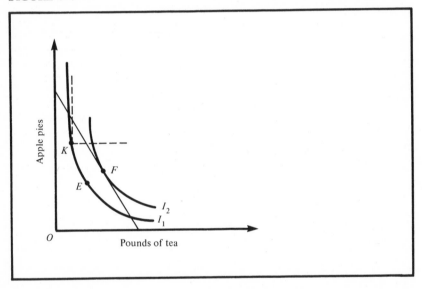

prefers. Which basket is this on the indifference map? Many indifference curves will touch or cross the budget line and thus enter the attainable set. Two, I_1 and I_2, are shown on Figure 3–7. Clearly, every point (basket) on I_2 is preferred to, or ranked higher than, every basket on I_1. This must be true because F is preferred to E. Transitive logic requires that every other point on I_2, being indifferent to F, must also be preferred to E, and these points in turn are also preferred to other points on I_1 because the latter are indifferent to E.

So when one is maximizing, any point on I_2 is not only preferred to any point on I_1, but must be chosen in any contest between the two. An inspection of Figure 3–7 reveals that only one point in the attainable set, Point F, lies on I_2 and that every other point in the attainable set must lie on a lower indifference curve. Hence F is preferred above all other points or baskets in the attainable set and must be the chosen basket. Point F lies at the tangency between the budget line and an indifference curve, so in geometric terms, to find this tangency is to maximize, or optimize, as our postulates have defined it.

A little more thought will make it clear that no point that is in the interior of the attainable set can be a maximum point. Starting from any point like K in Figure 3-7, it is always possible to find still another point in the attainable set that is in the quadrant above and to the right of K. Such a basket will contain more of both goods. It must be preferred to K. Only a point *on* the boundary will have no points above and to the right that are still in the attainable set. Hence only a boundary point can be a maximum point.

CONVEXITY

So far we have drawn indifference curves as if they were convex to the origin as in Figure 3-7, but we have not explicitly eliminated the posssibility that they might be concave as in Figure 3-8. If they were concave, F would not be the maximizing basket. Basket H is in the attainable set and obviously it is preferred to F; that is, it lies on a higher indifference curve than the one that goes through F.

Basket H, however, has a peculiarity that leads to an interesting conclusion. It contains only one of the two commodities. Even if we departed from geometry and considered all m possible commodities, the mathematics would still yield the same conclusion. If indifference

FIGURE 3-8

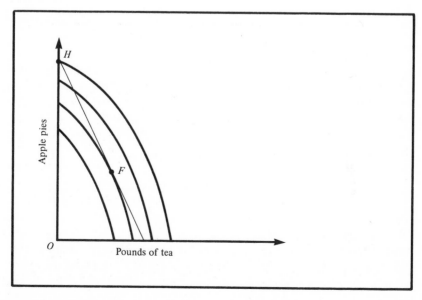

curves are concave to the origin, economic man will choose a pattern of consumption that involves spending all his income on one good and buying zero amounts of all the others. Our model is designed to predict the behavior not just of economic man, but of real people. Therefore, we are led to predict that individuals will limit their consumption to a single commodity. This is a testable proposition about human behavior. Even casual observation suggests that it does not pass the test. People do not behave that way.

FIGURE 3–9

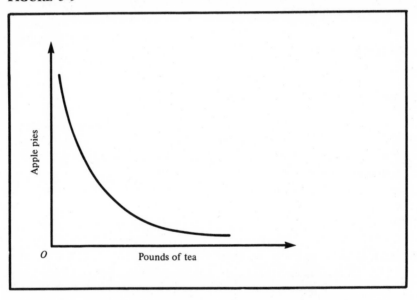

We might, of course, try to salvage the model by saying, "Yes, but people are not rational in the way our economic man is and that is why they consume more than one good." This will not make us very happy, for it seems as if any definition of rational ought to be consistent with variety in our consumption pattern. Any man who consumed only one commodity would be thought quite odd. It is much better just to give up the possibility of concave indifference curves and make them convex to the origin. We can say concave curves are not useful because they lead to statements about human behavior that can easily be observed to be wrong.[9]

---

[9] The assumption of convexity is also meant to eliminate the possibility that indifference curves are straight lines. A straight indifference curve suggests that the two commodities are perfect substitutes for each other. If so, the differences between them are superficial from the consumer's point of view and they ought to be treated as a single commodity.

Convexity does not mean, however, that the indifference curve is a rectangular hyperbola as in Figure 3–9. The rectangular hyperbola looks very much like the indifference curves we have been using, but it has the special property that the legs of the curve get continuously closer to the axis as they get further from the origin. They never reach the axis, however, no matter how far they are extended; they are asymptotic. This curve is often used as an example of an indifference curve because it has some simple mathematical properties that are very convenient. These properties, however, make it a special case that is not based in any necessary assumption about preferences, so we will not use it. We will permit indifference curves to reach either axis and, in certain cases, we will actually *want* them to get to the axis (See Corner Tangencies, Chapter 4).

ORDINAL AND CARDINAL

So far we have said only that any point on a higher indifference curve is preferred to any on a lower curve. This is no accident! This is all we mean to say. We might have said some higher points are twice as strongly preferred as some lower points (or give twice the utility or satisfaction), but we did not. Part of the reason is that real people seem not to know how strongly they prefer one consumption pattern to another, even when they are able to make a choice between them.

This question has been studied experimentally. For instance, suppose a particular individual buys a certain basket of goods in 1971 (call it X_{71}) and another in 1972 (X_{72}). Now measure the cost of both baskets in 1972 and suppose his 1972 income is large enough to buy either basket. Then the fact that he actually bought X_{72} in 1972 (when he could have bought X_{71}) is evidence that $X_{72}pX_{71}$.[10] This is evidence of the preference *order* of these two baskets. If the economist then asks the individual, "How great is your preference for X_{72} over X_{71}?" he has trouble getting an answer. People do not seem to know how to quantify their preferences. No units of preference are available, and there does not seem to be a mental distinction between the two baskets to which units might be attached. Economists have, therefore, decided to be content with information about the rank order of baskets, and the resulting preference pattern is called *ordinal*.

If we could attach a number of units of preference to each basket and use those numbers to rank baskets, we would call the preference pattern *cardinal*. Cardinal preferences were actually used by economists

---

[10] This technique has been developed into a theory of Revealed Preference that will be discussed more fully under that title later on in this chapter.

before the 1930s when they treated utility as a cardinally measurable characteristic of every basket of goods.[11]

There is another reason for sticking to ordinal preference: namely, that we do not need to attach a cardinal preference value to each curve in order to reach the usual conclusions of economic theory. In other words, at the present state of development, ordinal properties are enough to permit the deduction of all the usual propositions of economic theory.

With regard to indifference curves, one comment should be added. The ordinal relationship means that the distance between indifference curves is not an indication of strength of preference nor of how much better it is to move to the higher curve. In fact, the distance between two curves means, quite simply, nothing at all.

SATIATION

We have said little up to this point about satiation. Can people become satiated with one good? Can they become satiated with all goods? To be satiated with a good would mean that to get more of that one good and the same amount of all others would not put the individual on a higher indifference curve. Point S in Figure 3–10 represents such a situation.

At S the indifference curve is tangent to a horizontal line. A tiny bit more tea with the same amount of pie would leave our man on the same curve, no better off. We generally feel that this kind of satiation is possible for real people. Most of us have had the experience at some time of consuming one good at such a high rate relative to other goods that we felt no particular interest in a further increase in the *rate* of consumption of that good. We may, therefore, want, in the course of this analysis, to consider an assumption about satiation that permits indifference curves to have a horizontal tangent as at S and/or a vertical tangent as at U. We may even want the curve to have a positive slope to the right of S so as to indicate that more tea may in fact make him worse off unless he gets more pie to go with it.

COMPLETE SATIATION

Point R in Figure 3–10 represents satiation with all goods. Every other basket, whether it contains more pie or more tea or more of both (or less of either or both), lies on a lower indifference curve. This is a

---

[11] We even had a unit for the measurement of utility (satisfaction? happiness?) called a "utile." Similarly, psychologists have been tempted by the cardinal measurement of things like anger and frustration. Presumably frustration might be measured in "futiles."

FIGURE 3–10

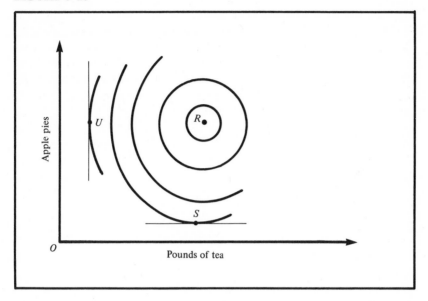

position of complete satiation. It is not one with which people have had much experience, consequently we seldom have use for an assumption that would lead to the closed indifference curves shown on Figure 3–10.

In fact, we generally limit discussion to the negatively sloped portions of indifference curves. Interesting economic questions usually involve states of the economy in which satiation is rare. Moreover, since maximizing has turned out to mean seeking the point of tangency between the boundary of the attainable set and an indifference curve, our analysis becomes much more complex if any kind of satiation is made possible.

REVEALED PREFERENCE

Indifference curves result from a fairly elaborate set of assumptions or axioms. These axioms determine the shape of the curves, but they cannot tell us where a particular basket might fall in the preference pattern of a particular individual. Neither axioms nor curves are directly observable. The axioms do assert that an individual can compare two baskets of goods and tell which one he prefers, and this suggests that we might construct an indifference map by asking some person a lot of questions. This approach makes economists nervous, because the answers people give depend so often on how they think the information will be used. We would all be more comfortable if we could describe and locate indifference curves by deduction from the observable *actions* of the individuals. This is exactly what the theory of revealed preference proposes to do.

The action that we propose to observe is the purchase of some basket of goods by a particular individual. For instance, we may observe his rate of consumption of various goods in 1970. Thus, we will have a set of quantities (per year) at 1970 prices and bought with 1970 in-

FIGURE 3–11

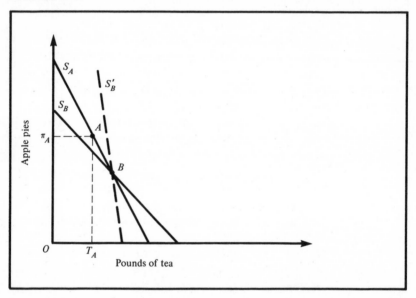

come. It will simplify the following argument if we use only two goods and geometry. The basket then becomes a point like A on Figure 3–11. The point A indicates that some person, call him Archer, actually bought π_A of apple pie in 1970 and T_A of tea. The purchase was made at certain prices for pie and tea and with a certain income, and these can be used to draw a budget line through A. This curve is exactly like the budget line drawn earlier in this chapter. This line represents a "price and income situation" that prevailed in 1970 and we have labeled it S_A on Figure 3–11 to indicate that these are the prices and income that lead to the actual purchase of basket A.

From the fact that Archer actually bought this basket, we will infer that he preferred it to any other basket in the attainable set. This set, determined by the price and income situation (S_A), includes all of the points on or below the curve labeled S_A on Figure 3–11. Basket B is one such basket and we want to infer that A is preferred to B because he could have bought B in 1970 when he actually bought A.

There may, however, be some price and income situation in which Archer will choose B. We will, in fact, assume explicitly that there is at least one price-income situation that will lead to the choice of B. Moreover we will assume there is a price and income situation for any basket that can be represented by a point on Figure 3–11. This is the first important assumption of the theory of revealed preference. We have labeled the price-income situation that leads to the purchase of B as S_B. Note that when B is chosen, it would not be possible to choose A. Basket A lies above the budget line S_B and hence at prices and incomes represented by S_B it would cost too much.

If baskets A and B represent the observed choices of some individual, then we can say that that individual is being consistent. When he chose A, B was attainable, so we infer that A is preferred to B. Later, when he chose B, A was not attainable, and so his choice of B gives us no reason to doubt that he still prefers A to B. We might not always be so lucky. Basket B might have been chosen in the situation represented by the dashed line S'_B. We would then have contradictory evidence about the preference relationship between A and B. A is apparently preferred to B in situation S_A and B is apparently preferred to A in situation S'_B. We would then describe these choices as inconsistent. Indeed, there is evidence from the study of the behavior of households that "almost all families made at least some inconsistent choices."[12] Economists have offered a number of explanations, but these have generally been difficult to test. There is evidence, however, that choices are more likely to be consistent if the alternatives (A and B in our example) are close together. More inconsistencies will appear when choice must be made among consumption patterns that are very different from the usual or typical pattern of the individual. At any rate, when inconsistency occurs, we cannot infer anything about the preference relationship between two baskets like A and B.

We must, therefore, recognize that the theory of revealed preference rests on the assumption that inconsistencies do not occur. We must assume that:

When A is chosen (situation S_A), B is attainable so that we can infer that A is preferred to B,

And that when B is chosen (in situation S_B) A could not be chosen, so that no inconsistency of choices exists.

<hr>

[12] Anthony C. Koo and Peter Schmidt, "Cognitive Range in the Theory of Revealed Preference," *Journal of Political Economy,* vol. 82, no. 1 (January–February 1974), p. 174.

When our observations meet these two conditions we will say that A is revealed preferred to B and use the symbol (r) for "is revealed preferred to." Thus: ArB. This is the second major assumption of the theory of revealed preference. It is really the assumption that individuals are consistent, meaning that their tastes and preferences do not change appreciably over the period of our observation of their purchases. Using these assumptions we can now develop something like an indifference curve from a sufficient number of observations of actual purchases.

FIGURE 3–12

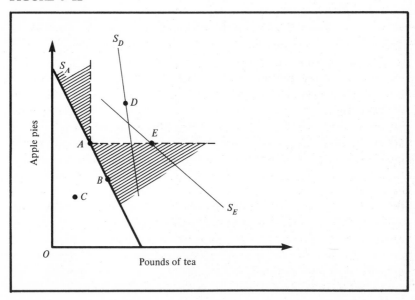

Start again with basket A, chosen by Mr. Archer in the price-income situation (S_A) as in Figure 3–12. On the assumptions made above, A is revealed preferred to any point on the line S_A or below it. This means that any such point (B and C are examples) will be chosen in some price-income situation (by the first assumption) and A will not be attainable in those situations (by the second assumption). We therefore can know the preference ordering between A and the rest of the attainable set from our observation that Archer actually bought A.

There is, in addition, another set of points whose relation to A is already clear. These are the points above and to the right of A. D and E are examples. In any price-income situation that leads to the choice of D or E, A will be in the attainable set and hence revealed inferior to D or E. In other words, as long as prices are positive, the lines S_D

and S_E must pass to the right of A.[13] We can, therefore, know A is revealed inferior to all points in the quadrant above and to the right of A from our observation that Archer actually bought A.

We still do not know anything about the points in the shaded area of Figure 3–12. Somewhere in there we can have points that are indifferent to A. It is through that area that an indifference curve would have to run, and this means that it would have negative slope. Instead of calling it an indifference curve, however, it would be better to think of it as a preference boundary. All baskets that are revealed inferior to A will lie below it and all that are revealed preferred to A will lie above it. This terminology merely stresses the fact that the preference boundary is built up from observations of actual behavior and hence is something quite distinct from the indifference curve deduced from a set of assumptions.

As just noted, the preference boundary will have negative slope. In addition it will be convex in the neighborhood of point A. We have assumed that in choosing A, the individual indicated his preference for A over any other points on the line S_A. This includes points on the line and very close to A, hence if we can locate a boundary through A, then it must lie above the line S_A on both sides of A. This boundary would thus be convex (when viewed from the origin) near A at least. Now negative slope and convexity are two of the characteristics of the indifference curves that we deduced earlier from assumptions alone. We can now argue that actual observations of individual consumption choices can be seen as evidence that people make choices as if they had something quite like an indifference curve in mind.

Further observations of actual purchases can lead to still more information about the preference boundary. Consider the point B on Figure 3–13. We know that A is revealed preferred to B, (ArB) from the assumptions and arguments already made. If we now observe that B is actually purchased when the price-income situation is S_B then we know that B is revealed preferred to all other points in the set on or below S_B. Point E in Figure 3–13 is such a point, hence BrE. We will assume that these choices are transitive, making this the third special assumption of the theory of revealed preference. It then follows that: ArB and BrE; hence, ArE. We have thus found another batch of points that must lie below the preference boundary through A. These are all the points in the small shaded triangle RBS (of which E is just one example). This triangle is part of the set whose relationship to A was

---

[13] As long as prices are greater than zero, S_D and S_E must have negative slope and therefore cannot go through A, let alone to the left of it. If the price of one good (tea) is zero, the line S_E would be horizontal and go through A. This would still indicate that A was available when E was chosen and E was not available when A was chosen, hence (ErA).

previously unknown, and was shown shaded in Figure 3–12. Use of a transitivity assumption has reduced that unknown area. We can reduce it still further by repeating the process described just above after observing the purchase of E in price-income situation S_E. Each additional observation will enable us to reduce the unknown area until we have approximated, as closely as we wish, the underside of the preference boundary through A.[14]

It is thus possible to approximate the preference boundary of a real individual by observing his behavior. In particular, we must observe his purchases of goods and services in a number of price-income situa-

FIGURE 3–13

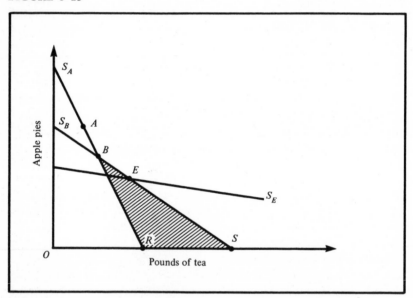

tions. A very large number of observations will be needed to pin down the precise location of even a few curves. It is not likely therefore that we will try to draw the preference boundaries for many individuals. Revealed preference is nevertheless very important because it suggests that individual behavior is consistent with something very like an individual indifference map. Clearly, economists can use indifference curves with more confidence, though we should not lose sight of the necessary assumptions on which revealed preference depends.

---

[14] It is also possible, by a similar process, to approximate this hypothetical preference boundary through A from above. In this case, observations are used to find sets of points that are revealed preferred to A and hence to lie above any preference boundary through A.

SUMMARY

This chapter has introduced the basic model of consumer choice. That model makes use of two curves, a budget line and an indifference curve. The budget line divides the set of consumption possibilities into two subsets, one of which is attainable. It fixes the boundary of the attainable sets by introducing two constraints on choice: the prices of goods and the size of money income.

The indifference curve also divides the consumption set, but does so on the basis of a ranking of consumption alternatives by preference. These curves have a number of important properties. They are:

Negatively sloped,

Smooth and continuous,

Non-intersecting,

Convex,

Ordinal in their relationship to each other.

These characteristics result from assumptions referred to in the text.

Using these curves, "maximizing" was discovered to mean choosing the basket of goods that occurs at the point of tangency of the budget line with the indifference curve. This basket will lie on the highest indifference curve that enters the attainable set. It is thus the preferred position, given the income and price constraints.

The next chapter will use this model to examine a number of propositions about the behavior of people making choices.

SELECTED READINGS

Hicks, John R.   *Value & Capital* (Oxford: The Clarendon Press, 2d Ed., 1946), Ch. 1 and 2.

Lancaster, K.   "A New Approach to Consumer Theory," *Journal of Political Economy,* vol. 74 (1966), pp. 131–57.

Leiberstein, Harvey.   "Bandwagon, Snob, and Veblen Effects in the Theory of Consumer Demand," *Quarterly Journal of Economics,* vol. 64 (1950), pp. 183–207.

Walsh, V. C.   *Introduction to Contemporary Microeconomics* (New York: McGraw Hill, 1970), Ch. 1–3.

Chapter 4

Extending the theory of choice

INTRODUCTION

The choosing, consuming, economic men who populated Chapter 3 can be made to tell us about demand. With a theory of demand we can find out a number of interesting things about exchange and how it affects welfare. As we move in that direction, however, we will come across several important ideas—the rate of substitution, income and substitution effects and corner tangencies. We will, therefore, spend Chapter 4 on these ideas and leave demand itself for Chapter 5.

THE RATE OF SUBSTITUTION

At any point on an indifference curve our man in Economics can give up a little of one good and, by getting the right additional amount of the other, stay on the same curve. We will call the ratio between what he gives up and what he gets "the rate of substitution." In Figure 4–1 we have in mind that he could switch from basket A to another basket, A', very close to A, that contains a little less pie and just enough more tea to leave him on the same curve. We have exaggerated the difference between A and A' to make the argument easier. The changing amounts of pie and tea suggest a substitution of tea for pie which we will call the Rate of Substitution and write $RS_{T\pi}$.[1] We can estimate this

---

[1] This concept is often called the Marginal Rate of Substitution, but the term marginal is really unnecessary since this is a "rate" of substitution anyway. See Peter Newman, *The Theory of Exchange* (Englewood Cliffs, N.J.: Prentice-Hall, 1965), p. 31.

FIGURE 4–1

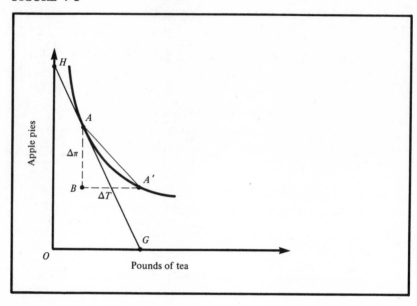

rate by dividing the loss of pie ($\Delta\pi$) as shown on Figure 4–1, by the gain in tea (ΔT), thus:[2]

$$RS_{T\pi} = \frac{\Delta\pi}{\Delta T}.$$

$\Delta\pi$ represents a loss of pie and should be preceded by a minus sign thus making $RS_{T\pi}$ a negative quantity. It is customary, however, to ignore the sign and to treat the rate of substitution as positive.

The ratio $\Delta\pi/\Delta T$ has another meaning as well. It is the slope of a straight line from A to A'. It can be seen by looking at the figure that as $\Delta\pi$ becomes smaller and smaller, A' moves closer and closer to A and the slope of AA' will come closer and closer to the slope of the line HAG, which is tangent to the indifference curve at A. In fact, it is one of the major theorems of calculus that, if $\Delta\pi$ is allowed to approach zero as a limit, then the slope of AA' will approach the slope of HAG as a limit. We will, therefore, define the rate of substitution of tea for pie ($RS_{T\pi}$) at any point on the curve (like A), as the slope of a tangent at

---

[2] It sometimes appears to students more logical to put ΔT on top of the ratio and let $\Delta\pi$ be the denominator. Economists did not do this because they wanted the RS to behave like an earlier, somewhat similar concept, marginal utility. The marginal utility of any good diminishes as the amount of that good is increased, and the $RS_{T\pi}$ is, therefore, defined so that it too will diminish as we move down the curve increasing the amount of tea. See the discussion that follows.

FIGURE 4-2

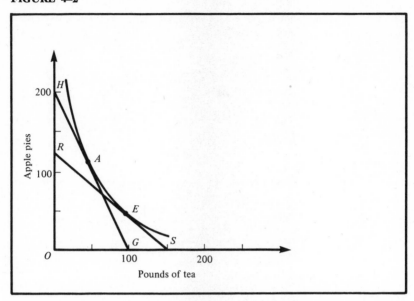

that point, rather than as a ratio of small changes in pie and tea. It should be added that we will make use of these mathematics many more times before we are done, for the slope of many economic curves has a significant meaning.

Now we can find a value for the rate of substitution at A using Figure 4–2 as follows:

$$RS_{T\pi} = \text{Slope of } HAG = \frac{OH}{OG} = \frac{200}{100} = 2.$$

If we look at E on Figure 4–2, it is clear that a tangent at that point will not be so steep. The rate of substitution of tea for pie decreases as the amount of tea increases. We get this result because we have made indifference curves convex to the origin. Hence at E we have:

$$RS_{T\pi} = \text{Slope of } RES = \frac{OR}{OS} = \frac{125}{150} = 0.83$$

We refer to this phenomenon as a "diminishing rate of substitution."

If we think, on the other hand, of moving up the curve substituting pie for tea, then we can talk about the rate of substitution of pie for tea ($RS_{\pi T}$) and it, too, will be seen to diminish. At E, for instance:

$$RS_{\pi T} = \frac{OS}{OR} = \frac{150}{125} = 1.2.$$

The ratio OS/OR may look strange at first, but when we move up the curve we treat the slope of RES as the tangent of the angle it makes with the vertical axis, and OS is therefore the opposite side and OR is adjacent. At A:

$$RS_{\pi T} = \frac{OG}{OH} = \frac{100}{200} = 0.5,$$

so the $RS_{\pi T}$ is smaller at A than at E. It diminishes as the quantity of pie increases.

FIGURE 4–3

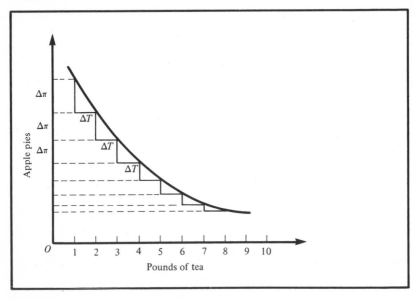

It might be added that diminishing rates of substitution do not seem to be unreasonable. Most of us believe from our own experience that added increments of any good become less and less attractive to us as we get more and more of that good *relative* to other goods. This can be clearly seen in Figure 4–3. As we move down the curve, the horizontal part of each stair step (ΔT) indicates one more pound of tea. The vertical part indicates the amount of pie ($\Delta\pi$) we could give up to get one more pound of tea and still remain on the same curve. As we move to the right, getting more tea, it obviously becomes less and less valuable to us, for the amount of pie we could give up gets smaller and smaller. This is exactly what we mean when we say that the rate of substitution of tea for pie diminishes. This result is entirely due to the assumption that indifference curves are (strictly) convex.

WELFARE AND THE RATE OF SUBSTITUTION

This does not end the concern of economists with the rate of substitution. It is used in the formulation of the conditions for maximization of economic welfare. These conditions often appear as an equality between two rates of substitution. For example, the $RS_{T\pi}$ discussed above is a rate of substitution in preference. It appears at point A on

FIGURE 4–4

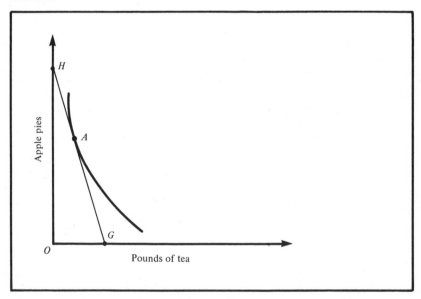

Figure 4–4 as the slope of the line HAG which is tangent to the indifference curve of A.

The line HAG can also represent a budget line. As a budget line it has a slope equal to the price ratio $P_T/P\pi$. Therefore at the point A:

$$RS_{T\pi} = \frac{P_T}{P_\pi}$$

We can view the ratio $P_T/P\pi$ as the rate at which an individual *can* substitute tea for pie by buying less pie and more tea. Furthermore we can view $RS_{T\pi}$ as the rate at which an individual is willing to substitute pie for tea, meaning that substitution at that rate will leave him on the same indifference curve. At A where the budget line is tangent to the indifference curve the individual is maximizing by making what he can do equal to what he wants to do.

In competitive markets all individuals face the same prices, hence the budget line has the same slope (P_T/P_π) for every one. As each person tries to maximize given these prices he or she seeks the point of tangency of the budget line with his or her highest indifference curve. The result will be that everyone makes the rate of substitution along their indifference curve equal to the common budget line slope. Therefore everyone who maximizes will have the same $RS_{T\pi}$ (if he or she consumes some of both goods) and we can say that equal rates of substitution between pairs of goods are a condition of a welfare maximum under competition.[3]

THE INCOME EFFECT

Up to this point whenever we have talked about income, we have assumed it to flow at some given rate. This fixed rate, along with fixed

---

[3] In Figure 4–1, the loss of $\Delta\pi$ will put the individual at B on a lower indifference curve. The model we are using tells us nothing about points A and B except that A is preferred to B. At one time, however, economists treated utility as a measurable quantity, hence one could say that a move from A to B caused a loss in utility equal to $\Delta\pi$ multiplied by the marginal utility per unit of pie. Marginal utility (MU_π) is the amount by which total utility is changed per unit change in the quantity of pie. From B the individual can get back on the original indifference curve by getting ΔT. Hence

$$\Delta\pi \cdot MU_\pi = \Delta T \cdot MU_T.$$

Utility lost by giving up $\Delta\pi$ must equal the utility gained from ΔT. If we rearrange this expression, then:

$$\frac{\Delta\pi}{\Delta T} = \frac{MU_T}{MU_\pi}.$$

The first term is the slope of the line AA' on Figure 4–1., and as pointed out above, it approaches the slope of HAG as $\Delta\pi$ approaches zero. Hence:

$$RS_{T\pi} = \text{Slope of } HAG = \frac{MU_T}{MU_\pi}.$$

In an older language, the rate of subscription of two goods is equal to the ratio of their marginal utilities, and at equilibrium:

$$R_{ST\pi} = \frac{MU_T}{MU_\pi} = \frac{P_T}{P_\pi}.$$

If we rewrite the last two terms, then:

$$\frac{MU_T}{P_T} = \frac{MU_\pi}{P_\pi}.$$

The first term, MU_T/P_T, is the marginal utility of a dollar's worth of tea. At equilibrium we can say that the marginal utility from spending a dollar must be the same whether it is spent on pie or tea. Thus the condition for an optimum is that the individual finds that one more dollar of income gives him the same utility no matter how he spends it. This language implies a cardinal measure of utility, however, and has been dropped as economists have shifted to the purely ordinal indifference curves.

prices for pie and tea, enabled us to define the attainable set shown as
the triangle *OHAG* in Figure 4–5. If we now relax the income constraint—that is, let the income assume other values—then the attainable
set will change in size. As income is increased from $500 per month to
$600 per month, but prices remain the same, we get a new budget line,
MES, and a new optimum position at *E,* which is on a higher indifference curve than *A.* (We find this new budget line by finding its end
points. Point *S* is the new income divided by the price of tea (Y/P_T).

FIGURE 4–5

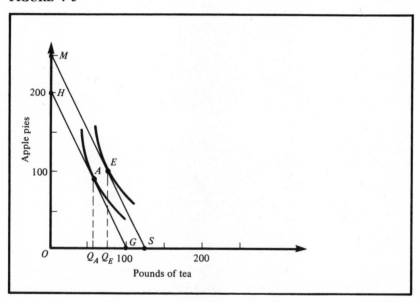

Since P_T has not changed, then *S* will be at $600/$5 = 120 pounds of
tea. The other end is found the same way using the price of pie as
denominator.)

What effect does this move have on the consumption of tea? In
Figure 4–5 it is obvious that the individual will want more tea and we
will attribute the increase $(Q_E - Q_A)$ to an "income effect." Since the
income effect usually results in increased consumption as income rises,
we call the goods (like tea in this example) normal goods, but abnormal
goods are possible. They may be goods like rice that bulk very large in
the diet of a poor family because they are cheap. As family income
rises, the family may want to reduce absolutely the quantity of rice it
consumes and instead consume more of other goods. Figure 4–6 represents this kind of behavior toward what we will now call an "inferior

FIGURE 4–6

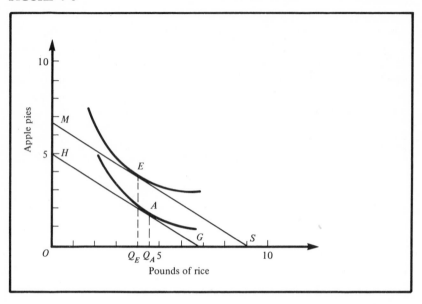

good" to distinguish it from a "normal good." The optimum amount
of rice falls from Q_A to Q_E at the higher income.

ENGEL CURVES

On Figure 4–7 we have added more budget lines based on larger
incomes and we get more optimum points (R and C). A line through
these points, called an "income-consumption curve," summarizes the relationship between income and tea consumption as income changes. (It
is also an income-consumption curve for the pie that is measured on
the vertical axis.) To make this information more convenient to use,
economists often plot just two of the variables, tea consumption and
income, together on one diagram. We have done this in Figure 4–8,
where consumption of tea is measured on the vertical axis and income
on the horizontal. Reading from Figure 4–2 we find that when income
is $500 per month, about 55 pounds of tea (Q_A) will be consumed,
and we plot this information on Figure 4–8 as point A'. Adding more
points by the same method will trace out the curve $A'E'R'$, which is
called an "Engel curve" after Christian Lorenz Ernst Engel, a German
statistician of the 19th century.

Engel curves are a common analytic tool in the study of consumption.
The Engel curve in Figure 4–8 indicates that as income grows, consumption also grows, but less than proportionately. The curve is con-

cave when viewed from below. (If income and tea consumption expanded in the same proportions to each other, the curve would, of course, be a straight line.)

Food eaten at home behaves like tea in this example, but food eaten out does not. In consumption studies we are often interested in what happens to groups of commodities like "food eaten at home," rather than individual goods like tea. We still use Engel curves in these studies, but it is necessary to change the nature of the curve somewhat to make

FIGURE 4–7

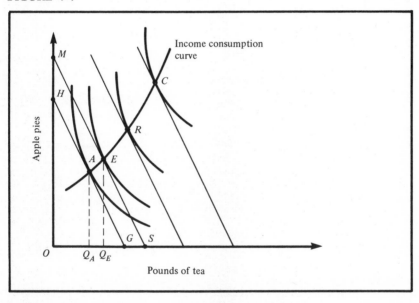

this possible. There are no physical units with which to measure "food eaten at home" so we switch to expenditures on food eaten at home. From Figure 4–5 we can find the expenditure on tea when income is $500 per month. The income of $500 locates the budget line HAG and since basket A is then chosen, expenditure on tea will be ($P_T \ Q_A =$ 5×55 units $= \$275$). To this we will add expenditures (when income is $500 per month) on all other goods that are part of food eaten at home. This gives a total expenditure in dollars (E_A), which is measured along the vertical axis in Figure 4–9. A is then a point on what we will call an Engel expenditure curve, and if we make the same calculations at all other income levels (prices of goods do not change), we get the whole curve ($A''E''R''$).

It can be seen from the shape of this curve that expenditure on food eaten at home increases as income increases but in smaller proportion.

FIGURE 4–8

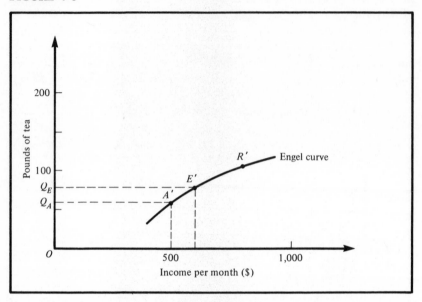

Though this relationship does not hold for "eating out" it holds for all food items taken together. This was one of the original findings of Christian Engel and it is still true today. It means that food production need not grow as rapidly as income rises in a developing economy. Manufactured goods on the other hand may have an Engel expenditure

FIGURE 4–9

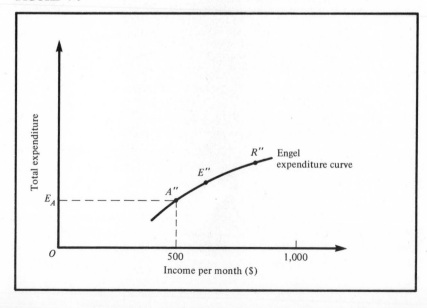

curve that is convex from below, indicating that their consumption grows more rapidly than income as income rises.

THE SUBSTITUTION EFFECT

Having seen what happens when the income constraint is relaxed, let us also investigate what happens when we relax the price constraint.

FIGURE 4–10

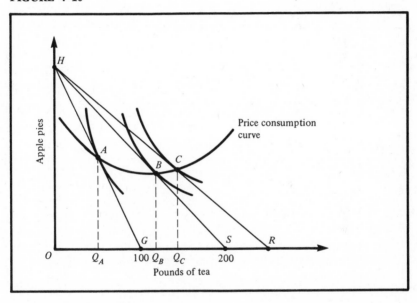

We will let the price of tea vary while income and the price of pie are held constant. In Figure 4–10 we have represented this situation when

$$Y = \$500 \text{ per month,}$$
$$P_\pi = \$2.50 \text{ per pie,}$$

and we have drawn in several budget lines. For the first of these, *HAG*, $P_T = \$5$. A lower price for tea ($P_T = \$2.50$) moves the boundary of the attainable set to the right and indicates a preferred basket at *B*. In this case, tea consumption will be greater at *B* than at *A*. It will increase from $Q_A = 50$ pounds to $Q_B = 125$ pounds.

We can still add more budget lines, *HCR* for example, to Figure 4–10 by introducing still more prices for tea while holding the price of pie and money income constant. There is an optimum point on each of these budget lines and they can be connected by a line like *ABC* on Figure 4–10. This line is called a price-consumption curve. It reveals what happens to the quantity of tea that the consumer wants to consume as the price of tea changes. It thus contains the information necessary to the construction of an individual demand curve, and we will return to it in Chapter 5.

The conclusion that tea is substituted for pie when its price goes down is not surprising, but the situation is actually more complex than it appears to be. At B, economic man is on a higher indifference curve because the fall in price has increased the size of the attainable set. Basket A is now inside the boundary HBS, which means he could buy

FIGURE 4–11

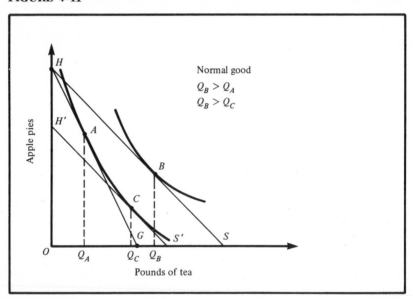

A and have income left over. We are talking about "goods," so the left-over income can be spent in such a way as to make him better off. We may want to say that "on a higher indifference curve" means "better off" or possessed of "larger real income."[4] We must therefore recognize that A and B differ because both income and substitution effects are involved. (The combined effect, the shift from A to B when the price of tea changes, is sometimes called the "total price effect.")

Geometry can be used to separate these two effects. On Figure 4–11 we have drawn two budget lines; HAG represents the first price of tea ($\$5$ per pound), and HBS represents a second price ($\$2.50$ per pound). Basket A is the basket that the consumer will choose when tea is $\$5$ per pound and basket B is the one he will choose at the lower price.

---

[4] The notion that "on a higher indifference curve" means "having a higher real income" will be discussed in the section Real Income later in this chapter.

Suppose that the consumer is at B because the price of tea is now $2.50. We can imagine a reduction in his money income that will put him back on his original indifference curve, the one through A. To show this on Figure 4–11 we move the budget line HBS to the left until it is just tangent to the original curve at C. In this location it is labeled $H'CS'$.

We will take the view that baskets A and C represent the same real income because they lie on the same indifference curve. However, A and C show the effects of different prices for tea. The slope of the budget line is determined by the ratio of prices, P_T/P_π. HAG, which goes through A, represents a price of $5 per pound. Thus:

$$\frac{P_T}{P_\pi} = \frac{\$5.00}{\$2.50} = 2 \text{ (along } HAG)$$

$H'CS'$, which goes through C, is parallel to HBS. This means it represents the same price ratio as HBS, thus

$$\frac{P_T}{P_\pi} = \frac{\$2.50}{\$2.50} = 1 \text{ (along } H'CS').$$

Since baskets A and C represent the same income but different prices for tea, we can argue that the shift in consumption of tea from Q_A to Q_C is due to the fall in the price of tea. The consumer substitutes tea for other goods (pie) when the price of tea falls relative to other goods. The shift from Q_A to Q_C is due to *the substitution effect of a change in price.*

Baskets B and C can also be compared. They both represent the same price for tea ($2.50) because HBS and $H'CS'$ are parallel. B represents a higher real income, however, because it lies on a higher indifference curve. The shift from Q_C to Q_B is therefore due to *the income effect of a change in price.*

Finally, the shift from Q_A to Q_B, which is the total effect of a change in the price, can now be seen to be made up of two parts: a substitution effect and an income effect.

We should note that the substitution effect always produces an increase in consumption of the good that has become relatively cheaper; that is $Q_C > Q_A$ always.[5] This result is made certain by the convex shape of indifference curves. As the price of tea falls relative to other goods, the budget line becomes less steep. Consequently it can only have a tangency with the same indifference curve to the right of A, because the slope of the indifference curve also gets less steep to the right of A. The conclusion that a relatively cheaper good will always

---

[5] This conclusion is called the "Slutsky theorem" after Eugene Slutsky, who proved that the substitution effect always produces a change in consumption of a good that is in the opposite direction from the change in its price.

be substituted for one whose price has not changed probably seems reasonable to most of us, but it is not the reason for the assumption that indifference curves are convex. (The discussion of convexity is in Chapter 3.)[6]

The substitution effect is always inversely related to the change in price, but we already know that the income effect can be either directly or inversely related to the change in income. We must now consider both normal and inferior goods in the context of the income effect that

FIGURE 4–12

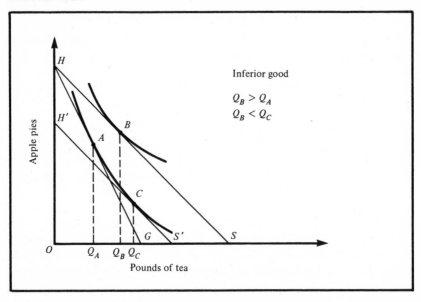

is due to the fall in the price of tea. In Figure 4–11, tea is a normal good ($Q_B > Q_C$), but what happens if we introduce an inferior good? We know that the relation between C and B is what must change. Tea consumption at B must be smaller than it is at C when the good is inferior ($Q_C > Q_B$). This possibility is indicated in Figure 4–12. The income effect is offsetting to the substitution effect.

---

[6] Textbooks sometimes say that the substitution effect is always negative. If we separate the income and substitution effects mathematically, then the sign of the term representing the substitution effect is always negative. When geometry is used, however, the term negative may lead to ambiguity. It sometimes suggests that quantity is always reduced. This will certainly be true if only rises in price are considered. It is, of course, reversed for a fall in price. It is best, therefore, to say that the change in quantity is always *inversely* related to a change in price. A student who wants to see the mathematical analysis of these effects should look at James M. Henderson and Richard E. Quandt, *Microeconomic Theory*, 2d ed. (New York: McGraw-Hill, 1971), pp. 24–28.

This suggests, of course, that some case might arise in which the income effect is so strong as to overwhelm the substitution effect and lead to an actual reduction in the consumption of the good that *falls* in price. Such a case is diagrammed in Figure 4–13. The good is not just inferior, it is a "Giffen good," named for the man who brought such goods to our attention. Giffen goods are said to be relatively inexpensive goods that, therefore, bulk very large in the consumption pattern of the poor—potatoes or rice, perhaps. The poor consume much of this good

FIGURE 4–13

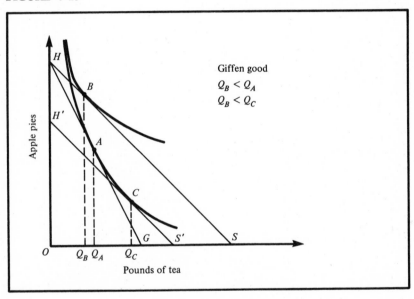

because only thus can they get enough to eat. If, however, the good falls in price, the poor consumer can buy quite a lot of it and still have income left for other foods. *Real* income is larger and this poor consumer may then want to reduce consumption of this good and let other goods replace part of it. There is some debate about whether such goods exist in the real world. They are at least extremely rare. We will discover later that a Giffen good will have a demand curve with positive slope, a phenomenon that is sometimes called Giffen's paradox.

REAL INCOME

We have been acting as if staying on the same indifference curve meant staying at the same level of real income (or welfare, or well being). This is not an unreasonable way to proceed. We are talking about choice, and each curve represents baskets among which the chooser is indifferent. To say that the chooser is indifferent between two baskets is to indicate that he does not feel one of them would make him better off than the other. Consequently, to say that the chooser prefers a basket on a higher curve is to imply that he feels it will make him better off than the other, and we can use the phrase higher real income to describe a shift to the higher curve.

When we begin to talk about a compensating adjustment in money

FIGURE 4–14

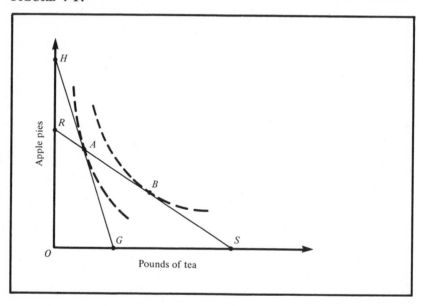

income that would put the individual back on the same curve following some change, however, we have to remember that indifference curves are not observable in real people. We would be hard pressed to decide whether any particular change in money income was enough to ensure that real income remained constant. We must, therefore, find an alternative definition of real income whenever we want to make actual changes (taxes or subsidies) for real people. When real income is defined so that different indifference curves indicate different levels of real income, it is called "Hicks real income." The alternative definition that we will now develop is called "Slutsky real income." J. R. Hicks, Eugene Slutsky, and perhaps R. G. D. Allen are the progenitors of modern demand theory.

Suppose that some set of prices and money income are represented by budget line *HAG* in Figure 4–14. Then a real individual may want to buy basket *A*. When he buys *A* he indicates that he prefers it to any other basket in the attainable set. Any adjustment of income and/or prices that still permits the purchase of *A* using the entire money income *could* be construed as providing the same real income. The line of attainable combinations labeled *RBS* is an example.

Basket *A* can still be purchased, but the difference in slope between *HAG* and *RBS* indicates a change in the relative prices of pie and tea and may require another level of money income as well. We are making some specific basket of goods (*A*) our measure of real income. Since it is just possible to buy *A* in each case, we are arguing that *HAG* and *RBS* represent the same real income under different price and money income conditions. In terms of our earlier theory, we could argue that the individual can get on a higher indifference curve by moving to *B*, but we cannot observe this result for real people because we cannot observe indifference curves. Real income defined in this way is often used in empirical studies and will also be of some interest when we come to derive the demand curve itself.[7]

---

[7] Substitution effects can be analyzed using this new definition of real income. The analysis concludes that the substitution effect leads to a change in quantity inversely related to the change in price, but it also indicates that the substitution effect may be zero.

Suppose the initial prices and money income produce the budget line *HAG* below. We have taken this figure from Figure 4–11 in the text, but have left out the (unobservable) indifference curves. We assume *A* is the preferred basket under these conditions. Now suppose there is a fall in the price of tea so that *HBS* becomes the new budget line, and some point (*B*) the new preferred basket. The increase in income is clear in that the consumer can buy *A* at the new prices without spending all of his income. *A* lies inside the new attainable set. Now using the Slutsky definition of real income, we can draw *H'AS'*. It reflects the

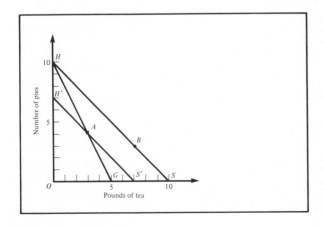

INCOME VARIATION

We have been able above to separate the income and substitution effects of a fall in price by making a hypothetical change in money income. Using the Hicks definition, the change in money income must be just large enough to put the individual back on his pre-price-change indifference curve. In Figure 4–15 (taken from Figure 4–11) the money income change shows up as a shift of the budget line from *HBS* to *H'CS'*. The size of the money income change involved can be measured

FIGURE 4–15

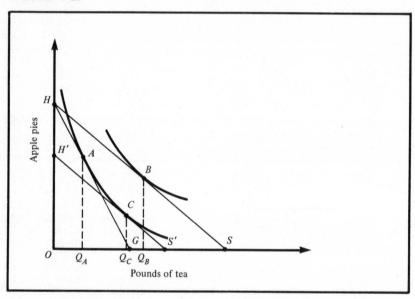

by noting that before the change the individual could buy *H* apple pies and after the change he can only buy *H'* apple pies. Since we have a given price for the pie, then the income change is:

$$\Delta Y = P_\pi \, (H - H').$$

---

lower price for tea by being parallel to *HBS*, but it provides the old real income in that there is just enough money to buy basket *A* at the new prices.

Where will the new preferred position lie? The answer is at *A* or between *A* and *S'*. All baskets between *A* and *H'* were available when *A* was chosen under the first set of prices. Consequently we can infer that *A* is preferred to all those points. We cannot tell what basket between *A* and *S'* will be chosen and must recognize that basket *A* may still be the preferred basket even under the new price conditions. Notice that if any point to the right of *A* is chosen, the substitution effect still leads to a change in quantity desired that is in the opposite direction to the change in price.

We will call this change in income a "compensating variation in income." We see it as the amount of money necessary to compensate the individual for bearing the income effects of a change in the price of tea.

It is easier to see why the term "compensate" is used if we think of the case in which the price of tea rises rather than falls. The *rise* will shift the individual to a lower indifference curve, and the money income change would be the amount necessary to compensate him for this shift by putting him back on the original curve. No matter which way

FIGURE 4–16

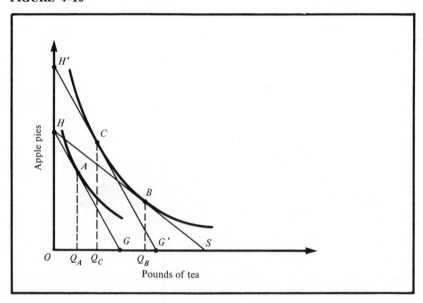

the price changes, however, we use the term "compensating variation" when we want *the amount necessary to return the individual to his original indifference curve (at the new prices).*

This careful definition of the term "compensating variation" is necessary because it is possible to consider a different hypothetical income change in this situation, and the size of the change need not be identical. In Figure 4–16 we indicate the same fall in the price of tea that shifts the budget line from *HAG* to *HBS* and permits the individual to get to *B* on a higher indifference curve. There is obviously a hypothetical change in money income that has an equivalent effect on his well-being. We can imagine an increase in money income that shifts the budget line *HAG* to a new position, *H'CG'*. This shift maintains the old price of tea and therefore describes a change in money income that has an income effect that is equivalent to the income effect of the fall in the price of tea. In other words, both the fall in the price of tea and this "equivalent income variation" put the individual at the same indifference curve. The size of the necessary income variation can be measured as $\Delta Y = P_\pi (H' - H)$ in Figure 4–16. We have explained this variation by considering a fall in the price of tea, but whether the price falls or rises, the equivalent variation is *the amount necessary to put the individual on the new indifference curve (at the old prices)*.

This may sound as if we have two names for roughly the same thing, but that is not the case. For any particular change in the price of tea, the compensating variation need not be the same size as the equivalent variation. The total effect of the price change is the quantity $Q_B - Q_A$ on Figures 4–15 and 4–16. This total effect is, of course, partly an income effect and partly a substitution effect. In Figure 4–15, where we measured the compensating variation, the substitution effect appears as $(Q_C - Q_A)$ along the lower indifference curve. In Figure 4–16 the substitution effect appears as $(Q_B - Q_C)$ along the higher curve. These two curves represent different levels of well-being, or real income or welfare for the individual. There is no reason to suspect that he will substitute tea for pie in the same proportions at the higher level as at the lower level. We would not be surprised to learn that the relationship between the two goods changes when real income changes. That is, our tastes, as they affect demand for those goods, are different when we are richer rather than poorer.

However, if the total effect $(Q_B - Q_A)$ is the same, and part of that effect, the substitution effect, is different at different real income levels, then the income effect must also be different. An equivalent variation in income is not likely to be equal to a compensating variation.

This distinction has lately become quite important in the study of pollution and other spillovers. Consider the case of a noisy airport. If the noise is considered to be undesirable, it reduces the well-being of individuals who live near the airport. If two individuals are alike in all other relevant respects, then the one near the airport will be on a lower indifference curve than the one who cannot hear the planes.

The notions developed above can give us two measures of the amount by which a nearby resident would be better off if the noise disappeared. Getting rid of the noise would put him on a higher indifference curve. His real income would be larger once the noise was gone. How much would we have to reduce his money income to return him to his old real income level once the noise was gone? Since this is an amount necessary to restore the old income level under the new (noise-free) conditions, it is what we have called a *compensating* income adjustment. It is a measure of the amount necessary to compensate the individual for putting up with the noise.

On the other hand, once the noise is gone and an individual is on a higher indifference curve, we can determine how much added money income it would take to keep him there if the noise returned. Since this is a case of holding him at the new real income level in the face of a return to the old (noisy) conditions, this is an *equivalent* income adjustment.

These two need not be the same. Indeed, they are not likely to be the same. The value of a noise-free environment is likely to rise as real income rises. That is, it will not stay the same after an individual has shifted from one indifference curve to another. Hence the implications for public policy may be quite different if we are considering what to do about a noise that already exists than if we are considering some action that will create a new noise. This is only one among a number of problems connected with pollution that can be analyzed by the economist. We will take the subject quite a bit further in Chapter 15.

CORNER TANGENCY

So far all the attainable sets we have used have had a point of tangency with an indifference curve that was somewhere along the budget line, but not at either end of it. The result is that we have only considered optimum baskets that contain some of both goods. There is another possibility. Shown in Figure 4–17 are indifference curves with a shape that puts a point like H on the highest curve. This situation will arise when the price of tea gets higher and higher. If we hold income

FIGURE 4–17

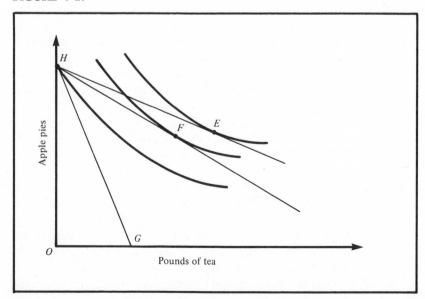

and the price of pie constant, then the budget line gets steeper and steeper. As it gets steeper the point of tangency may move upward to the left from E to F to H. Given the prices represented by the budget line HG, tea is now so expensive that a maximizing economic man will get on the highest indifference curve at the H where he buys no tea at all. We refer to this point as a corner tangency, although the two curves may not be tangent at H in the usual sense. Basket H contains no tea at all. (It seems to contain nothing but apple pie, but this is misleading. If we included more than two goods in the model, then a corner tangency indicates only that one good is missing from the basket.)

The indifference curves shown in Figure 4–17 have the usual shape, but we have let them go until they touch the vertical axis. A movement to the left along one of these curves involves an increase in pie and a reduction in tea. Even though the proportion of pie to tea approaches infinity as the curve approaches the vertical axis, the curve does not suggest satiation in pie. To show satiation with pie it would have to bend up until a tangent at some point is vertical, as was explained in Chapter 3. Instead, these indifference curves meet the vertical axis at an angle.

How can we interpret this shape in terms of consumer preferences? It means that tea is not essential to the consumption of pie. Even when an individual has no tea at all (along the vertical axis), a little more pie will put him on a higher indifference curve. It will still make him better off. This must be true of most commodities at reasonable levels of consumption. Figure 4–17 also suggests that if we keep moving up the vertical axis, indifference curves may get steeper and steeper where they touch the axis and that eventually one will have infinite slope at that point. When that point is reached, it will indicate a quantity of pie that produces satiation though no tea is available. As suggested in Chapter 3, it is likely that most goods have this characteristic as well.

A corner tangency is therefore a way of increasing the realism of the model because we know from our own experience that most consumption patterns do not contain positive amounts of every commodity. In fact, observation suggests that there can be many corner tangencies in connection with any real consumption pattern because there are so many commodities that do not enter the consumption pattern of each of us.

Realistic or not, these situations are inconvenient when we try to use geometry and consider only two goods. They interfere with the derivation of demand curves and the analysis of exchange. We can handle them well only if we are willing to use more complicated mathematics, so we will assume them away in the rest of these chapters by specifying that all tangencies are "internal" tangencies.

Perhaps a note of caution should be added. A corner tangency should not be confused with the earlier discussion on concave indifference curves.[8] The conclusion there was quite different. We argued that concave curves would lead to baskets of goods containing *only* one commodity. Here we have argued that corner tangencies indicate baskets of goods that leave out one good completely. The former prediction is quite inconsistent with our observation of real people; the latter prediction can be easily and frequently observed.

SUMMARY

This chapter deals with a variety of topics. Each of these is an extension of the basic model of consumer choice introduced in Chapter 3, and each is very useful to the economist.

The rate of substitution has one of its most important uses as a device for specifying the conditions for an economic welfare maximum. It is the rate at which an individual can substitute one good for another while staying on the same indifference curve. One of the conditions for a welfare maximum is that at the maximum point, the rate of substitution be the same for everyone.

The notion of dividing the effect of a change in price into an income effect and a substitution effect is very important in the study of consumer expenditure patterns. It leads to the income-consumption curve and the price-consumption curve, each of which can be used to explain changes in the way consumers allocate their incomes among groups of commodities.

This notion also leads to the definition of real income either by reference to indifference curves (Hicks) or by reference to particular baskets of goods (Slutsky). Both definitions are helpful in discussion of the use of taxes or subsidies to alter consumption patterns. Much use has also been made of these notions in the analysis of environmental problems.

We are now ready in Chapter 5 to have a look at demand itself and discover that the demand curve is a very simple summary of this whole elaborate model of consumer behavior.

SELECTED READINGS

Ferguson, C. E. "The Substitution Effect in Value Theory: A Pedagogical Note," *Southern Economics Journal,* vol. 26 (1960), pp. 310–14.

Friedman, Milton. *Price Theory* (Chicago: Aldine Publishing Company, 1976), Chapter 2, pp. 12–64.

---

[8] See the section Convexity in Chapter 3.

Hicks, John R. *A Revision of Demand Theory* (Oxford: Clarendon Press, 1956).

Mishan, E. J. "Theories of Consumer Behavior, A Cynical View," *Economica,* vol. 28 (1961), pp. 1–11.

Newman, Peter. *The Theory of Exchange* (Englewood Cliffs, N.J.: Prentice-Hall, 1965), Chapter 2.

Chapter 5

Demand, elasticity, revenue

INTRODUCTION

Finally we come to demand itself. The preceding analysis of choice has imbedded in it the basis of demand. We can proceed deductively from indifference curves and budget lines to the demand curve. This deduced curve will have all of the familiar characteristics introduced and discussed in Chapter 2. Its shape is a simple summary of the whole model of consumer choice. It is the main item from consumer theory that will be carried forward into equilibrium analysis.

THE DEMAND CURVE

Demand refers to the quantity of some good that an economic man is willing to buy at each possible price. "Willing," of course, implies that demand is some function of the pattern of tastes and preferences, the pattern that gives shape to the indifference map itself. A particular set of indifference curves, as in Figure 5–1, rests on a particular set of tastes and preferences.

"Willing" in this case also includes "and able." Thus demand is some function of money income, used as in Chapter 3 to fix the boundary of the attainable set. In Figure 5–1, we have drawn three attainable sets using an assumed income of $500 per month and three different prices for tea. The boundary of each set starts from H, since we hold the price of pie constant while considering the demand for tea. In this way we introduce constant prices for other goods. That is the third important constraint on the common demand curve. We have *money income, tastes and preferences,* and *prices of other goods* all under control when we use the indifference map and the budget line. We shall be able to investigate the relationship between price and quantity demanded when income, tastes, and the prices of other goods are held constant.

FIGURE 5–1

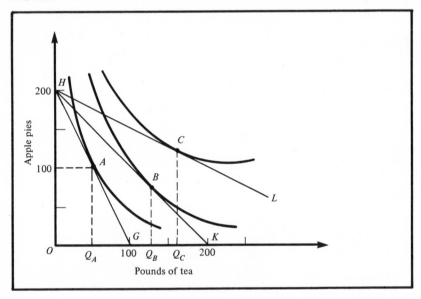

Basket *A* of Figure 5–1 is already familiar. It represents a consumption of 100 pies and 50 pounds of tea (Q_A) when the price of tea is $5 per pound. It gives us a price and a quantity for tea that go together and can be plotted together. In Figure 5–2, we have measured *price* on the vertical axis, but left the quantity of tea as before on the horizontal axis. Basket *A*, with 50 pounds of tea at $5 per pound, becomes point *A*. Going back to Figure 5–1, the attainable set with boundary *HK* represents a lower price for tea of $2.50 per pound. (Basket *K* is the basket that can be bought if nothing but tea is purchased when the price of tea is $2.50 and income is still $500 per month. It contains 200 pounds of tea.) At this lower price, consumption of tea will be larger and the optimum basket, *B*, contains about 130 pounds (Q_B). We thus have another price-quantity pair that can be plotted on Figure 5–2, this time as point *B*. If we consider other prices for tea (budget line *HL* represents a price of $1.25), we get other attainable sets and other price-quantity pairs that can be transferred to Figure 5–2. Enough repetitions of the process will trace out the whole demand curve.

This is the usual demand curve. It has negative slope, indicating that larger quantities are demanded at lower prices. This inverse relationship of price and quantity is called the "Law of Demand," and is one of the oldest propositions of economic theory. It does not seem to be inconsistent with our own real experience. People seem to be willing to buy

FIGURE 5–2

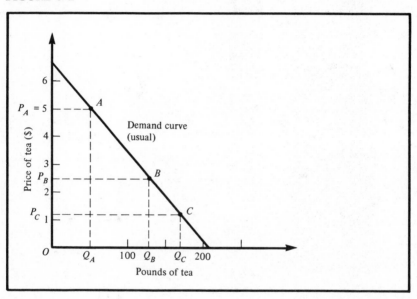

larger quantities of almost any good at lower prices, "other things being equal." (The latter phrase will need to be expanded somewhat as we go along.) We have guaranteed that demand curves obey the Law of Demand by making the assumption, back in Chapter 3, that indifference curves are convex to the origin. That assumption produces a substitution effect yielding larger consumption at lower prices. (We will, of course, have to take account of the possibility of inferior goods soon since they may, in rare cases, result in demand curves with positive slopes.)

As we compare different points on this demand curve, we are assuming income, tastes, and prices of other goods to be the same at all these points. Any change in any of these parameters will shift or rotate the whole curve.[1] For instance, a rise in income will almost certainly move

---

[1] Economists have adopted the convention of referring to different points on the same curve as revealing differences in "quantity demanded." A "change in demand" is used when they want to indicate a shift in the whole curve. It is very wise for a student to get used to using these terms in this conventional way.

the whole curve up to the right. This is because most goods are normal goods as defined in Chapter 4.

The demand curve just derived is based on the assumption that there are only two goods. We can, however, introduce all other goods and still use the geometry of Figure 5–1. The way to do this is to let the vertical (pie) axis represent combined units of all other goods instead of pie. This change is shown on Figure 5–3. Each unit on the vertical axis is a one-dollar bundle of all goods except tea in some given

FIGURE 5–3

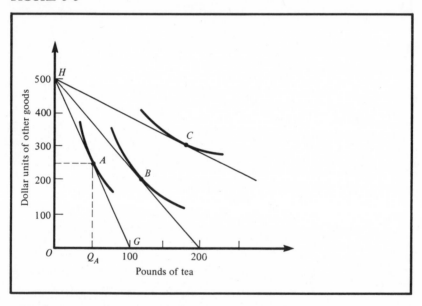

proportions to each other. The basket H now represents the number of one-dollar bundles that can be bought if no tea is purchased and all income ($500) is spent on other things. The line HAG is still a budget line with the same meaning as before. Basket G is the amount of tea that can be bought if all income is spent on tea.

The individual will, of course, choose some maximizing basket, A perhaps, which contains some tea (Q_A) and about 250 one-dollar units of all other goods as shown in Figure 5–3. Thus, point A relates a quantity demanded of tea (Q_A) to a particular price for tea, the price used to derive budget line HAG. This price-quantity pair is a point on the demand curve for tea and can be plotted as before on Figure 5–2. The rest of the demand curve can be plotted by choosing other prices for tea and drawing additional budget lines. Along each budget line there will be a maximizing point that indicates a quantity demanded to go with each price. Points B and C in Figure 5–2 are price-quantity pairs that were plotted this way, and the whole curve has the same general shape as it did before.

MONEY INCOME

As we have just noted, the demand curve is drawn with money income fixed, and this needs more discussion. The analysis of income and substitution effects indicates that the larger quantities demanded at lower prices depend on both these effects. The substitution effect *always* works to increase the quantity demanded at lower prices. The income effect can, on the other hand, work to reduce quantity demanded at lower prices when the good being considered is inferior. For a strongly inferior good, the income effect may overwhelm the substitution effect (see Figure 4–13) and produce a fall in quantity demanded as price falls. As a result, the demand curve of a very inferior good will have positive slope at least along some part of its path, and we will know we are dealing with a Giffen good. Empirical evidence of positively sloped demand curves has been scarce, however, and so most economists feel that Giffen goods are logically possible, but not very probable.

REAL INCOME

The Giffen-good problem disappears if we hold real income constant all along the demand curve. This becomes clear in Figure 5–4

FIGURE 5–4

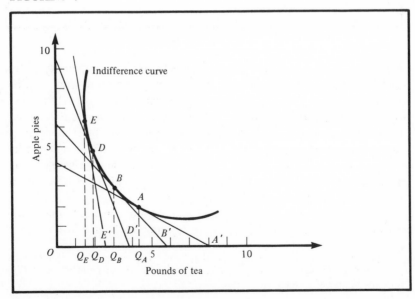

where real income is held constant by considering only alternative baskets that lie on the same indifference curve. We are thus holding "Hicks real income" constant and you should recall the argument of Chapter 4 that gave reasons for using a particular indifference curve to represent a particular level of real income.

In Figure 5–4, baskets *A, B, D,* and *E* are alternatives that are possible at the same level of real income and different prices for tea. The budget line *AA'* indicates the lowest price and *EE'* the highest. Each

FIGURE 5–5

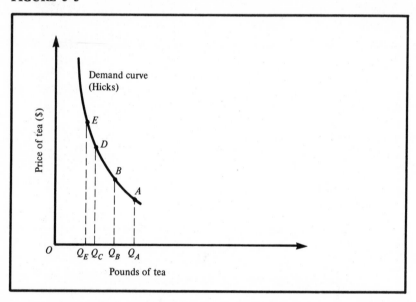

basket, *A, B, D,* and *E,* associates a price for tea with a quantity of tea and so we can, as before, transfer the information to a diagram similar to the one in Figure 5–2 and get a very similar demand curve. We have done this in Figure 5–5.[2] It will still have a negative slope; that is, the quantity demanded will still be larger at lower prices, but this result is now entirely due to the substitution effect. We have eliminated the income effect. Since the substitution effect always leads to increased consumption at lower prices, a positively sloped demand curve is no longer possible and the Giffen-good case disappears.

It should be noted that if we hold real income constant along a demand curve, something else will have to vary. In Figure 5–4 it is the

---

[2] This demand curve is curved, but that is not important. If the indifference curve of Figure 5–4 had somewhat different curvature, the demand curve of Figure 5–5 could be straight.

price of pie that varies and this can easily be seen by extending the budget lines *AA'*, *BB'*, etc., until they touch the vertical axis. With money income constant, the fact that each line touches at a different point means that the price of pie is different for each budget line. We are thus relaxing the assumption of fixed prices for other goods.

HICKS AND SLUTSKY AGAIN

The demand curve in Figure 5–5 uses, as its definition of real income, a concept that we have called "Hicks real income." This means

FIGURE 5–6

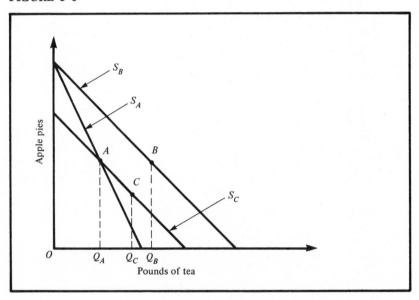

that a given level of real income is identified with a particular indifference curve, and holding real income constant means staying on that curve. We can, however, derive a demand curve along which "Slutsky real income" is constant. This is important because the necessary information for such a curve can be obtained from observations of the behavior of individuals, whereas indifference curves are never directly available to us.

In Figure 5–6, the line S_A indicates a particular price-income situation in which a consumer chooses basket *A*. S_A is a budget line drawn just as before[3] and we may think of an indifference curve that is just

---

[3] See Chapter 3, The Budget Line.

tangent to S_A at A. We cannot, however, observe the indifference curve and have left it off the figure. The rest of this argument in no way depends on such a curve. If we now consider a lower price for tea with the same money income, we get a new price-income situation describing the new budget line S_B with B as the new chosen basket. Basket B represents a larger real income by the Slutsky definition, because in the situation S_B it is possible to buy basket A without using all of one's income. The Slutsky definition uses basket A as a measure of real income.

If we want to see the effect of the new prices without any income change, we must move S_B to the left until it goes through A. The resulting line S_C represents the new prices because it is parallel to S_B and the old (Slutsky) income because it goes through A. The consumer would have just enough money income to buy his old choice, basket A, even though he must pay the new prices.

We do not know exactly what basket he will choose in the price-income situation S_C. We do know that he will choose A or some point to the right of A along S_C. (Any point to the left of A could have been chosen when A was originally chosen and so must be less desirable than A.[4]) However, there is a way to estimate the location of this new basket (call it C). We shifted the budget line from S_B to S_C by making a hypothetical reduction in money income, hence the position of C relative to B depends on an income effect. It is possible to estimate the income effect on a good like tea by observing the response of consumers to changes in their incomes. The placement of point C on Figure 5–6 suggests that we have at least determined that tea is a normal good. This is clear from the fact that $Q_B > Q_C$.

Baskets A and C can now be used to get information about two points on a demand curve for tea. Some price of tea was used to locate the line S_A. At that price (P_A) the basket A was chosen, hence the quantity Q_A was purchased. The price-quantity pair (P_A, Q_A) describes one point on the demand curve as shown in Figure 5–7. The line S_C depends on a lower price for tea (P_B) though it represents the same (Slutsky) real income as S_A. It results in consumption of the quantity Q_C. (P_B, Q_C) is thus another price-quantity pair that lies on the demand curve in Figure 5–7. By continuing this process, we could get enough points to trace out the whole curve. It is a curve that has the special characteristic that "Slutsky real income" is constant along it. It thus reveals the quantity of tea that will be demanded at each price of tea when money income is made just large enough to buy basket A at that price of tea. The prices of all other goods in basket A have of course been held constant.

---

[4] See Chapter 4, footnote 7.

FIGURE 5–7

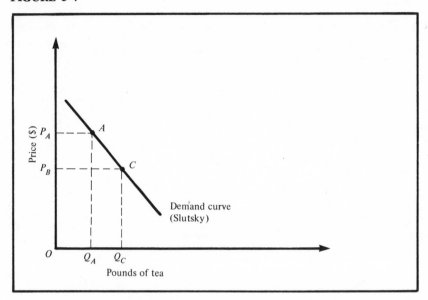

THREE DEMAND CURVES

We have now introduced three demand curves. The first curve, Figure 5–2, holds money income constant at all points along the curve. The second holds Hicks real income constant and is shown on Figure 5–5, and the third holds Slutsky real income constant, as in Figure 5–7. We can thus say:

The first or usual demand curve shows quantity demanded at each price when tastes and preferences, *money income,* and prices of other goods are held constant. Real income, no matter which way we define it, varies along the curve.

The second or Hicks curve shows quantity demanded at each price when tastes and preferences and *Hicks real income* are held constant. Prices of all other goods are permitted to vary.

The third or Slutsky curve shows quantity demanded at each price when tastes and preferences, *Slutsky real income,* and the prices of other goods are held constant. Money income is permitted to vary.

Each of these curves has its uses in economics that depend on the availability of empirical data and on whether the problem being considered is an applied or a theoretical problem. We will generally use the first type in the rest of this book.

ELASTICITY

We now turn to one of the best known characteristics of demand, namely, its price elasticity. Price elasticity is a number used to summarize the relationship between price and quantity demanded along a particular demand curve. It is a measure of the difference in quantity demanded at two different prices. Since the demand curve comes by deduction from indifference curves, we should also be able to deduce the character of price elasticity from the indifference map, and that is a good place to start.

FIGURE 5–8

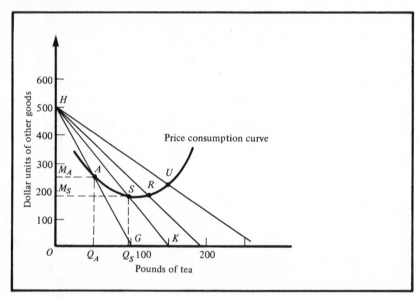

Figure 5–8 presents an indifference map with dollar units of all goods except tea on the vertical axis. Point H represents the total number of one-dollar units of all other goods that can be purchased if no income is spent on tea. It is thus total money income as well. The slope of the budget line now depends on the price of tea. We can find point G by dividing money income by a certain price of tea, P_A. We thus get the budget line HAG along which A is the maximizing basket. The consumer will want Q_A of tea when its price is P_A and will have about \$250 (M_A) left to spend on all other goods. A lower price for tea ($P_S < P_A$) will produce a new budget line, HSK, and a new chosen basket, S. (We have left out the indifference curves that are tangent at A and S and at R and U as well in order to keep the drawing uncluttered.) We can continue this process through baskets R and U, tracing out the price-

consumption curve. This curve will provide the necessary information about elasticity.

For instance, if we compare baskets S and A in Figure 5–8, it is clear that economic man will spend less on other goods at S ($M_S <$ M_A). Thus at S he is spending a larger part of his income on tea even though its price is lower. He buys more tea, of course, but the quantity must be much larger. He must increase his purchase of tea more than in proportion to the fall in its price because the total income spent on tea is larger. This is what we mean when we say demand is price-elastic. A 1 percent difference in price is accompanied by a more than 1 percent difference in quantity.[5]

We are thus comparing quantity demanded at two different prices that lie on the same demand curve. These prices are alternatives that exist under the same set of given conditions. If we consider very small price differences, then we can introduce a formula consistent with the notion presented in the previous paragraph that approximates the elasticity at a point on the curve as follows:

$$\text{Elasticity} = \eta = \frac{\text{Percent change in quantity}}{\text{Percent change in price}} = \frac{\Delta Q/Q}{\Delta P/P}.$$

ΔQ is the change in quantity so that $\Delta Q/Q$ is the percentage change in quantity and similarly for price. If we let ΔP become very small and approach zero as a limit, this formula gives the elasticity as a rate of change of quantity demanded due to price changes, measured at any particular point on the curve. It is called the point elasticity formula[6] and it has one quite important characteristic. It is independent of the units used to measure either prices or quantities. For instance, a change in price from dollars to francs will change both P and ΔP in the same proportion so that the ratio $\Delta P/P$ will be unaffected.

---

[5] Sometimes economists will say, "Demand is elastic if a 1 percent *fall* in price results in a 2 percent *rise* in quantity demanded." This language should be used with care since "rise" and "fall" imply a beginning price and then an adjustment of that price as time passes. If we consider changes that take place over time, we may find that the given conditions are changing and we are no longer on the same curve. Elasticity is defined, however, along a single curve—meaning under a given set of circumstances. It compares two alternatives that are available at the same time.

[6] There is another measure of elasticity called the "arc" elasticity. It permits the calculation of the elasticity of a segment or arc of the demand curve from information about price and quantity at both ends of the segment. It is, however, of little use to economists. When demand curves are obtained from observations of demand for some real commodity the process usually involves fitting a curve to the observations. It is then relatively easy to find the elasticity of such a fitted curve at any point on it. On the other hand, in analytical studies of demand we do not generally have specific prices and quantities to use in calculating the elasticity and we do not usually want a precise number for the elasticity in any event. For these reasons the formula for arc elasticity has not been included.

ELASTICITY ALONG A DEMAND CURVE

Looking back at the price consumption curve in Figure 5–8, it is clear that we have used the negatively sloped portion between S and A to make the argument so far. Along that portion a 1 percent difference in price is matched by a more than 1 percent difference in quantity. Only in this way can the proportion of income spent on tea be larger

FIGURE 5–9

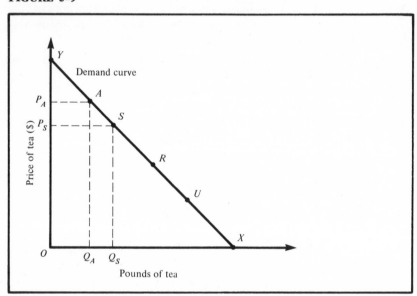

at S, even though the price of tea is lower at S. We can therefore say that between S and A,

$$\text{Elasticity} = \eta = \frac{\Delta Q/Q}{\Delta P/P} > 1.^{7}$$

On Figure 5–9 we have drawn a demand curve derived from the indifference map of Figure 5–8 using the same technique presented earlier in this chapter. Points A and S will appear on this demand curve and we will now argue that the curve is relatively elastic ($\eta > 1$) along the segment AS.

On the other hand, between R and U in Figure 5–8, the price-consumption curve has positive slope. The proportion of income spent on all other goods is increasing ($M_U > M_R$). The amount of income

---

[7] The student who has followed the arithmetic will know that elasticity is negative ($\eta < 0$). It is customary to ignore the negative sign, however, and treat elasticity as positive. We use the absolute value of η.

spent on tea must therefore be smaller, even though more tea is bought. Hence the increase in tea purchased must be in small in proportion to the fall in price. The percentage change in quantity of tea is smaller than the percentage change in price.

We can write

$$\eta = \frac{\Delta Q/Q}{\Delta P/P} < 1$$

and call the demand curve relatively inelastic along this portion. The demand curve of Figure 5–9 has such a portion from R to U.

SOME EVIDENCE

We have argued entirely from the U shape of the price consumption curve up to this point, but we can go further and ask whether real demand is likely to behave in ways consistent with a U-shaped price consumption curve. Actually a fairly simple appeal to our own casual experience will provide a good answer to this question.

Suppose we consider letting the price of some good approach zero. Will a real person limit his consumption of that good to a finite amount that we could represent by a point like X on Figure 5–9? Certainly! How fast can you drink beer? Two bottles per hour? Four? Eight? Clearly there is a limit to the rate of consumption of any good. If still more is taken then storage and disposal problems arise.

Thus an appeal to experience suggests that the demand curve should cross the axis at some point like X, and points below the horizontal axis can be read as consumption rates at negative prices; that is, subsidies. What can we say about elasticity at X? If we rearrange the equation used to define elasticity as follows, we can answer the question.

$$\eta = \frac{\Delta Q/Q}{\Delta P/P} = \frac{\Delta Q}{Q} \cdot \frac{P}{\Delta P} = \frac{\Delta Q}{\Delta P} \cdot \frac{P}{Q}.$$

In the expression on the right $\Delta Q/\Delta P$ has some finite value at X. It represents the slope of a curve that we have agreed should cross the axis at X.[8] The ratio P/Q, however, will be equal to zero at X because $P = 0$. Therefore we conclude that

$$\eta = \frac{\Delta Q}{\Delta P} \cdot \frac{0}{Q} = 0$$

at X.

---

[8] $\Delta Q/\Delta P$ is actually the reciprocal of the slope of the demand curve. On Figure 5–10 ΔP and ΔQ are the legs of a small triangle. As argued earlier, if ΔP is permitted to approach zero then the ratio $\Delta P/\Delta Q$ will give the slope of the curve at A. Thus $\Delta P/\Delta Q$ is the slope of the curve and the reciprocal of $\Delta Q/\Delta P$.

Now consider the other end of the demand curve. We can be sure there is some price for tea (and every other good) so high that a real person will entirely forego consumption of that good.[9] This suggests that the demand curve ought to cross the vertical axis as it does at Y in Figure 5–9. We can also deduce that elasticity will approach infinity at Y by using the same equation used just above:

$$\eta = \frac{\Delta Q}{\Delta P} \cdot \frac{P}{Q}.$$

P/Q now becomes larger without limit as we approach Y because Q, the denominator, is approaching zero. We must conclude, therefore, that the elasticity of the usual demand curve approaches infinity as higher and higher prices are considered.

ELASTICITY AND GEOMETRY

With $\eta = 0$ at one end of a demand curve and approaching infinity as we get near the other end as indicated on Figure 5–10, we can expect it to assume all values between zero and infinity somewhere along the curve. There is a simple geometric equivalent to the elasticity that can be used to make clear this steady shift in value along the curve. We have defined the elasticity at a point on a demand curve as

$$\eta = \frac{\Delta Q}{\Delta P} \cdot \frac{P}{Q}$$

when we let the change in price (ΔP) become as small as possible. It is possible to use this formula to prove that the elasticity at A on the demand curve YAX in Figure 5–10 is equal to the ratio of the two line segments labeled y_1 and y_2; that is,

$$\eta = \frac{y_1}{y_2}.$$

(We have labeled a number of line segments in Figure 5–10 with the x's and y's to make the following argument easier to follow.)

Imagine a small rise in price from the price P_A. This is labeled ΔP on Figure 5–10 and is accompanied by a small decrease in quantity labeled ΔQ. While both of these quantities have been exaggerated to make the figure easier to read, it is clear that they form the legs of a small triangle that is similar to the larger triangle $P_A YA$. From a theorem

---

[9] A good like salt may seem to be an exception. Some minimum amount is necessary to keep us alive. Nevertheless, as its price gets higher and higher relative to income and the prices of other goods, it seems likely that we will reduce our consumption. If the price goes high enough we are likely to reduce our consumption below the minimum necessary to life rather than go on with a consumption pattern that has little in it but salt.

FIGURE 5-10

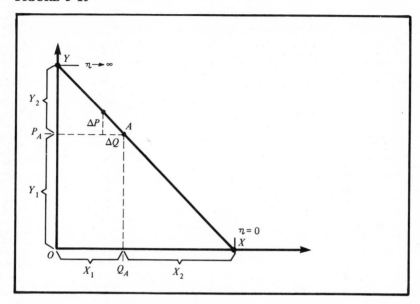

of geometry about similar triangles, we know that the ratio of the two legs of the small triangle $(\Delta Q/\Delta P)$ is equal to the ratio of the corresponding legs of the larger triangle. Thus

$$\frac{\Delta Q}{\Delta P} = \frac{P_A A}{P_A Y},$$

and since $P_A A = x_1$ and $P_A Y = y_2$ we can write

$$\frac{\Delta Q}{\Delta P} = \frac{x_1}{y_2}$$

and then put this into the formula for elasticity:

$$\eta = \frac{x_1}{y_2} \cdot \frac{P}{Q}.$$

However, at point A, where we are trying to measure the elasticity, we have values for both price (P_A) and quantity (Q_A) that can be used in the formula just above. Since $P_A = y_1$, and $Q_A = x_1$, we can insert these symbols in the formula for elasticity to get

$$\eta = \frac{x_1}{y_2} \cdot \frac{y_1}{x_1} = \frac{y_1}{y_2}.$$

This is what we set out to prove. Using this ratio, it is clear that $\eta = 1$ at the middle of a straight line demand curve because then y_1

would be equal to y_2. As we consider points below the middle of the curve, like B in Figure 5–10, y_1 becomes smaller and smaller, ultimately going to zero. So the ratio y_1/y_2 must go to zero. Above A, y_2 gets smaller, approaching zero, and so the elasticity moves from $\eta = 1$ toward $\eta = \mathcal{8}$.

We have now concluded that the usual demand curve (a) has negative slope, (b) reaches both axes, and (c) has a full range of values for η. Economists usually draw it as a convex line like the solid line in Figure 5–11. There are *no* objections, however, to giving it any of the

FIGURE 5–11

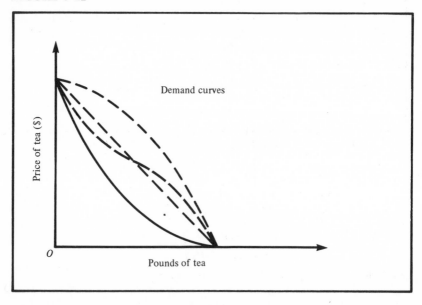

other shapes indicated by dashed lines. We have made no assumptions that eliminate these possibilities, and we have not appealed to any experience that contradicts them. In an empirical study the data gathered may, of course, suggest that one is more likely than another for *some particular commodity,* but we will not make any general argument that eliminates these possibilities.

So far we have discussed only the price elasticity of demand, but it is possible to measure the price elasticity of supply as well. This is a measure of the response of quantity supplied to differences in price measured along a single supply curve. It will therefore be defined at a point as:

$$\eta_S = \frac{\text{Percent change in quantity supplied}}{\text{Percent change in price}} = \frac{\Delta Q/Q}{\Delta P/P}$$

when the change in price (ΔP) is permitted to approach zero. This elasticity will of course be positive since ΔP and ΔQ both shift in the same direction. It is also true that price elasticity varies along the supply curve with the curve usually becoming less elastic as we move to the right.

OTHER ELASTICITIES

Economists sometimes use the concept of elasticity to indicate a relationship between two different commodities. For instance, we would expect a change in the price of margarine to have some effect on the demand for butter because we think of them as substitutes. The measurement of the cross-elasticity of demand will give us some idea of the importance of this effect. Specifically, we want to measure the percent difference in quantity demanded of butter when the price of margarine changes by 1 percent. This is a definition of the cross-elasticity of the demand for butter as a function of the price of margarine. We write the formula as follows:

$$\eta_{BM} = \frac{\Delta Q_B / Q_B}{\Delta P_M / P_M},$$

where Q_B is the quantity of butter demanded and P_M is the price of margarine.

This measure can take any value from large negative values to large positive values. In the case of butter and margarine, we expect a positive value for η_{BM}. We expect that as the price of margarine rises, the demand for butter will also rise because they are substitutes for each other. (It will become clear further on that they may be good substitutes at some prices and very poor substitutes at others.)

The cross-elasticity of the demand for automobiles as the price of gasoline changes is likely, on the other hand, to be negative. These two goods are compliments and a rising price for gasoline makes the automobile less desirable.

The usefulness of the concept of elasticity and cross-elasticity is illustrated by a recent study of the demand for rail versus truck transportation for delivering apples and cherries to market.[10] It was found, for instance, that when rail freight charges varied,

a.   the elasticity of demand for rail service $= -12.57$;
b.   the cross-elasticity of demand for truck service $= 3.56$.

---

[10] Walter Miklius, Kenneth Casavant, and Peter Garrod, "Estimation of Demand for Transportation of Agricultural Commodities," *American Journal of Agricultural Economics,* May 1976, p. 216.

The first of these, (a), is the price elasticity of rail transportation. It indicates that as price rises by 1 percent, quantity demanded will fall by about 12½ percent. We would thus describe the demand for rail transportation, when $\eta = 12.57$, as relatively elastic.[11] We have called this measure the price elasticity of demand, but it is often called the "own-price elasticity of demand" as well. The latter term avoids some ambiguity when more than one price is considered. It makes clear that what is measured is the elasticity of demand for some good as a function of its "own" price.

The second statistic above, (b), involves the demand for another good, truck transportation, as a function of changes in the price of rail transportation. It is thus an example of a cross-elasticity of demand. It indicates that when the price of rail transportation rises by one percent, then the quantity demanded of truck transportation will rise about 3½ percent. Again, this is a change in the direction expected because we believe that truck transport is a substitute for rail transport in hauling agricultural produce. In this case we have been careful to note the sign of η since that is what distinguishes a substitute from a complementary good.

The study we are considering also introduced a number of other variables, and an example will help make clear the range of uses for the concept of elasticity. It was calculated for instance that when the transit time by rail increased, then cherry growers would reduce their demand for rail transport and increase their demand for truck transport. The two elasticities are

$$\text{Rail transport} = -5.56;$$
$$\text{Truck transport} = +4.12.$$

This means that a 1 percent increase in the time it takes the railroad to get the cherries to market will reduce the demand for rail transportation by about 5½ percent and increase the demand for truck transportation by a little over 4 percent. The usefulness of this kind of information to a railroad or a trucking company that wants to increase its haulage of agricultural products is obvious.

Another very common use of the concept of elasticity is called the income elasticity of demand. We can calculate the percentage change in quantity demanded by a consumer as his income changes by 1 percent. The formula will be

$$\eta_Y = \frac{\text{Percentage change in quantity}}{\text{Percentage change in income}} = \frac{\Delta Q/Q}{\Delta Y/Y}.$$

---

[11] As usual, we ignore the minus sign when indicating the price elasticity of demand for some good.

From what we already know about the income effect, it is obvious that this measure will be positive for a normal good and negative for an inferior good.

These examples suggest the range of application of the concept of elasticity. It can, as a matter of fact, be used to describe the relationship between any two variables we may want to consider. It is therefore a very valuable tool for the economist.

SUBSTITUTES

Substitutes, or their lack, are used by economists to explain the elasticity of a particular demand curve. It is argued that demand for any good will be more elastic if good substitutes are available. People, it is said, can turn to the substitute when the price of the good rises, and so the quantity demanded may be significantly smaller at the higher price. It is, however, very hard to define a substitute. We often refer to physical qualities and are thus led to suggest that tea is a good substitute for coffee. But this is obviously not true of a great many Americans who would rather drink nothing than substitute tea for coffee. On the other hand, an Englishman may stick to his tea and refuse to substitute coffee even when it is very cheap relative to tea.

This last reference to price will, however, lead us to a more useful notion about substitution; that is, substitution is mostly a matter of relative prices. Butter and margarine are usually considered to be good substitutes for each other "in use" because they have similar physical characteristics, but if butter costs $5 per pound and margarine 50¢ per pound, then it is unlikely that they will be good substitutes in the market. Few people will switch from margarine to butter even when margarine experiences a significant (large percentage) rise in price. Its demand is price-inelastic at *these prices*.

If, however, margarine costs $4 per pound when butter costs $5 per pound, the reverse can easily be the case. The suggestion is that there is a price for any good that is high enough to make other goods look like substitutes and hence to make demand price elastic. This is true even when the two goods are not particularly good substitutes "in use." For instance, we do not think of movies and football games as substitutes for clothing, but it is clear that at quite high prices we will economize our consumption of entertainment and get our entertainment by spending our income on a host of other goods, perhaps including clothes.

Thus, even a firm that is a monopoly by virtue of being the sole producer of some good will find that the demand for that good becomes price-elastic at some set of prices that are high enough. Moreover, we can reverse this whole argument and point out that there is always a set of prices so low that the demand becomes inelastic. This discovery that the inelastic portion of the demand curve will be found at the "low price" end is, of course, completely consistent with the conclusions about elasticity that were derived from the indifference map in Figure 5–8.

As long as we are making arguments about the model by reference to our experience with reality, we ought to add another "real" consideration. Time also has its effect on the elasticity of *real* demand curves. This is because we get committed to certain consumption patterns and stick to them through force of habit. We do not readily change the habit even in the face of a price rise, but given some time to think about it and to try some of the possible substitutes, we may finally switch a substantial portion of our consumption to the substitute. Thus a demand that seems relatively inelastic at the time the price is changed may become much more elastic after a few months.

MARKET DEMAND

We have just deduced an individual demand curve from indifference curves and the budget line. Indifference curves and budget lines had been deduced still earlier from a carefully formulated set of assumptions. The individual demand curve, however, is not the basic datum for the firm. That role is played by the market demand curve, which is a summation of all individual curves.

FIGURE 5–12

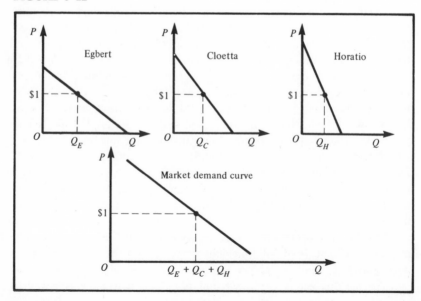

The summation of individual demand curves uses a technique called horizontal addition. Figure 5–12 shows the individual demand curves for Egbert, Cloetta, and Horatio. On these curves we can find the quantity demanded by each of them at a price of $1. For instance, Egbert will take Q_E, Cloetta Q_C, and Horatio, Q_H. If these three are the only buyers in this market, then we can add up $Q_E + Q_C + Q_H$ to get a market demand at $1 as shown on the graph below. If we continue this process over enough prices, we trace out the whole curve.

You will recall that when we discussed individual demand, we mentioned the possibility of a positively sloped curve, the Giffen-good case. It must now be clear that before a market demand curve can have positive slope, this good must be a Giffen good for most individual demanders. This reduces still further the probability that we can actually find a Giffen good.

So far we have acted as if all consumers are individuals, but often they are not. An "individual" demand curve may come from a household. Several different indifference maps will belong to the household. Somehow the preferences represented in those maps are reconciled inside the household and we treat the household as a single unit with an indifference map from which a household demand curve can be derived.

TOTAL REVENUE

A market demand curve indicates the quantity demanded by the entire market at each possible price. It is thus possible to talk about the total revenue that might be realized by a firm or group of firms selling in this market. We can define Total Revenue as follows:

$$Total\ revenue = Price \times Quantity,\ or\ TR = P \cdot Q.$$

(Total revenue is not profit, of course, since some account must still be taken of costs before profits can be known.) Total revenue varies with price. At Y on the demand curve in Figure 5–13, TR is, of course, zero, because $Q = 0$ and so $PQ = 0$. TR is also zero at X because $P = 0$. We have indicated this on Figure 5–14 by letting the total revenue curve come down to zero at both Y' and X' output levels.

Toward the bottom of the demand curve the elasticity is less than one. This means that a 1 percent difference in price will correspond to a *less* than 1 percent difference in quantity. When P is 1 percent higher, Q is less than 1 percent lower, and hence PQ gets larger as we move to higher prices. We also know that near the top end of the curve, where the elasticity is greater than one, a 1 percent lower price is matched by a *more* than 1 percent larger quantity, so that PQ gets larger as price falls.

Thus if we start from X in Figure 5–13, considering higher and

FIGURE 5–13

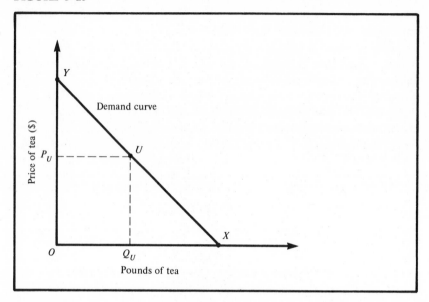

higher prices, *TR* grows; if we start from *Y,* considering lower and lower prices, *TR* grows. It reaches its maximum at the point where the price elasticity of demand equals one. At that point a 1 percent higher price is matched by a 1 percent smaller quantity, and *PQ* is constant (for very small changes in *P*) as at *U* in Figure 5–13. The total revenue

FIGURE 5–14

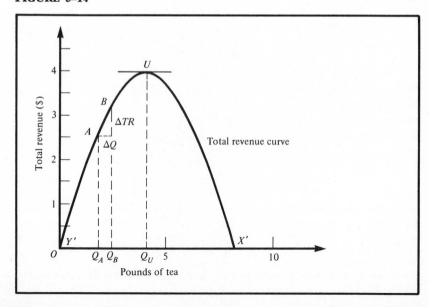

curve will therefore have the general shape of graph in Figure 5–14, and sellers face a market in which there is a price (and quantity) that maximize total revenue.[12]

Suppose we consider for the moment the total revenue curve of a single firm. If that firm is a monopolist in this market, meaning that it is the only seller, then it faces by itself the market demand curve of Figure 5–13. It can sell the quantities indicated at each price along that curve and its total revenue is therefore the one derived from that demand curve and shown on Figure 5–14.

FIGURE 5–15

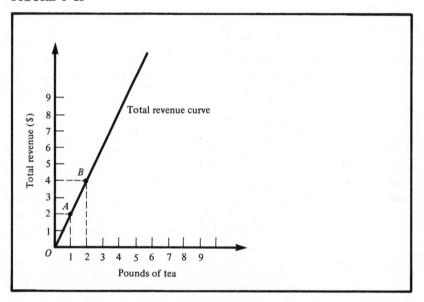

What if, on the other hand, this firm is merely one small firm in a large market? It may assume that it can sell any quantity it wishes without having an effect on price. This means that it views P as a constant in the expression $TR = PQ$, and total revenue varies only as Q varies. The total revenue curve will then appear as shown on Figure 5–15. When the firm sells one unit (at a price of $2, for instance, at A on Figure 5–15), then

$$TR = P = \$2.$$

When two units are sold (at B)

$$TR = 2P = \$4.$$

---

[12] The student should also notice that total revenue is equal to the area of a rectangle under the demand curve at each price. When the price is P_v in Figure 5–13, then total revenue is equal to $P_v \cdot Q_v$, which is the area of the rectangle labeled OP_vUQ_v.

Thus the total revenue curve becomes a straight line whose slope is determined by the price (P). This total revenue curve will be useful later when we discuss the profits of a competitive firm.

MARGINAL REVENUE

We now go back to consider total revenue along a market demand curve. If there were only one seller in this market, he would have to recognize that price will change as he tries to sell different quantities in this market. Both P and Q will change as he moves along this curve and $TR = P \cdot Q$ will change as well. We call the difference in TR between two points on the curve the marginal revenue. On Figure 5–14, compare the quantity Q_A with a somewhat larger quantity $Q_B = Q_A + \Delta Q$, where ΔQ is a small increase in quantity demanded due to a small reduction in price. The difference in total revenue is shown along the curve as ΔTR. Marginal revenue (MR) is then approximately equal to the added revenue (ΔTR) divided by the added quantity (ΔQ). Thus

$$MR = \frac{\Delta TR}{\Delta Q}.$$

Marginal revenue will be expressed as some number of dollars per pound of tea.

Actually we need a somewhat more careful definition of marginal revenue, which in turn will lead to a very simple geometric representation of it. A small section of the total revenue curve is shown in Figure

FIGURE 5–16

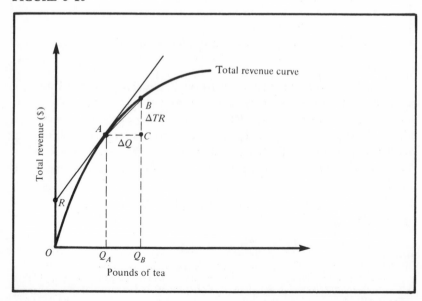

5–16. Start again with the quantity Q_A and consider a somewhat larger quantity Q_B. Again, therefore, marginal revenue is approximately

$$MR = \frac{\Delta TR}{\Delta Q}.$$

From high school geometry you may recall that the ratio $\Delta TR/\Delta Q$ is the ratio of "the opposite side over the adjacent side" in the triangle ABC and that it is therefore a measure of the slope of the straight line AB, which is the hypotenuse of that triangle. Thus, we can identify marginal revenue with the slope of the line AB. If we now let ΔQ become smaller and approach zero, we can use a theorem from calculus mentioned earlier to prove that the slope of the line AB will approach the slope of the tangent line at A. This is the line AR in Figure 5–16. We will therefore define marginal revenue at any point (like A) on the total revenue curve as equal to the slope of a tangent to that curve at that point. Marginal revenue is thus a rate of change. At A it is the rate at which total revenue increases as quantity sold increases when the change in quantity sold is very small.

The fact that marginal revenue can be measured by the slope of tangents to different points along a total revenue curve will make it easy for us to "see" how marginal revenue changes as quantity expands. For instance, on Figure 5–14 we can see that marginal revenue is zero at the quantity Q_U because a tangent to the total revenue curve at U will be horizontal. At points near the origin, the tangents will be fairly steep, indicating that marginal revenue is large. It is also clear that marginal revenue will decline steadily as we move up the total revenue curve toward U, where it is zero. Beyond U the tangents will have negative slope so the marginal revenue must be less than zero. We have thus concluded that marginal revenue will start at some fairly large positive value and decline steadily as we move along the total revenue curve until it reaches zero and then become negative. Remember that the total revenue curve in Figure 5–14 was derived from the demand curve in Figure 5–13. Both figures have quantity on the horizontal axis. We can therefore put both demand and marginal revenue on the same figure. We have done this on Figure 5–17, making marginal revenue positive but declining up to the output Q_U and negative after that.

Figure 5–17 also indicates that the marginal revenue curve lies below the demand curve everywhere. This means that for any quantity demanded (except zero).

$$MR < P.$$

This is clear at the quantity Q_U because we know from Figure 5–14 that the $MR = 0$ at U and that the price (P_U) must be greater than zero because at U because total revenue is positive. It is not difficult, however,

FIGURE 5–17

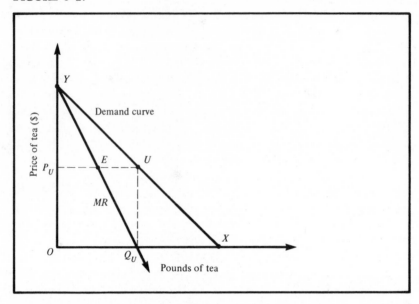

to establish that marginal revenue is less than price everywhere. Suppose that quantity demanded at some price (P_1) is 100 units and suppose that 101 units are demanded at a slightly lower price $(P_1 - \Delta P)$. We can find the marginal revenue from one more unit[13] as

$$
\begin{aligned}
MR &= TR_{101} - TR_{100} \\
&= 101\,(P_1 - \Delta P) - 100\,P_1 \\
&= 101\,P_1 - 101\,\Delta P - 100P_1 \\
&= P_1 - 101\,\Delta P.
\end{aligned}
$$

The last expression indicates that marginal revenue will always be the initial price *minus* a quantity that represents a small reduction in price on all units. This reduction is necessary because the demand curve has negative slope and so the additional units can be sold only if the price is reduced a little.

One more note about the location of the marginal revenue curve will be useful. In addition to noting that it must cross the horizontal axis at Q_U on Figure 5–17 and that it must lie everywhere below the demand curve, it can be shown that it must start at Y and bisect any horizontal line drawn from the vertical axis out to the demand curve. Thus, on

---

[13] Note that we are now considering the marginal revenue of a one-unit increase instead of treating it as a rate of change at a point. This makes it possible to use arithmetic instead of calculus in the argument that follows.

Figure 5–17, E must be halfway between P_U and U, and Q_U must be halfway between the origin and X. Proof of this proposition using geometry is not difficult, but it is very cumbersome and we have therefore omitted it. With this information, we can draw the marginal revenue curve for any straight line demand curve, and with minor modifications we could use it to find the marginal revenue along a "curved" demand curve.

SUMMARY

The individual demand curve is derived directly from the budget line and the indifference map. It usually indicates the quantity that will be demanded at each price when individual money income, tastes and preferences, and the prices of other goods are given. Each of these given conditions is built into the indifference curves and budget lines we have used.

Price elasticity is the statistic most commonly used to describe particular demand curves. It is a measure of the effect on quantity demanded of a difference in price, other things equal. More generally, elasticity can be used to summarize the relationship between any two related variables. Supply elasticity, cross-elasticity, and income elasticity are common examples.

Market demand curves are just the sum of individual demands, but once we have a market demand curve, it is possible to begin talking about the revenues that will accrue to firms selling in that market.

Total revenue is the amount that could be realized at each price by a single firm selling in a market. Because of the characteristics of demand, total revenue increases from zero to some maximum amount and then falls back to zero as output expands.

Marginal revenue is the rate of increase of total revenue as output increases. It has a number of important characteristics. It is less than price at every output. It is zero at the output for which total revenue is a maximum. It is positive when the demand curve is elastic and negative when it is inelastic. A cut in price will increase total revenue as long as marginal revenue is positive.

In Chapter 5 we have talked about demand as deduced from the assumptions of the theory of choice. If, instead, we try to describe the demand for some real commodity by observation of people's purchases in the market, we run into a host of very complex statistical problems. Though these problems have never been solved to our complete satisfaction, demand is frequently measured statistically. Such measurements have provided repeated tests of the analytic demand curve developed in this chapter. This demand curve is consistent with what we know from actual measurements of demand.

SELECTED READINGS

Baumol, William. "On Empirical Determination of Demand Relationships" in *Economic Theory and Operations Analysis* (Englewood Cliffs, N.J.: Prentice-Hall, 1977), pp. 227–47.

Bailey, M. J. "The Marshallian Demand Curve," *Journal of Political Economy,* vol. 62 (1954), pp. 255–61.

Friedman, Milton. "The Marshallian Demand Curve," *Journal of Political Economy,* vol. 57 (1949), pp. 463–95.

Knight, F. H. "Realism and Relevance in the Theory of Demand," *Journal of Political Economy,* vol. 52 (1944), pp. 289–318.

Mock, Ruth P. "Economics of Consumption." In *A Survey of Contemporary Economics,* edited by Bernard F. Haley, Chapter 2 (Homewood, Ill.: Richard D. Irwin, 1952). © 1952 by Richard D. Irwin, Inc.

Robinson, Joan. *The Economics of Imperfect Competition* (New York: Macmillan, 1933), pp. 29–40.

Schultz, Henry. *The Theory and Measurement of Demand* (Chicago: The University of Chicago Press, 1938), pp. 5–58.

Chapter 6

Exchange

INTRODUCTION

We are now ready to extend consumption theory in such a way that one can see some of its most important implications. We will do this by examining a simple exchange of two goods between two people. The results nevertheless will be impressive and make it easier to understand the commitment that many people have made to perfect competition.[1] Moreover, the analysis will contain many of the key characteristics of economic theory at its best, even though the example is very simple. There are mathematical techniques that can extend this analysis to include production, even of many goods, and exchange of those goods by many people, but all of this would not change the basic characteristics that show up in this simple case.

A SIMPLE EXCHANGE ECONOMY

Let us start by thinking of two individuals named Archer and Bascomb. They will be the only traders in the market. They will buy from

---

[1] We will make use of the assumption of perfect competition in the analysis of exchange. This does not mean that we think that real markets are perfectly competitive. They are not. However, we have the same use for the competitive assumption that the physicist has for a world without friction. Abstracting from friction enables him to predict what will occur in certain situations. His predictions are often very close approximations of what actually does occur in the corresponding real situation. He uses a "frictionless world model" because it is a successful model, and we will use a perfectly competitive model because it is more successful than any other that economists have as yet invented. However, this argument for perfect competition has been a source of much controversy among economists and so we will give it a fuller discussion in Chapter 13.

and sell to each other. Next, let us limit ourselves to a two-good world
of pie and tea. The reasons are the same as before; namely, that we
want to use geometry as an aid to understanding, but we will try not
to derive any conclusions that would be false in an m-good world.
Since we exclude the possibility of production in this simple model,
we will assume that the total amount of pie and tea are given as in
Figure 6–1. The axis OT represents the total amount of tea available, and $O\pi$ does the same for pie. We can indicate that Archer has a

FIGURE 6–1

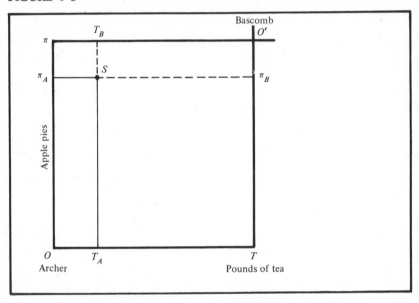

certain quantity of each of these goods by indicating a point like S.[2]
The basket S is the equivalent of a one-period income for Archer consisting of an amount of pie (π_A) and an amount of tea (T_A). It represents the quantities available to Archer before trading begins. We are
thus putting Archer at the origin and measuring his basket from there.

Now since we have only two people and fixed quantities of both
goods, everything that does not belong to Archer must belong to
Bascomb. The point S also indicates his income as measured from the
upper right-hand corner. He has π_B and T_B. The box $OTO'\pi$ is therefore
the complete consumption set. This diagram is called an Edgeworth-
Bowley box. It differs from the consumption set of chapter 3 only in
that we have specified the total amount of each good available. The

---

[2] Actually Archer receives a certain flow of each good, not a one-time stock.
This is, of course, consistent with the way we have viewed goods up to this point.

basket S, therefore, lies on an indifference curve (A_1) as in Figure 6–2. This is Archer's indifference curve and is convex to the origin (O). Since basket S also represents an income for Bascomb, it lies on one of his indifference curves (B_1) as well.[3]

The set of points (baskets) that lie in the area between these two curves is now a very interesting set. These baskets are in the "better-than-S set" for Archer, meaning that they lie above A_1, which is his indifference curve through S. They are also in the "better-than-S set"

FIGURE 6–2

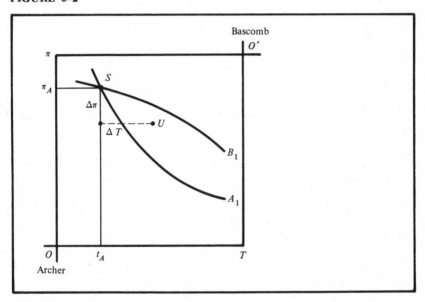

for Bascomb for the same reasons. Both people would be better off at any interior point of this set. We want to examine the possibility that they will exchange their way into this set, and we will therefore call it the trading set.

Consider basket U on Figure 6–2, for instance. It represents a different distribution of pie and tea between the two people. They can get to U from S if Archer is willing to trade some pie ($\Delta\pi$) for some tea (ΔT) and Bascomb agrees to the exchange. Given the assumptions we have made about these people (optimizing, etc.), there is good reason to expect them to trade. Both will be better off (on higher indifference curves) at U. The trading set, however, is a very large set. We need to

---

[3] To simplify this analysis, we use the "more-to-less" axiom instead of one that permits satiation. This has the effect of giving indifference curves a negative slope everywhere inside the consumption set of Figure 6–2.

ask whether we can expect exchange to lead to any of the points in the set or only to some of them, or perhaps only to one.

Basket N on Figure 6–3 will give some of the information we seek. The thing that makes N useful is that the indifference curves of Archer and Bascomb are tangent at N. If, as the result of exchange, our two people got the distribution of pie and tea represented by N, no further exchange would take place. Any move in any direction from N would make at least one of the two worse off, and some moves would make

FIGURE 6–3

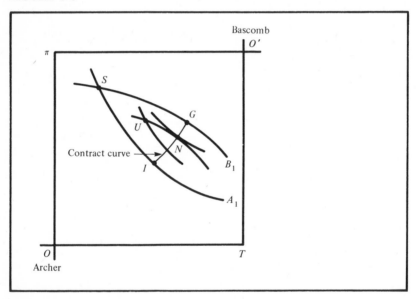

them both worse off. At least one of them would object to any further exchanges. We therefore call N an efficient trade. It is efficient in the sense that no further trades could make one better off without making the other worse off. There is a set of such points along the line ING, and we can call this line the set of efficient trades or the contract curve. All the points on ING are points of tangency between one of Archer's indifference curves and one of Bascomb's curves.

An important thing to notice is that under our assumptions, trade will continue until an efficient trade is made. Any other basket inside the trading set, U for instance, will have its own trading set formed by indifference curves, and further exchanges will take place.

It is customary to call the set of efficient trades a set of Pareto optima. Pareto was an Italian economist whose work encouraged the use of this definition of efficiency in economic theory. We can say of a

Pareto optimum that every exchange has been made that will put one individual on a higher indifference curve without putting any other individual on a lower curve. Or we can say a Pareto optimum indicates the highest possible curve for one individual, given any particular curve for the other. Each of these statements includes the assumption of a given stock of goods to be exchanged. We will adapt this definition of efficiency to other theoretical situations that include production. It will be particularly useful in Chapter 18 on General Equilibrium.

EXCHANGE RATES

The set of efficient trades, line *ING* in Figure 6–3, is, of course, only a small part of the trading set associated with basket *S*. It consists, however, of many points, and we do not as yet know what path toward *ING* our exchangers will take. We can extend the analysis if we introduce a budget line in somewhat different garb. We will treat it as a rate of exchange of pie for tea. In Figure 6–4, the line *SX* represents an exchange rate, $\Delta\pi$ for ΔT, as Archer sees it. If we said to Archer, "You may trade with Bascomb on these terms (along the line *SX*)," then he could start from *S* and move down the line giving up pie and getting tea in a given proportion represented by the ratio $\Delta\pi/\Delta T$. This is the equivalent of the price ratio that determines the slope of the usual budget line. It gives the price that must be paid to get more tea in the form of the pie that must be given up.

FIGURE 6–4

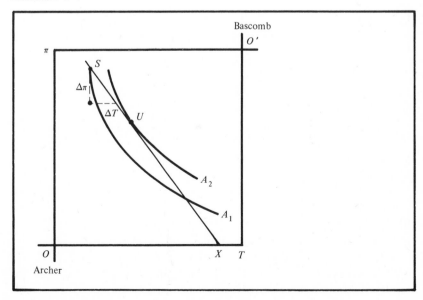

SX is, for Archer, the boundary of an attainable set. He will move along it looking for the basket that will get him on the highest indifference curve. Basket U is the optimum basket at this price ratio because one of his indifference curves is just tangent to SX at U. SX, however, is not the only ratio of prices we can consider. In Figure 6–5 we show four different ratios, SW, SX, SY, and SZ. From Archer's point of view, SW represents a very high price for tea. If he considers exchange with Bascomb along this line, he will have to give up quite a lot of pie for a little more tea. In fact, the price of tea is so high he cannot make any

FIGURE 6–5

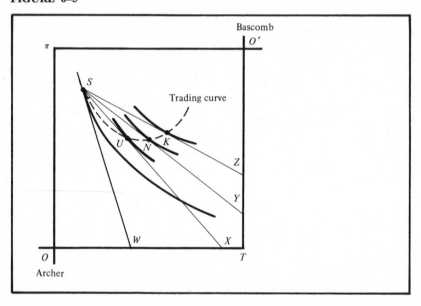

trades that put him on a higher indifference curve than the curve through S. The budget line SW does not enter the trading set.

SX enters the trading set, as we noted above, and basket U is the optimum trade for Archer at that rate of exchange. SY represents a still lower price for tea and an optimum basket at N, and SZ still another with optimum at K. In fact, the dashed line SUNK indicates the optimum trade for Archer at every price as tea gradually falls in price relative to pie. It is Archer's trading curve. Bascomb will also have a trading curve with similar shape (when viewed from O', of course) as shown in Figure 6–6. For Bascomb, who at S has much tea and little pie, the budget line SZ represents a high price for pie. The swing of the price line through SY and SX represents falling prices for pie, and he moves along his trading curve (SNL) getting on higher and higher indifference curves through exchange.

It is clear from looking at the geometry of Figure 6–6 that the two trading curves must cross each other at a point like N. The shapes of these curves are the result of our assumptions, especially the convexity assumption, so the intersection N could be deduced logically from those assumptions. We will, however, be content with the argument that we have drawn trading curves that are consistent with these assumptions and that we can "see" that they will intersect.

What can we say about basket N? In the first place, it lies on Archer's trading curve and on Bascomb's trading curve, so we know they both

FIGURE 6–6

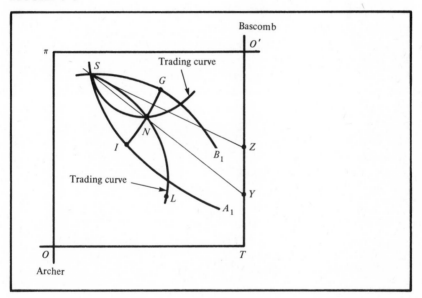

will be willing to make trades that bring them to N. Furthermore, we can draw the budget line SNY. Its slope represents a rate of exchange between pie and tea that will lead both Archer and Bascomb to want to trade along it until they reach N. At N, Archer has an indifference curve that is just tangent to SNY, the budget line. We know this because it is true of every point that lies on Archer's trading curve. It is also true for Bascomb that he has an indifference curve tangent to SNY at N, and for the same reason. However, if both indifference curves are tangent to SNY at N, then they must be tangent to each other there, indicating that N is an efficient trade. Any further trading will make at least one person worse off and some will make both worse off.

Thus, this analysis leads to some very interesting and important conclusions. The first of these is that there is a set of prices, a rate of exchange between pie and tea (SNY), that will lead to an efficient trade.

This is clear from the geometry of the figures we have used. It can also be logically deduced from the assumptions we have made. Such a set of prices will exist even if we expand to m commodities. If these "right" prices are established in some way, free exchange will then lead to an efficient trade; that is, all exchanges will be made that can make someone better off without making someone else worse off. These arguments, of course, put great stress on the importance of prices. They help explain why a system of free exchange is often called a price system.

We know, however, from our earlier discussion, that N is not the only efficient trade. The set of efficient trades is the line ING of Figure 6–3, also shown in Figure 6–6. Can we say where along that line the two trading curves will intersect? That depends on their shape, which in turn depends on the shape of both Archer's and Bascomb's indifference curves. If N is close to G, we say that Bascomb's tastes are such that he had little bargaining power in his exchange with Archer.[4] He was much more eager to trade because of his preferences for pie and tea. "Bargaining power" is a somewhat misleading term here. It does not refer to anything except the shape of the indifference curves; that is, to the pattern of tastes and preferences of each individual.

We have now come up against one of the limits of our analysis. We are using only two people. In trading with each other, they are like monopolists in that neither can shop around for other sources of the commodity he wants. If there were more traders on each side of the market, the outcome would be somewhat different. As long ago as 1881 the economist Edgeworth proved that as more and more traders are added, the line ING gradually shortens to a single point. Adding traders shifts the analysis from a bilateral exchange, a type of monopoly situation, to a perfectly competitive situation.

To summarize, we know now that if the prices are "right," then free trade will always lead to an efficient trade *and* that the "right" prices do exist. We still need to know that there is some market mechanism that will discover the "right" prices and present them to buyers and sellers. It should be very vigorously stressed that:

> These conclusions derive logically from the assumptions we have made in Chapter 3 about how choices are made.

Other assumptions will lead to other conclusions, and empirical tests can either support our conclusions or, by not supporting them, suggest that our assumptions are not very useful and ought to be replaced.

---

[4] If the equilibrium point N turned out to be very close to G, this would not mean, however, that Archer is somehow better off than Bascomb. Indifference curves cannot be used for direct interpersonal comparisons of welfare.

DISCOVERING THE RIGHT PRICES

A full and rigorous treatment of the discovery of "right" prices is beyond our needs and talents at this point, but it is useful to see how economists have handled the question. The process seems at first to demand tremendous amounts of knowledge. Any umpire who wanted to establish the "right" prices would need to know the preference patterns of all traders and their initial quantities of both (all) goods. This ac-

FIGURE 6–7

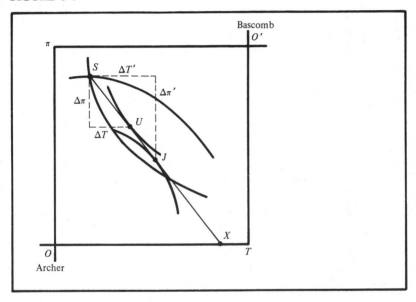

cumulation of knowledge is clearly beyond the limits of human capacities in any real situation. We could not expect the problem to be solved that way in real markets. If, however, we are willing to consider a kind of trial-and-error process, we will find that the *model* requires much less information, and that it appears to be a much more realistic description of actual markets.

Imagine an umpire who "cries" the price of pie and tea when the market opens. His first set of prices, represented by SX on Figure 6–7, can be chosen at random though his real counterpart, the businessman who posts his prices on Monday morning, will be partly guided by his experience during the preceding weeks. Now let Bascomb and Archer each indicate their willingness to trade at those prices. Archer will offer pie ($\Delta\pi$) in exchange for tea (ΔT) so as to get from S to U in Figure 6–7. He will thus be construed as having a demand, at prices represented by SX, for ΔT pounds of tea. Bascomb, on the other hand, will wish to trade from S to J. He will offer $\Delta T'$ of tea to get $\Delta\pi'$. He will, in other words, be construed as willing to supply $\Delta T'$ at these prices. Obviously the supply of tea exceeds the demand $(\Delta T' > \Delta T)$. There is "excess supply" of tea.

In real markets we generally observe that when some good does not sell fast enough and an inventory is accumulated, the seller is likely to lower the price. It therefore seems reasonable to tell our umpire to "cry" a new set of prices making the good for which there is excess supply lower in price and any for which there is excess demand higher in price. Thus tea should go down in price relative to pie in this example. This change will make the price line less steep than SX and will, after a number of tries, bring it close to SNY, the efficient trade of Figure 6–6.[5] Similarly, a real businessman might adjust price in a series of steps that brought him close to an equilibrium position; that is, closer to the point where his customers are willing to buy at that price all that he is willing to sell at that price.

It is most important to observe that our model does not demand any knowledge of preference patterns or initial endowments. All it demands is a knowledge of quantities supplied and demanded at each price as that price becomes the effective price. Moreover, this model does not seem to be a grossly unrealistic description of some real markets, so that we might conclude—indeed, economists do conclude—that there is a similar reduction of the need for knowledge in real markets. The conclusion is, of course, very much dependent on the existence of real market structures that do not inhibit the adjustment of prices and quantities and, of course, the conclusion is subject to empirical test in any real market.

DEMAND AND SUPPLY CURVES

In Figure 6–5 we considered the way Archer will respond to a change in the price of tea. When the price of tea is represented by the slope of the budget line SX, he will want enough more tea so that he gets to the maximizing point U. We can say that Archer has a demand for tea at this price. SY represents a lower price for tea, and Archer will demand a larger quantity so that he can move to the new maximum N. Thus at each point along the trading curve we have a price-quantity

---

[5] If the good in question is what we called a Giffen good in Chapter 3, then the convergence of this trial-and-error process to a unique and efficient trade becomes much more complex. This is because raising the price of a good that is in excess demand will not reduce the quantity demanded. For a thorough discussion of this problem, see Peter Newman, *The Theory of Exchange* (Englewood Cliffs, N.J.: Prentice-Hall, 1965), pp. 93–99.

pair. We have the information necessary for the construction of a demand curve for tea. The construction process can be carried out just as it was in Chapter 5 except that we will express the price of tea as the amount of pie that must be offered for one unit of tea.

Finally, note that when Archer demands more tea, he offers to trade pie. He is willing to supply some quantity of pie at a price represented by the slope of the budget line. *SX* indicates one price and *SY* a higher price. He will offer more pie at the high price because he will want to move from *S* to *N*, rather than from *S* to *U*. Each point on the trading curve indicates a price-quantity pair that lies on his supply curve for pie. We have ruled out production, so this curve only describes his willingness to supply out of his current income of pie and tea. In the next chapter we will introduce production, but even this supply curve has all the necessary general characteristics.

EFFICIENCY AND EQUITY

A movement from *S* to *ING* in Figure 6–6 represents an increase in economic efficiency. That is, exchange makes it possible for both individuals to be better off—to move further up on their preference scales as represented by indifference curves. And the move up is possible without any additional inputs or costs (assuming the trading process itself to be costless). Changes of this kind may be the result of shifts in production as well as exchange. Any change that increases output from the same inputs will also be called efficient.

A movement along the line *ING* represents a redistribution of income and raises problems of equity. It could be achieved by a tax and a subsidiary. Bascomb could be taxed some amount of pie and tea that could then be paid to Archer as a subsidy. There are an infinite number of economically efficient positions between *I* and *G*, but from the point of view of equity, some may be bad and some good.

Thus, if one starts with point *S*, which can be any point in the box not on the contract curve, one can deduce that free exchange will lead to some point along *ING*. Both people will be better off in the sense of being on higher indifference curves. If we feel that people *ought* to be able to choose and to get into chosen positions, then we can call points on *ING* "better" than *S*.

ING may be "better" than *S*, but it may not be "best." By imposing taxes and subsidies either before or after exchange, *any* point in the box can be achieved. How might we judge some other point like *J* in Figure 6–8, for instance? If we think it is better than any point between *I* and *G*, we are making an explicit value judgment about it. We are saying simply that we believe the distribution of income at *J* is "better" than any distribution that lies between *I* and *G*. This is an individual

statement about our feeling that Archer and Bascomb will be treated
with greater fairness at the distribution of income represented by *J*. Another distribution of income (perfectly equal) can be represented by
point *E*, which comes exactly in the middle of the box. It has appealed
to many people as an ideal, but it obviously has not appealed to everyone. Discovery of the best point is dependent on the choice of values.
People differ, and so may you and I. Both of us are likely to rank *ING*
ahead of *S* if we are both willing to use indifference analysis, but we are

FIGURE 6–8

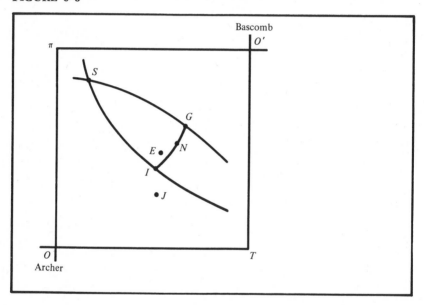

not likely to rank *J* in the same way unless we share other value judgments. (The same can be said for the ranking of *I* relative to *N* or *G* or
any other point on the line *ING*.)

Thus, the concept of an efficient trade provides a very fascinating
tool for comparing alternatives and policies that lead from one economic state to another. It is, however, dependent for its usefulness in
this respect on a situation in which at least one person can be made
better off without anyone being made worse off. For policies that are
proposed once we are on the contract curve, it is no use at all. Any
change that necessarily makes someone worse off requires a value judgment about the injury to some, relative to the benefit to others. Some
aspects of injury and benefit may be objective and open to measurement, but such measurements are never likely to be sufficient for policy
decisions. Some value judgments will remain essential.

SUMMARY

The argument of this chapter reaches the conclusion that free exchange will lead to an efficient allocation of goods among individuals. Efficient merely means that there are no further exchanges that would put one individual on a higher indifference curve without putting someone else on a lower curve.

There exists a set of "right" prices that are consistent with an efficient allocation, and it is possible to imagine a kind of cut-and-try process that would lead to these prices. The necessary process involves a significant economy of information over any attempt to set the right prices by fiat.

The assumptions necessary to generate an efficient distribution of goods among individuals are not sufficient, however, to generate an equitable distribution. This last outcome will require value judgments about different distributions of income in addition to the usual assumptions.

We will now leave demand and consumers without examining the actual determination of equilibrium prices. This is because demand by itself is not enough. We also need a theory of production to which we turn in the next chapter.

SELECTED READINGS

Knight, F. H. *Risk Uncertainty and Profit* (New York: Houghton-Mifflin Co., 1948), Chapter 3.

Newman, Peter. *The Theory of Exchange* (Englewood Cliffs, N.J.: Prentice-Hall, 1965), Chapter 3.

PART III

PRODUCTION

Chapter 7

Production: Isoquants

INTRODUCTION

As everyone knows, economics is all about supply and demand. Exchange occurs between suppliers and demanders. We draw simple pictures of people coming to market with something to exchange for something else. Each individual is potentially both supplier and demander and may change roles as prices change. When the price is high, he may decide to exchange all he has of some good and keep none for himself. At lower prices he may keep some or all for his own use. Sometimes real-world situations are closely analogous to this simple view. A man may decide, for instance, to sell his own labor or to keep some of it as leisure, and consume it himself. Or a farmer may decide to sell the vegetables from his garden or to let his family consume them. But most of the time the real world seems more complex. Demanders, instead of coming to markets with stocks of goods to sell or keep, come with their money incomes and come to buy.

More important for this chapter, suppliers do not usually come to market with some *given* quantities of goods to exchange; they must instead choose how much of each good to produce and bring to market. Clearly we need to support the supply side of exchange with an analysis of production. We will use this chapter and several more to "explain" production.

Production theory, like demand theory, is seen by economists as a part of a general theory of choice. Production choices can be divided into two kinds, each reflecting the type of information available.

Our first step will be to analyze choice in the framework of the technical conditions under which production is possible. We will adapt what the engineer knows to the uses of economics. This is the subject of Chapters 7 and 8, and part of Chapter 11.

The second step will be to add a knowledge of prices to our knowledge of technology. We will develop a set of cost curves and analyze their impact on choice making in Chapters 9 and 10.

Finally, we will bring all of this production information together with demand and look for equilibrium prices and quantities. This process begins with Chapter 13.

PROFIT MAXIMIZING

In building the model of consumer choice, we had to create a fiction called "economic man." He became our man in economics, and we forced him to make choices under our rigid rules. Now we must create another fiction called "economic firm." It will be our agent in productive choice making, and we will define a set of rules to guide its choices. Notice that economic firm is not the name of a set of buildings and equipment, although we will imagine it to make choices about those things. Nor is this firm a real firm any more than economic man lives and breathes. It is just a name for an abstract chooser. Once again we are developing a concept to make it easier to think clearly and logically about a complex world. And once again we will justify the effort only if the concept is useful in predicting events in that complex world.

In predicting production choices, economists have had the most success by starting with the general view that choice is guided by the desire to maximize "something" subject to certain constraints. Thus, the economist says:

> We assume that economic firm makes choices as if it were trying to maximize profits.

Real firms seem to have this motive, but clearly they have other motives as well. Sometimes they seem to be trying to maximize sales or rates of growth, or job opportunities for the wife's nephews. Much effort is being made by economists to draw some of these other goals into the model, but the effort has not yet been very successful. It still appears that profit maximizing is the best initial approach. The profit-maximizing assumption has, however, generated a great controversy among economists. It is worth exploring this controversy for the light it throws on the profit motive and also for the data it provides on the actual behavior of real business people. We have therefore included an extended discussion as the subject matter of Chapter 12.

We should also note that even though real firms usually choose to produce many commodities at once, we can simplify our discussion by limiting economic firm to the production of *the* one good that maximizes its profits. What we have to say can later be extended to multi-product firms when necessary and without much change in the outcome.

THE PRODUCTION FUNCTION

The term "production function" refers to the physical relationship between inputs and the resulting outputs. For any real firm, the basic constraint on its choices is the current state of technical knowledge about these relationships in our society. The whole body of production functions includes all of our technical knowledge about production. A change (or improvement) in the state of technology implies the discovery of some new production function.

Production is really a transformation of some things (inputs) into other things (outputs). The making of sheet steel into a fender is obviously production, and so is making a mountain in northern Michigan into sheet steel. But transporting a good to market is also production. It transforms, for instance, an automobile in storage in Detroit (input) into an automobile in a dealer's showroom (output). One hardly need start out to buy a car to realize these are quite different things. The key to the concept is transformation. Not all of it occurs in factories.

If output is, then, a function of inputs, we can express the production function symbolically thus:

$$X_V = F(x_1, x_2, \ldots, x_n),$$

where X_V is output of firm V and $x_1, x_2, \ldots, x_n$ are the inputs. The F represents the technical aspects of the transformation. It is a symbol for the current state of technical knowledge.[1]

THE PRODUCTION SURFACE

Our desire, however, is not so much to understand what is really a complex technological process as to arrange the relationships between inputs and outputs in such a way that they are useful to economists. It will help to consider a simple example. It takes some apples, some

---

[1] This formula makes no mention of the possibility that one input may impinge on another in ways that affect output. Thus output may not depend in a *simple* way on the quantities of inputs used. In an auto factory, the fender-stamping machine may make so much noise as to interfere with the output of machinists working on some other part of the car. Moreover, the firm may find that its efforts to produce refrigerators as well as automobiles has an effect on the output of cars. These effects are generally called externalities (or spillovers) and are so pervasive that an extended discussion is included in Chapter 14. In this chapter we will assume they do not exist.

flour, some seasonings, some heat, and some work by a baker to produce an apple pie. The "firm" can choose to buy a basket of these
ingredients, or inputs, and then start making pies. Again, geometry is
a help in understanding concepts if we can limit the number of variables. With mathematics we could handle the production function using
all these inputs, but it is more revealing at first to limit ourselves to two
inputs and one output and make use of geometry.

Assume, therefore, that apple pie has only two inputs: the baker's

FIGURE 7–1

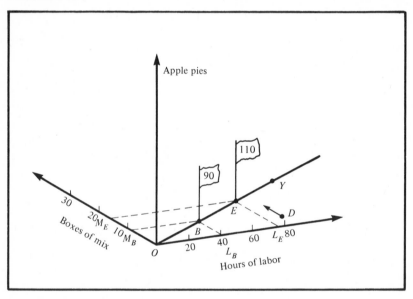

time in hours of labor, and boxes of apple pie mix. Thus the output
of a firm is a function of the input of labor and pie mix, and we can
write:

$$X_V = F(L, M).$$

A basket that contained about 40 hours of labor per week (L_B) and
8 boxes of pie mix per week (M_B) can then be represented by a point
like B on the base plane of Figure 7–1. The base plane represents the
production set, the set of all possible baskets of inputs among which
the firm can choose.[2]

Imagine that we set up a flag pole at B that is high enough to show

---

[2] Note that all quantities of labor and mix will thus be zero or positive. We
have no economic meaning for negative rates of input and would have to say so
explicitly if we were handling this analysis by mathematical techniques.

the number of pies (90) that can be made with the stuff in basket *B*. An engineer may know of several "ways" to utilize the inputs in any basket to get outputs. Some ways will yield a greater output from the given basket of inputs than others. Our assumption that economic firm is profit-maximizing clearly requires that it use the way that yields the greatest output. The flag pole will thus show the *maximum* number of pies that can be produced with basket *B*.

It would not be surprising if basket *E* could produce more pies than *B*. After all, it contains more of both inputs. A flag pole for basket *E* should be higher than the one at *B*. If a flag pole were put up from every point on the base plane to represent the pie output of the basket at that point, then the tops of all those poles would look from a distance like the surface of a hill. This is called the production surface, and we must now say something about its shape.

THREE VIEWS

The shape of the hill describes the way in which output varies as inputs vary. If we draw a line on Figure 7–1 from the origin (*O*) through the points *B* and *E,* we have marked out a particular set of baskets. What we want to know is the way in which output changes from basket to basket along that line. The changing pattern of output gives a profile to the hill directly above the line. Someone standing at *D* and looking in the direction indicated by the arrow would see this profile clearly. Any other line we can draw across the base plane of Figure 7–1 will indicate another set of input baskets, and these, in turn, will have outputs that trace out a profile of the hill that lies directly above that line.

This is important because certain lines on the base plane, meaning certain sets of input baskets, have special economic meaning. Each of these special lines represents certain constraints that force the firm to choose among the baskets that lie on that line. Traditionally, there have been three patterns of constraints that economists believe to be important. The shape of each line and the constraints that each represents are easier to see if we present the base plane in two, rather than three dimensions, as in Figure 7–2. The figure gives a view of the hill from directly above it. The output axis does not appear on the figure, but both input axes do. Output would have to be measured as a vertical distance straight up from the page on which the figure is printed.

Now consider the line *OBEY,* which is in the same position on Figure 7–2 as on Figure 7–1. This line represents the first important pattern of constraints. We will call it a long-run expansion path. The key constraint is that the quantities of the two inputs are in a given proportion to each other in every basket that lies on the line. The basket E has more of both inputs than basket B, but the ratio of mix to labor is about 1:5 in both.

The line $DART$ on Figure 7–2 represents another important constraint. This line is called a short-run expansion path and the key constraint is that every basket on the line has about 18 boxes of mix (measured on the vertical axis as the distance OD). The amount of labor in a basket gets larger and larger as we move along the line to the right, but mix remains constant.

FIGURE 7–2

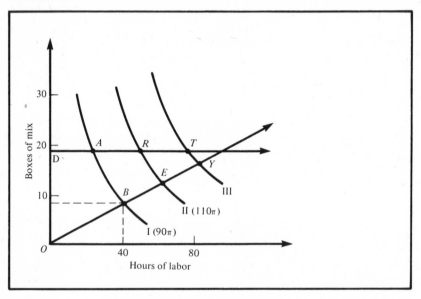

The third line is called an isoquant and several examples appear on Figure 7–2 labeled I, II, and III. The key constraint here is that the output of every input basket that lies on any one of these lines is the same. Take curve II, for instance. Baskets R and E both lie on this line. E has more labor and less mix than R, but as indicated on the figure, both have the same output of 110 apple pies.

It is perhaps easiest to take up the explanation of the third line, the isoquant, first. We will therefore postpone a discussion of the long- and short-run expansion paths until the next chapter.

THE ISOQUANT

If we were sitting on top of a flagpole at B' in Figure 7–3, we might get up and walk along the tops of poles until we get to H', or going the other way, to E'. We could choose our path around the production surface in such a way that we maintained the same altitude. This is equivalent to holding output constant along the path. Baskets B, H, and E (shown on the base plane) all have the same maximum output.

If we then climbed down the pole and painted a line on the ground connecting all such baskets, it would look like EBH. This is an iso-quant, or equal-quantity line. It is, of course, analogous to an indifference curve that shows equal preference, except that we can attach

FIGURE 7–3

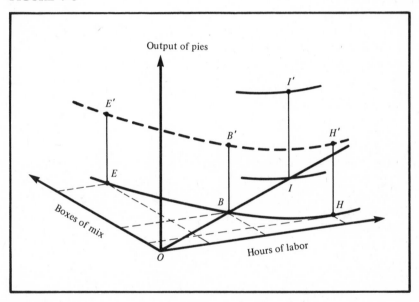

a cardinal number to it that indicates the number of units of output. Cardinal numbers are possible because we can count pies where we could not count or measure preference. In the same way we can draw another isoquant through any and every point on the base plane until we have a whole family of isoquants that we will call an isoquant map.

It is very important to realize that isoquants drawn this way require the assumption that labor and pie mix are substitutes for each other in making pies. Some substitution is possible in most real production processes. The same number of pies can be made with less mix by using more labor, if the added labor is use to reduce waste by more careful peeling and coring of apples and more careful handling of flour. Of course, there are some limits to these substitutions in the real world, but we will start by assuming the possibility of "continuous substitution," meaning that the same output can be obtained from any point on the isoquant. Later we will consider some assumptions that restrict substitution and add realism to this model.

Note that assuming continuous substitution also requires the assumption that inputs are perfectly divisible. It must be possible to consider using a little less mix and a little more labor to get the same output, where "little" can be very small indeed. These two assumptions are responsible for two of the characteristics of the isoquants we use for the rest of this chapter. These curves are both smooth and continuous. They have no sudden bends or kinks and they have no gaps. These characteristics have been very convenient when calculus has been used in economic analysis. They are by no means essential, however, and we will discuss less demanding assumptions in Chapter 11. Now, let us consider the shape of an isoquant and the reasons for that shape.

NEGATIVE SLOPE

In Figure 7–4 the base plane of Figure 7–3 has again been presented in just two dimensions. Line *EBH* obviously has negative slope as far as *H*, but why? First, we will insist that a basket like *I*, which has more of both inputs, can be made to yield more pies than *B*. This assumption plays the same role in production theory that "more is preferred to less" played in consumption theory. If *I* yields more pie than *B*, then *B* and *I* cannot lie on the same isoquant, and so isoquants

FIGURE 7–4

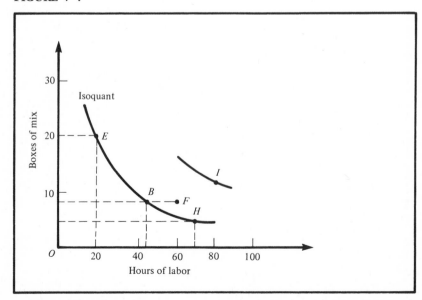

cannot have positive slope everywhere. Moreover, we will insist that a basket like F also yields more pie than B, for it contains more labor and no less pie mix, so an isoquant cannot be horizontal (or vertical, for the same reason). The reasons in both cases are technological; that is, real production processes seem to yield greater output from greater inputs for at least some levels of production. We will, therefore, give the isoquant a negative slope over *some* portion of its path.

NONINTERSECTION

For reasons of logic, we will not let two isoquants cross each other. If on Figure 7–5 one ran through AI and another through AB, we would have to say:

Basket I makes as many pies as basket A;
Basket A makes as many pies as basket B;
therefore,
Basket I must make as many as basket B.

This is, of course, another example of transitive logic. We have a transitivity assumption in production theory just as we did in the consumer preference model. When isoquants intersect, it leads to a contradiction just as it does when indifference curves intersect. The statement just above that basket I must make just as many pies as basket B is contradicted by the assumption that basket I will in fact

FIGURE 7–5

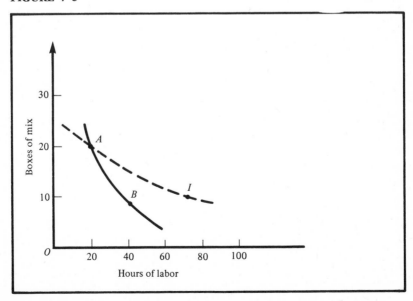

make more pies than B because it contains more of both inputs. We must, therefore, rule out the possibility of intersection of isoquants.[3]

MARGINAL PRODUCT

Imagine now a basket F as in Figure 7–6, that holds the same amount of pie mix as basket B and one additional unit of labor. We have assumed that more inputs yield more output and basket F, there-

FIGURE 7–6

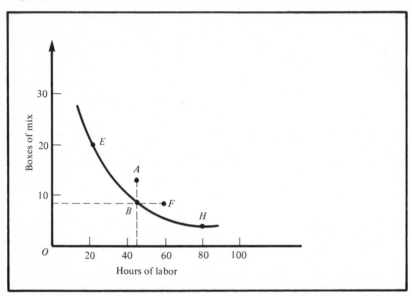

fore, lies on a higher isoquant. Suppose that output along the higher isoquant is larger by two apple pies. These two pies must then be attributed to the additional unit of labor. We will call them the marginal product of labor and use the symbol MP_L. Marginal product is the addition to total product per additional unit of input.[4]

Obviously we could also approximate the marginal product of mix (MP_M) at point B in the same way by looking at basket A, which lies directly above B. (The symmetrical arrangements of points A, B, and

---

[3] Isoquants may not be tangent either. The argument against tangency is identical to the one just presented against intersections.

[4] Marginal product, like other marginal concepts, is actually a rate of change. It is the rate at which total product increases as inputs are increased. We can find its value at any point on the total product curve; it will be equal to the slope of a tangent to the total product curve at that point. This approach will be used in Chapter 10.

F in Figure 7–6 should not be interpreted to mean that the marginal products of labor and mix must necessarily be the same at *B*.)

RATE OF TECHNICAL SUBSTITUTION

The concept of marginal product can now be used to explain the meaning of an important term, namely, the rate of technical substitution. Starting from the basket *B* on Figure 7–7 we can take some mix

FIGURE 7–7

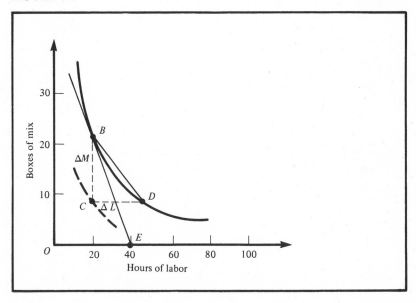

(ΔM) out of the basket. This will take us to basket *C*, which by assumption must lie on a lower isoquant. How much smaller will output be along this lower curve? If we had removed just one box of mix from basket *B*, then output would be smaller by the marginal product of mix (MP_M). Since we actually removed the quantity ΔM, output will decline by $\Delta M(MP_M)$.

Given our assumption about substitution among inputs, we can now get back into the original isoquant, the one through *B*, by adding some amount of labor (ΔL), also shown on Figure 7–7. The added labor will yield added output that can be measured by $\Delta L(MP_L)$, and since we are back on the same curve, the net change in total output is zero. Thus, the output lost by using less mix must be exactly made up with output gained from adding more labor. Therefore:

$$\Delta M(MP_M) = \Delta L(MP_L).$$

This last expression can be rearranged as follows:

$$\frac{\Delta M}{\Delta L} = \frac{MP_L}{MP_M} .$$

The first term of this new expression has a special meaning in the geometry of Figure 7–7. It is a measure of the slope of the straight line, *BD*. Once again, if we let the quantity ΔM become very small and approach zero, we can use a theorem from calculus that says the slope of the straight line *BD* will approach the slope of the tangent to the isoquant at *B*, which is labeled *BE*. We will therefore equate the ratio $\Delta M / \Delta L$ (when $\Delta M \to 0$) with the slope of a tangent at a point and call it the rate of technical substitution.[5] At *B* this slope reveals the rate at which labor can be substituted for mix, leaving output constant. We will use the symbol RTS_{LM} to mean the rate of technical substitution of labor for mix and write:

$$RTS_{LM} = \frac{\Delta M}{\Delta L} \text{ (when } \Delta M \to 0).$$

LAW OF VARIABLE PROPORTIONS

This argument can now be extended to establish a very important characteristic of the isoquant. Using the facts (see above) that:

$$\frac{\Delta M}{\Delta L} = \frac{MP_L}{MP_M} \text{ and that } RTS_{LM} = \frac{\Delta M}{\Delta L} ,$$

we can conclude that

$$RTS_{LM} = \frac{MP_L}{MP_M} .$$

If we can explain what happens to the marginal product ratio on the right as we move down the isoquant, we can then explain something about the changing slope (RTS_{LM}) of the curve.

Take first the marginal product of labor (MP_L). It will not be surprising that the marginal product of labor declines as we move down the curve. At *B* on Figure 7–7, a modest amount of labor has a fairly large quantity of mix to work with. A little more labor at this point will find plenty of mix to work with, and we can expect it to be used effectively; that is, its marginal product will be large. Further down the curve, however, there is more labor trying to work with less mix.

---

[5] This phrase is often preceded by the term "marginal." Here as in the case of the (marginal) rate of substitution of Chapter 4, the extra term is redundant. The rate of technical substitution will also have a negative sign because ΔM is a reduction in mix. Again, however, we will ignore the sign and treat it as a positive number.

Additional units of labor may be hard pressed to find something useful to do without getting in the way of the workers already there. The marginal product of labor is likely to be much smaller.

This argument is an informal statement of the best known law of economics, the Law of Variable Proportions, also called the Law of Diminishing Returns. It can be carefully stated thus:

> If the proportion of one input (labor in this case) is continuously increased relative to the other(s), a point will be reached where the marginal product of that input will decrease. Once it begins to decrease it will not reverse itself and it can go to zero and even to negative amounts.[6]

We believe that this law describes a physical characteristic of all production. It is not really an economic law at all in the sense that it can be derived from our assumptions. It is intsead a characteristic of the physical world in which we live. It in no way depends on costs or prices or on the current state of our technical knowledge. It is a characteristic of all technologies and applies in all types of economies.

When one input, for instance, land, is fixed in quantity and another, labor, is variable, we are likely to refer to the law by its other name, the Law of Diminishing Returns. The prediction about output is the same, namely that after some point, diminishing marginal products will appear. The fact that one input is fixed and the other is variable, is irrelevant. The crux of the matter is that proportions between inputs change, and it is the change in proportion that brings about the decline in marginal product. Even when both inputs are being increased, but at different rates, the change in proportion will lead to decreasing marginal product for the one that increases most rapidly.

Along the isoquant, this law means that the marginal product of labor will decline from left to right. The proportion of labor to mix is rising continuously and diminishing returns are to be predicted. There is an additional characteristic of this law that should be noted. It is reversible. This means that if we move up along the isoquant from right to left, the proportion of labor to mix is decreasing and we will find marginal product of labor rising. Hence moving down the curve will mean decreasing the MP_L because the ratio of labor to mix is increasing, and moving up the curve will reverse both of these changes. This result is indicated on Figure 7-8.

The law of variable proportions applies in the same way to the marginal product of mix (MP_M). As we move down the curve to the

---

[6] Sometimes decreasing average product is used in the definition instead of decreasing marginal product. This changes the output level at which "diminishing returns set in." The result can be seen along the average and marginal product curves presented in Figure 10-5. It is more common, however, to use marginal product and to indicate that diminishing returns begin when the marginal product begins to decline.

FIGURE 7–8

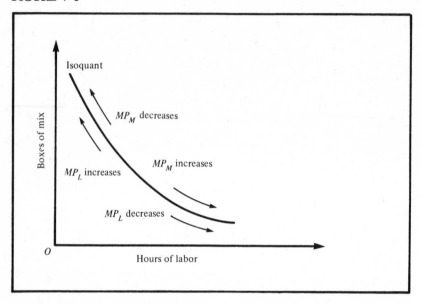

right, baskets of inputs contain more labor and less mix. We have described this as an increase in the proportion of labor to mix (L/M) in applying the law of variable proportions. However, we can also describe it as a *fall* in the proportion of mix to labor (M/L). Thus, as we move down the curve, the ratio of mix to labor gets smaller, and as we move up it, the ratio gets larger. Moving up the curve to the left, the increasing proportion of mix to labor must affect the marginal product of mix. Mix and every other input must obey the law of variable proportions, so that we can expect the marginal product of mix to decline as we move up the curve. Moreover, the law is reversible for mix, just as it was for labor, so that decreasing MP_M as we move left is replaced by increasing MP_M as we move right. This behavior is also indicated on Figure 7–8.

These conclusions are based on the physical law of variable proportions, but they have important implications for the economic concept of the rate of technical substitution. Recall first that

$$RTS_{LM} = \frac{MP_L}{MP_M}.$$

Now, moving down the isoquant brings about a fall in the MP_L and a rise in the MP_M; hence, the rate of technical substitution diminishes. The rate of technical substitution is, of course, equal to the slope of the isoquant, so that slope must therefore decrease as we move down

FIGURE 7–9

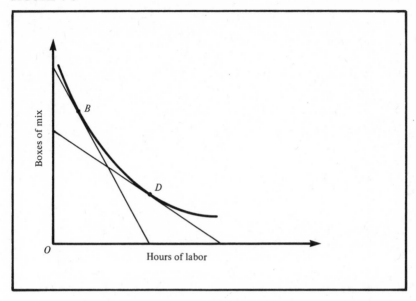

the curve to the right. To make this happen, we must draw the curve convex when viewed from the origin. Thus, in Figure 7–9 the slope of the tangent at D is less than the slope of the tangent at B.[7] We will therefore make the assumption of convexity a specific part of our model of production, and in so doing we guarantee that the isoquants will be consistent with the law of variable proportions.

OTHER SHAPES

Sometimes in the real world two inputs must be used in fixed proportions. In Figure 7–10 we use wheels and axles with a proportion of two to one to produce camping trailers at R or S or T or at any point on a line from the origin going through R, S, and T. Production takes place only on this line because each basket of inputs on the line contains twice as many wheels as axles.

It is tempting to draw an isoquant horizontally along TW, for instance, indicating that if more wheels were used with the same number of axles, output would be unchanged. The extra wheels would be wasted. Similarly, the section TX might suggest that with more axles but no more wheels, output would remain the same. However, since the only point on either TW or TX that is of any interest is T itself,

[7] We are, as before, ignoring the fact that both of these slopes are negative and treating the RTS_{LM} as a positive quantity.

FIGURE 7–10

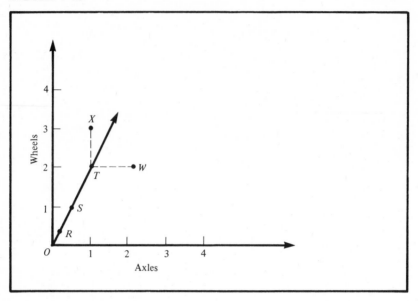

we probably ought to ignore the rest of it. In fact, if the two inputs cannot be used except in fixed proportions to each other, it seems sensible to treat them as one input. We could put both wheels and axles on one axis and call the combination of one axle and two wheels a "running gear." We would then dispense entirely with diagrams like Figure 7–10.

It is also possible to imagine two inputs that are perfect substitutes for each other. They could replace each other in the production process at some fixed rate, like two for one, without affecting output. Perhaps sugar and saccharin used in the manufacture of some sort of baked goods can be an example. If they are perfect substitutes, their marginal products do not change as the proportions between them change. The law of variable proportions is suspended and the rate of technical substitution is a constant. The isoquant that describes this situation is a straight line with slope determined by the now constant rate of substitution as in Figure 7–11. Again, one is tempted to suggest that if the two inputs are really perfect substitutes for each other, then the differences between them are (at least in this production process) superficial. A difference that makes no difference is no difference. We might just as well treat them as a single input. And so we will, putting this single input (with two names) on one axis only. We can then dispense with diagrams like Figure 7–11 as well.

FIGURE 7-11

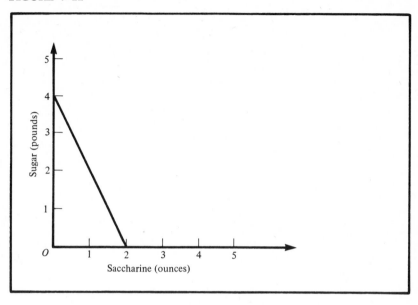

SUMMARY OF CHARACTERISTICS

The discussion so far has indicated the basic shape of isoquants. An isoquant represents a single level of output produced by various baskets of inputs. It is analogous to a contour line on a map of the production surface. Its basic characteristics are that:

a. An important segment will have negative slope simply because we have assumed that more inputs will usually yield more output. We will modify this characteristic somewhat in the next section.

b. Isoquants will not intersect each other. This prevents a contradiction that would otherwise arise between two of our assumptions.

c. The isoquants presented so far are smooth and continuous because we have assumed that continuous substitution between inputs is possible. This assumption will be radically modified before we are done.

d. Isoquants are convex when viewed from the origin because we believe that the law of variable proportions is a physical characteristic of all production processes. No completely adequate empirical proof of this law has ever been carried out. Nevertheless, we believe it to be one of the constraints of every economic system, no matter how the system is organized. Communist, capitalist, socialist, and Robinson Crusoe type economies must face its implications. It in no way depends on costs and would hold even if all goods were free, though no one would really care.

e. Each isoquant can be assigned a cardinal number indicating the output that is constant along it.

We will add a bit more to this list as we go along.

THREE STAGES OF PRODUCTION

As noted above, the marginal product of either input can drop to zero when it is used in quantities that are very large relative to the

FIGURE 7–12

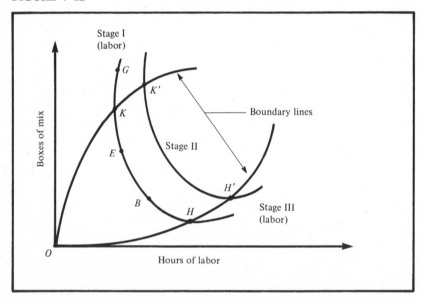

quantities of other inputs. Point *H* on Figure 7–12 reflects this possibility. At *H* so many units of labor are trying to work with so little mix that workmen are a hindrance to each other. A little more labor will add nothing to output. Its marginal product is zero. If still more labor is used, then it is possible that output will actually fall. The marginal product of labor can become negative. If we extend the isoquant to the right of *H* under these conditions, it will have to bend up, indicating that we have to use additional mix with the added labor if we expect to maintain the same output level. A similar thing occurs with regard to pie mix if we consider the isoquant extended above *K* in Figure 7–12. We are thus arguing that an isoquant will not have negative slope everywhere, but will be positively sloped to the right of *H* and above *K*.

The portion of the isoquant beyond H is said to be in the third stage of production (for labor) and the line OHH' is drawn as the boundary of Stage III. The analogous area beyond K is called Stage I. We are interested in defining these stages and boundaries because no firm that wished to minimize the cost of a given output would want to operate in either stage. It would not willingly hire so much labor to work the pie mix on hand that it moved into Stage III where $MP_L < 0$. This is just a matter of logic. The cost of the additional labor, the wage, could not be met from the sale of its marginal product because the latter is less than zero. So also, no (profit-maximizing) baker would buy so much pie mix that $MP_M < 0$ and he found himself in Stage I. Another box of pie mix would be so much in his way as to reduce the number of pies he could bake.

However, a baker might upon occasion find himself at G, with too much mix, because of a contract with his supplier made in the past when the technical conditions were different. If he wants to keep the same output he will throw some mix away immediately. He will move back to K rather than try to use the redundant mix even though he has to pay for it. If he tries to use it and produce at G, he will just have to work more himself—an added cost—in order to get the same number of pies as he can get at K. He can at least save some of his own labor by throwing away some mix. Thus, we can conclude on logical grounds that the negatively sloping portion of the isoquant is usually the most interesting part.

If our example had been an agricultural one, we would describe a movement along the isoquant toward H as farming land more intensively. We would be putting more and more labor on the land. H, which lies on the boundary of Stage II and Stage III, is sometimes referred to as the intensive margin, and any productive process that uses much labor relative to other factors is called labor-intensive. Similarly then, to reduce the amount of labor on the land, is to approach the extensive margin.

We have indicated that the marginal product of labor is zero at Stage II–Stage III boundary. Can we say anything about the average product? Output remains the same all along this isoquant, and as we approach H at the boundary we are using less and less pie mix. Since the average product of pie mix is just output divided by the amount of mix, the average is a maximum at H, where the smallest amount of pie mix is used and, incidentally, where the marginal product of labor is zero. A similar argument would establish that the average product of labor is a maximum at the Stage I–Stage II boundary, where the marginal product of pie mix is zero.

The argument just developed concludes that production will take place in Stage II if the firm seeks to minimize costs. In a later chapter we will develop the additional argument that production will occur at a level that equates marignal cost and marginal revenue. Fortunately, these two prescriptions do not contradict each other. We will find that marginal cost equals marginal revenue in Stage II.

SUMMARY

This lecture has developed the characteristics of isoquants. They are summarized above and turn out to be very similar to the characteristics of indifference curves. Perhaps the most important difference is that isoquants can have a cardinal index but indifference curves can only be arranged in order from most to least preferred.

Isoquants are used in this chapter to divide the production surface into three parts or stages. Only one of these stages, Stage II, is consistent with profit-maximizing because one input has zero or negative marginal product in each of the other two stages. The appearance of negative marginal product stems from the law of variable proportions.

In the analysis of indifference curves, there was a constraint on income that made it impossible for economic man to go beyond the attainable set to higher and higher curves. We could therefore be primarily interested in the shape of indifference curves as they crossed the budget line. Economic firm, however, can move up or down the production surface in its efforts to maximize profits merely by buying more or fewer inputs. No isoquant is out of reach and we must therefore examine the "expansion paths" that lead from one isoquant to the next in some detail. We will do this in the next chapter.

SELECTED READINGS

See list at end of Chapter 8.

Chapter 8

Production:
Expansion paths

INTRODUCTION

The baskets of inputs that lie along the isoquant described in the preceding chapter all have the same output. A firm operating on this curve is therefore choosing among different ways to produce that output. This is an important choice, as we will discover when we introduce costs and let the firm look for the least costly "way" to produce a given output. Nevertheless, it is only a part of the choice problem faced by the firm. An economic firm must also decide which isoquant, meaning which level of output, will maximize its profits.

One of the paths along which a firm can move to higher or lower isoquants is described by the line *OBEY* in Figure 8–1. A movement along this line requires an increase or decrease in all inputs but does not permit any change in the proportions between inputs. Thus, basket E contains more labor and more mix than basket B, but the ratio L_E/M_E is equal to the ratio L_B/M_B. We will refer to any movement like the one from B to E as a "change in scale." Changes in scale are in fact possible along any positively sloped ray from the origin. Several others are indicated by short arrows on Figure 8–1. They differ from each other only in that the slope of each indicates a different ratio of labor to mix that will be held constant along it.

If a firm wishes to increase its scale of operations by moving along one of these paths to the right, it has to be able to increase all inputs. Real firms find that it takes more time to increase some inputs than others. For instance, if the electric company needs more unskilled labor it can probably hire that labor in a few days, but if it needs greater water storage space for use in generating electricity, then the additional dam may take years to construct. These two examples are extremes, and there will usually be many inputs, each with its own time constraint, that lie somewhere between these extremes.

The needed time is measured from the point at which the decision to hire the additional input is made to the point at which output is in-

FIGURE 8–1

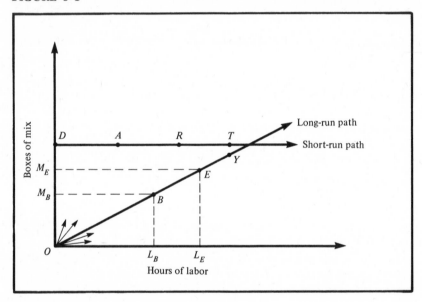

creased by the use of that input. Since the decision to make a change in scale requires time enough to increase *all* inputs, including the one with the longest lag between decision and output effect, we view a change in scale as a long-run decision. Any of the rays on Figure 8–1 can then be called a long-run expansion path. Notice the term "long-run" describes the decision itself. It indicates that even though the decision is made now, it will be some long period of time before that decision can affect output.

We should not, however, think that the input with the longest time constraint is always the physical plant of the firm. In a medical practice, it is the doctor himself who is likely to be the relatively fixed input. He can increase his use of office space, X-ray machines, or medical technicians in a fairly short period of time, but his own capacity is fixed. He must wait until his son is trained or until he can find a suitable partner. Professional skill is the fixed factor here. Similarly, it would not be hard to imagine a business in which land would be the fixed input.

Before we turn to the analysis of the long-run expansion path, one note of caution is necessary. We will act as if the firm can buy in the market whatever quantities of inputs seem likely to maximize its profits. Thus, the entire production set is in the attainable set. We are assuming that there are no imperfections in the capital market that affect the firm's choice of the profit-maximizing basket of inputs.

RETURNS TO SCALE

If a firm decides to make a change in scale, it will be because of what will happen to its total output. We must, therefore, describe the way in which output changes along a ray like $OBEY$ on Figure 8–1. It is easiest to "see" the shape of the total output curve, or to use a more common term, the total product curve if we go back to three dimensions as in Figure 8–2.

Along the path $OBEY$ each basket is assumed to produce some output.[1] We can measure the output from the basket B as the distance B to B', which is equal to Q_B marked on the vertical axis. Similarly, at E output is Q_E, and so on. The line $OB'E'Y'$ is the profile of the production surface that we want to examine.

Between the origin (O) and the point B' the path appears to get steeper and steeper. This means that output is increasing faster than inputs are added to the production process; that is, when inputs have doubled, output will have more than doubled. We say the curve shows "increasing returns to scale." Increasing returns occur mainly because the additional inputs permit a *division of labor* and capital. The division of labor is one of the best known concepts in economics. When a firm is small, one individual may perform many different tasks. It is generally true that his output would rise if he could specialize in just one of them. Moreover, he loses a certain amount of time just switching from one to the other. In a larger firm, each individual (and machine) can have only one task, and even that task may be subdivided into particular operations. The result is that men learn the limited task very well. For men it is the case that practice makes more nearly perfect. It also becomes possible to design each machine to fit a task. The resulting rise

---

[1] It is sometimes suggested that baskets near the origin (O) yield no output at all. They seem to have so little labor and mix that no pies can be produced. However, these inputs are not finite quantities, but rates of input over time. Even if a basket provides apples at the rate of one apple per week and a pie takes four apples, we can *usually* get output by accumulating enough apples to make one pie per month. Thus, we will assume that as soon as we have small positive rates of input we will begin to get small positive rates of output.

FIGURE 8–2

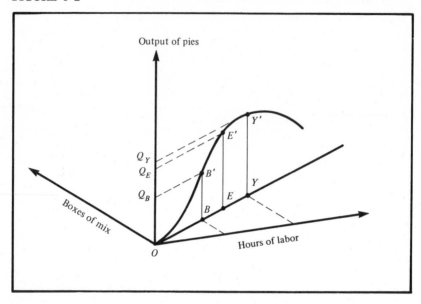

in productivity of both men and machines makes the total product curve bend up between O and B' on Figure 8–2.

The factors that lead to increasing returns seem, however, to have some physical limits so that the firm reaches some output like Q_B where the path begins to bend the other way. Increasing returns are coming to an end and the curve is now dominated by a new problem that produces "decreasing returns to scale." This is basically the problem of control and coordination of larger and larger collections of inputs. The span of control of a single manager or entrepreneur is limited. We are looking at a long-run expansion path, and that implies an increase in management along with all other inputs, but this turns out to be impossible. To take a military example, suppose that the management of one platoon is a full-time job for one lieutenant. If there are two platoons, then there will be two lieutenants. We seem to have doubled both inputs, but the management problem appears to have more than doubled. Each officer must now take some time off from his full-time platoon management job to coordinate the activities of the two platoons. If this is not done, they will end up some dark night shooting at each other.

It is now clear that what we have in mind when we talk about doubling all inputs is that we will double the *capacity* to manage. We need a lieutenant who can run two platoons because he thinks twice as fast, communicates twice as fast and so on, and hence, can handle twice as many men. Human beings, however, do not expand that way. Doubling the number of lieutenants did not double the capacity to manage. We have not doubled all inputs in the relevant sense and therefore the proportion between management capacity and troops has actually changed.[2]

When the proportion between inputs changes, the effect on output is determined by the law of variable proportions. This law tells us to expect that output will *not* double when we double the number of soldiers and the number of lieutenants because the ratio of the number of soldiers to the command (management) capacity has increased.

This is the same law that had so much to do with the shape of isoquants in Chapter 6. (It also has an effect on the short-run expansion path that we have yet to discuss.) We can conclude from the argument just above about soldiers and lieutenants that what we have called "decreasing returns to scale" reveal in fact another situation in which the law of variable proportions is at work.

Thus, returns start to decrease at B' on Figure 8–2 and continue decreasing to the right along the curve. At Y' the total product curve reaches its maximum point. "Returns" have decreased to zero, meaning that the marginal product of another input package of labor and mix is zero. This is a very important property of the production function. If there is a maximum total output for any production process, then a profit-maximizing firm will not expand beyond that point, and there is an effective upper limit on the size of the firm. This means, among other things, that General Motors will not try to take over the world as long as it remains interested in profits. Changes in technology often shift the maximum (Y') up and to the right, making the firm larger in that it uses more inputs and produces greater output, but changes can also push firms in the other direction as well. The transportation of many commodities by truck instead of railroad is an example of this reverse trend. Trucking companies tend to be much smaller than railroad companies simply because the technology they use is different.

Beyond Y' the total product curve in Figure 8–2 turns down. This is a way of saying that the quantities of inputs being managed by the firm have become so large and unwieldy that management loses con-

---

[2] Management is not the only source of this problem. All inputs are subject to physical constraints that will be important in certain processes. It will then be true that doubling the number of units of an input will not double the capacity of that input to contribute to output. For instance, doubling the number of machines used may not effectively double their contribution to output even when all other inputs they work with are also doubled. If they generate noise or heat, then the space they require may have to be more than doubled in order to keep them efficient. A single machine standing by itself can dissipate heat in all directions. If, however, another machine stands right beside it, then heat may not be effectively dissipated in that direction and the plant space may have to more than double when two machines have twice the heat to dissipate.

FIGURE 8–3

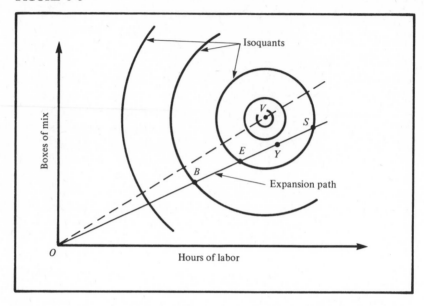

trol of production. The marginal product of additional input bundles is negative. A firm could conceivably go so far beyond Y' that total output would fall to zero, but of course this part of the curve is not very interesting to profit-maximizing firms.

In summary, one can say that:

> From O to B' we have "increasing returns to scale." The marginal product of an input bundle of mix and labor inputs (MP_I) is positive and it is increasing.[3] Increases in returns are due to the division of labor and specialization by men and machines.
>
> From B' on to the right we have "decreasing returns to scale." The marginal product of input bundles (MP_I) is decreasing. At Y', $MP_I = O$, and beyond Y' it is negative, and total output falls.

You should also note that if we start from Y' and go in either direction, we go to lower output levels. This means that we will cross a given isoquant (output level) no matter which way we go. The isoquants must go clear around the hill to its "back side." They must be closed curves as in Figure 8–3. The basket Y will have the largest output on the path $OB'E'Y'$, and this is where it will touch the highest isoquant that is touched by the line $OBEY$. To the right of Y, this path will again cross lower isoquants as at S. Nevertheless, Y may not have the

---

[3] Here, as elsewhere, we can identify marginal product with the slopes of tangents to the total product curve. It is easy to "see" that between O and B' the tangents get steeper, meaning that MP_I gets larger.

largest output when all baskets of inputs are considered. The largest
output, V on Figure 8–3, may lie on a different expansion path (OV).

OTHER POSSIBLE SHAPES

The S-shaped path that appears as the line $OB'E'Y'$ in Figure 8–2
is believed by economists to be quite realistic. Data derived from the
observation of real production processes suggest that a firm will at first

FIGURE 8–4

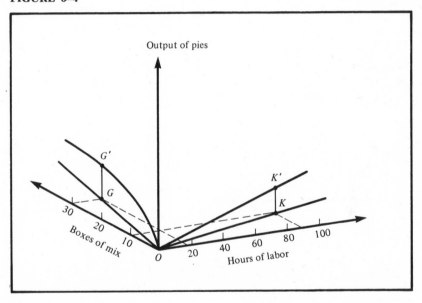

realize increasing returns as it expands output, but that if it expands
far enough, it will experience decreasing returns and ultimately falling
total output. Mathematically, however, this S-shaped path is cumbersome, and economists have often introduced some simplifications. One
important simplification has been to eliminate the possibility of increasing returns by assuming that the production set is convex or even
strictly convex. For instance the profile directly above the ray OG in
Figure 8–4 is strictly convex. A whole production surface that is strictly
convex will look like a dome, and every expansion path will show decreasing returns to scale everywhere. Though we have used the word
convex before, we are now giving it some added meaning and it needs
a more careful definition.

The curve OG' in Figure 8–5 is meant to be a profile of a production
surface. It has the same general shape as the line OG' in Figure 8–4.

but it is presented in two dimensions instead of three. All possible outputs from the baskets that lie along the line OG in Figure 8–4 are now represented by points on the curve OG' in Figure 8–5. The curve thus encloses a subset of the production set, and we want to know when that subset is convex. If we take any two points in that set—x_1 and x_2, for instance—we can connect those points with a straight line. The set will be convex if any point on that line (x_0) is also in the set. In this case the point x_0 is in fact *inside* the set, meaning that it is not a boundary

FIGURE 8–5

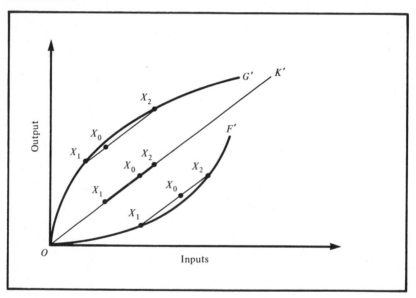

point, so this set is "strictly" convex. Thus, a set is strictly convex if any point on a straight line that connects two other points in the set is itself an interior point of the set.

By contrast, if the straight line OK' on Figure 8–5 also represents the boundary of a production set (also taken from Figure 8–4), it is easy to see that x_0 can be on the boundary. This set is therefore said to be convex but not strictly convex. Finally, notice that a set that shows increasing returns to scale, OF' in Figure 8–5, will put the point x_0 outside the set. The curve OF' is again drawn as the profile of a production surface and all possible outputs lie on or below this line. (See, for example, the section from the origin (O) to B' of the total product curve $OB'E'Y'$ in Figure 8–2.) Since OF' is the upper boundary of this set, then the point x_0 lies above this boundary. It is outside the set, and the set does not meet our definition of convex. Therefore, if a production set is convex, it cannot show increasing returns to scale anywhere along its upper boundary.

Looking back at Figure 8–4, if the curve OG' constitutes a useful simplification of the total product curve, then the curve OK' represents still greater simplicity. As noted above, such a set is convex, but not strictly convex, and by far the easiest to handle mathematically. The whole hill will look like a half cone with its vertex at O and is called a convex cone. The key characteristic of the curve OK' is that a proportional expansion of all inputs will lead to an expansion of output in the same proportion. For example, if every input is doubled anywhere along the curve, output will also double, and we can use the term "constant returns to scale" to describe the behavior of output along this curve.

SOME COMMENTS

We have thus introduced the possibility of three long-run expansion paths and we should now make a few comments about each.

a. The most realistic path, $OB'E'Y'$ in Figure 8–2, is often used in informal discussion of production. It can be easily represented geometrically, but is difficult to represent mathematically so it is not so likely to be used when a rigorous analysis is desired.

b. Increasing returns to scale appear on this "realistic" path at low levels of output. If increasing returns existed everywhere along an expansion path, competition among firms would be impossible. This is because output expands faster than inputs where the inputs are the real costs. The largest firm will, therefore, have the lowest average costs and be able to undersell its competitors. Indeed, the existence in the real world of production functions with long increasing-returns sections is offered by econoimsts as an explanation of "natural monopolies." These are monopolies that, in the layman's language, seem to involve economies of mass production. More will be said about these monopolies in Chapter 15.

c. Constant returns, as in the path OK' of Figure 8–4, are the easiest to handle mathematically and are most commonly used where elaborate analytic models are being developed. This has been especially true with regard to models of economic growth. This curve will be carefully considered in Chapter 11.

d. However, constant returns make the whole question of firm size indeterminate. The output of a commodity would be equally profitable to any size of firm (under competition). This is true because doubling inputs would double output. Hence, both costs and revenues would double and profit per unit of output would be the same no matter what size the firm. In the real world, however, we are often very much aware of industries in which existing firms seem to cluster about an average size.

e. We account for this size factor by assuming strict convexity, which gets us a hill like OG' in Figure 8–4. This latter surface is open to very rigorous, if somewhat more difficult, analytics than the constant-returns hill.

LINEAR PROGRAMMING

Economists have usually assumed that any point on the production hill can be reached by walking up some path; that is, they assume that inputs can be combined in any proportion because they are infinitely divisible into small units *and* that technical knowledge is always sufficient to permit their use in any proportion. Outside of that and the assumption about convexity, the exact shape of the hill is said to be a technical problem in the province of engineers.

But the engineers, unfortunately, do not seem to see the problem that way at all. The production problem seems to them one of choosing between two (or more) different "ways" of doing things. Each way involves relatively fixed proportions of inputs. That is, each "way" corresponds to a given expansion path, and there appear to be only a few paths open at any one time. Also, each path appears to be linear; that is, to exhibit constant returns to scale, at least over an important range of outputs.

Economists now approach this engineer's view of production by using the mathematics of linear programming. The resulting models are addenda to the neo-classical theory of production that is so important as to warrant a full discussion. This discussion will therefore be included as Chapter 11 after cost curves have been developed along more conventional lines.

THE SHORT-RUN EXPANSION PATH

It is possible to look at the *long-run* expansion path as a set of alternative baskets of inputs among which the firm must choose. It can make its choice now, but it will be some time before that choice can have an effect on output. This is because *all* inputs must be increased (or decreased) along the long-run path. Some inputs take more time than others, but even the slowest to change must change if the decision is a long-run decision. The electric company that decided to expand its output by building a new dam and acquiring all of the necessary generators and power lines that go with it, makes a good example. The dam itself will probably be the input that takes the longest time to complete.

Once a long-run decision has been made, the firm must wait for it to affect output. The electric company must make do with the existing dams until the new one is complete. It can, however, vary other inputs. It may be able to get greater output by using its existing facilities for longer hours. This will require more labor, perhaps more fuel for some of its plants, probably more management personnel, and so on. It will find that it can increase the rate of delivery of coal to its steam generating plant in a few days. Thus, it can make a decision today about coal that can have its effect on output three or four days hence. If it needs more labor, that may take a little longer, and to find especially skilled management personnel may take still longer.

All of these are short-run decisions, though some take longer than others to affect output. In fact, every decision except the decision to build the dam is a short-run decision. Thus, the firm must make a whole series of short-run decisions. These decisions take effect at various times, ranging from almost immediately to times far in the future, almost as far in the future as the long-run decision. Looking at the problem this way makes the distinction between long and short run seem arbitrary, but it is as a matter of fact quite useful. It will be especially useful in the discussion of cost curves that follows this chapter, and again when we discuss the character of equilibrium in Chapter 13.

A short-run decision is always a decision to make a "change in the proportions" among inputs. (By contrast, the long-run decision is a decision to make a "change in scale.") Proportions change because at least one input is fixed and it is decided to increase or decrease one or more of the others. For the simplified situation in which there are only two inputs, the short-run path looks like $DA'R'T'$ in Figure 8–6. This path appeared in two dimensions on Figure 8–1, where its relationship to the long-run path can be noted.

In Figure 8–6, the amount of mix is unchanging, and the choice concerns the amount of labor to use with the mix. The baskets that lie along the straight line $DART$ can be viewed as alternatives among which the firm can choose in order to determine its output while it waits for any long-run choice about the amount of mix to become effective. Since proportions change, this would suggest that the Law of Variable Proportions should be at work. So it is!

From D to A', the marginal product of labor increases as the baker gains time enough to be efficient; that is, to specialize—rolling all the crusts at once, peeling all the apples at once, and so on. Further up the hill beyond A', there is too little mix, and the baker spends much of his time trying to stretch the flour and apples into more and more pies. Another unit of labor is partly wasted and the marginal product of labor declines. This is the range over which the law of variable proportions makes itself felt.

Ultimately, the baker will get all the pies possible by careful peeling

FIGURE 8–6

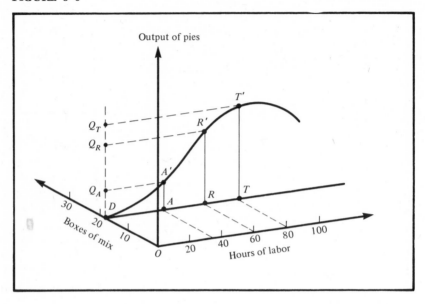

of apples and rolling of dough, and another hour of his time will add nothing to output. The marginal product of labor is now zero (as at T'). Adding still more labor will reduce total output below Q_T as bakers interfere with each other. If, ultimately, too many units of labor are trying to get at the fixed amount of mix, then a point may be reached where no pies at all are produced. Output along the production function can return to zero beyond T'. Thus, the shape of this path is primarily determined by the law of variable proportions.

STAGES OF PRODUCTION AGAIN

When we looked at isoquants in Chapter 7 we found that there was only one segment of the production function where a profit maximizing firm would want to operate. We called this segment Stage II, and it can now be shown that the short-run production function also has a Stage II with essentially the same meaning. This should not be too surprising since isoquants, short-run total product curves, and long-run total product curves are simply alternative ways of looking at the same production surface.

This argument starts with the total product curve shown in Figure 8–7. This is the usual S curve like the one labeled $DA'R'T'$ on Figure 8–6. The horizontal axis indicates that units of labor are being added to the fixed input, mix. Mix is assumed to be fixed at ten boxes and the

FIGURES 8–7 and 8–8

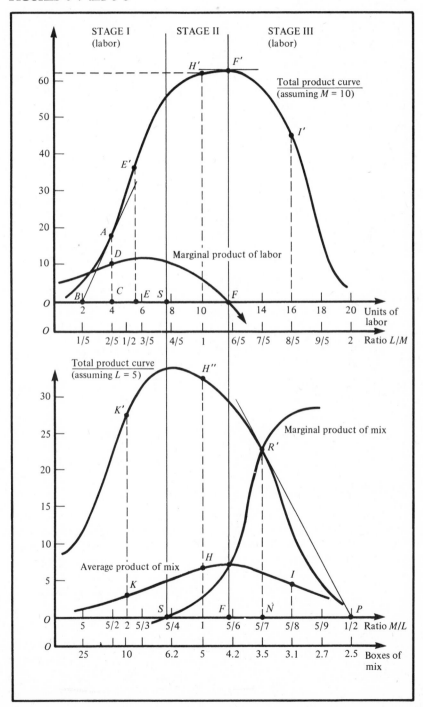

total product curve indicates the output of each combination of inputs. The first thing to do is to derive the marginal product of labor from this curve. At each point along the total product curve, marginal product of labor (MP_L) is equal to the slope of a tangent drawn at that point. This idea first appeared in Chapter 4, where we related marginal revenue to total revenue. In Figure 8–7 we have actually drawn a tangent to the total product curve at A as an example. It forms the small triangle ABC. The slope of that tangent (which is the hypotenuse of the triangle) is the ratio of the opposite side of the triangle (AC) to the adjacent side (CB). The value of this ratio appears to be approximately equal to

$$\frac{AC}{AB} = \frac{18}{2} = 9.$$

Hence we can say that when four units of labor are being used, a small increase in the labor input will expand output at the rate of nine apple pies per unit of labor. This information is shown in Figure 8–7 as point D on the marginal product (of labor) curve.

The rest of the curve can be approximated in the way point D was found. Starting from the left, tangents to the total product curve get steeper and steeper until E' is reached. Thus the MP_L curve must rise until about 5½ units of labor are being used. From there on it will fall, reaching zero at about 11½ units. One can see that the tangent at that point (F) is horizontal, that is, it has zero slope and $MP_L = 0$.

The point F' on the total product curve is an important point, precisely because the marginal product of labor is zero. Using labor in excess of 11½ units (when using 10 units of mix) will add nothing to output. No matter how low wages are, there will be no added output to be sold to help pay those wages. We have reached the Stage II–Stage III boundary, where the ratio of labor to mix becomes so large that labor is redundant. No profit-maximizing firm will want to hire more labor if it increases the labor-mix ratio beyond $L/M = 11.5/10$.

We attribute this outcome to the law of variable proportions. As this law indicates, the *proportion* of labor to mix (L/M) is an important determinant of output. In Figure 8–7 we have related output along the total product curve to units of labor, but we could replace those units with L/M ratios. Since there are assumed to be 10 boxes of mix, we get ratios as indicated on the scale just below the horizontal axis. Using ratios along the horizontal axis puts the emphasis in the right place, that is, on the effects of changes in the proportions between inputs.

Whatever the ratio L/M, we can view that ratio as a ratio of mix to labor as well. Thus when ten units of mix are used with three units of labor, we can describe the ratio as

$$L/M = 3/10 \text{ or } M/L = 10/3 \,.$$

This second ratio is laid out along the horizontal axis in Figure 8–8. From right to left along this scale, it is clear that mix is increasing relative to labor: the ratio M/L is getting larger. Therefore, according to the law of variable proportions, the marginal product of mix (MP_M) should ultimately decline. We will now show that this is just what happens by deriving the marginal product of mix curve from the production information contained in Figure 8–7.

The first step is to realize that the total product curve in Figure 8–7 can give us the average product of mix associated with each input ratio. For instance, when

$$L/M = M/L = 1,$$

total product equals about 61 apple pies (point H on Figure 8–7). Since mix is fixed at 10 boxes, this means an average output per box of mix of about 6.1 pies, and this is shown as point H on Figure 8–8. Also, when

$$L/M = 8/5 \text{ and } M/L = 5/8,$$

output appears to be about 45 apple pies (I' on Figure 8–7), or 4.5 pies per box of mix. We show this information as point I on Figure 8–8. If we continue this process for every input ratio we get the whole curve labeled average product of mix on Figure 8–8.

This curve shows the average product of mix associated with each input ratio (M/L). The size of the average product depends on the ratio and is independent of which input is variable. We can therefore view Figure 8–8 from right to left as an example of production when labor is fixed and mix is the variable input. We will do this by assuming some given quantity of labor (five units) and finding the amount of mix necessary to give the right M/L ratio. Thus when $M/L = 1$, the units of mix must be 5 as indicated along the bottom scale on Figure 8–8.

It is now easy to get a new total product curve. We know how many units of mix are used and the average product of mix. Thus when 5 units of mix are used ($M/L = 1$), average product is 6.1, so total product is $5 \cdot 6.1 = 30.5$, shown as point H'' on Figure 8–8.[4] Similarly, when 10 units of mix are used ($M/L = 2$), then the $AP_M = 2.7$ and total product is 27, shown at K' on Figure 8–8. If we continue this process for every input ratio, we will get the curve labeled total product on Figure 8–8.

The final step is to derive the marginal product of mix from this total product curve. We will do this in the same way we did earlier for

---

[4] There is a tacit assumption here that total product depends only on the input ratio. The AP_M is assumed to be the same at that ratio whether 5, 10, or 1,000 units of mix are used. In other words, there are assumed to be no increasing or decreasing returns to scale. This is a useful assumption here because we are analyzing the effects of changes in proportion, not changes in scale.

the marginal product of labor. Thus the marginal product at any given point is equal to the slope of tangent to the total product curve at that point. At R' the tangent has a slope equal to the ratio

$$\frac{R'N}{NP} = \frac{22}{1} = 22;$$

hence the MP_M at R' is 22 apple pies per box of mix. This slope is negative but we will treat it as positive because we are moving along the total product curve from right to left. We are increasing the input of mix, and total product is rising, hence both values are positive. $MP_M = 22$, and it is shown this way at R' on Figure 8–8. If we apply this process all along the total product curve we get the whole curve labeled marginal product of mix.

This curve obviously goes to zero at S, and this becomes the boundary of Stage I and Stage II. To move to the left of this boundary is to add units of mix whose marginal product will be zero or perhaps negative. Mix is now redundant and the profit-maximizing firm will not be interested in entering Stage 1. Production will therefore take place somewhere between points S and F. The proportion of labor to mix (or mix to labor) that will maximize profits will lie somewhere between

$$\frac{L}{M} = \frac{7.5}{10} \text{ and } \frac{L}{M} = \frac{11.5}{10}.$$

When we get to the discussion of cost curves we will be able to pin down the exact point in Stage II that maximizes profits. (This will of course require that we also know something about revenues).

EXPANSION AND GROWTH

There is one thing that these expansion paths are not! They are not historical growth paths for individual firms. They do not describe what happens as a new firm begins small and with the passage of time grows into a large firm. Clearly, growth patterns do exist and are very important, though they are more important to managers than they are to economists. Expansion paths, on the other hand, mark out the alternatives that exist at a particular time, not the alternatives that will appear to the firm in sequence as time passes. They are alternaives among which a firm will choose in order to maximize profits, and they depend on what is known about the technology of production, not on the history of the individual firm.

PRODUCTION POSSIBILITIES

There is a way to consider the production of more than one good at a time with some particular set of inputs. It involves the development of a curve called the production-possibilities curve. The required change in our viewpoint is modest. When we developed the isoquant in Chapter 7, each basket contained two inputs and one output. Since most firms produce many outputs with many, many inputs, this is a particular simplification of reality made in order to facilitate the use of geometry. If we now consider baskets that include *two* outputs as well as two inputs, we have a different simplification but one that we can still handle with geometry. It is, however, about as far as geometry can take us.

FIGURE 8–9

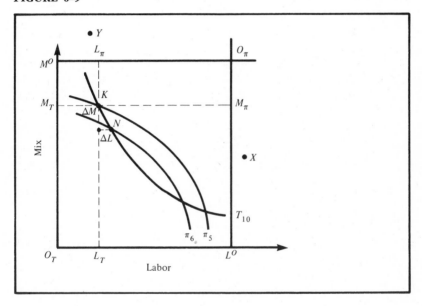

In Figure 8–9 we have drawn an isoquant for the production of tea labeled T_{10}. At K the firm can use some mix (M_T) and some labor (L_T) to get an output of ten pounds of tea indicated by the fact that K is a point on the isoquant T_{10}. Now suppose that the firm has some given amount of both labor and mix and cannot increase that amount. The given amount of labor is shown as L^0 on Figure 8–9 and the given mix as M^0. These limits mean that the firm must choose among points inside the box $O_T M^0 O_\pi L^0$. Any points that lie outside the box, like X and Y, require more labor or more mix than is available. The points inside the box constitute the production set under these constraints. These constraints are being introduced so that we can ask what it means to maximize output from fixed inputs. We will look at this question first from the point of view of a single firm, but in Chapter 18 we will use the same techniques to talk about production in the whole economy when supplies of labor and other inputs are given.

Looking back at Figure 8–9, it is clear that at K only part of the total labor is being used to make tea. The rest can be used to make pie. It is measured from O_π at the upper right-hand corner of the box and is labeled L_π on the top edge of the box. Similarly, the mix available for pie making is measured from O_π and labeled M_π. How much pie can be made with L_π of labor and M_π of mix? This will be revealed by a pie isoquant through K. The isoquant map for pie has been rotated 180° from the usual position for such maps, and then the origin has been

FIGURE 8–10

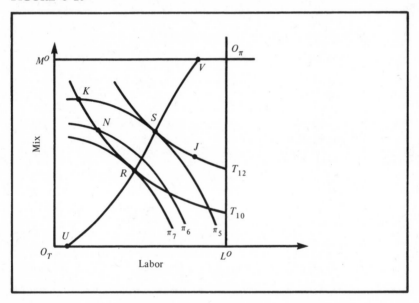

placed at O_π. The resulting isoquant (π_5) has the usual convex, negatively sloped shape in relation to its origin O_π.

The point K on Figure 8–9 indicates an output of ten pounds of tea (T_{10}) and five apple pies (π_5). Is this the maximum output of pie when ten pounds of tea are produced? The answer is no! At N the firm can still make ten pounds of tea, but pie output is increased from five (π_5) to six (π_6). The increase comes from reallocating the inputs between pie and tea production. As shown in Figure 8–9, ΔM of mix is shifted from tea to pie production and ΔL of labor is shifted from pie to tea production.

In Figure 8–10 it is clear that the reallocation of inputs can go on until the firm gets to R. At R, pie output is at the highest level (π_7) that is possible without reducing tea output below the ten pounds produced along the isoquant T_{10}. Any larger output of pie will lie on an isoquant that is completely below the isoquant T_{10}, and hence it can only be reached by reducing the output of tea below ten pounds. In finding the point R we imagined the firm to start from K and move along T_{10}, but no matter where it starts, J for instance, it can find a similar maximum point (see S).

There are certain things we can say about points like R and S. They are points of tangency between a tea isoquant and a pie isoquant. Given that each set of isoquants is convex to its own origin, there must be a

FIGURE 8–11

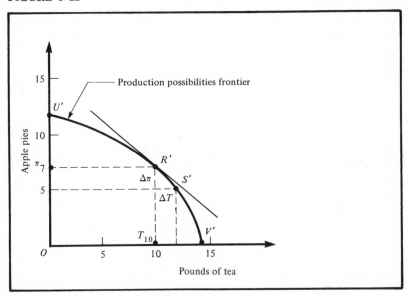

whole set of such tangencies. The line UV in Figure 8–10 is drawn through this set of points.

If the firm is using any allocation of inputs between pie and tea production that can be represented by a point off this line, then it can always reallocate so as to move to the line and increase one output without reducing the other and without increasing total inputs. (If a firm is producing at any point on this line then any move along the line or off the line must reduce at least one output and may reduce both.)

The line UV of Figure 8–11 thus describes a particular set of production possibilities. It indicates the maximum amount of pie that can be produced with any given amount of tea from a fixed set of inputs. This information is often presented in the form shown in Figure 8–11. We can transfer point R from Figure 8–10 to Figure 8–11, where it appears at R'. At the point R' pie output is shown to be seven when tea output is ten. Similarly, S maps into S'. If all the points on the line UV in Figure 8–10 are mapped onto Figure 8–11 we get a curve like $U'V'$. This curve is called the production possibilities curve. On and below it lie all possible output combinations using the given set of inputs (L^0 and M^0). If the firm moves along this curve, say from U' to R', it is reallocating inputs in such a way as to get less pie and more tea, but always getting the maximum amount of pie for any given amount of tea.

As the firm moves down this curve it is transforming pie into tea. As it moves from R' to S' it gives up $\Delta\pi$ and shifts resources, so as to add ΔT to its output. Pie is being transformed into tea at the rate $\Delta T/\Delta\pi$. We will call this ratio the "rate of transformation" of pie into tea and write

$$RT_{\pi T} = \frac{\Delta T}{\Delta \pi}.$$

Again using the mathematics we have so often used before, if $\Delta\pi$ is made very small then the ratio $\Delta T/\Delta\pi$ approaches the value of the slope of a tangent to the curve at R'. Hence we will define the rate of transformation of pie into tea at any point on the curve as the slope of a line tangent to the curve at that point.

At U' in Figure 8–11, all the resources are being used to make apple pie. This means that resources that are especially well adapted to the production of tea are nevertheless being used to make pie. It cannot be expected that they add much to the output of pie and would produce substantial quantities of tea if shifted from pie to tea production. Thus, if we start at U' and move some small quantity of inputs from pie to tea production, we expect the loss of pie output to be small and the gain in tea output to be large. The rate of transformation of pie into tea ($RT_{\pi T}$) is large. Presumably the resources that are best adapted to tea production would be shifted first. Consequently as we move down the curve toward V', less and less effective resources are being shifted and so the gain in tea is smaller and the loss of pie is greater. The result of this argument is that the production possibilities curve must be concave when viewed from the origin as in Figure 8–11, indicating that the rate of transformation of pie into tea declines as we move down the curve.[5]

We will come back to the production possibilities curve and the rate of transformation in Chapter 18 on general equilibrium. At that point, we will take the supply of inputs for the whole economy as given so that the curve will indicate production possibilities for the whole economy.

---

[5] The rate of transformation is a negative number here because $\Delta\pi$ is a reduction in pie and is therefore treated as negative.

SUMMARY

Production and technology are, of course, much more complex than we have indicated. The material considered here is an abstraction guided by economic considerations. We have selected those aspects of the engineers' knowledge of production that we believe to be the constraints on choice by economic firm. If we have overlooked something important, our predictions about real prices and quantities of outputs will be wrong and we will have to rebuild the model.

The next step in the presentation of the theory of production is to introduce the prices of inputs and develop the cost curves of production. This we will do for the long run in Chapter 9 and for the short run in Chapter 10.

It can be said as a brief summary of the last two chapters that we have thought of the production possibilities for any good as a hill. The height of the hill represents output and each point on the hill corresponds to some combination of inputs. Moreover, we have been particularly interested in three kinds of paths over the surface of that hill. One of these goes up the hill along the path of a ray through the origin. This is the long-run expansion path, along which proportions among inputs are constant. The second goes up the hill along a path parallel to one of the input axes. This is the short-run expansion path, along which some input is physically constant in quantity. The last goes around the hill at a given height like a contour line. This is the isoquant, and the constant height represents a constant level of output. Each of these paths has an importance for existing theories of production choices that will become clearer as we consider costs and equilibrium.

SELECTED READINGS

Carlson, Sune. *A Study on the Pure Theory of Production* (London: P. S. King, 1939).

Cassels, John M. "On the Law of Variable Proportions," in *Explorations in Economics* (New York: McGraw-Hill, 1936), pp. 223–36.

Chamberlin, E. H. "Proportionality, Divisibility, and Economies of Scale," *Quarterly Journal of Economics,* vol. 62 (1948), pp. 229–62.

Machlup, Fritz. "On the Meaning of the Marginal Product," *Explorations in Economics* (New York: McGraw-Hill, 1936), pp. 250–63.

Tangri, O. P. "Omissions in the Treatment of the Law of Variable Proportions," *American Economic Review* (1966), pp. 484–92.

Chapter 9

Costs in the long run

INTRODUCTION

A long-run choice is a choice to expand (or contract) output by choosing a new basket of inputs that has more (or less) of every input. In Chapter 8 we examined the effect on output of shifting from one such basket to another. This led to the long-run expansion path as presented again in Figure 9–1. We now want to convert this information about physical inputs and outputs into information about the costs of production.

We can simplify the following discussion if we make a first assumption that the firm is a competitive buyer of inputs. This means, of course, that it can expect to buy any quantity of any input at current market prices. This assumption is fairly realistic for inputs that are not specialized to the production of this firm. Thus, IBM can expect to hire all the janitors it wants without bidding up their wage (price), but computer mathematicians are likely to be another story. As the firm or its industry expands, a specialized input will rise in price. This is the problem we wish to avoid at the moment.

PROPORTIONS AGAIN

An economic firm, about to make a long-run choice, will find that the choice has two aspects:

a. It must pick an appropriate level of output as its goal. That is another way of saying it must decide how high up on the production hill to go. This is the *problem of scale*.

177

FIGURE 9–1

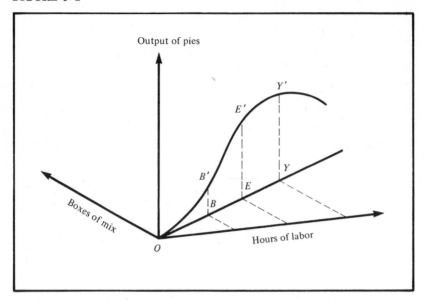

b. Then it must decide what combination of inputs to use in producing
   that level of output. In other words, once up the hill to the desired
   output level, it must decide how far around the hill and in which
   direction it should walk to get the right input combination. This is
   the *problem of proportion,* the proportion between inputs.

If we postpone the problem of scale and take up the problem of
proportions first, we find a simple answer to the proportions problem
based on input prices. It requires an answer to this question: "How can
the firm produce *any* chosen output at the least cost?" Suppose the
chosen scale of output is 90 pies, represented by the isoquant *ECD* in
Figure 9–2. If labor costs $1 per hour ($P_L = \$1$) and pie mix costs
$2 per box ($P_M = \$2$), then basket *D* will cost 70 dollars (60 hours of
labor at $1 each and 5 boxes of mix at $2 each). Basket *D* will produce
the chosen output of 90 pies, but there are a number of other baskets
that can be bought for the same money. Basket *X,* for instance, which
holds 70 hours of labor, and basket *Y,* with 35 boxes of mix, can be
had for $70. In fact, any basket on the line *YDX* can be bought for $70.
All baskets on this line cost the same, so we call it the *isocost curve.*

The slope of the isocost is determined by the ratio of input prices. We
can find one end of it by dividing the cost ($C = \$70$) by the price of
labor (C/P_L). This is basket *X*. Similarly we can find basket *Y* as
C/P_M. The slope of the curve is the tangent of the angle it makes with
the horizontal axis at *X*. Therefore,

FIGURE 9–2

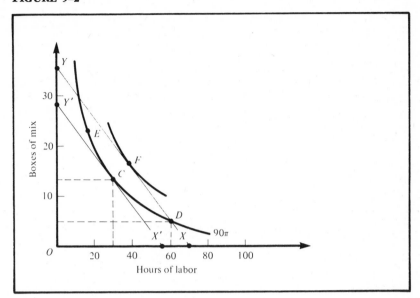

$$\text{Slope of } YDX = \frac{OY}{OX} = \frac{C/P_M}{C/P_L} = \frac{C}{P_M} \cdot \frac{P_L}{C} = \frac{P_L}{P_M}.$$

Thus the slope of an isocost curve is equal to the ratio of input prices (P_L/P_M). The isocost curve is an analogy for the budget line in consumer theory.

If $70 will buy any basket on YDX, it will, of course, be enough to buy basket F, which can make more than 90 pies because it lies on a higher isoquant. If we can make *more* than 90 pies for $70, then we probably can make 90 pies for less than $70. Neither basket F nor basket D is the least-cost way to make 90 pies. Since the *slope* of line YDX is determined by the prices of labor and pie mix, we can move it to the left to $Y'CX'$, leaving its slope unchanged by keeping P_L and P_M constant. The total cost, however, is reduced. Baskets along $Y'CX'$ cost only about $55 at the prices we are using. Basket X' contains about 55 units of labor at $P_L = \$1$ for a total cost of $55. $Y'CX'$ is tangent to the 90 pie isoquant at C. Thus we know that 90 pies can be made at C with 12½ boxes of mix and 30 hours of labor at a cost of $55. If we try to spend any less (move the isocost curve any further to the left), no available basket will have enough inputs to make 90 pies. We can make 90 pies more cheaply with basket C than with any other *as long as* the price of pie mix and labor do not change. This makes it clear that the least-cost combination of inputs for any output is determined by the ratio of input prices that gives the isocost curve its slope.

Notice what happens if the price of pie mix rises and that of labor falls. Any given expenditure will buy less mix than before (when it is all spent on mix) and more labor (when it is all spent on labor). The isocost curve will be less steep (see line *UBZ* in Figure 9–3). The "all-labor" basket (*Z*) will lie to the right of *X'*. *UBZ* represents an isocost curve that also permits production of 90 pies. The point of tangency is rolled around the 90-pie isoquant from *C* to *B*. Thus, for any level of output chosen by the firm, the input price ratio will tell it how to find the least-cost combination of inputs.

FIGURE 9–3

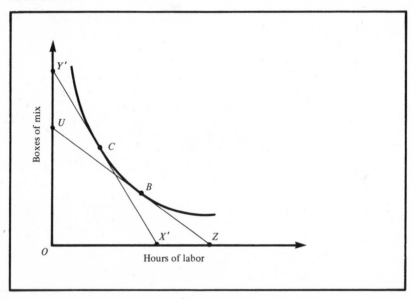

There is another way of looking at the least-cost problem and seeing the importance of the input price ratio. Remember that the slope of the isoquant (the RTS_{LM}) at *C* (or any other point) can be expressed as a ratio of marginal products at that point (MP_L/MP_M).[1] The slope expressed this way is, of course, negative; but we will ignore the sign. The slope of the iso*cost* is P_L/P_M as noted above, and so at *C*, where the isocost and isoquant are tangent,

$$RTS_{LM} = \frac{MP_L}{MP_M} = \frac{P_L}{P_M}.$$

The terms on the right can be rewritten thus:

---

[1] See Chapter 7, The Law of Variable Proportions.

$$\frac{MP_M}{P_M} = \frac{MP_L}{P_L}.$$

If, as this expression suggests, we divide the marginal product of mix by the price of mix, we get the marginal product of a dollar's worth of mix. Similarly, MP_L/P_L is the marginal product of a dollar's worth of labor. What would it mean if

$$\frac{MP_M}{P_M} > \frac{MP_L}{P_L};$$

that is, if the marginal product of a dollar's worth of mix was greater than the marginal product of a dollar's worth of labor? It would mean that the firm could spend a dollar less for labor and a dollar more for mix and watch its output go up without any increase in cost. If a larger output can be produced at the same cost, then the same output can be produced at lower cost. Obviously, we cannot have a least-cost combination of inputs when

$$\frac{MP_M}{P_M} > \frac{MP_L}{P_L} \text{ or when } \frac{MP_M}{P_M} < \frac{MP_L}{P_L}.$$

The least-cost combination can occur only if these two ratios are equal, that is, when

$$\frac{MP_M}{P_M} = \frac{MP_L}{P_L}.$$

This equality holds at the point of tangency between isoquant and isocost as noted above, and so the least-cost combination of inputs occurs at that tangency.

CORNER TANGENCY

The isocosts and isoquants we have been considering always have a point of tangency somewhere between the two axes. The least-cost combination of inputs always includes some positive amount of each of the inputs, and we would reach the same conclusion if we expanded the number of inputs beyond two. In real production processes, however, we can think of situations in which some input can be used or done without. Crops can be grown with or without fertilizer. Is there any way we can represent this real situation in the model?

To do so we will have to use isoquants of a somewhat different shape. Consider the isoquant in Figure 9–4. Let us suppose it represents possible combinations of cornstarch on the horizontal axis and boxes of all other inputs to apple pie on the other axis. As we approach point A, moving along this isoquant to the left, the amount of cornstarch approaches zero and the amount of all other inputs becomes very large

FIGURE 9–4

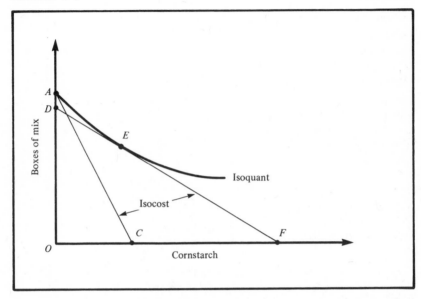

in proportion to cornstarch. We can, however, produce pie without cornstarch, so we need not expect the marginal product of all other inputs to approach zero just because their proportion to cornstarch is very large. This isoquant will not become steeper and steeper until its tangent is vertical indicating that all other inputs have become redundant relative to cornstarch.

The firm will still try to find the least-cost combination of inputs. If it is faced with an isocost curve like *AC,* then *A* is clearly the least-cost combination here. Any isocost parallel to *AC* but to the left of it will not intersect the isoquant at all; that is, it will not include enough inputs to produce that output. Any isocost to the right of *AC* will produce that output, but at higher cost. Thus *A* is the least-cost basket, and it includes no cornstarch at all. So pie will be made without cornstarch. Point *A* is called a corner tangency, or a corner solution.

It is also obvious that a fall in the price of cornstarch sufficient to produce a new isocost like *DEF* will lead to a new least-cost basket of inputs at *E* that does include cornstarch. The point *E* is an "internal" tangency of the kind we have used before. We will continue to use internal tangencies because they make the geometry of our analysis much easier. But the corner tangency does provide a way of handling a situation that must be very common in the real world; a situation in which the production of some good uses none of one or more inputs.

SCALE

Switching from the problem of proportions to the problem of scale, suppose we started out from the origin (O) in Figure 9–5 to walk up the hill until we got to a level that represents an output of five pies (B' perhaps). Then we could walk around the hill until we found the least-cost basket for making five pies. If the firm decided to make five pies per week, this would be the only basket of interest. We can repeat this process for every possible output level. A firm, seeking least cost at

FIGURE 9–5

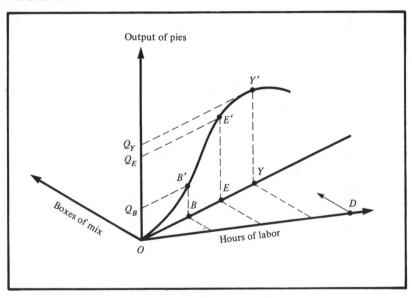

every output and therefore moving along this set of points, may not be led on a "straight" path up the hill. That means that both scale and proportion may have to change along the path. However, it will be easier to examine changes in scale by themselves if we assume the path will look like $OB'E'Y'$ in Figure 9–5. Along this path the firm will use the two inputs in fixed proportion. Thus along this path only scale is changing. It is a long-run expansion path, and we can now convert it into a long-run cost curve.

THE COST CURVES: TOTAL COST

In Figure 9–5, each basket along the path, such as O and B and E and Y, has in it certain quantities of pie mix and labor. They are in fixed proportion to each other so that we can view a movement along *OBEY* as adding bundles or packages of mix and labor in a given proportion to each other. We can then present the curve in two dimensions by putting these bundles along the horizontal axis. The curve will look like Figure 9–6. This is the view one would get by standing at *D* on Figure 9–5 and looking in the direction of the arrow. The curve *OB'E'Y'* appears as the profile of the production surface directly above the line *OBEY*.

This is a convenient way to look at this curve if we want to get a total cost curve. In fact, this curve is one kind of cost curve. It shows the number of bundles of inputs necessary to produce each output. It takes

FIGURE 9–6

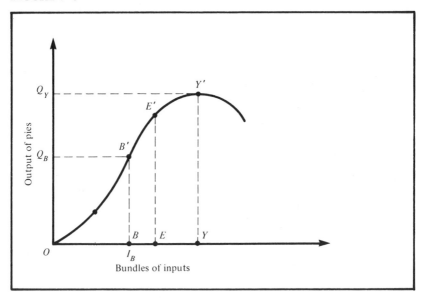

I_B bundles of inputs to produce Q_B units of output on Figure 9–6. I_B is the cost of that output expressed in physical units of inputs, meaning that this many bundles of inputs must be purchased and used up in order to produce Q_B.

When we talk about cost curves, however, we make a small change in our point of view. So far we have been concerned with the amount of output that can be obtained from each basket of inputs. We thus viewed output as dependent on the choice of an input basket, and following a convention in mathematics, we put the dependent variable (output) on the vertical axis. In the discussion of costs, however, we view output as the independent variable. The firm chooses an output and then asks how big a basket of input bundles it will have to buy in order to produce that output. This makes input costs the dependent variable and so by convention they are put on the vertical axis. This means that the two axes are reversed as in Figure 9–7.

The final step is to convert the input costs into dollars. The basket I_B has some units of labor and some units of mix. Each of those inputs has a price. We can therefore find out what it will cost to buy the basket I_B and every other basket along the vertical axis in Figure 9–7. This merely involves a change in scale along that axis from bundles of inputs to costs of inputs in dollars as shown on Figure 9–8.

FIGURE 9–7

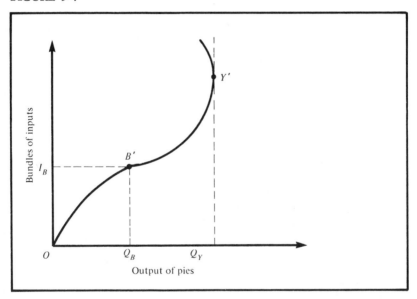

We have thus traced out the long-run total-cost curve (LTC). This curve is relevant only for long-run choices because it must be possible to choose any quantity of any input if economic firm is to be able to stay on this curve. It is *physically* possible to use any quantity of any input since, as noted earlier, inputs are rates of flow over time.[2] When costs are introduced, however, we complicate the problem. The real markets in which inputs are bought and sold may not permit the purchase of very low rates of input. It may not be possible for a small auto producer to rent a fender-stamping machine on a part-time basis. He

---

[2] It should be remembered here that technology may not permit the combination of inputs in any proportion whatever, but we have abstracted from this problem by assuming that the production function is continuous. We will not depart from this assumption until we get to linear production functions in Chapter 11.

FIGURE 9–8

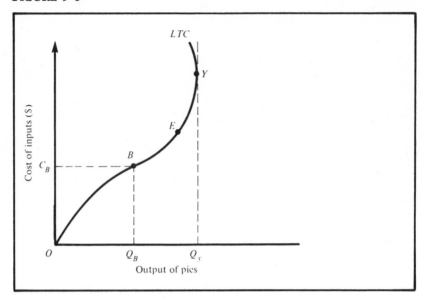

may have to buy it and absorb its full cost or make fenders some other way. If he has to buy it outright, then the average cost of making fenders will go down as he makes more per hour up to the point where he reaches the "capacity" of the machine. This factor will add to the economies of scale along the first part of the curve from O to B. It is time, therefore, to introduce the concept of economies of scale.

ECONOMIES OF SCALE

We have suggested above that there are a number of factors that make the long-run total-cost curve look concave from below between O and B in Figure 9–8. A machine with twice the output capacity may not cost twice as much to buy and install. The type of machine itself may change as output rises. Men with wheelbarrows will be replaced by trucks especially designed for quick loading and unloading. The most important factor, however, is the increasing returns to scale that we noted along the corresponding portion of the long-run total product curve. We summarize the effects of all these factors on the cost curve by saying that firm experiences "economies of scale" between O and B.

Similarly from B to Y we are looking at what we will now call "diseconomies of scale." The primary explanation of diseconomies of scale lies in the decreasing returns to scale that are also a physical characteristic of the total product curve and were discussed in Chapter 8.

MARGINAL COST

A firm ought to increase its output as long as each additional unit of output adds more to its revenues than it adds to costs. This sounds logical and is, in fact, a logical consequence of assuming that an economic firm wishes to maximize profits. We can imagine our firm currently producing 90 pies per week and contemplating an increased output of one pie per week. The choice problem will be the same whether the firm is currently at 90 pies or a thousand, or even zero. Selling that extra pie under competitive conditions will add P_π, the price of one pie, to its revenues. We have already begun to call this addition to total revenue marginal revenue.

In order to make that one more pie, inputs will have to be increased. This is true because economic firm will get the maximum output from whatever basket of inputs it uses. It cannot get more unless it buys a larger basket. These added inputs are the added costs of getting one more pie and are called by the economist the marginal cost. We can find out how large the marginal cost of pie (MC_π) is by subtracting the total cost of 90 pies from the total cost of 91 pies. We could thus move along the total cost curve of Figure 9–8 determining the marginal cost of a one unit output expansion at every point on the curve by subtracting total cost at one point from total cost at the next.

Marginal cost at any output, however, can also be represented by the slope of a tangent drawn to the total cost curve at that output. The marginal cost at E in Figure 9–9 is the slope of the tangent OE. The

FIGURE 9–9

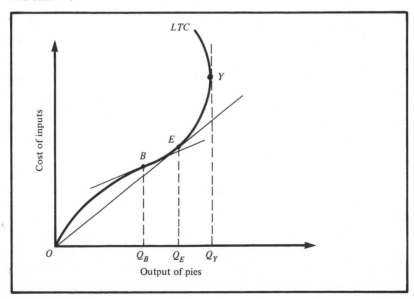

argument in support of this statement was first made in Chapter 5, where we explained how to represent marginal revenue at any output as the slope of a tangent to the total revenue curve at that output. You may want to look back at that section (Marginal Revenue).

It may seem strange that a slope can measure a cost so it may help to calculate the marginal cost at some point like B on Figure 9–10 where part of the total cost curve from Figure 9–9 is shown. We will assume some value for the total cost at B. This is C_B on the vertical axis and we will assume it to be $550. We will also assume some output at B, say $Q_B = 1,000$ apple pies. Now extend the tangent through B back

FIGURE 9–10

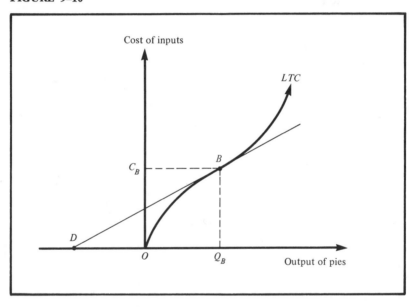

to the left until it reaches the horizontal axis at D. The slope we want is a measure of the angle this tangent makes with the horizontal axis. The measure of this slope is the ratio of the side opposite this angle over the side adjacent. The side opposite is the distance from Q_B to B, which is equal to C_B. The side adjacent to the angle is the distance from D to Q_B, which appears to be approximately equal to $2Q_B$. Therefore

$$\text{Slope of tangent } DB = \frac{C_B}{2Q_B} = \frac{550}{2,000} = 0.275 .$$

Thus on Figure 9–11 we can show the marginal cost at output Q_B as $MC_B = 27.5$ cents.

What will the long-run marginal cost curve (*LMC*) look like? We can apply this information about the slopes of tangents to Figure 9–9 and thereby describe completely the marginal cost curve shown on Figure 9–11. Starting from zero, we find the total cost curve quite steep, but its slope declines all the way to *B*. Thus we would expect marginal cost to start high and decline as in Figure 9–11 until it is at its lowest point at the output Q_B. This is the point of inflection of the total cost curve, and from here on the slope of total cost will become steeper.

FIGURE 9–11

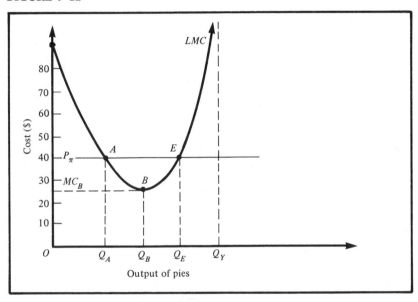

Notice, however, that the total cost curve does not have a horizontal tangent at *B* and so marginal cost does not equal zero at its lowest point.

To the right of *B*, the total cost curve becomes steeper and steeper, so marginal cost must rise. Under the convexity assumptions about production, we know that the production surface has a peak, meaning that there is some maximum total output. This is the output Q_Y in Figure 9–9. More inputs can be used, but total output cannot be increased further. The total cost curve has a vertical tangent at *Y* (and since output falls as still more inputs are used, the curve bends back on itself). Moreover, if the total cost curve becomes vertical at some output (Q_Y), then marginal cost, its slope, must become infinite. The marginal cost on Figure 9–11 just becomes larger and larger as that output is approached.

THE LOGIC OF MR = MC

Now that we know the shape of the marginal cost curve, let us return to the logic of profit maximizing. The simplest statement of the logic of this situation is that the firm will want to expand as long as the added costs are less than the added revenues. In technical words, it will expand from its current level of output, if marginal cost is less than marginal revenue ($MC < MR$).[3] Suppose we now put a simple marginal revenue curve on Figure 9–11 so we can know both MC and MR at every level of output. The MR curve will look like the line from P_π to E. This shape indicates that additional units of output can be sold at a going price (P_π), no matter what the level of output of this one firm. Thus, marginal revenue equals price at every output. This is a special assumption about marginal revenue and, as we shall discover in Chapter 13, it holds when the firm is assumed to be perfectly competitive.

A firm currently producing Q_B would, under these conditions, want to expand output until it reached Q_E. At first the added items of output would add about 27.5 cents to costs ($MC_B = 0.275$), but about 40 cents to revenues ($MR_\pi = P_\pi = 0.40$). The firm is better off by 12.5 cents. As it expands toward Q_E, its marginal cost rises and the gain from each addition to output grows smaller but is, nevertheless, still *positive*. Finally, at Q_E the gain is zero and beyond Q_E, $MC > MR$ and the "gain" is negative. To stop short of the output Q_E is to miss some possible gain. To go beyond is folly.

THE LONG-RUN SUPPLY CURVE

Since we have established that a profit maximizing firm will produce the output for which $MC_\pi = MR_\pi = P_\pi$, we can easily find its supply curve. We need only move along the marginal cost curve until it intersects the price line as at E in Figure 9–11 and then read off the profit-maximizing output (Q_E). We describe Q_E as the quantity that this firm will be willing to supply at the price P_π. If we find this quantity for all other possible prices, we have found the supply curve.

Therefore, the long-run marginal cost curve is, in fact, the long-run supply curve for this firm. At each price the firm would choose to produce the quantity whose long-run marginal cost (LMC) is equal to the price.

Since we are talking about long run decisions, however, *part* of the long-run marginal cost curve should not be included in the supply curve. The amount of every input is variable in the long run and that means

---

[3] Any student who has forgotten the meaning of marginal revenue should see Chapter 5.

there is the possibility of zero input and hence zero output. This firm can elect, in the long run, to go into some other business. Certainly this firm will not be willing to make a long-run choice to produce pie unless the price is expected to be high enough to cover all costs. There needs to be at least one level of output at which total revenue covers total cost. Do not confuse this argument with the one that immediately preceded it. Picking the output for which $MC = MR$ is picking the output that maximizes profits, but the maximum profit may not be greater than zero. In some businesses the largest possible profit is a small loss. In that case, the $MC = MR$ output will produce the smallest possible loss, and that's all. It does not guarantee profits.

Total revenue, of course, depends on price. The higher the price at which each item is sold, the larger will be the total revenue. We must

FIGURE 9–12

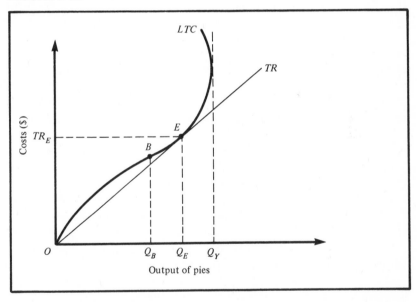

ask whether P_π on Figure 9–11 is high enough so that total revenue will cover total costs at the profit-maximizing output or at any output. The easiest way to answer this question is indicated in Figure 9–12. *LTC*, of course, indicates the total cost at each output level, so we need only add a total revenue curve. At each level of output, total revenue is equal to the price of output multiplied by the quantity of output $(P \cdot Q)$. The curve will be a straight line that slopes upward toward the right like *TR* in Figure 9–12. When output is Q_E, then total revenue is TR_E. The slope of the total revenue curve is, of course, the tangent of the angle that it makes with the horizontal axis. Using "the opposite side over the adjacent side," or "the rise over the run," we get:

$$\text{Slope of } TR = \frac{TR_E}{Q_E} = \frac{P_\pi Q_E}{Q_E} = P_\pi .$$

TR_E is a measure of the side opposite the angle at the origin, and Q_E of the side adjacent. We can say that the slope of the total revenue curve under competitive conditions is equal to price.

Let us now assume that the price P_π of Figure 9–11 (about 40 cents) is just large enough to yield the total revenue curve shown on Figure 9–12. There is then one output (Q_E) for which total revenues are large enough to cover total costs. The output Q_E is not only the profit-maximizing output where $MC_\pi = MR_\pi, = P_\pi$, but it is also an output that the firm would be willing to plan for in the long run because $TR_E = LTC$. Any price higher than P_π will yield a TR curve that is steeper and has many outputs for which long-run total costs can be covered.

Any price lower than P_π, however, will lead to a TR curve that lies completely below the long run total cost curve (LTC). There will be no output for which total costs can be covered. The firm will be unwilling to stay in this industry in the long run if the price is below P_π. Hence all of the marginal cost curve below P_π in Figure 9–11 is irrelevant. The quantity supplied at any price below P_π will be zero, and only that portion of the marginal cost curve from E to the right should be counted as part of the long-run supply curve. This is the way the supply curve is shown on Figure 9–13.[4] At all points on this supply curve the firm can expect that total revenues will cover long-run total costs. It will be willing to make the long-run decision to enter or remain in this industry, and its output will be determined somewhere between Q_E and Q_Y by the actual price that prevails.

To say that the firm will expect to cover all costs in the long run is to say more than is immediately obvious. It will want to earn a reasonable return on its investment, and the owner will expect compensation for any services he extends to the business. Compensation of the owner for services is clearly a cost, and we expect it to be already in-

---

[4] You will notice that some prices like P_π in Figure 9–11 will cross the long-run marginal cost curve at two different outputs. The firm will not be interested in the first of these, the one on the left. If it were to choose that output, it would immediately find that an expansion of output would make $MC < MR$ and hence add to profits. It would, therefore, move on out to the second crossing in order to maximize profits.

cluded in the long-run total cost. But we usually think of return on investment as coming out of profits, not as a cost. This is the way an accountant would prepare the profit and loss statement.

The economist, however, lists this return as cost. Return on investment is merely that payment necessary to induce capital to enter this business. It is a payment to capital just as wages are a payment to labor. A real firm will not make a long-run decision to enter or expand its investment in this business unless it expects to earn an adequate return.

FIGURE 9–13

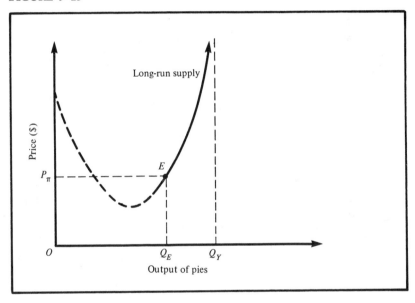

Therefore, this return should also be made part of the total cost curve used above. For these reasons, profits to the economist are something quite different from what they are to an accountant. Profits for the economist occur only when total revenues *exceed* total costs when the latter include a "normal" or adequate return on investment. The definition of normal or adequate may be quite difficult in any real situation, but the treatment of normal returns as costs is quite useful to economists.

AVERAGE TOTAL COST

We have just derived a long-run marginal cost curve from the total cost curve. A long-run average cost curve is also easy to derive from the total cost curve. Deriving it geometrically or arithmetically amounts to the same thing. For instance, in Figure 9–14, average cost at an output, Q_E for instance, is just total cost (C_E) divided by total output (Q_E). Thus, Long Run Average Total Cost at E is:

$$LAC = \frac{C_E}{Q_E}.$$

We know from the geometry we have already used several times that the latter term is a measure of the slope of the line OE. Thus, long-run average total cost at any point on the total cost curve is equal to the

FIGURE 9–14

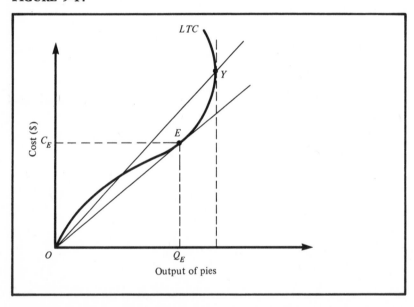

slope of a ray from the origin through that point. (Note that average cost is the slope of a ray to a point whereas marginal cost is the slope of a tangent at that point. These two are the same at E, but more about that later).

Clearly, if we plot the LAC curve, it will be U shaped as in Figure 9–15. Starting from zero on Figure 9–14, the slope of each ray will be fairly steep, but get less and less steep until the one through point E is reached. This indicates that average total cost is declining but reaches its lowest point when output is Q_E, as drawn in Figure 9–15. After that, it will rise toward a maximum represented by the slope of the ray OY in Figure 9–14.

It is well now to remember that economies and diseconomies of

FIGURE 9–15

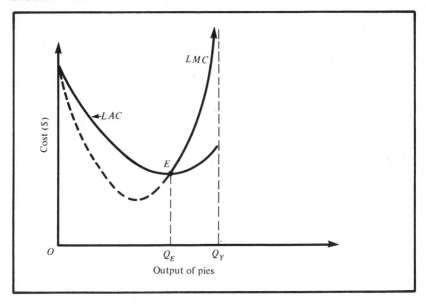

scale provide the reasons for the U shape of the long run average total cost curve.[5]

a. Take the decreasing average cost section first. It has its basis in the increasing returns section of the production function. We attribute increasing returns to the possibilities of division of labor and specialization that go with expanding the size of the firm. These factors are said to produce "economies of scale," or in the layman's language, economies of mass production.

b. Increasing returns turn into decreasing returns, however. The advantages of specialization are finally mostly realized and the volume of resources to be managed by the firm becomes unwieldy. Gradually management becomes more and more ineffective. Decreasing returns in production mean rising average costs, and these are "diseconomies of scale." They ultimately dominate, and the *LAC* curve rises more and more steeply.

---

[5] There is another source of economies and diseconomies of scale that we have not considered. When one industry expands its scale of operations, it sometimes generates economies of scale in some of the firms that are its suppliers. As the auto industry expands, there may be economies of scale for the firm that manufactures starter motors. If so, the latter can fall in price, lowering the cost of building an automobile. Since this kind of change in costs is likely to affect every firm in the industry as the whole industry expands, it probably is best to handle it as a downward shift in the entire *LAC* of the individual firm. We will have another look at this situation in Chapter 13 when we discuss the way in which an industry adjusts to equilibrium size.

If we put both *LAC* and *LMC* on the same diagram as in Figure 9–15, they will be related to each other in an important way. They will cross each other at E, where average cost is a minimum.[6] For all outputs less than Q_E, $LMC < LAC$, and for all outputs greater than Q_E, the reverse is true. One can see on Figure 9–14 that the slope of a tangent to the total cost curve and the slope of a ray are the same at E because the ray is just tangent to the curve at that point. Therefore $LMC = LAC$ at E. It can also be seen in the same figure that rays are steeper than the tangents up to E. As a result, these two curves are located in relation to each other in the way indicated on Figure 9–15.[7]

COSTS AND CONVEX PRODUCTION FUNCTION

Up to this point we have developed all of the cost curves around the S-shaped production function of Figure 9–1. Economists think this

---

[6] Average cost and marginal cost will also tend to the same value as the curves approach the vertical axis (see Figure 9–15). One can "see" that this is likely from the figure below, where a small segment of the total cost curve near the origin has been enlarged. At A the slope of the tangent (MC) is much smaller than the slope of the ray (AC). At B the difference in slope is reduced and at

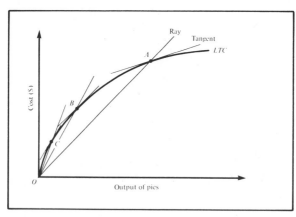

C it is reduced still further. It appears that the difference will gradually disappear; that is, the two slopes will become the same and $MC = AC$ at zero output.

[7] These two curves have sometimes been presented as rising toward infinity near the vertical axis. To be consistent, the total cost curve would have to be made vertical as it approaches the origin. A vertical total cost curve means that the firm must incur some costs before it gets any output. No doubt many real firms have this experience when they begin production of a new product. They must acquire plant and equipment and pay staff for some time before output begins. However, this phenomenon does not belong on a total cost curve. The total cost curve is not a growth-through-time curve for a firm that starts from scratch. It is, rather, a summary of the cost conditions that the firm can expect at each output level once it has adjusted to that level. If it considers choosing zero output it is because all variable costs can be reduced to zero at that output. We have therefore presented a total cost curve that has a finite positive slope at the origin.

function is fairly realistic, but it is analytically frustrating because of its complexity. What would cost curves be like if the production function were assumed to be strictly convex, or perhaps linear? We will examine strict convexity here and linearity in Chapter 11.

The convex expansion path as developed in Chapter 8 is reproduced in Figure 9–16. It is a slice out of an inverted bowl with its highest

FIGURE 9–16

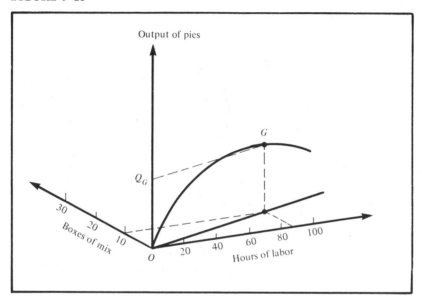

point at G. What does the total cost curve of such a production function look like? It is clear that decreasing returns to scale set in immediately and that marginal product becomes zero at G. Thus output is expanding less rapidly than inputs are added at every point along the curve, and the total cost curve will bend upward as in Figure 9–17. Diseconomies of scale appear everywhere along the curve.

Diseconomies mean that the total cost curve (LTC) gets steeper and steeper as output expands. Therefore marginal cost, which can be represented by the slope of LTC, must continuously increase as output expands. As output approaches the maximum possible (Q_G), the marginal cost increases without limit. (Obviously the added cost (MC) of getting a little more than the maximum possible output is infinite.) The LMC is given this shape in Figure 9–18.

Average cost can be represented as before by the slope of a ray through the origin. Clearly at every point the slope of a tangent exceeds the slope of a ray, hence at every output $LMC > LAC$. We have drawn in both a ray and a tangent at H in Figure 9–17 as an example,

FIGURE 9–17

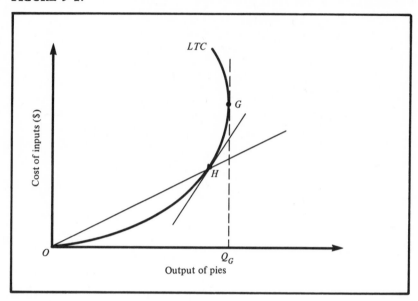

FIGURE 9–18

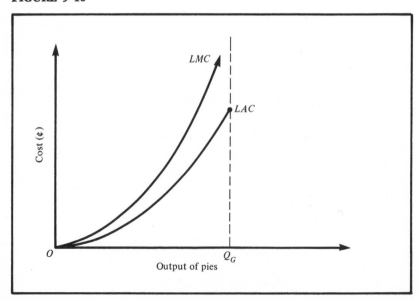

and then drawn the average cost curve (*LAC*) below the marginal cost curve (*LMC*) on Figure 9–18.

SUMMARY

This chapter has led to the development of a long-run supply curve for an individual firm. This curve, which is actually one portion of the marginal cost curve, turns out to be dependent on the physical conditions of production and the prices of inputs.

Actually the supply curve is a very simple summary of a fairly elaborate combination of product and cost curves. It rises as output increases. It approaches infinity as output approaches its maximum value, and there will be no output at all from the firm when price falls below a certain level. This shape is mainly the result of the decreasing returns to scale that appear along the production function.

Now we are ready to describe the making of long-run choices as an interaction between these supply conditions and possible sets of demand conditions. Such will be the topic of Chapter 13. But before that we will analyze short-run supply conditions in Chapter 10 and spend some time with constant returns to scale in Chapter 11.

SELECTED READINGS

See list at end of Chapter 10.

Chapter 10

Costs in the short run

INTRODUCTION

In Chapter 9 we developed the cost curves needed by an "economic" firm that is trying to reach a decision that involves changes in all inputs. We concluded that the firm would have to decide *now* what scale (level of output) would maximize profits and what combination of inputs would be "least-cost" at that output. All of this must be decided now, but the new rate of production cannot begin until the change in the relatively fixed factors is completed. This may take some time; a few months perhaps for a small retail business, many years for a hydroelectric generating plant. Thus long-run choices are visualized as choices made now that determine what will be possible at some point suitably far into the future. The passage of time makes it important to recognize that for real firms, choices are made on the basis of *expectations* about the prices of inputs and outputs and the state of technology once the change is completed.

Those expectations can fail to be realized. By the time the plant is complete and production ready to begin, the firm may already regret its long-run choices. If, for example, prices of either inputs or outputs are different from what they were expected to be, the choices will now turn out to have been more or less seriously wrong. The firm must decide to make some additional change in its scale of operation; that is, to make a *new* long-run choice based on new expectations. But again time will have to pass before these new choices can be reflected in the output of the firm. What to do in the meantime? That is the short-run problem. Short-run choice becomes then a choice made *now* about how to operate the existing plant and equipment or other fixed inputs until such time as the long-run changes can be completed.

What choices can be made in the short run? No choice can be made about the rate of at least one input, but the rate of use of any of the other inputs requires a short-run choice. We can simplify the analysis that follows by supposing that the rate of input of each of the others can be changed instantaneously. Real firms, however, cannot make instantaneous changes and seem to face a whole family of short runs that get longer and longer until they merge into the long run. The entrepreneur, looking ahead, will see that he can hire or fire unskilled labor and expect the decision to be effective in a week or two; that he can negotiate a new contract for the delivery of raw materials that will change their rates of delivery in a few months; that he can start a search for some highly specialized employee with the expectation of having him at work six months from now, and so on. Finally, he will see that he can start construction of a new plant that will be in operation in a few years. Thus the short run becomes longer and longer until it becomes the long run.

SHORT-RUN TOTAL COST

Chapter 7 introduced the production function as a physical relationship between inputs and outputs. We now want to use that relationship to deduce the shape of the short-run cost curves. We will use mix as a fixed input and labor as variable. Changes in output can be brought about only by changing the quantity of labor so the expansion path looks like *DART* from Chapter 7. We have reproduced this diagram as Figure 10–1.

The amount of mix is fixed as 15 boxes per week, presumably because of some contract with the supplier that cannot be changed soon. As we move to the right from *D,* the amount of labor is increasing so the proportion of labor to mix is rising. The law of variable proportions tells us the general shape of *DA'R'T'*. As the labor-mix ratio rises, the marginal product of labor may increase at first. Ultimately, however, it *will* decrease and it may go to zero and even become negative. The curve bends up from *D* to *A'* while marginal product is increasing and then bends back from *A'* to *T'* as marginal product declines toward zero.

To convert these physical facts into costs we need to indicate a price for labor and a price for mix. We will use $P_L = \$1$ and $P_M = \$2$. With mix fixed at 15 boxes we have a fixed cost of $30. There is an unnoticed ambiguity about the fixed input here. We have assumed that

mix is delivered at 15 boxes per week so that its *cost* is clearly fixed. A
real firm, however, would not have to use all of it. Some could just be
thrown away, an act that would not reduce the cost of mix but might
reduce some other costs. As an example, look at *"G"* on Figure 7–12
and the accompanying discussion. The production function in Figure
10–1 does not consider this possibility. It is based on the assumption
that the input of mix is fixed in the physical-use sense as well. This is
the approach we will use in deriving the cost curves. If someone wants
to consider a situation in which an input is physically variable but fixed
in cost, he will have to draw a new production function. He can, how-

FIGURE 10–1

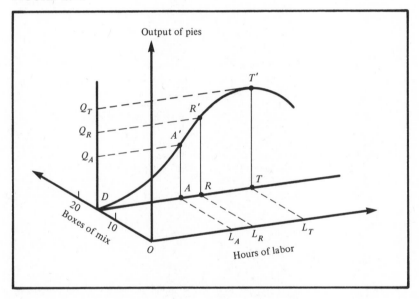

ever, derive the cost curves by the same technique from this new
production function.

To get a short-run total cost curve we proceed just as we did when
deriving long-run total costs in Chapter 9. The first step is to draw the
short-run total product curve of Figure 10–1 in two dimensions; see
Figure 10–2. The labor input is measured along the horizontal axis
and mix is assumed to be fixed at 15 units. The next step is to reverse
the axes in order to indicate that costs (the necessary units of labor and
mix) are now to be viewed as dependent on the choice of output level.
The dependent variable, costs, will therefore go on the vertical axis.
Instead of measuring the physical units of labor along the vertical axis,

however, we will convert to dollars' worth of labor by using a price for labor P_L. Thus the cost of output Q_A is equal to:

$$L_A \cdot P_L = C_A,$$

where L_A is the amount of labor used to produce that output.

The general shape of this curve, labeled VC on Figure 10–3, comes directly from the total product curve in Figure 10–2. That curve, in turn, got its shape, as explained in Chapter 8, from the law of variable proportions. It should be added, however, that the curve in Figure 10–3 includes only the labor costs. In finding it we used only the price of labor (P_L), and since labor is the variable input here we will call this curve the variable cost curve (VC). If at some point we need to consider all costs, then we will add the fixed costs of mix to this curve. Since the amount of mix does not change and neither does its price, we

FIGURE 10–2

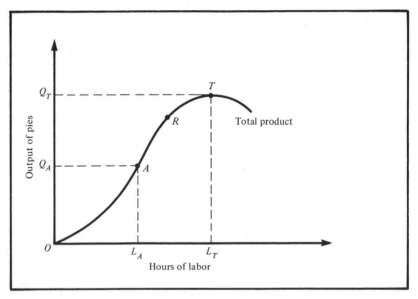

have a constant (15 P_M) to add at every output level. This gives the dashed line on Figure 10–3 labeled STC for short-run total cost.

From here on, the derivation of marginal cost and average cost can proceed exactly as it did along the long-run total cost curve in Chapter 9. We will not repeat that argument. Instead, we will go back to the production function to show the direct relationship of marginal and average costs to physical production. This will give us a second way of deriving marginal cost and average cost; neither of the curves, however, will be changed in any way by the new technique.

FIGURE 10–3

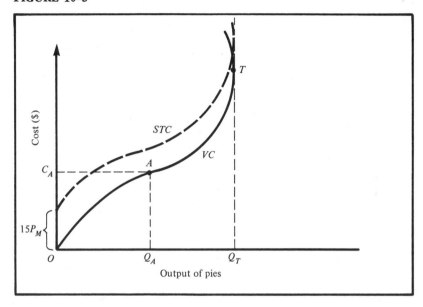

MARGINAL PRODUCT

On Figure 10–4 we present the total product curve again. It is, of course, a total product curve (TP) when various amounts of labor are used with the fixed amount of mix. As we have seen several times already, a marginal quantity can be represented by the slope of a

FIGURE 10–4

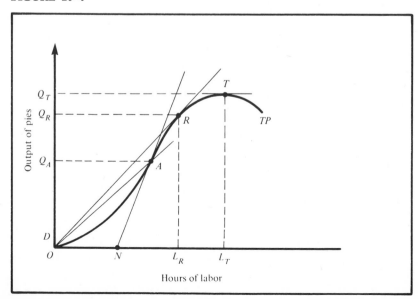

tangent to the corresponding total quantity curve. We should therefore be able to find a marginal product curve using this total product curve. In this case when we move from left to right, the amount of labor is increasing relative to mix and the total product curve shows the effect on output of successive hours of labor. The slope of this curve will therefore be the marginal product of labor (MP_L). It will be represented at output Q_R, for instance, by the slope of the tangent OR or at Q_A by the slope of the tangent NA.[1] If we imagine tangents drawn to each point on this total product curve starting at D, we can see that their slopes will get steeper and steeper until A is reached. At A the marginal product of labor as shown on Figure 10–5 is therefore at its maximum.[2]

FIGURE 10–5

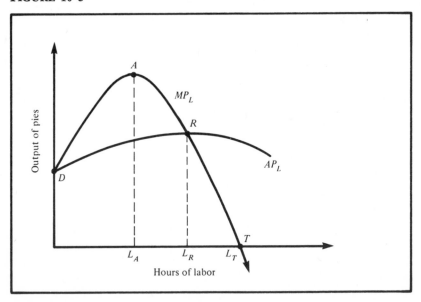

From A to T, the slope of the total product curve is decreasing, which means that marginal product will decline. At T the slope of a tangent to the total product curve is zero, so marginal product is zero. Beyond T it is negative. We have given the marginal product curve this shape in Figure 10–5, but there may be one part of the curve that looks confusing. Why does the marginal product fail to start from zero at D? This is because marginal product is a "rate" of change in total product.

---

[1] The relationship between a marginal curve and its corresponding total curve was first discussed in Chapter 5.

[2] In Figure 10–5 we have enlarged the output scale along the vertical axis so that we can more readily see the shape of the curves.

The rate at which total product increases need not be zero even when production is just beginning.

AVERAGE PRODUCT

The average product curve can also be derived geometrically from the total product curve of Figure 10–4.[3] At any point like R it is the slope of a ray drawn from that point through the origin, OR in this case. One can see that if we start to draw all possible rays beginning at the origin, they will get steeper and steeper until R is reached. Here the ray OR will be just tangent to the curve. Thus average product increases continuously up to the point where L_R units of labor are being used and that is the way we have drawn it in Figure 10–5. Since the ray is identical to the tangent at R, both ray and tangent have the same slope, and that means that MP_L and AP_L must be equal to each other at this output. To the right of R the rays become less and less steep; that is, average product is declining. Looking at Figure 10–4, it is not hard to "see" that a tangent will have a steeper slope than a ray for any point up to R and the reverse will be true from there on. Thus in Figure 10–5 we have drawn $MP_L > AP_L$ up to the point $R;$ $MP_L = AP_L$ at $R;$ and $MP_L < AP_L$ to the right of R. Marginal curves will always cross average curves where the average is either maximum as in the case of average product, or minimum as in the case of average cost.[4]

SHORT-RUN COSTS

As we have argued above, total product and total cost are two ways of looking at one relationship. They both reveal the cost of various outputs in terms of the inputs that must be used up. From the total product curve we have just derived a marginal product curve, and it should therefore lead us to a marginal cost curve. The marginal product curve indicates the rate at which output grows (or shrinks) as units of the variable input are added. At each point along the curve a unit of labor has some marginal product. A day's work may add ten apple pies to output. Each of those apple pies "costs" some part of a day's work. If the firm paid $8 for the day's work, then it costs about

---

[3] In Chapter 9, an average cost curve is derived from a total cost curve. The technique is the same for all total and average quantities.

[4] Average product and marginal product on Figure 10–5 have been given the same value (D) at the vertical axis. This is because a ray and a tangent will tend toward the same slope as we consider points closer and closer to the origin along the total product curve. We have made this argument before in footnote 6 in Chapter 9, using a total cost curve, and the geometry is much the same. It also means that the marginal cost and average cost curves will start from the same point in Figure 10–7.

80 cents to add one apple pie to output. This cost of getting one more unit of output (pie) by adding to the inputs (labor) is called the marginal cost.

Marginal cost obviously depends on marginal product. When the marginal product of a day's work is large, the marginal cost of a pie is relatively small, and vice versa. These two concepts, marginal product and marginal cost, are inversely related to each other. If we know the price of a unit of labor, perhaps $P_L = \$1$ per hour, and if we also know the marginal product at the highest point on its curve in Figure 10–5, say $Q_A = 5$, then we can find the marginal cost as follows:

$$MC_\pi = \frac{P_L}{MP_L} = \frac{\$1.00}{5} = 20\cancel{c}.$$

Do not think this is a cheap pie. Twenty cents is not the cost of this pie, but only the cost of increasing total output, expressed as the added cost per pie when the firm is already producing the quantity Q_A.

If we apply the formula just above all along the marginal product curve of Figure 10–5, we can deduce the shape of the marginal cost curve. When input is L_A it will be at a minimum because marginal product (the denominator of the fraction above) is at its maximum. It is drawn this way on Figure 10–6. As output rises from Q_A toward Q_T, marginal cost approaches infinity for the obvious reason that the marginal product of labor is approaching zero. If another unit of labor adds

FIGURE 10–6

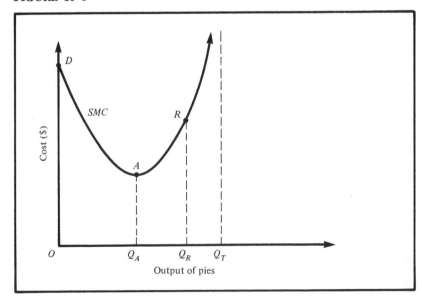

nothing to total output, then the cost of getting another unit of output by using more labor is infinite. For outputs smaller than Q_A, the marginal cost rises toward D. The marginal product of an hour of labor is quite small at D because labor is quite scarce relative to mix, but we have not made it zero. Therefore the marginal cost at D is large but not infinite. The whole marginal cost curve has the same U shape that we found for long-run marginal costs in Chapter 9 (see Figure 9–11). This is not surprising. We derived them by different routes, but from the same source. That source is the production function, whose long- and short-run expansion paths look very much alike.

We need to wrap this up by getting an average variable cost curve directly from the average product curve of Figure 10–5. At output Q_R, average product is a maximum, which we will assume to be three pies per unit of labor used. If labor costs \$1 per hour, then

$$AVC_\pi = \frac{P_L}{AP_L} = \frac{\$1.00}{3} = 33\tfrac{1}{3}\text{¢}.$$

Now this is the *average variable cost,* not the marginal cost. We mean that in producing the output Q_R, the labor cost per pie has averaged about 33 cents.

The formula above indicates that at Q_R, where average product is a maximum, average variable cost will be at its minimum, as shown in Figure 10–7. It will rise as output approaches Q_T because average

FIGURE 10–7

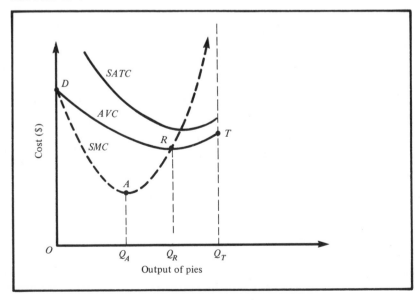

product falls, but it does not rise toward infinity. At Q_T, there is a given total output and a given number of inputs (see L_T and Q_T in Figure 10–4), so average product will have a finite positive value:

$$APL = \frac{Q_T}{L_T}.$$

If average product is finite, then so is average variable cost in the formula just above and the AVC curve reaches some finite value at T on Figure 10–7, instead of rising toward infinity, as the marginal cost curve does. Average variable cost also rises to the left of Q_R as average product gets smaller.

There is one final observation to make. At output level Q_R, the marginal cost and the average variable cost are equal. This occurs, of course, because average and marginal product are equal at this output, too. As we have noted before, for any variable such as cost or revenue or profit, its marginal curve will cross its average curve either at the peak or the trough of the average curve. It is the peak in the case of average product and the trough in the case of average cost.

VARIABLE COSTS AND TOTAL COSTS

The curve in Figure 10–7 is the average variable cost curve. The formula used to derive it takes account of the cost of labor (P_L), but does not make use of the cost of the fixed factor, mix. If we add in the average fixed cost, we will get the short-run average total cost ($SATC$) also shown on Figure 10–7. The formula is

$$SATC = \frac{P_L}{AP_L} + \frac{FC}{Q},$$

where FC is the fixed cost and Q is the output level for which average total cost is being calculated. Since the fixed cost is a positive number, it is clear that $SATC > AVC$ at all outputs. It is also clear that as we move to the right output gets larger so that average fixed cost (FC/Q) gets smaller and the two average cost curves come closer together.

In Figure 10–7, the two average curves can be compared, but it is also useful to look at the two total curves in Figure 10–8. The variable cost (VC) turns out to be a perfect image of total cost (STC) moved down the diagram by an amount equal to the fixed cost. At each level of output the curves have the same slope; that is, the marginal cost curve will be the same, whether derived from the total cost curve or the variable cost curve. This is not surprising! Marginal cost, the *added* cost of producing a little more, must depend on variable costs, not fixed costs. It would make no sense to talk about adding to something that is fixed. It is, in fact, the variable costs that give total cost its reverse S-shape

FIGURE 10–8

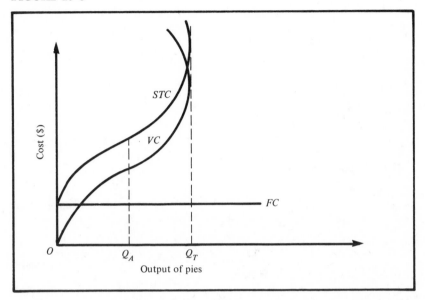

when they are added to the fixed costs, so it is variable cost that determines the slope (that is, the *MC*) of both curves. Note that we use the letters *VC* for variable costs and *FC* for fixed costs without using an *S* to indicate short-run. This is, of course, because the distinction between variable and fixed cost is meaningful only in the short run. In the long run, all costs are variable.

THE SUPPLY CURVE

The long, busy ramble through cost curves that we have now completed has a purpose. That purpose is to lay the groundwork for output and input choices by economic firm. We can summarize the pattern of those choices in the form of a supply curve. We have noted before that economic firm will not expand output beyond the point where one more unit of output adds as much to costs as it adds to revenues when it is sold. The added cost of producing one more unit is the marginal cost, which we derived above. If we assume perfect competition for a moment, then the added revenue is just the price at which output can be sold. Thus for any given price of apple pies (P_π), we can simply move along the marginal cost curve until $SMC = P_\pi$. For instance, in Figure 10–9, if the price of pie is P_π, the output will be Q_R. If the price is somewhat higher (P_π'), then output will be larger (Q_S). The short-run marginal cost curve thus reveals the quantity that economic firm

FIGURE 10–9

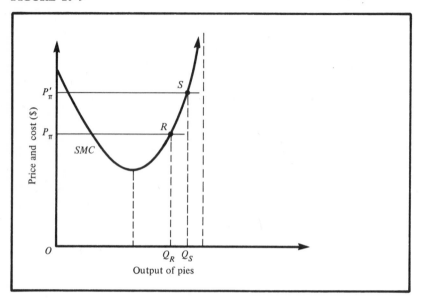

Output of pies

will be willing to supply at each possible price. Since this is what we mean by supply and what we ask the supply curve to tell us, we can conclude that the marginal cost curve is the supply curve of the individual firm.

We have, however, overlooked one exception. A firm might decide in the short run to produce nothing at all. There could be an advantage to going out of business. All variable costs could be reduced to zero; not the fixed costs, of course. They are fixed! They will have to be paid anyway. However, if the total revenue is not enough to pay all of the variable costs at the chosen output, it is better to get out of business and eliminate those costs. Then the losses will be limited to the amount of the fixed costs. On the other hand, if total revenues exceed variable cost even a little bit, then the excess will help pay part of the fixed costs and reduce the losses.

Total revenue will only be large enough if the output selling price (P_π) is high enough. How high must the price be for total revenue to be high enough to cover the variable costs? Since total revenue is equal to the price times the quantity sold, we can write:

$$TR = P \cdot Q.$$

Also we can write the variable costs as

$$VC = AVC \cdot Q.$$

For the firm to stay in business in the short run:

$$TR \geqslant VC.$$

Substituting from above:

$$P \cdot Q \geqslant AVC \cdot Q.$$

Dividing both sides by Q we get:

$$P \geqslant AVC.$$

In words, there must be at least one output level where the price of pie is equal to the average variable cost. If we put the marginal cost curve and average variable cost curve together again as in Figure 10–10, it is

FIGURE 10–10

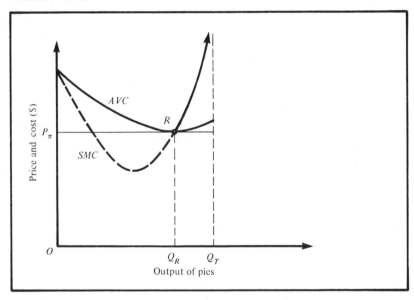

clear that the price of pie must be at least P_π if the firm is to stay in business.

It is clear that a price lower than P_π will be less than the average variable cost at every level of output. Since the firm would then be better off out of business, the sections of the marginal cost curve below and to the left of R are not part of the supply curve. In other words, the quantity supplied at any price below P_π will be zero. We can say in summary that the short-run supply curve of a single firm is that portion of its marginal cost curve that lies above its average variable cost curve. It is presented in Figure 10–11. It starts at R and rises toward infinity as output increases toward the maximum Q_T.

FIGURE 10–11

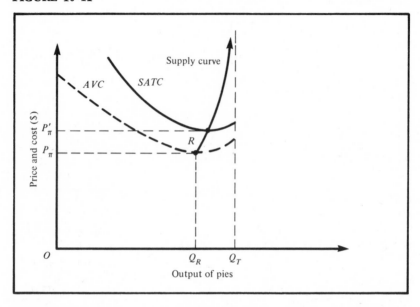

At any price P_π or above, the firm will be willing to continue to operate, but we must bear in mind the fact that it will cover its variable cost but not necessarily its total costs. If we add an average total cost to Figure 10–11 ($SATC$) we can see that the price must be at least P_π' to eliminate all losses. If it does not get that high, then the firm will have have to consider a long-run decision to leave the industry while it continues to operate in the short run.

STAGE II AGAIN

The argument just made has produced a supply curve. The supply curve indicates the quantity the firm is *willing* to produce at certain prices. Back in Chapter 7, however, it was argued that the firm would *not be willing* to operate in Stages I or III. These two statements will be consistent with each other if the supply curve turns out to be in Stage II. Fortunately, it does.

It is easy to find the Stage II–Stage III boundary on Figure 10–11. This boundary occurs where the marginal product of labor goes to zero. As the marginal product of labor approaches zero, we now know that the marginal cost of output approaches infinity. Consequently, the supply curve on Figure 10–11 is approaching the Stage II–Stage III boundary as it approaches the output Q_T. This is eminently sensible since no firm would want to expand output beyond the point where the marginal cost of additional units of output has become infinite.

The other boundary is not quite so easy to locate but is, nevertheless, just as sensible on profit-maximizing grounds. Looking back at Figures 8–7 and 8–8, you will notice that the Stage I–Stage II boundary occurs where the marginal product of the other input, mix, is zero. In Stage II both inputs yield decreasing marginal product as the input is increased and the stage ends where each marginal product has decreased to zero. This is not the only way in which those boundaries are symmetrical. Notice that when the $MP_L = 0$ on Figure 8–7, then the AP_M is a maximum on Figure 8–8. We have not shown the average product for labor on those figures, but it too would be a maximum when the $MP_M = 0$.

This means that the AP_L is a maximum at the Stage I–Stage II boundary. Since average product and average variable cost are inversely related, this means that average variable cost will be a minimum at that boundary. Thus the Stage I–Stage II boundary appears on Figure 10–11 at the output Q_R where the average variable cost curve reaches its lowest point. As we have already argued, no firm would want to produce a quantity less than Q_R at a price less than P_π (even though $MC = MR$), since that price would not provide enough revenue to cover the variable costs.

We can thus conclude that the supply curve begins at the left boundary of Stage II and ends at its right boundary. We can predict that the profit-maximizing firm will want to operate in Stage II, whether we are looking at its product curves as in Chapter 8 or its cost curves as in this chapter. Where it will finally produce, within that stage, will depend on the price of output, for it will seek the output level that makes

$$P_\pi = MR_\pi = MC.$$

THE INDUSTRY SUPPLY CURVE

The short-run supply curve of the individual firm that we deduced above is not the final curve. We want now to get a short-run supply curve for the whole industry by adding together the supply (marginal cost) curves of each of the firms in that industry. They are added horizontally; that is, for each price of output we find the quantities supplied by each of the firms at that price. The curve will, therefore, be shaped like the individual firm curve, but be located much further to the right. Quantity supplied will be zero for the whole industry until the price becomes high enough so that some firm is able to cover its variable costs and begin to produce.

In order to convert the product curves into cost curves in the first part of this chapter, we had to assume certain prices for inputs. We have treated those prices as given and fixed ever since. When we begin to combine individual supply curves into an industry supply curve, however, this may not be a realistic thing to do. If a *real* firm is a small part of a large industry, then rises and falls in its output will probably have no effect on input prices. Thus far, the assumption looks quite realistic, but we must recognize that all firms in a competitive industry have many common characteristics. They probably use roughly similar technologies and generally hire similar inputs and sell to the same consumers. Consequently, many changes in demand or supply conditions that stimulate one of them to expand output will stimulate most of the others. Is it realistic to expect that a whole industry can expand without affecting input prices?

FIGURE 10–12

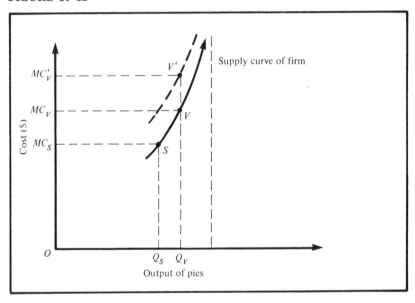

The answer depends on the extent to which the inputs are specialized to the industry. Almost any industry could expand without affecting the price of some standardized input like janitorial services. On the other hand, the computer industry can hardly expect the price of computer mathematicians to remain fixed as it expands. Thus our model should permit analysis of what happens when input prices rise.

Suppose one firm in an industry decides to expand output on Figure 10–12 from Q_S to Q_V; its marginal cost will rise to MC_V. This rise is due to the fall in marginal product as output expands. It is internal to the firm. If the expansion is due to a change in demand or some other change that affects all firms alike, however, then the price of some input, labor for example, may be higher at V. Suppose the price of labor rises from P_L to P_L'. The marginal cost at V must then also be larger. Using the relationship developed earlier in this chapter:

$$MC_V = \frac{P_L}{MP_L} < MC_{V'} = \frac{P_L'}{MP_L}$$

This change will of course affect the industry supply curve. As shown on Figure 10–13, a price high enough to call forth the output Q_V, from each firm in the industry must now be equal to MC_V' rather than MC_V and this means a price equal to $P_\pi' = MC_V'$ on Figure 10–13. The supply curve of the industry is not the solid line from S through V. That curve shows only the effect of the decline of marginal

FIGURE 10–13

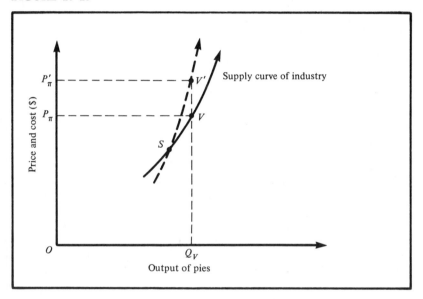

product as output expands, and it assumes that the price of labor is constant. When the price of labor cannot be assumed to be constant, then the supply curve will look like the dashed line from S through V': it will rise more steeply because it shows the effects of declining marginal product *and* rising input prices.

Though we will not examine the question in detail, we should also be aware that changes in the prices of some inputs will bring reorganization of production within the firm. The firm will try to find substitutes for those factors that become relatively more expensive. This too will cause the marginal cost curve to assume a position somewhat different from the one we deduced directly from the marginal product curve of the individual firm with fixed input prices.

THE SHORT RUN AND THE LONG RUN INTEGRATED

In Chapter 9 we discussed long-run choices as being those in which the firm could plan to use any amount of any input. The alternatives among which it can choose can be described as points on a long-run curve that indicates the cost of every level of output. This curve can be either the total cost curve of Figure 9–13 (*LTC*), or the average total cost curve of Figure 9–14 (*LAC*). One of these can be easily derived from the other, and it does not matter much which one we use here. Perhaps the average total cost curve will ease somewhat the following explanation.

Long-run average cost (*LAC*) is a U-shaped curve as in Figure 10–14. There are net economies of scale at first and net diseconomies

FIGURE 10–14

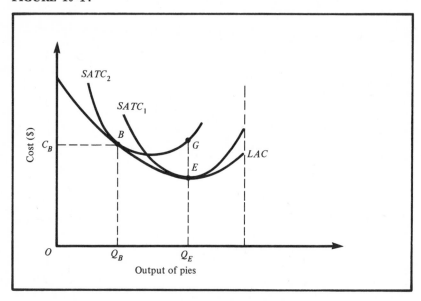

later. Suppose the economic firm makes the long-run decision to build a plant big enough to produce Q_E at minimum cost. It will then realize most of the economies of scale and not many of the diseconomies, so that the average cost of a unit of output will (in the long run) be the lowest possible under existing technology.

Once that decision is made and the firm has had time to acquire the necessary inputs and put them to work, the firm must make short-run choices. The future has arrived, and the firm has to decide whether to operate right at Q_E or somewhere above or below. If the prices of inputs and output turn out to be exactly as expected when the long-run choice was made, then output Q_E will be just right. It is not likely, however, that all expectations will be realized. Some adjustment around output Q_E is very probable. The firm must then ask the question: "What happens to costs if we make a short-run decision to increase output some-what beyond Q_E?"

This short-run decision cannot, of course, involve any change in the input of the fixed factors, but it can call for an increased input of the variable factors. At outputs greater than Q_E, average costs will rise be-cause some inputs are fixed in the short run and the proportion of fixed to variable inputs must change when output expands. Thus the law of variable proportions works against the firm, and the resulting curve for short-run choices ($SATC_1$) rises more steeply than the long-run curve (LAC).

In a competitive industry, a firm will be motivated to choose Q_E as its long-run output[5] because that is the low point on its LAC curve, but at any particular point in time it may find itself somewhere else on this curve. It may be stuck at Q_B with a plant represented by $SATC_2$ while it waits for the new plant to be completed. No matter where the firm is at the moment, it will have to make short-run decisions about output. The effects on costs of those short-run decisions will then be described by curves like $SATC_1$ and $SATC_2$. There is, in fact, such a curve for each point on the long-run average cost curve (LAC) and the latter constitutes a sort of envelope of all the short run curves.[6]

---

[5] Support for this statement will be found in Chapter 13, where long-run com-petitive equilibrium is discussed.

[6] The point of tangency between long-run and short-run average cost curves will come at the lowest point on the short-run curve only when scale is Q_E (see Figure 10–14). This is because we want the LAC to show the minimum average total cost for each level of output. At B, for instance, on the figure below, $SATC_2$

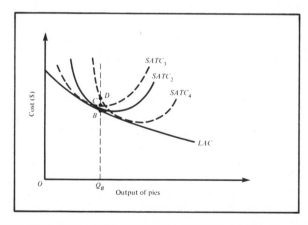

is the curve that gives minimum average cost for output Q_B. Both smaller ($SATC_3$) and larger ($SATC_4$) fixed plants will have higher average cost for that output, indicated at C and D. The plant represented by $SATC_2$ may offer the cheapest way to produce the output Q_B, but Q_B is not the cheapest output level for this plant. The former is the concept we want the long-run average cost curve to show, not the latter.

ANOTHER VIEW

Figure 10–15 permits a comparison of the costs of operating two different sizes of plant. One is the long-run optimum size and is represented by the short-run average cost curve labeled $SATC_1$. The other is less than optimum and indicated by $SATC_2$. If the firm decides to produce the output Q_E it can do so at a much lower average cost with the larger plant. The cost difference is measured by the vertical distance between E and G.

This information can be put on an isoquant map and then another important aspect can be made quite clear. The basic curve in Figure 10–14 is the long-run average cost curve (LAC). It indicates the change in average cost as the firm expands its scale (output) by increasing all inputs. A ray like $OBEY$ on Figure 10–15 is a similar

FIGURE 10–15

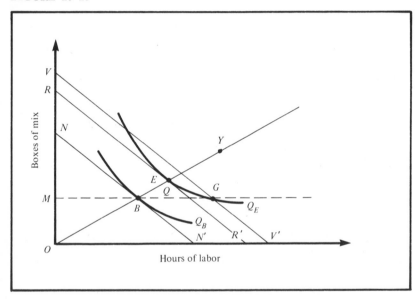

but not quite identical curve. We can read off the changes in scale (output) by noting each isoquant crossed. We can also see the growth of total costs as $OBEY$ crosses one isocost curve $(NN', RR', $ etc.) after another, but we cannot read the average total cost directly.

Suppose point B on this ray is a point of tangency of an isocost curve (NN') and an isoquant (Q_B). The ray $OBEY$ is thus a long-run expansion path because it goes through points of least cost for every output at given input prices.[7] These prices have determined the slope of the isocost curve and thus located the tangency point B. Since we know total cost at B from the isocost, and total output at B from the isoquant, we can find the long-run average cost. This is the same quantity that already appears as C_B in Figure 10–14. We are asking point B to represent the same basic information in both figures. In effect, we have started with a single long-run production function, assumed certain prices, and then developed two different pictures of the costs of production as output is expanded. One of these is LAC in Figure 10–14 and the other is $OBEY$ in Figure 10–15.

Suppose now that the firm decides to produce the output Q_E with a plant that is smaller than optimum. (Perhaps the short-run output price is so high that $MC = MR$ at the output Q_E). In Figure 10–14 this means moving along a short-run cost curve like $SATC_2$ from B to G. The point G indicates a high average cost of production for the firm. It could reduce its costs by expanding its scale, but cannot do this in the short run because some input is fixed. If mix is the fixed input, then Figure 10–15 will also show the short-run expansion of output as a move from B to G. At G the isoquant indicates an output of Q_E, and total cost is indicated by the isocost VV'. Clearly the firm could get the same output at lower cost by moving back along the isoquant from G to E, but it cannot do this because it cannot increase its use of the fixed factor—mix—in the short run. Thus, both figures indicate the advantage to the firm of a long-run increase in scale.

This brings us to a point of some interest for economic welfare. The long-run advantage of the firm is also a long-run advantage to society. At point E on Figure 10–15, the isocost is tangent to the isoquant. The slope of the isocost is the price ratio P_L/P_M, and the slope of the isoquant is the marginal product ratio MP_L/MP_M.[8] Therefore at the point of tangency (E):

$$\frac{P_L}{P_M} = \frac{MP_L}{MP_M},$$

which can be rewritten as

$$\frac{MP_L}{P_L} = \frac{MP_M}{P_M}.$$

----

[7] We argued in Chapter 9, that the least-cost combination of inputs will be indicated by a point of tangency between an isocost curve and an isoquant. Consequently, every point on LAC in Figure 10–14 must correspond to such a tangency point on Figure 10–15.

[8] A full discussion of these slopes and the least cost for a given output appears in Chapter 9.

Now this is the condition for a least-cost combination of inputs. It does not hold at G, the short-run equilibrium. Here the isocost is steeper than the isoquant, so

$$\frac{P_L}{P_M} > \frac{MP_L}{MP_M}$$

and therefore

$$\frac{MP_M}{P_M} > \frac{MP_L}{P_L}.$$

The second inequality makes the argument very clear. The marginal product of a dollar's worth of mix (MP_M/P_M) is greater than the marginal product of a dollar's worth of labor (MP_L/P_L). If the prices of labor and mix represent opportunity costs, meaning that these inputs could earn these prices elsewhere by producing other goods, then too many dollars' worth of labor are being used here. The firm could reduce its use of labor by one dollar and output would go down by the marginal produce of that dollar's worth of labor. It could then return to the same output level by buying more mix, but it would not need a full dollar's worth of mix because the marginal product of a dollar's worth of mix is larger. Society could get the same output for fewer dollars' worth of inputs, and some inputs could be released to add to the output of other things.

The nature of the short run, of course, keeps this from happening. The firm wants to buy more mix and use less labor (to move from G to E on Figure 10–15), but it takes time to increase the input of the fixed factor. The firm will make a long-run decision to make just such a move. We predict this decision because of the assumption that the firm tries to maximize profits. Moreover, what the firm does in its attempt to maximize profit leads to a more efficient use of resources from the point of view of the society.

SUMMARY OF COST CURVES

In the last two chapters we have introduced many curves. It will be hard to remember all of them unless it is recognized that they are all aspects of one curve, the total cost curve. Not only that, but they can all be derived from the total cost curve by very simple arithmetic. The example that follows will help make these relationships stand out.

The example starts with a total cost curve. This curve indicates the total costs of production at each level of output. If this is a long-run total cost curve, we can proceed immediately to the calculation of average cost, marginal cost, etc. Let us assume, however, that it is a short-run total cost curve so that some part of the total cost is fixed and some part is variable. The numbers used in this example are hypothetical, but they have been chosen so as to reflect a total cost curve with the usual reverse S-shaped shown in Figure 10–3. In Figure 10–16 the first row indicates various levels of output. The second row indicates the total cost at each of those levels of output.

Now, if we assume that the fixed cost is $10, then we can find the variable costs immediately by subtracting $10 from total cost at each output. This gives us row 3 on Figure 10–16. Both curves are plotted on the same figure. The vertical distance between the total cost curve and the variable cost curve should be equal to $10 at every point. If one

FIGURE 10–16

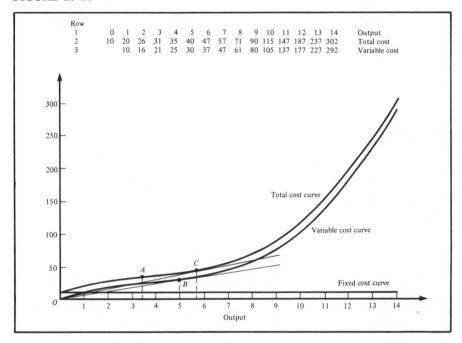

Row																
1	0	1	2	3	4	5	6	7	8	9	10	11	12	13	14	Output
2	10	20	26	31	35	40	47	57	71	90	115	147	187	237	302	Total cost
3		10	16	21	25	30	37	47	61	80	105	137	177	227	292	Variable cost

wants to show the fixed cost curve, it will appear as a horizontal line $10 for every output.

Marginal cost is the rate at which total cost increases as output increases. If we expressed the total cost curve as a mathematical function then we could find that rate of increase at any point along the function. This would be equivalent to finding the slope of a tangent to the function, and that is the relationship between marginal cost and total cost that we have been using. We cannot, however, find that slope with simple arithmetic. We will therefore use a different technique.

We will change the definition of marginal cost so that it is the addition to total cost caused by a one-unit increase in output. Thus, when output goes from 2 units to 3 units, total costs go from $26 to $31, and marginal cost is therefore $5. Figure 10–17 shows this small segment of the total cost curve. We get marginal cost as the change in total cost per unit change in output; hence:

$$\frac{\Delta TC}{\Delta Q} = MC = 5.$$

Since ΔQ *is* always equal to one in this example, then marginal cost is always equal to ΔTC. Thus on Figure 10–18 when output goes from zero to one, total cost goes from 10 to 20 and marginal cost is ten. This technique is used to get row 4. The value thus obtained represents an approximation of the marginal cost along a segment of the curve

FIGURE 10–17

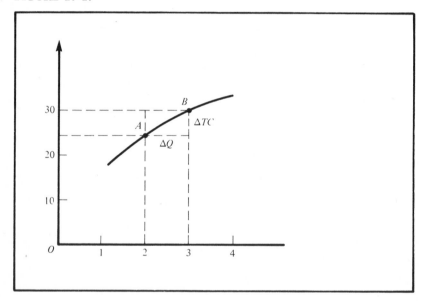

from zero units of output to one, and we have therefore put the marginal cost ($10) halfway between those two outputs. The resulting curve, also shown on Figure 10–18, has just the shape expected.

There are two measures of average cost that are important in the short run—average variable cost and average total cost. To find average variable cost, we simply divide the variable cost, row 3 on Figure 10–19, by output, which is row 1. The result is set out in row 5 and shown on the figure.

Average total cost is, of course, the total cost from row 2 divided by output, and this result is shown on row 6 of Figure 10–19.

FIGURE 10–18

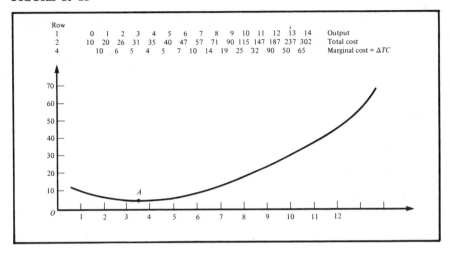

Row																	
1	0	1	2	3	4	5	6	7	8	9	10	11	12	13	14		Output
2	10	20	26	31	35	40	47	57	71	90	115	147	187	237	302		Total cost
4		10	6	5	4	5	7	10	14	19	25	32	90	50	65		Marginal cost = ΔTC

POINTS OF INTEREST

The first interesting point comes at A on the total cost curve in Figure 10–16. This is the point of inflection on that curve, where it shifts from being concave from below to being convex from below. It is the point, therefore, where marginal cost has its smallest value and is shown as point A on Figures 10–18 and 10–19.

Next, look at point B on the variable cost curve on Figure 10–16. This is the point where a ray through the origin is just tangent to the

FIGURE 10–19

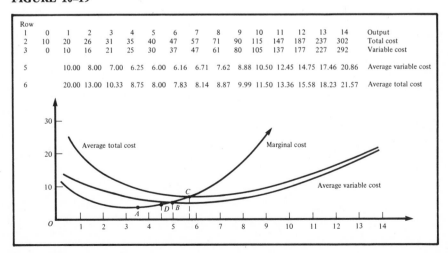

Row																	
1	0	1	2	3	4	5	6	7	8	9	10	11	12	13	14		Output
2	10	20	26	31	35	40	47	57	71	90	115	147	187	237	302		Total cost
3	0	10	16	21	25	30	37	47	61	80	105	137	177	227	292		Variable cost
5		10.00	8.00	7.00	6.25	6.00	6.16	6.71	7.62	8.88	10.50	12.45	14.75	17.46	20.86		Average variable cost
6		20.00	13.00	10.33	8.75	8.00	7.83	8.14	8.87	9.99	11.50	13.36	15.58	18.23	21.57		Average total cost

variable cost curve. It must, therefore, be the point of minimum average variable cost and so it is (see *B* on Figure 10–19). Since it is the lowest point on the average variable cost curve, then it must also be the point where that curve is crossed by the marginal cost curve. If we add the marginal cost curve from row 4 to Figure 10–19, this turns out to be true.

Finally, look at point *C* on the total cost curve of Figure 10–16. This is the point of tangency of a ray from the origin. It must therefore be the lowest point on the average total cost curve and the point where that curve is crossed by the marginal cost curve. Both of these things appear clearly on Figure 10–19.

The supply curve will be the marginal cost curve from *B* to the right on Figure 10–19. This is the portion that lies above the lowest point on the average variable cost curve. It means that the price of output must be at least $6 before this firm will produce any units at all. If the price of output was only $5, the firm could find a point where $MC = P$ at *D* on Figure 10–19, but it is clear that $P < AVC$ at *D*. Since variable costs cannot be covered, the firm will go out of business in order to reduce its variable costs to zero.

Our study of both long- and short-run cost curves is now complete. The most important aspects of the whole analysis are summarized in the shape of the long- and short-run industry supply curves. They include almost all of the information we will now use in Chapter 13 to determine equilibrium prices and quantities under competitive market conditions. First, however, we will look at production functions that show constant returns to scale to see why they have become more important in recent years.

SELECTED READINGS

Friedman, Milton. "Theory and Measurement of Long Run Costs." In *Readings in the Theory of the Firm,* edited by G. C. Archibald (Baltimore: Penguin, 1971).

Haldi, J., and Whitcomb, D. "Economies of Scale in Industrial Plants," *Journal of Political Economy,* vol. 75 (1967), pp. 373–85.

Henry, William R., and Haynes, W. Warren. *Managerial Economics: Analysis and Cases* 4th ed. (Dallas, Texas: Business Publications, Inc., 1978), Chap. 6.

Stigler, George J. "The Economies of Scale," *Journal of Law and Economics,* vol. 1 (1958), pp. 54–71.

Viner, Jacob. "Cost Curves and Supply Curves." In American Economics Association, *Readings in Price Theory* (Homewood, Ill.: Richard D. Irwin, Inc., 1952).

Chapter 11

Modern production theory

INTRODUCTION

The key to modern production theory lies in its assumptions about the shape of the production function. As we have already noted, neoclassical economists sometimes find it useful to assume that the function is strictly convex, thus eliminating increasing returns to scale. Modern theory goes one step further and reduces the function to a very simple mathematical form—the convex cone. This simplification is the result of an assumption of proportionality; namely, that any proportional increase in every input will produce an increase of output in the same proportion.[1] Thus, decreasing returns to scale are also eliminated, and production is characterized by constant returns to scale at every level of output. Every long-run expansion path will have the same shape as OP_1 in Figure 11–1, and the whole surface will look like a cone sliced in half along its axis and laid on its flat side with its apex at O. This shape is in marked contrast to the inverted soup bowl or the dome shape used in earlier theories.

Even though the long-run expansion path is linear, the short-run path is still made subject to the law of variable proportions. At M on Figure 11–1, the basket of inputs has mix but no labor and no output. Moving to the right along the curve MA, labor input increases and so does output, but the latter increases at a decreasing rate. Marginal

---

[1] Such a function is said to be linear and homogeneous in the first degree, which is a mathematician's way of saying that it displays constant returns to scale.

FIGURE 11-1

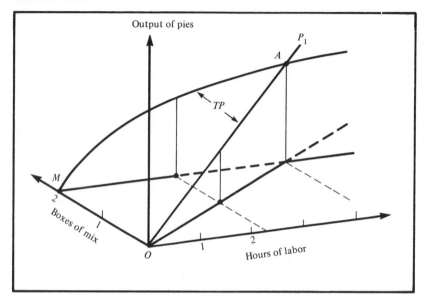

product of labor, indicated by the slope of tangents to the curve *MA*, decreases continuously along the curve.

The adoption of this kind of function permits the application of a new kind of mathematics, whereas earlier models were adapted to the use of the calculus. The best known portion of the new mathematics is linear programming, a set of techniques developed just after the end of World War II. A new mathematics does not, however, mean a completely new economics. Linear theory still contains "a recognizable core and may be regarded as a restatement of a central part of conventional economic theory," to quote Professor Hicks.[2] That core is the view that choice should be treated as an effort to maximize or optimize some variable—profit, for instance—subject to constraints. Linear theory readily fits this mold.

We will use the constant-returns-to-scale production function in this lecture to analyze optimizing production choices by economic firms. We will assume that these firms will try to maximize profits subject to constraints in the form of input and output prices and fixed quantities of some inputs. Since these are the kinds of choices we have just been discussing in connection with other types of production functions, we will perhaps get a better insight into the significance of linear assumptions.

[2] John R. Hicks, "Linear Theory." In *Surveys of Economic Theory*, edited by E. A. Robinson (New York: St. Martin's Press), vol. 3, 1966, p. 75.

Constant returns to scale are also assumed by economists when their models are likely to be very complex. Models of economic growth are a case in point. They are generally so elaborate and complex that the mathematical simplicity of a linear expansion path is an important consideration.[3]

Finally, linear techniques can be adapted to the solution of specific management problems in business and government. The first such application came shortly after World War II and had to do with the procurement problems of the U.S. Air Force. These techniques have since been applied to many other problems, and at least two of the applications have been developed into standard textbook examples. These examples are generally called the "diet problem" and the "transportation problem," and since they reveal aspects of linear theory not considered here, they are highly recommended to any interested student.[4]

GREATER REALISM

Making output a linear function of inputs is not the only important new element in this model. We will also assume that knowledge of technology suggests several different techniques for producing a given good, but does not provide an infinite number of different "ways" to make the good. This is a significant break from earlier assumptions. The production function of Chapters 7 and 8 made every combination of inputs a possible choice for the firm. It was tacitly assumed that a production technique exists for every bundle of inputs, no matter what the proportions among them. There thus seemed to be no need to make choices among techniques or production processes, but only to choose among input bundles.

Nevertheless, an engineer dealing with production problems will think he has to choose among alternative ways of doing the job. Each way or process seems to be characterized by some relatively fixed proportion between inputs, and the number of processes that are known is, in fact, finite. He may, for instance, have to choose between a complex machine run by one highly skilled workman and a couple of helpers or several relatively unspecialized machines, each operated by a skilled general machinist. It is unlikely that he can use just any proportion of

---

[3] Two particular linear functions have been commonly used in the literature: the Cobb-Douglass function and the CES function. See C. W. Cobb and Paul H. Douglass, "A Theory of Production," *American Economic Review,* supplement, vol. 17 (1938), pp. 139–65; and Kenneth J. Arrow, Hollis G. Chenery, Bagicha Mihhas, and Robert M. Solow, "Capital-Labor Substitution and Economic Efficiency," *Review of Economics and Statistics,* vol. 43 (1961), pp. 225–40.

[4] C. E. Ferguson, *Microeconomic Theory,* 3d ed. (Homewood, Ill.: Richard D. Irwin, Inc., 1972), pp. 370–86.

men and machinery that happens to lie between these two limits without completely wasting some of one input or the other. In other words,
some possible bundles of inputs contain the wrong quantities for use
with any known technique. We will thus be making a move in the
direction of realism if we assume that production of any good is possible only by a finite number of different processes, and that the firm
will have to choose among them.

A simple situation of this kind is presented in Figure 11–2. The lines

FIGURE 11–2

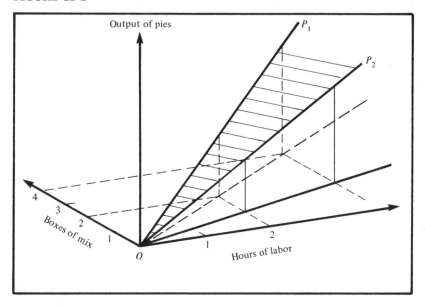

OP_1 and OP_2 represent two different processes of production. Each is
itself linear, so that in a move along OP_1 we are increasing both inputs
in the same proportion and watching output also expand in that proportion. Let us suppose that OP_1 represents a process for making apple
pie by combining mix and labor in a ratio of one to one (1:1). Then
OP_2 is in turn a process that combines inputs in the ratio 1:2. We might
imagine that in this second process mix is handled more carefully so
that there is less waste. We would expect to get more pies per box of
mix, but to have to use more labor per pie to do so. The firm is able
to use either of these processes and must choose between them on
profit-maximizing criteria.

Real firms, choosing among several processes, will often choose to
use more than one and, in fact, profit maximization may require that
output come in some proportion from two processes at once. We will

want the model to admit this possibility. It turns out that different combinations of the two processes, P_1 and P_2 of Figure 11–2, always yield a point on a plane connecting OP_1 and OP_2. This is the shaded area. It will be somewhat easier to explain why this is so if we shift from a three-dimensional diagram to one with only two dimensions as in Figure 11–3. We will imagine that we are looking down on the production

FIGURE 11–3

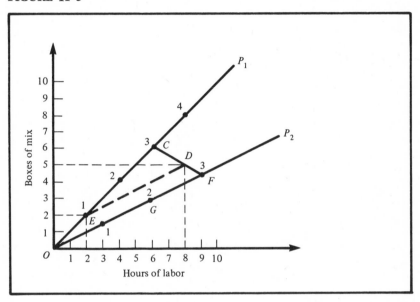

surface of Figure 11–2 from above. Processes OP_1 and OP_2 will appear as rays through the origin. The slope of OP_1 is determined by the 1:1 proportion among inputs, and OP_2 has a 1:2 slope.

Suppose that the firm wants to produce an output of one dozen pies. This will require some input of both mix and labor. If we set the requirements in this example at two boxes of mix and two units of labor per dozen pies when using process P_1, then we can mark output levels along OP_1. An output of one dozen pies comes at E, where input is two boxes of mix and two units of labor. When we have four of each input, we must have two dozen pies because of the linear assumption, and we get three dozen at C, where six units of each input are used. For process P_2, let us set the necessary inputs at 1½ boxes of mix and 3 units of labor per one dozen pies and mark off an output scale along OP_2 also. Thus each of these processes indicates a fixed relationship between three variables: input of mix, input of labor and output of pie. These relationships are presented in Table 11–1.

TABLE 11–1

Process P_1			Process P_2		
Output of pie	Inputs		Output of pie	Inputs	
	Labor	Mix		Labor	Mix
0	0	0	0	0	0
1	⅙	⅙	1	¼	⅛
6	1	1	6	1½	¾
12	2	2	12	3	1½
24	4	4	24	6	3
·	·	·	·	·	·
·	·	·	·	·	·
·	·	·	·	·	·

This table describes all the possibilities using either process by itself, but we also want to know what can be done using both processes at the same time. Suppose for the moment that total output is to be three dozen pies and that the firm starts producing one dozen by process P_1 so that at E on Figure 11–3 it is using two boxes of mix and two units of labor to get one dozen pies. This information is shown across the first row of Table 11–2. Let it then produce the other two dozen pies

TABLE 11–2

Process	Output	Inputs	
		Mix	Labor
P_1	1 dozen	2	2
P_2	2 dozen	3	6
$P_1 + P_2$	3 dozen	5	8

using process P_2. It will move along OP_2 until it reaches G on Figure 11–3, where it will be using three boxes of mix and six units of labor to produce two dozen pies. This information is also in Table 11–2, row two.

In Figure 11–3, output with process P_2 is represented by the distance OG. We can add the two processes geometrically by moving OG upward to the right until it lies along ED. The slopes of OG and ED are the same to indicate that both represent the use of inputs in the proportions called for by process P_2. Point D should now correspond to the last line of Table 11–2, the line that shows the sum of outputs and inputs of the two processes.[5] Inspection of Figure 11–3 shows that it does. Point D indicates the use of five boxes of mix and eight hours of labor to get three dozen pies. The crucial point is that there is no single technological process that can be used to get three dozen pies out of five boxes of mix and eight units of labor. Only a combination of two processes will do it.

On Figure 11–3, the line CDF is an isoquant. It indicates all the combinations of inputs that can be used to get three dozen pies. The proportion of output produced by each process varies as we move from C, where only P_1 is used, to F, where only P_2 is used. It should

FIGURE 11–4

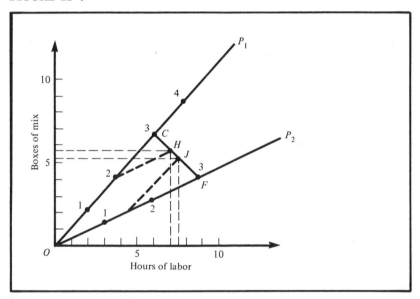

be clear from the geometry of Figure 11–3 that any point on the isoquant CDF can be obtained from some combination of the two processes. This result is made certain by our linear assumptions, but if the student is still unconvinced, he may want to work out the production of three dozen pies using P_1 to make two dozen and P_2 to make one dozen (point H in Figure 11–4), or using P_1 to make 1½ and P_2 to make 1½ (point J). He should find the sum of the inputs needed by each

[5] This addition of processes requires one more assumption, sometimes called the Axiom of Additivity. We must assume that using some of the resources in a second productive process in no way interferes with the output of the first and vice versa. The two outputs can be added to get total output and respective inputs can be added to get the total of each.

process to be the same as indicated by the appropriate point on *CHJF*, the isoquant on Figure 11–4.

THE ISOQUANTS

Let us now expand the number of processes to a convenient but still fairly small number. We will then get a production surface like the one shown in Figure 11–5. Q_1, Q_2, and Q_3 are isoquants derived in the

FIGURE 11–5

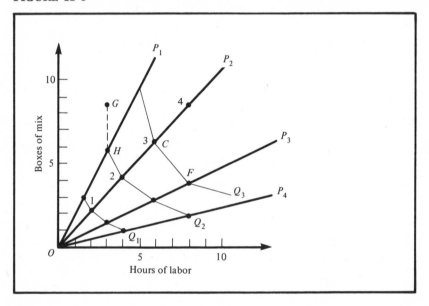

same way we got *CDF* of Figure 11–3 and have exactly the same meaning as the ones we used in earlier chapters except that they are no longer smooth curves. They have kinks, which will present some special problems before we get to the end of this chapter. Points in the space above OP_1 and below OP_4 will involve waste of one input or the other. There is no process or combination of processes that will permit inputs to be used in the proportion indicated by G, for instance. It would therefore be misleading to extend the isoquants out into those areas.

The isoquants of Figure 11–5 are convex to the origin, and this is no accident. If we suppose for a moment that one might be concave, as at B in Figure 11–6, then we will find we have come across what is called an inefficient process. Baskets A, B, and C are on the same isoquant, hence they yield the same output. It is clear from the analysis

FIGURE 11-6

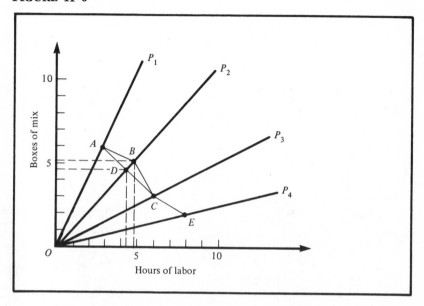

above that basket D can also be used by using some combination of processes P_1 and P_3. It lies on the line ADC, so it will produce the same output as either A or C. Therefore D yields the same output as B but uses fewer inputs. The process P_2 is inefficient when compared to a combination of P_1 and P_3. It will no longer be considered by the firm, and the remaining isoquant $ADCE$ will be convex.

KINKS

Isoquants obtained in this manner have one special characteristic. They have kinks in them instead of being smooth curves. What is the importance of kinks? Look for a moment at the smooth isoquant of Figure 11-7. We have drawn an isocost curve (ZZ') so that it is tangent at X_1. Under the cost conditions and input prices indicated by ZZ', the firm will choose to buy the basket of inputs represented by X_1. Now suppose that relative input prices change so that a new isocost curve (YY') is generated. We predict that the firm will shift to the input bundle X_2. Bundles X_1 and X_2 are assumed to yield the same output. This means that there is assumed to be a technology that makes it possible to produce that output (as a maximum from each bundle of inputs) with the input proportions indicated by the locations of X_1 and X_2. Now the change in relative input prices can be imagined to be very small, in which case X_1 will be very close to X_2. Will there always

FIGURE 11–7

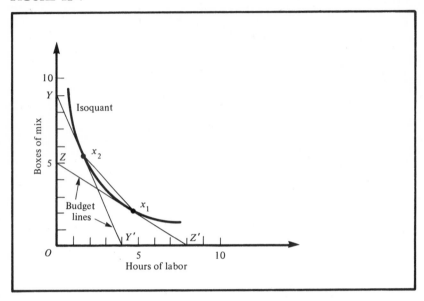

be a technology ready for use, no matter where X_2 is located? The engineer says "No! Production is possible at some point like X_1 in Figure 11–7 or at X_2 using another technology, but all points in between lie on the straight line from X_1 to X_2 and can be obtained only by using some combination of these two technologies."

This means, finally, that the choice of which process (technology) to use is itself an important economic choice. It is a choice that disappears when isoquants are smooth because each bundle of inputs is (tacitly) assumed to have its own maximum output. It appears clearly when kinked isoquants are used because it is necessary to ask which process or combination of processes will get the maximum output or profit from any given bundle of inputs.

PRODUCTION CHOICES

We now want to consider two simple examples of the way an economic firm will choose. The student should be warned in advance that even though these examples have the key characteristics of linear programming problems, they tend, nevertheless, to make the process seem trivial. Part of the reason is that we want to be able to use geometry, so we must restrict the number of variables included. This seems worthwhile because for most of us a geometric solution will be more revealing of the general character of the problem than would be the equivalent arithmetic solution. The latter quickly exceeds the capacity of human beings as the number of variables is increased anyway, and the calculations must be made by a computer. It is the volume of computations that gets out of hand, however, and not the difficulty of the computations. Anyone who is interested can quickly master the arithmetic of the "diet problem" or the "transportation problem" as presented in many textbooks.

The examples used here will also seem too simple because they do not explore the many extensions of linear programming. The latter have much to do with making it important and permitting its application to a multitude of real problems. However, they add too much to the difficulty and too much to the length of the discussion to be included in a general treatment of micro-theory.

FIRST EXAMPLE

In the discussion above, we used only two inputs and we will continue to use labor and mix to make apple pie in these examples. We will also propose that the firm has a choice among four different production techniques, usually called "activities" or processes. Each process or activity permits the combination of inputs in fixed proportion to produce an output and requires that any proportional increase in all inputs expands output in the same proportion. Thus process P_2 on Figure 11–8 requires two boxes of mix and two units of labor to make one dozen pies. Ten boxes of mix and ten units of labor used in process P_2 will then make sixty pies, and so on. Figure 11–8 presents four such processes.

If we look at P_2 for a moment, it will become clear that there are no constraints in this model that limit the size of firm under competitive conditions. If the firm can sell one dozen pies (at the competitive price) and pay the costs of mix and labor used, then it can produce two or ten or a thousand dozen at the same profit (or loss) per dozen. Both revenues and costs expand in exactly the same proportion because input and output prices remain constant under competitive assumptions. This was not true for the production functions considered earlier in this book. The firm in earlier examples ultimately encountered decreasing returns to scale, meaning that costs would increase faster than revenues, and losses would ultimately appear. Linear models, therefore, will not be useful in analyzing decisions about the *scale* of operations of the firm. The decision about scale has been described above as the long-run decision, so linear models must be confined to short-run choices; that is, to choices about the proportions among inputs.

In the short run you will recall there is an additional constraint on the behavior of the firm; namely, that one input at least is in fixed

FIGURE 11–8

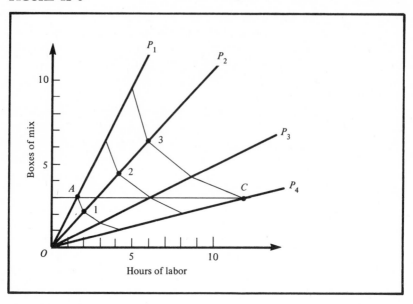

supply to the firm.[6] In our simple example, let us suppose that the amount of pie mix is fixed at three boxes. We therefore mean to indicate that the firm can use any process (P_1 through P_4) up to the level where it requires three boxes of mix. It can also use any *combination* of processes up to the point where three boxes of mix are required. Thus all possible input-output combinations lie within or on the boundary of the triangle *OAC* in Figure 11–8. We refer to all the points in this set as "feasible solutions" to the problem of choosing the optimum.

Now we must establish a rule to serve as the basis for the choice of the optimum point from the feasible set. One might expect in advance that the rule will be profit-maximizing because we are analyzing production choices. Linear programming problems always involve maximizing something subject to constraints, and thus fit well into the usual form of economic theorizing. (The problem, of course, can be expressed as minimizing something subject to constraints, too. For ex-

---

[6] In fact, linear theory often starts with the assumption that all inputs are fixed. We will consider this case using earlier production functions when we talk about the market period, a period too short to permit variation of any input. It will be assumed that this means no variation in the level of output as well, so that no production decision seems to be required. Linear theory takes a more general view; namely, that output can be varied by not using all of some of the inputs. This possibility does not appear readily in the framework of earlier production functions because each bundle of inputs is assumed to yield a particular output, and questions about *ways* of combining given inputs to get output do not arise.

ample, we can seek the maximum output from given costs or the minimum costs of a given output. We proceed in the same way no matter which way the problem is put.)

Suppose for the moment however, that we consider how to get maximum total output from the feasible set OAC in Figure 11–8. This is a simple optimizing rule and is easier to handle than profit maximizing at first. We can express it thus:

$$\text{Total output} = Q_1 + Q_2 + Q_3 + Q_4,$$

where Q_1 is the quantity of pie that we may decide to produce by process P_1, and similarly for Q_2, Q_3, and Q_4. When we indicate that total output is to be maximized, we are setting up the above equation as the "objective function," the function to be maximized in the language of linear programming. The solution in this case will be very simple. We need only put the isoquants on Figure 11–8 and then pick out the feasible solution that lies on the highest isoquant. It appears from the geometry of our simple example that the firm will maximize output when it uses process P_4 to produce at the rate of three dozen pies at C.

We should perhaps express the constraints explicitly now. The one we are most conscious of is the limit imposed on the use of mix. In process P_2, we assumed that it took two boxes of mix for every dozen pies. Then if Q_2 is the number of dozen produced by process P_2, $2Q_2$ will be the total mix used by process P_2. The other process lines have been drawn on Figure 11–8 in such a way that process P_1 needs three boxes of mix per dozen pies, process P_3 needs 1.5 boxes of mix per dozen pies, and P_4, one box per dozen. We can now write the "mix" constraint as follows:

$$3Q_1 + 2Q_2 + 1.5Q_3 + 1Q_4 \leqslant M = 3.$$

Thus the total mix used may not exceed three boxes of mix (M).

There is still another set of constraints that is not so obvious. We must specify that output by each process must be zero or larger. We do not even think of the possibility of negative output because we have no economic meaning for the idea. But a computer, not constrained by economic principles, might offer solutions that included use of some process at a negative rate. Most real linear programming problems are much more complex and hence are assigned to computers for solution. We must therefore include among our instructions the following:

$$Q_1 \geqslant 0; \quad Q_2 \geqslant 0; \quad Q_3 \geqslant 0; \quad Q_4 \geqslant 0.$$

These are called the non-negativity constraints.

The problem is now ready for the computer and it is also now expressed in the usual form of a linear programming problem. It has an objective function that can be written as follows:

$$\text{Total output} = Q_1 + Q_2 + Q_3 + Q_4.$$

This function is to be maximized subject to the following constraints:

$$a_1Q_1 + a_2Q_2 + a_3Q_3 + a_4Q_4 \leqslant M,$$

where a_1, a_2, a_3, and a_4 represents the amount of mix per dozen pies required by each process; and the additional constraints that:

$$Q_1 \geqslant 0; \quad Q_2 \geqslant 0; \quad Q_3 \geqslant 0; \quad Q_4 \geqslant 0.$$

We know M and the values of the coefficients (a_1, a_2, a_3, a_4), so we could solve this problem using arithmetic, but using the geometry of Figure 11–8 was certainly easier. It told us immediately that C was the optimum basket of inputs and three dozen pies the maximum output.

Now add one more constraint. Suppose the firm also has a fixed quantity of labor for some short-run period. If labor is fixed at five units, as in Figure 11–9, then output is maximized at E. E lies on the

FIGURE 11–9

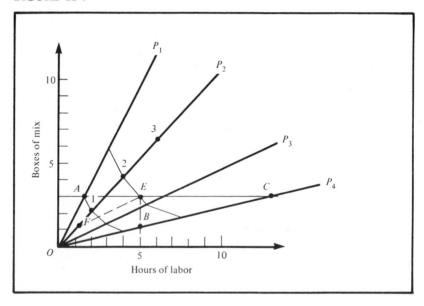

highest isoquant to enter the new feasible set $OAEB$. Output will be two dozen pies to be produced by a combination of processes P_2 and P_3. Inspection makes it appear that about ¾ dozen should be made by P_2 (OF) and 1¼ P_3 (FE). If, on the other hand, the labor available exceeded 13 hours, the feasible set would expand to $OAEC$. The optimum would still be at C using 13 hours of labor. The rest of the labor would be idle even though it had to be paid for.

A VARIATION

Now perhaps we ought to make the problem a little more complicated by introducing profit-maximizing as the objective function. To do this we will have to get some measure of the revenues from the sale of output and some measure of the costs of production. Revenues are dependent on the price of pie (P_π), which we will set equal to $1 (and assume competition so that $P_\pi = \$1$ for every output of this firm). Profits will, of course, be revenues less costs, but in this case the cost of mix is a fixed cost. Since it does not change and is the same for every feasible output, it cannot influence the choice among feasible outputs. If profits are a maximum before the fixed cost is paid, then they will be a maximum (or losses will be a minimum) after they are paid. We can ignore fixed costs in our objective function.

Labor costs, however, are not fixed, so we must find out where the difference between revenues and labor costs is maximum and then we will have the maximum profit point. Set the price of labor at $P_L = \$3$ and look at process P_2. It takes two units of labor costing $6 to make one dozen pies, which will bring a revenue of $12, or a profit of $6 per dozen pies produced by process P_2.[7] If we continue to use the processes laid out in Figure 11–9, we can see from the location of the isoquants that process P_3 takes three units of labor per dozen pies, yielding a profit of $3 per dozen. P_4 yields no profit at all because it takes four units ($12 worth) of labor to make a dozen pies. P_4 now begins to look like an uninteresting process. P_1 uses about 1⅓ units of labor for a profit of $8 per dozen.

Now we can write the objective function as follows:

$$\text{Profit} = 8Q_1 + 6Q_2 + 3Q_3 + 0Q_4,$$

where Q_1, Q_2, Q_3, and Q_4 are the number of dozen pies produced by each process. The constraints are the same as in the earlier example except we are not putting any constraint on the supply of labor. Therefore:

$$a_1Q_2 + a_2Q_2 + a_3Q_3 + a_4Q_4 \leqslant M,$$

where

$$a_1 = 3, a_2 = 2, a_3 = 1.5, a_4 = 1;$$

and

$$Q_1 \geqslant 0; \quad Q_2 \geqslant 0; \quad Q_3 \geqslant 0; \quad Q_4 \geqslant 0.$$

---

[7] This is, of course, "profit" before the fixed cost of mix is met. It is this quantity that should be maximized, but fixed costs may exceed even the maximum. In that case, maximizing what we are loosely calling profits will, in fact, minimize the losses.

To solve this using geometry instead of arithmetic, we need to convert this information into a set of isoprofit curves. Then we can pick the point within the feasible set (triangle OAC) that lies on the highest isoprofit curve. Take a profit of $12, for instance. We would get that profit using P_2 when two dozen pies are produced, since process P_2 yields a profit of $6 per dozen. This is point E in Figure 11–10. Similarly, a $12 profit would require an output of four dozen pies if they were made by process P_3, indicated by point G. The linear assumptions mean that all points on the line EG also yield $12 of profit because each is reached by some combination of the two processes in which

FIGURE 11–10

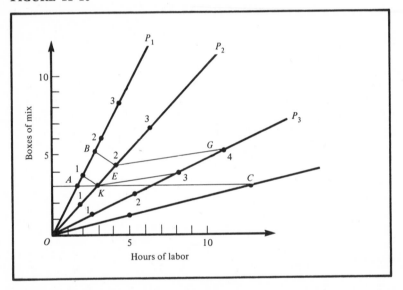

costs are the sum of labor inputs to each process and revenue is the sum of values of the two outputs. For process P_1, the isoprofit of $12 should appear at 1.5 dozen pies (B). (P_4 can be ignored because it involves zero profit and will not be considered by the firm.)

If we add a whole family of isoprofit curves by this process, they will all have the same shape. It is clear that the highest one that enters the feasible set anywhere will do so at K and indicate that profits will be maximized when approximately 1.5 dozen pies are produced entirely by process P_2.

These isoprofit curves are based on the assumptions we have made about the technical conditions of production by each of the processes and the assumed prices of inputs and output. If we made slightly different assumptions about technical conditions, we might get an isoprofit curve that has a segment lying right along the boundary of the feasible set as between K and F in Figure 11–11. In this case, the firm could use either process, P_2 or P_3, or in fact, any combination of the two to maximize their profits. The maximum is the same for every point from K to F.

FIGURE 11–11

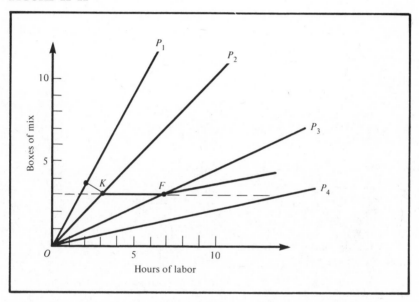

SECOND EXAMPLE

Another simple, though fairly realistic, example can be examined if we imagine a small firm starting out on the production of a new good and being told by its banker that it can borrow only a given amount for the production of this good. This example will reveal some ambiguities introduced by the kinks in the isoquants.

Since the firm is small, the price of inputs will be taken as given and together with the borrowed money made to generate an isocost curve like ZZ' in Figure 11–12. The firm can, in other words, buy any combination of the two inputs that lies on ZZ'. If the firm has open to it four productive processes represented by P_1, P_2, P_3, and P_4, then it will produce at G. Here the attainable set of input combinations is touching the highest isoquant. So far this problem is very much like the problem of finding the most output for given costs as discussed in Chapter 9, but this situation is more complicated.

There are kinks in the isoquants and two kinds of complications

FIGURE 11–12

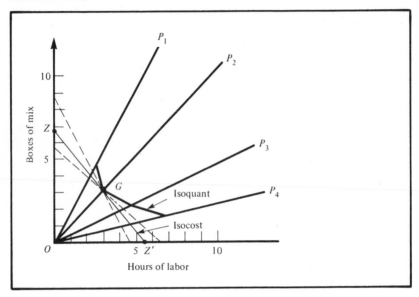

may arise. For instance, in Figure 11–13, the boundary of the attainable set lies along one of the straight facets (*GH*) of the isoquant. In this case the firm can use either process P_2 or P_3 or any combination. The model does not yield a unique optimum under these particu-

FIGURE 11–13

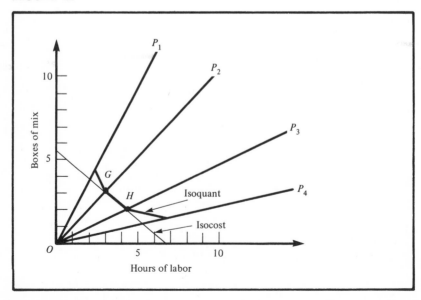

lar input prices and total costs. On the other hand, it is easy to see that point G in Figure 11–12 may be the optimum under many different price and cost constraints. The dashed lines indicate two other examples. Both of these complications can arise only because we have not enforced convexity conditions sufficiently strong to produce smooth isoquants.

SUMMARY

Though the examples we have used are extremely simple, they have the main characteristics of typical linear programming problems; namely,

> The functions are linear; the constraints are inequalities; the output using each process is greater than or equal to zero; and there is an objective function that is to be maximized.

These characteristics derive from the three special assumptions made at the beginning:

1. The assumption of proportionality; i.e., constant returns to scale.
2. The assumption of a finite number of processes.
3. The assumption of additivity of processes.

The second of these is generally defended on the ground that it adds to the realism of the production model. It makes the economist's view of the production function appear more like that of production managers and engineers.

The first assumption, however, abandons both increasing and decreasing returns to scale. Economists are convinced that both exist in real situations. Therefore, this assumption is valuable only if there exists some fairly wide range of outputs over which returns to scale are relatively constant. This range may be preceded by increasing returns at lower output levels and followed by decreasing returns at higher output levels. It must, however, be wide enough so that an important number of production decisions fall within that range.

The third assumption is patently untrue in the real world. It implies that when two or more processes are used simultaneously they in no way interfere with each other. The real world provides numerous counter-examples. Nevertheless, in the absence of any exact knowledge of the effect on P_1 of each possible output from P_2, we are forced to make this assumption in order to make a solution possible. This amounts to assuming away many "externalities" in production. This is not the only context in which externalities are important, and all conclusions about welfare are clouded by the necessary use of the assumption. The matter will be considered further in Chapter 14.

We have considered linear programming in the context of production choices already familiar from our analysis of other types of production functions. This is, perhaps, a help in understanding linear models, but it does have the disadvantage of concealing the full power of linear programming to deal with complex practical problems. The usual textbook examples—the diet problem, the multiproduct firm problem, the transportation problem—do this much better, and the interested student should have a look at such an example. At that point he will find another aspect not revealed by our examples. Solutions involve very large amounts of simple mathematics. They are laborious.

SELECTED READINGS

Baumol, William J. "Activity Analysis in One Lesson," *American Economic Review,* vol. 48 (1958), pp. 837–73.

Baumol, William. *Economic Theory and Operations Analysis* (Englewood Cliffs, N.J.: Prentice-Hall, 1977), Chapter 12.

Dorfman, R. "Mathematical or Linear Programming: A Non-mathematical Exposition," *American Economic Review,* vol. 43 (1953), pp. 797–825.

Chapter 12

Profits and firms

INTRODUCTION

In a private-enterprise economy, the entrepreneurs are said to be motivated by the desire for profits. In the preceeding chapters on production and costs we have explicitly relied on this motive. We will carry this argument further in later chapters, until we can predict that under perfect competition in the long run, this motive leads to an optimum allocation of resources. The character of that optimum is described in some detail in Chapters 13 and 19.

A planned public-enterprise economy may also decide to seek such an optimum allocation of resources. If so, it will need an alternative motive or perhaps a set of rules and incentives that can substitute for the profit motive as a criterion for choice. The fact that these alternatives are not explored in this book should not obscure the extent to which production (and consumption) theory can be useful to a central planning board. Much of economic theory becomes useful whenever the goal of "maximizing something, subject to constraints" is accepted by choice-makers. This is true even though what is to be maximized is not profit.

Thus, while micro-economic theory is not necessarily biased toward private enterprise systems, it is nevertheless traditionally biased that way. Noncapitalist alternatives to the profit motive are not usually considered in a textbook such as this and will not be considered here. They have been studied extensively in socialist countries of Eastern Europe, and a substantial body of information exists.

We will, however, consider a number of proposals for the introduction of alternatives to the profit motive that appear to exist in private-enterprise economies. These motives divide models of the firm into three groups: *marginalist models,* which assume a simple profit-maximizing motive; *managerial models,* which assume maximization but introduce variables other than profit; and *behavioral models,* which give up maximization as an assumed motive altogether. We have a few additional things to say about the marginalist model and its profit motive before we go on to the others.

THE PROFIT MOTIVE

Profit is defined simply as total revenue minus total cost:

$$TR - TC = \text{Profit (or loss)}.$$

This is a quantity that a real firm will want to know at the end of its business year. It can presumably find out from its accountant the size of its profit or loss. The accountant, however, will not measure the profit (or loss) the way an economist does. This is because the economist uses a different definition of total cost. He argues that some payment must be made to the owners of the firm if they are to be willing to provide equity capital for use in the firm. This payment ought, therefore, to be recognized as a cost. It is the cost of the services of capital, just as a wage is the cost of the services of a workman. It is thus considered when profit-maximizing choices are being made.

It should be remembered from Chapter 10 that the return to capital will *not* affect choices when capital has been invested in the firm in some highly specialized form. Highly specialized means that it cannot be readily adapted to other uses and hence that its earnings in other uses are very low or nil. This is the short run, and these are the fixed or sunk costs of a short-run period. Choices will then be made in the light of variable costs and not total costs, and any return to capital can be viewed as a residual after all other costs are met. The choice among alternatives will be unaffected by the size of this residual even if it is expected to be zero.

Aside from this short-run case, the economist includes a "normal" return to capital as a cost of production. What is a normal return? The answer comes from the argument above. It is an amount just large enough to draw capital away from other uses and into the firm. This is an opportunity-cost definition of the normal return. It depends on the amounts that could be earned by this capital in other uses adjusted for any differences in risk between uses.

In some circumstances total revenue may exceed total cost even though the latter includes the normal return. The excess, called economic profit,[1] also belongs to the providers of equity capital, to the owners of the firm. Both normal returns and profits may be paid out in the form of dividends, or they may be retained in the firm. When they are retained and invested in the firm, they increase the value of the equity of the owners.

Later we will argue that in a long-run competitive equilibrium, capital will receive a normal return, but economic profits will be zero. This conclusion does not change the description of the profit motive, however. We want to predict the choices of firms. These choices must be made in the light of expected profits since they are made before actual profits can be known. We argue that firms will choose the alternative that maximizes expected profits even when the expected maximum is zero or a minimum loss, and even when the profits realized sometime later are smaller than those expected.

OTHER GOALS

The assumption that firms try to maximize profits is a very simple one. It has this simplicity in common with many other assumptions, such as economic man and perfect competition. There is no question that simplicity is a virtue in theoretical assumptions, and no assumption should be rejected on that ground alone. Nevertheless we are sometimes made uneasy by such elegant simplicity and this is one such case.

One of the reasons for this uneasiness is not a legitimate one. It comes from confusing "economic firm" with real firms run by human beings called businessmen. The economic firm of the last few chapters is only a theoretical construct. It is used to predict, for instance, the effect on price of alternative taxes such as excise and corporate income taxes. We value economic firm as a construct only if those predictions are correct.

This construct is not to be used, however, and is not adequate to predict the actual behavior of business persons running their firms. What this means is that the "theory of the firm" does not offer a realistic description of the actions of real business persons. Neither does it describe their motives as they see them. The language that we use sometimes suggests the real firm and the real people, but this is unfortunate, and is unintended. Taken seriously, it leads directly to the uneasy feeling that theory is too simple to be useful. Shortly we will look at certain efforts by economists to describe and analyze actual business behavior. It will then be seen that these efforts, which have had some success, are

---

[1] Since we will argue in Chapter 13 that economic profits are zero in a long-run *competitive* equilibrium, we tend to think of economic profits as "monopoly profits" and sometimes use the closely related concept of "economic rent." Monopoly profit and economic rent are discussed in Chapter 17.

directed at other kinds of questions and predictions. They do not yet replace the "economic firm" in the uses for which it was designed.

However, as Prof. Machlup has persuasively argued there is an area in which criticism of the simplicity of economic firm and profit maximizing motive seems legitimate.[2] If, in an industry, the number of real firms is small, then the idiosyncrasies of managers may not "average out." Successful prediction of the outcome of a tax change may require substantial information about decision processes inside individual firms. We will look at some proposals for dealing with these situations under the heading Managerial Models. Then we will complete this chapter with a discussion of Behavioral Models of the firm in which the intent is to understand choice by a firm as an internal social and political process.

One final note on motives is needed. It is not the function of positive economic theory to tell firms what their motives *ought* to be. Business motives are what they are, and the economist is concerned with what he can predict about prices and other variables. Opinions about what business motives *ought* to be are value judgments that arise because the implications of some motives are seen as good and the implications of others as evil. Each of us may hold views of this kind, but at this point we are interested only in motives, observed or assumed, and the observable outcomes that each can predict.

MAXIMIZING SOMETHING ELSE

When many real firms produce quite similar products, it is generally argued that there is little chance for the peculiarities of a manager to affect outcomes. These peculiarities are in part averaged out. In addition, the range for their exercise is narrowed because of the "competition." In some industries, however, it is thought that a wider range of choice is open to managers and that this range includes alternatives that may be primarily of interest to the manager alone. Several factors may create this situation. An oligopoly firm, because of its negatively sloped demand curve and because of the small number of its rivals, may open up such possibilities to its management. The separation, in large corporations, of management from ownership is also a possible source of managerial discretion. It has even been argued that large size alone is a sufficient condition. Economists are not yet prepared to say which factors are important and how important they are. Nevertheless, we have some quite useful models of the behavior of managers with discretion.

---

[2] Fritz Machlup, "Theories of the Firm: Marginalist, Behavioral, Managerial," *American Economic Review,* vol. 57 (March 1967), p. 1.

One of these models starts by recognizing that managers seem to be concerned with sales, in fact with the size of total sales, i.e., total revenue. No doubt this concern appears where larger sales mean larger profits, but it has been argued that sales are often desired in their own right and will be pursued even when this means smaller profits.[3] Declining sales may have a number of undesirable consequences for the firm. They may make it harder to borrow funds; they may lead to the loss of distributors and retail outlets; they may require reductions of staff. This list could be expanded, but it is probably long enough to make a concern with sales appear reasonable. As Professor Baumol has observed, "Almost everytime I have come across a case of conflict between profits and sales, the businessmen with whom I worked left

FIGURE 12–1

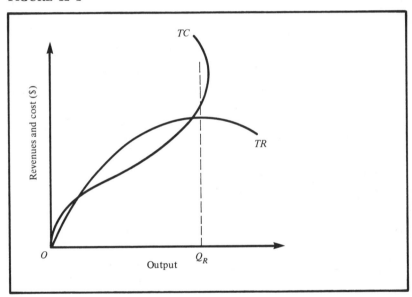

little doubt as to where their hearts lay. . . . A program which proposes any cut in sales volume, whatever the profit considerations, is likely to meet a cold reception."[4]

This argument is posed as a conflict between two maximization goals; total revenues (sales) and profits. It is not generally possible, however, for the firm to pursue revenues to the exclusion of profits. It is easy to see, as in Figure 12–1, that when total revenues are maxi-

---

[3] William J. Baumol, *Business Behavior, Value and Growth* (New York: Macmillan, 1959), pp. 45–48.

[4] Ibid., p. 4.

mized at Q_R they may be less than total costs. This can occur even though $TR > TC$ at some outputs and profits are possible.[5]

Baumol therefore proposes that profits be introduced as a constraint on revenue-maximizing rather than as the variable to be maximized in its own right. We can draw a profit curve as indicating positive profits over the range of outputs for which $TR > TC$. In Figure 12–2 profits

FIGURE 12–2

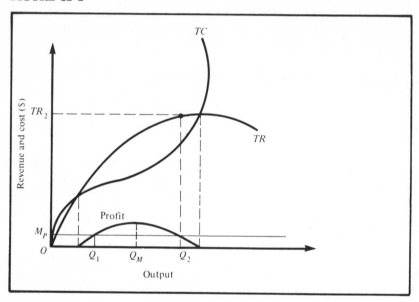

are maximized at the output Q_M. Using profits as a constraint means setting a minimum profit figure, say the amount represented by the horizontal line M_P. There is still a range of outputs for which profits exceed this minimum. This is the range from Q_1 to Q_2.

How might the firm decide on the size of M_P? Baumol suggests that it is determined by the need for the firm to raise capital. The firm may be an oligopolist in its own industry, but it is likely to have to behave competitively in the large capital market. Thus the competition for funds will determine the minimum amount that must be paid to the investors (owners) in the firm.

---

[5] The total cost curve is a typical long-run TC curve from Chapter 9. The total revenue curve, however, rises to a peak and then falls off because we are assuming a large firm with few rivals (an oligopoly firm) and therefore a negatively sloped demand curve. As we move to the right along this curve the number of units sold is increasing but the price at which they are sold is declining. A total revenue curve of this kind first appeared in Chapter 5, and the student may want to look back at that explanation.

It is now clear that while profits are maximized at the output Q_M, the firm can still expand to output Q_2, increasing total revenues to TR_2 without having profits fall below the minimum constraint (M_P). Q_2 is thus the output that maximizes revenues subject to the constraint that profits be a least M_P. If we raise the minimum profit constraint above M_P, then Q_2 moves closer to Q_M, where profits are maximized. Thus the two models, revenue-maximization subject to a profit constraint and simple profit-maximization come closer in their predictions about output as the size of the minimum profit increases.

Earlier in this chapter we argued that fixed (sunk) costs have no effect on output decisions. This conclusion is a logical implication of the profit-maximization assumption. It can be deduced as in Chapter 9 that profits are maximized at the output for which marginal cost equals marginal revenue. Fixed costs, simply because they are fixed, do not enter the calculation of marginal cost and hence have no effect on the determination of the (profit-maximizing) output. It has been observed, however, that a change in fixed costs has sometimes been the occasion for examination of output and price decisions by real firms. Changes in output may follow such an examination. The revenue-maximization model offers a possible explanation.

Suppose that the change in fixed costs takes the form of a rise in property-tax payments on the fixed plant and equipment. The new tax payment will be larger at every level of output, but marginal cost is unaffected, and we would normally expect output to be unchanged. If, however, the firm is maximizing sales subject to a profit constraint, then a change in output may be just what the economist should predict. The rise in taxes will shift the total cost curve to TC' as in Figure 12–3. This will in turn shift the profit curve downward. The output Q_3 will now provide the largest revenues consistent with a minimum profit of M_P. Thus the revenue-maximization model predicts a fall in output and a rise in price for an oligopoly that experiences a rise in its fixed costs.

By now it is easy to see why the revenue-maximizing model is appealing to economists. To begin with, it fits completely within the logical framework of economic theory. It is merely a special case of maximizing subject to constraints where profit is, unexpectedly, the constraint and sales the maximand. Moreover it enables us to draw total sales directly into micro-economic theory. This is pleasing because businessmen are known to be much concerned about total sales and thus we can have a more "realistic" model. And finally, it enables us to rationalize and predict the observed phenomenon of a price and output response to a change in fixed costs. This phenomenon was clearly irrational from the point of view of a simple profit-maximizing model.

Baumol's total revenue model is not the only model that promises these delights. O. E. Williamson has built a utility-maximizing model of

FIGURE 12–3

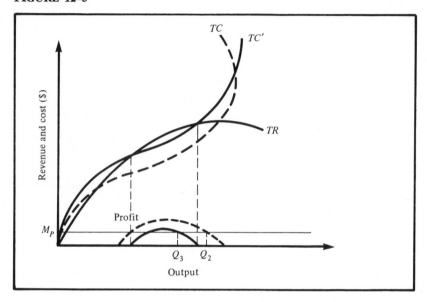

managerial behavior.[6] The model is intended for firms in which management is sufficiently independent of the owners to be able to pursue some
of its own goals. The model consists of a "manager's utility function,"
which makes utility a function of profits, size of staff controlled, control of the firm's investable resources, and a set of managerial perquisites
like expense accounts and fancy offices. It is then proposed that the
manager will maximize this utility function subject to certain constraints, such as a minimum profit constraint. While we will not look at
this model in any detail, it is clearly within the maximization tradition
of micro-economic theory. Like Baumol's model, it is designed to
extend the range of variables that might be maximized and to consider
additional variables that might be introduced as constraints. What we
want to do next is to consider several approaches that lie completely
outside the maximizing framework, models that go under the general
title, Behavioral Models.

SATISFICING

Economic theory has been criticized on the ground that making
choices in such a way as to maximize, demands unrealistically large

---

[6] O. E. Williamson, *The Economics of Discretionary Behavior: Managerial
Objectives in the Theory of the Firm* (Englewood Cliffs, N.J.: Prentice-Hall,
1964).

amounts of information and unrealistically high computational skills. Economic theory does not, of course, propose that real people, even when they manage real firms, actually make choices that way. It only argues that we can predict outcomes such as the direction of a price change by assuming that choices are made that way. This "as if" technique has been very useful to economists, but we would still like to know how real people choose.

If real people actually try to choose so as to maximize, it is clear that the demands for information and computational abilities are indeed very high. A person will have to know the attainable set of alternatives among which he can choose. He must then know the set of payoffs attached to each alternative, and finally, he must have a function that orders all of the payoffs by preference. There are many ways that any of these requirements may fail to be met in a real situation. For example, one may know only a part of a set of alternatives. One may shop around for a used car, and discover that several dealers have the desired model. Shopping around, however, costs time and money, so a complete survey of all dealers is unlikely. Next, the connection between an alternative and its payoff may also present problems. The precise condition of each car is uncertain. The uncertainty can be reduced, but not eliminated, by paying an independent mechanic to look at it. Finally, it may be very hard to rank the payoffs because each alternative has a number of payoffs that cannot readily be combined. In buying a car, one is concerned about mechanical condition, condition of tires, the condition and perhaps color of the upholstery, the condition of exterior paint and its color, responsibility of the seller, etc. Each car will meet these criteria in different degrees, and there is no obvious way to combine them into a single index so that a car with good paint and bad tires can be readily compared to one with good paint of the wrong color and fair tires.

It has been observed that real people seem to recognize that they cannot meet such elaborate demands for information and skill, and, therefore a real car buyer may decide not to pay more than $1,000 for a car that is in reasonably good condition and take any color but chartreuse. This person is setting "aspiration levels," to use a term from psychology. Instead of trying to find the lowest price, he settles for the first car that is priced at or below $1,000 and meets the other two minimum criteria as well. This will reduce the cost of searching for alternatives. Less will need to be known about the payoffs associated with each alternative and payoffs are easier to compare for purposes of preference-ranking. In fact, the aspiration levels divide the alternatives into two sets: those that equal or surpass the levels and those that fall below. Search continues until one alternative that lies above the boundary has been found, and then the choice is made.

For choices made this way, economists have come to use the term "satisficing" in contrast to maximizing. A business firm may set aspiration levels with regard to profits, sales, output, and other variables. Economists have therefore built models of satisficing behavior in real firms that we will now examine. These models have had some success in predicting the behavior of managers. Nevertheless, as we will argue toward the end of this chapter, maximizing and satisficing models do not directly contradict each other. They do not in fact predict the same kinds of events, and as a result their predictions are not easily compared.

BEHAVIORAL MODELS

When satisficing replaces maximizing as the assumed form of behavior, a contrasting view of the firm becomes very interesting. The most important aspect of this "behavioral" view is its description of the process by which choices are made. An entrepreneur who maximizes can be described very simply. He stands before a set of alternatives whose profit outcomes are known and picks the one that maximizes profit. Nothing more is said about how he makes up his mind. He then makes his choice effective by paying employees to carry it out.

In the behavioral view, the entrepreneur is replaced by management, a group of individuals responsible for running the firm. Where the entrepreneur was an abstraction useful for making certain predictions, the managers are real people. Choices result from a group decision process. Members of the group have their own objectives, and their own views about what is good for the firm. These views are likely to be expressed as aspiration levels, not objective functions to be maximized. Each manager, depending on his position in the management hierarchy, will have some power to influence the choice. Making a choice means forming a coalition of individuals with sufficient power to enforce the decision on the rest of the firm.

Coalition-forming is basically a political process. The coalition will be held together by a combination of compromises on policy and side-payments to members. The compromises are necessary because the final choice must be acceptable to people with divergent views about what is best for the firm. The side-payments are designed to gain support for a compromise that may not be really satisfactory to anyone. Side-payments may take the form of support for the pet projects of key members of the group, or they may be grants of perquisites such as fancy office, larger subordinate staffs, and new titles. (One of the most interesting aspects of this process is that these side-payments may be inconsistent with the basic goals of the firm, including the specific choice that made them necessary.)

Over time, this decision process will set the basic goals of the firm with regard to production, sales, inventories, market shares, and of course profits. These goals are likely to be stated as norms, for instance a minimum profit figure, or a hoped-for gross sales figure during the next period. They do not usually support the single dominant goal of profit-maximization. They are aspiration levels that are supposed to be consistent with survival and/or prosperity of the firm and perhaps of present management as well. Research in the area suggests that current aspiration levels are very closely related to the firm's recent experience. The gross sales objective may be a simple extrapolation of last year's sales that is adjusted for inflation and raised to reflect some rate of growth in sales that has been noted in the past few years. Failure this year to achieve a goal may lead to a reexamination of the goal itself and to an evaluation of the performance of the various divisions of the firm. As a result, the operation of the firm may be "improved" for the next year and/or the goal may be reset at what now appears to be a more realistic level.

BEHAVIORAL RESEARCH

The decision process outlined above takes place in the upper levels of management. It may then lead to the development of certain rules that are designed to bring behavior in the firm into correspondence with the goals. These rules are simple ways of making oft-repeated decisions like deciding the price of a new item to be sold in a retail store. One of the most familiar of these "rules of thumb" suggests that the retail price of an item will be set by marking up the wholesale price by some fixed percentage.

The "mark-up rule" has been studied in some detail. One study[7] of a department store tested the proposition that the normal price of a good can be predicted by dividing the wholesale price by 0.6 (a 40 percent mark-up) and then adjusting the result to the nearest price that ends in $.95. Normal price here means only that it is not a sale price or a price designed to clear out remnants, etc. This rule was then used to predict the normal price of a sample of 197 items purchased for resale by the department store during a particular time period. The prediction was observed to be correct in 188 out of 197 cases.

Another study[8] in a different store and city, some years later, gen-

---

[7] Richard Cyert and J. G. March, *A Behavioral Theory of the Firm* (Englewood Cliffs, N.J.: Prentice-Hall, 1963).

[8] William J. Baumol and Marco Stewart, "On the Behavioral Theory of the Firm." In *The Corporate Economy: Growth, Competition and Innovative Power*, edited by Robin Marris and Adrian Wood (Cambridge, Mass.: Harvard University Press, 1971).

erally supports this rule-of-thumb model. The actual mark-up turned out to be closer to 45 percent than 40 percent and the price was usually rounded to a full dollar rather than $.95. Nevertheless, there seems no reason to doubt that a simple rule of thumb is used in this store as well.

The rule-of-thumb studies just outlined have been remarkably successful in their efforts to predict. There is no reason to doubt that simple rules are used in some real firms and some reason to suspect that they are more widely used than research has so far established. These rules are said to be supportive of the general goals of the firm and to be revised when those goals are not met. The process of revision, however, has not been much studied by economists. We have little to say about the way in which changes in general business conditions as experienced by the firm lead to the adjustment of goals nor the way in which revision of goals themselves leads to the formulation of new rules of thumb. What we do have to say in this area comes chiefly from the study of aspiration levels by psychologists.

PROFITS VERSUS RULES

In describing the process by which goals are set and rules formulated, the economist may seem to be advancing a nonrational view of behavior in the firm. This is stated, of course, in the context of a literature that uses the term rationale in connection with profit-maximizing. This is not, however, a necessary implication. A rule of thumb may be a "rational" response, even in the narrow economic sense, to certain sets of conditions.

Take a case in which the cost of making a profit-maximizing choice is very high. In a department store, for instance, much will have to be known about the demand conditions for hundreds of items if the firm is to set the right price on each item. If the cost of information is included in selling costs, then a rule of thumb can result in larger profits than its alternative. A rule of thumb becomes a way to maximize in this situation.

Moreover, behavioral models may be seen as a description of rational behavior in a somewhat different sense. They describe the way in which real firms adapt to their environment. The decision process and its rules of thumb may enable a firm to survive, perhaps even thrive, in a situation in which information is limited and calculational skills inadequate. We may therefore want to describe satisficing as a rational response to these shortcomings.[9] This statement, of course, gives the word rational a reasonable but different meaning. It means successful adaptation, not

---

[9] This argument is developed at some length in Herbert A. Simon, "A Behavioral Model of Rational Choice," *Quarterly Journal of Economics,* vol. 69 (1955), p. 99.

maximization. This use of the word rational should not lead to the conclusion that we have reintroduced profit-maximizing. In fact, satisficing models have their value in predicting quite different kinds of outcomes, outcomes that cannot be predicted by maximizing models. This last point needs more discussion.

MARGINALISM AND BEHAVIORALISM

We have suggested several times that the marginalism and behavioralism models do not try to answer the same questions. Marginalism is designed to predict the allocation of resources in the whole economy. Behavioralism deals with allocation inside the firm. Marginalism makes no statements about allocation inside the firm. It does not, in fact, have a theory of the firm, in the sense of a theory of the way in which real firms act. The economic firm of marginalism is an abstract device, useful in predicting, for example, the character of a long-run competitive equilibrium or the price change that will result from a tax change. No observations of the actions of real managers can directly contradict this model because it makes no statements about their behavior.

Behavioralism, on the other hand, is specifically concerned with the behavior of real managers. So far the conclusions are not readily generalized beyond the individual firms used in each study. This is probably a temporary limitation. Much more important is the fact that any conclusions about the allocation of resources within the firm cannot be contradicted by a marginalist model because these conclusions imply (as yet) nothing about the allocation of resources outside the firm. The connections between the idiosyncrasies of particular managers and an optimum allocation of resources have not been explored. We can make this argument more revealing by considering some of the attempts to make the two models seem compatible.

FOR INSTANCE

It has been argued that real managers want to be marginalists but cannot be because the decision costs are too high. In one of the studies mentioned earlier,[10] it was pointed out that, "In the early 1920s some of the basic principles of inventory theory had already been discovered and reported in print. However, firms began to abandon simplistic rule-of-thumb control techniques only when improved statistical methods and the availability of computers made it possible to provide the data needed for implementation of optimal inventory principles." The use of linear

---

[10] Baumol and Stewart, "On the Behavioral Theory of the Firm," p. 119.

programming by individual firms provides several more examples of solving by a maximizing process, problems that were handled in other ways before it was invented in the late 1940s. This argument is attractive to economists because it suggests that reality will become more like theory with the passage of time. The argument and its examples are, however, merely suggestive. There is as yet no evidence that the improvement of calculating techniques and computers will make it possible to maximize in all choice situations, and it is not yet obvious that real managers would always choose to do so if they could.

Probably a more important argument is one that says marginalism is important inside the firm, just as it is outside, but that there is no equivalent of the discipline of the market inside the firm. The allocation of resources outside the firm results from the independent decisions of millions of individuals and firms. We will argue in Chapter 13 that those decisions are constrained by competitive markets in such a way that an optimum allocation of resources is achieved. One of the most important conclusions of economic theory has been that *de*centralized decision making will lead to an optimum if there are competitive markets. Inside the firm the equivalent of the market seems to be missing. If different divisions of the firm make independent decisions, there is no mechanism that makes these decisions compatible with some optimum.

Management, therefore, centralizes the decision process. The result inside the firm, as it would be outside the firm, is a tremendous increase in the need for knowledge and a large rise in the cost of decision making.[11] This supposedly makes necessary those techniques described by behavioralists: rules of thumb, side-payments, satisficing. Again, we have an argument that appeals to economists. It suggests that marginalism ought to be used and would be used if it could be used. It suggests that we should seek a set of rules that would make the decentralized decision makers inside the firm behave as if there were a market. However, no one has as yet proved that such a set of rules can be formulated.[12]

This argument also poses the problem mentioned above. It presumes to know what managers would do if only they could. Much of the evidence gathered by behavioralists does not support this presumption. Managers do not see themselves as frustrated marginalists nor do they appear to behave that way most of the time.

---

[11] The need for knowledge and the way in which that need is reduced by competitive markets is discussed in Chapter 13.

[12] In a very important article in 1938, Oscar Lange established that there is a set of rules that will guarantee a perfectly competitive-type optimum in a socialist economy. See Lange, Oscar, and Fred M. Taylor, *On the Theory of Socialism* (Minneapolis: University of Minnesota Press, 1938).

One more argument is worth considering. It has been said that rules of thumb are gradually adjusted over time until they produce very close approximations to the outcome of maximizing choice. It is also said that the level of profits that is satisficing is gradually adjusted upward over time until it approximates the level that would be achieved by maximizing. There is so far little evidence to support these statements. Neither marginalists nor behavioralists have models of the way in which goals or rules are adjusted within the firm in response to changes in conditions outside the firm. This argument cannot be supported without such models. At the moment, it expresses little more than a pious hope.

CONCLUSION

Thus one may say in conclusion that, up to now, marginalists and behavioral models are not in conflict because they do not deal with the same problems. They do not refute each other's hypotheses because they do not make hypotheses about the same phenomena. To quote again from Baumol and Stewart,[13] "It follows that a direct confrontation of the two approaches in terms of their predictive power is not easy to arrange and does not seem imminent." It is true, however, that the way resources are used within an individual firm determines in small part how they are allocated among uses in the economy. It is likely that some reconciliation of these two theories will ultimately be necessary. However, we cannot say that any of the arguments just considered seems most likely to be the basis of that reconciliation.

SELECTED READINGS

Boulding, Kenneth. "The Theory of the Firm in the Last Ten Years," *American Economic Review,* vol. 32 (1942), pp. 791–802.

Machlup, Fritz. "Theories of the Firm: Marginalist, Behavioral, Managerial," *American Economic Review,* vol. 57 (1967), pp. 1–33.

Oliver, H. M. "Marginal Theory and Business Behavior," *American Economic Review,* vol. 37 (1947), pp. 375–82.

Seitorsky, Tibor. "A Note on Profit Maximization and its Implications," *Review of Economic Studies,* vol. 11 (1943–45), pp. 57–60.

Simon, Herbert A. "New Developments in the Theory of the Firm," *American Economic Association, Papers and Proceedings,* vol. 52 (1962), pp. 1–15.

[13] Baumol and Stewart, "On the Behavioral Theory of the Firm."

PART IV

EQUILIBRIUM

Chapter 13

Partial equilibrium: Competition

INTRODUCTION

We have now examined two models of choice. We have analyzed the consumer choosing among baskets of consumption goods and services, and we have analyzed the producer choosing among baskets of inputs and outputs. We have applied to both consumers and producers the same set of restraints on behavior in the form of axioms of optimization. Thus these two models are in most ways symmetrical. Their differences lie primarily in assumed differences in their respective attainable sets.

One assumption made in the analysis of both models is the assumption that all prices are given. This was both necessary and convenient when we were considering consumption and production as separate activities. Nevertheless, it has been clear from the beginning that prices are some of the things we wish to explain. We cannot continue to fix their value, but must instead ask whether the interaction of consumption and production models is adequate for the determination of prices.

In answering this question, our first step will be a quite limited one; namely, to analyze the determination of one price when all prices but that one are assumed to be already determined. This is a partial equilibrium analysis. It will lead to a definition of the concept of equilibrium in a market and to the discovery that prices depend in part on whether we make a competitive assumption or consider some form of monopoly.

We will begin the analysis under the assumption of perfect competition. This means that we have in mind buyers and sellers who act as if their decisions have no effect on price. Thus perfect competition is not the property of any *real* market. It is, instead, an intellectual device or model that we hope will enable us to predict events in real markets. Economists have done more to explore the implications of the competitive model than of any other. Perfect monopoly has also been thoroughly examined, but other market models are much less well developed. We will consider monopoly in Chapter 15 and the other models, such as oligopoly and monopolistic competition, in Chapter 16.

PERFECT COMPETITION

Perfect competition is the name of the model that economists are most likely to use. The crucial assumption of this model is that the participants make their decisions about buying, selling, and producing as if those decisions would not affect prices. This has been said a number of ways. For instance, the buyers or sellers may be described as price takers, or they may be assumed to act as if the demand (or supply) curve is horizontal. Or it may be said that none has monopoly power, meaning the power to alter price by changing the rate of production, sale, or purchase.[1]

Economists have used this assumption to make predictions about the determination of prices and quantities in real markets. They have also used it to predict the characteristics of production and exchange in a long run equilibrium. These preditcions appear very attractive to many people with the result that they see perfect competition as a normative guide for policy. All of this has made perfect competition and its key assumption one of the most important elements in economic theory, and we must make a few more comments about it.

When we are talking about exchange under perfect competition, we mean to imply that buyers and sellers are in contact with each other and communicate their offers and supply prices to each other. In a real market, there may be factors that inhibit communication or that prevent buyers and sellers from making offers based only on the conditions of supply and demand considered in earlier chapters. When we make theoretical use of the concept of perfect competition, however, we abstract from these factors, and that is why a simple statement that demanders and suppliers are price takers is adequate.

Here, as elsewhere, however, our interest is not in theory for its own sake, but in theory as a device for predicting real events. For instance, the theory of perfect competition can be used to predict that within a

---

[1] One of the implications of this definition is that competitors are not "rivals." Competitors make their decisions in response to price and without regard to the likelihood that others will react or retaliate once the decision is made. Retaliation is the essence of the problem faced by an oligopoly, however, and we will refer to oligopolists as rivals. Thus oligopoly is rivalrous and competition is not, and it only confuses an argument to talk about intense "competition" among the big three auto firms.

market there will be a single price for each good and that that price will equal the marginal cost of production. We cannot expect that all sales in a real market will take place at exactly the same price, a price exactly equal to marginal costs. Nevertheless, we will want to know immediately whether price *approximates* marginal cost in some real market and whether we can identify certain characteristics of real markets that insure a close approximation.

This question brings to mind the nitty-gritty of real markets. Are real buyers and sellers sufficiently well informed? Do they collude with one another to gain advantage over others? Are there restraints on prices like fair trade laws or ceiling prices. Are there specified conditions under which sales must be made, such as an eight-hour-day law, for instance, or a government permit that must be obtained by the seller? This list could be expanded at length and economists have done much research in this area. The object of this research has been, and should be, to try to state the minimum requirements for mobility, knowledge, and other market characteristics that are necessary if a real price is closely to approximate the price predicted under perfect competition.

We know, for instance, that the number of sellers need not be indefinitely large *if* new firms can enter the market easily. We know that every seller need not shop around to every buyer *if* some minimum number is willing to shop around and if their shopping patterns overlap to cover the whole market. We can even estimate the size of that minimum number through the study of particular real markets.

These minimum conditions are usually complex statements about the interaction of several variables. An example will help make this clear. It is usually argued that perfect mobility of resources (including labor) is necessary for perfect competition in a market. Real markets, of course, never display perfect mobility, and one can ask what factors will encourage or discourage migration of individuals within a market. A recent empirical study suggests that the likelihood of migration decreases as distance increases, and then connects the significance of distance with the age and education of the migrants.[2] For instance, it appears that increasing distance reduces migration by reducing rapidly the information about job opportunities available to migrants. There are, however, a number of ways of getting information. Some are less affected by increasing distance than others, and it appears that these are more likely to be used by better educated individuals. It is therefore likely that mobility will be greater in any given market, the higher the education levels of potential migrants. Older individuals seem more

---

[2] Aba Schwartz, "Interpreting the Effect of Distance of Migration," *Journal of Political Economy*, vol. 81, no. 5 (September–October 1973), p. 1153.

likely to be affected by increasing distance than the young, but age seems to be a minor factor compared to education.

This example suggests that the conditions under which perfect competition is a successful predictor cannot be summarized by what are usually called the "conditions of perfect competition."[3] The latter are simplified, idealized statements that introduce immediate confusion. They appear to be conditions for the existence of perfect competition. Is "perfect" competition something that can exist? Do economists really *believe* in perfect competition? The answer to both questions is no! The economist uses the idea of perfect competition as an analytic device, not as a description of reality. Belief in the desirability of perfect competition as a policy goal is a judgment about the way things *ought* to be, not about the way they are. It is a judgment that can be made by anyone and may be made by some economists, but it is not necessary to the usefulness of perfect competition in economic theory.

With this in mind we can ask, "What can be predicted with the assumption that economic man acts as if his decisions about buying and selling have no effect on price?" The first step toward an answer will be to consider the market for a single commodity. We will take the price of tea out of the set of given conditions but continue to treat all other prices as fixed. This means that we can consider the quantities that will be demanded and supplied at every price. The price of tea will be determined by the conditions of supply and demand discussed in earlier chapters.

THE DEMAND CURVE

In Figure 13–1 we have presented the negatively sloped demand curve that grew out of our analysis of consumer behavior. Each point on the curve is an alternative price-quantity pair. All alternatives exist "at the same time," which is another way of saying "under the same conditions." These conditions include a preference pattern as represented

---

[3] The "conditions of perfect competition" can be listed as follows:

1. Perfect competition requires that every economic agent in the market be so small that it cannot exert a perceptible influence on price.
2. The product of any one seller in a perfectly competitive market must be identical to the product of any other seller.
3. A third condition is that *all* resources are perfectly mobile.
4. Consumers, producers, and resource owners must possess perfect knowledge if a market is to be perfectly competitive.

This list comes from C. E. Ferguson, *Microeconomic Theory,* 3d ed. (Homewood, Ill.: Richard D. Irwin, 1972). pp. 250–53. © 1972 by Richard D. Irwin, Inc. Prof. Ferguson added, "Glancing at the four requirements above should immediately convince one that no market has been or can be perfectly competitive." This is quite correct and should lead to the conclusion that the *conditions* of perfect competition are not of much use to the economist.

FIGURE 13–1

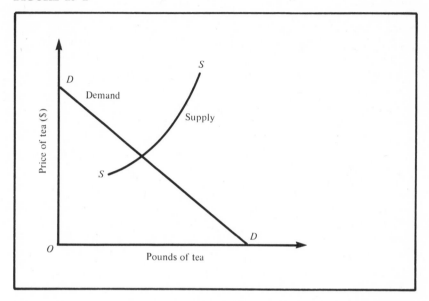

in the indifference map; income, which helps generate the boundary of the attainable set; and all other prices as noted above. This is a market-demand curve, meaning that individual demands have been added to-gether. In the eyes of sellers it is the set of all the possible price-quantity pairs that are possible under these certain conditions. If time is allowed to pass, then some conditions may change and the demand curve will be shifted.

THE SUPPLY CURVE

Figure 13–1 also presents a positively sloped supply curve, the sum-mary statement of our analysis of producer behavior. We have assumed that 100 identical firms make up this industry.[4] The supply curve of each firm involves the assumption that the price of the inputs is unaf-fected when the firm and the industry expand output. This may have been a reasonable assumption for most inputs for a small firm in a competitive industry, but as soon as we consider a fairly large industry

---

[4] The assumption often seems terribly unrealistic. We are aware that some managers are better than others, some business locations better than others, and so on. This is true enough, but if one location is really better in the sense that it gives a cost advantage to the firm that uses it, then under competition many firms will bid for that location. Its rent will be bid up until any cost advantage to its user disappears. Since this can happen to any input, the assumption is not as unrealistic as it at first appeared.

(or a monopoly firm), it is less plausible. As the industry expands, it becomes probable that at least some inputs will be bid up in price. Those most likely to be affected are those most specialized to the production of the commodity. Thus the industry supply curve will generally be steeper than the simple sum of individual supply curves. While we want to hold this idea in the back of our minds, we will nevertheless proceed on the assumption that all prices, including prices of inputs, are determined (with the exception of the price of tea, of course).

Consideration of the shape of the supply curve forces us to consider time again. It is still true, as in the case of demand, that points on the curve are alternatives that exist "at a point in time." They are price-quantity pairs that exist under the given set of conditions. Any change in these conditions will generate a new curve. In addition, however, each price-quantity pair represents a rate of flow of output that would be achieved after some time is allowed for adjustment to a particular set of conditions. The short run allows for adjustment of some inputs, and the short-run supply curve indicates rates of output associated with price after those adjustments have been made. The long-run curve reveals the results of adjusting all inputs and the market period curve, which we have not yet discussed, allows for the adjustment of none. From what we have learned about cost curves, we can expect that the supply curve will be more elastic at any price, the longer the "run." Thus we must choose the supply curve in relation to the problem we are considering.

EQUILIBRIUM IN THE MARKET PERIOD

Equilibrium is perhaps easiest to introduce if we start with the market period, a period of time so short that the firm cannot vary the rate of any input to production. Do real firms have to make decisions about how to act under such conditions? Perfect examples are hard to find. One might suggest, for instance, that once Christmas trees are all cut, or perhaps the strawberries are all ripe and harvested, that we have no way to increase the supply of them. The supply is absolutely fixed and cannot be varied even by storage of some until next year. On this view the supply curve will appear to be a vertical straight line at the amount of the existing supply as in Figure 13–2. The decision on price will then seem to depend entirely on demand.

If the demand is represented by DD, then a price of P_e will lead to the sale of all the Christmas trees. In a real market, the price P_e will usually be quickly discovered as dealers whose prices are higher find they are not selling many trees and dealers whose prices are lower realize they will be sold out long before Christmas. We will call this price the equilibrium price. At this price sellers will be able to sell all

FIGURE 13–2

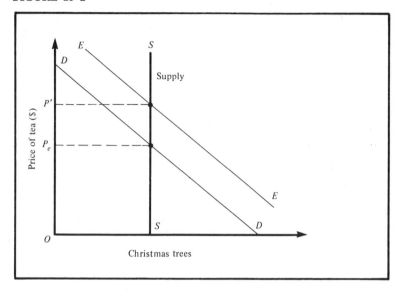

they want to and buyers can take home as much as they want to buy at this price. When a market is not in equilibrium, we assume that buyers and sellers adjust their prices toward equilibrium. The seller who is not selling all he wants to sell at the current price lowers that price and the buyer who cannot get all he wants offers to pay more. The market will thus feel its way to the equilibrium price.

All producer choices in the market period will be choices about price and not about rates of output. A shift in demand, to *EE*, for instance, will only shift the equilibrium price (to *P'*) and not change the quantity sold. However, the fixed-supply model is weakened if we introduce the possibility that the good can be stored. The supply curve will no longer be a vertical line. Sellers will compare the current price with an expected future price minus any storage costs and may decide not to sell now. Since different sellers will have different expectations about the future, they will not all withhold their supplies at the same current price. Probably the higher the current price, the greater the number of sellers who will decide not to store for an uncertain future. The supply curve will be a positively sloped curve very much like the one in Figure 13–1 except that it will extend downward to the left until it reaches the vertical axis. The intersection with the vertical axis will indicate a price just high enough to induce at least one seller to sell now rather than to store his goods. The introduction of storage does not, however, change the way we describe equilibrium. We will soon talk about that in some detail.

The realism of a fixed-supply model is further weakened by the realization that there are more inputs to the production of Christmas trees than the tree itself. Some of them are variable on very short notice; for instance, the number of salespersons employed on the lot or the number of red and green lights turned on to attract the public. Each of these affects the shape of the supply curve and assures that it will not be an absolutely vertical line. If the price rises, more help will be hired to set up trees and provide selling services so that the supply of trees is effectively increased. A tree in the big pile of bundled trees on the back of the lot is just not part of the supply until someone shakes it out, mounts it on a base, and sets it out where customers can see it. We must conclude, therefore, that the analysis of this extreme, "the market period," in which all inputs and hence supply are absolutely fixed, has its value in indicating the character of real cases that lie somewhere near that extreme. There are probably no real cases that fit exactly.

EQUILIBRIUM IN THE SHORT RUN

In Figure 13–3, we have the familiar demand curve and short-run supply curve. One can see again that P_e appears to be a special price under the conditions that produce those curves. At the price P_e, every seller can sell exactly as many pounds of tea as he wants and every buyer can buy exactly as many as he wants. Thus, if the price came to

FIGURE 13–3

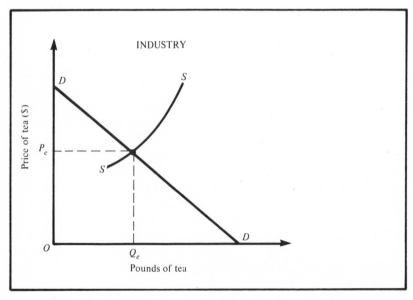

be P_e, no economic man operating in this market would have any desire to change his choices. This was true of P_e when we examined the market period too. It is the key characteristic of equilibrium, but the concept of equilibrium has other aspects, and we will return to it in a few pages.

The position of the individual firm can be seen clearly in Figure 13–4, where we have drawn a supply curve (SMC) that represents just

FIGURE 13–4

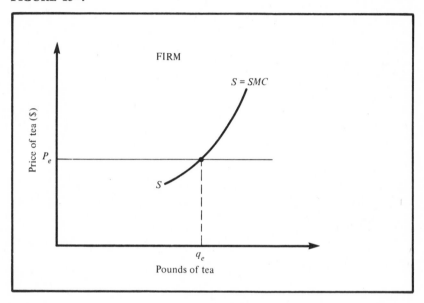

one of the 100 firms producing tea.[5] Hence the supply curve of Figure 13–4 is just 1/100 of the supply curve in Figure 13–3. Since we are assuming perfect competition, this firm expects to be able to sell any amount at the industry price (P_e). This does not mean that we think this firm or any real firm actually has a horizontal demand curve that could be represented by the line P_e. This line is merely a shorthand way of saying that this firm will choose its output level as if that choice could not affect the price (P_e). It is thus an indication that we intend for this choice to be a perfectly competitive one. The price P_e therefore, is the marginal revenue for this individual firm. The firm will maximize profits with an output q_e because at that output $P_e = MR = MC$. Under our simple assumptions, q_e is just 1/100 of the quantity (Q_e) sup-

---

[5] This is the short-run supply curve of an individual firm from Chapter 10 (see Figure 10–11).

plied by all firms and no firm will wish to change its plans as long as price remains at P_e.

SHORT-RUN PROFITS OR LOSSES

We now turn to the question of profits in the short run. The price P_e in Figure 13–3 is a price that equates supply and demand and, from the viewpoint of the firm in Figure 13–4, a price that maximizes profit. We cannot determine from either diagram, however, the size of those profits. Profits appear for the firm whenever its selling price is higher than its average costs of production. We are, of course, talking about profits in the economist's meaning of the term. A normal return on capital is not called profit and is included in total costs. When the price is higher than average total cost, then total revenue will exceed total costs. We can then say the return on capital is above normal or that the firm is making an economic profit.

FIGURE 13–5

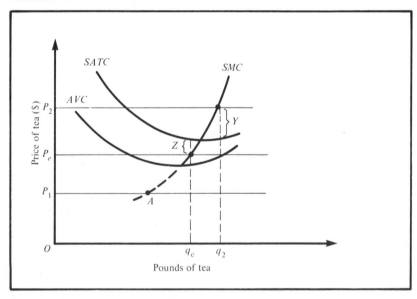

To find the size of these "above-normal returns," we need a short-run average cost curve for a single firm ($SATC$), as shown in Figure 13–5. On the assumption of competition, we again depict an equilibrium price as a horizontal line, P_e. The firm will choose to produce and sell the quantity q_e. However, the short-run average total costs ($SATC$) are not covered at this output and there is no output that would cover these costs when the price is P_e. The firm is losing an amount equal to Z on every item it sells. Maximizing profits means minimizing losses in this case. On the other hand, if the selling price were higher, P_2 for instance, the firm would produce a large output (q_2) and, more important, it would make an above-normal profit equal to Y on every unit it sells.

We must also say a few words about a price as low as P_1, though we have discussed this before in Chapter 10. At that price, average variable costs are not covered for any output. We could discover the output at which marginal cost equals marginal revenue, but this point (A), which would minimize losses, is not on the supply curve (SMC) of the firm. The firm can eliminate all of its variable costs by stopping production, and will, therefore, be unwilling to supply this good at any price that is less than the lowest point on its average variable cost curve.

Prices like P_e and P_2 are equilibrium prices in the short run, but because they involve either losses or above-normal returns, they have implications for the long run. Firms losing money will ask how to avoid these losses. Since this is a short-run equilibrium situation, they are presumed to have done all they can in the short run. They must turn to possible long-run decisions to solve their problem. If, on the other hand, they are making above-normal returns, it is new firms (to this industry) who will look to the long-run decisions that might give them a share of those returns.

ADJUSTMENT IN THE LONG RUN

We call these decisions long-run because they can specify a change in any of the inputs. As indicated before, we are not talking about the period of time necessary for these decisions to be carried out and output to be appropriately affected. Long-run describes the type of decision being made rather than the time period itself.

Let us assume that one aspect of the long run has already been handled by these firms. They have decided to become optimum-sized firms. This is a reasonable assumption because firms would want optimum size even if the short run yielded profits instead of losses. The motivation for optimum size is entirely a matter of profit-maximizing. By assuming optimum size for all firms, we can now concentrate on the long-run response to short-run conditions.

If firms are losing money in the short run—if the price is P_e as in Figure 13–5, for instance—then we expect that they will decide to withdraw from this industry. Their capital can earn a normal return elsewhere and in this case a normal return is higher than they now get.

In fact, we define what we mean by a normal return as the return that capital could earn in other industries under similarly risky conditions.

Now if we imagined all of the firms deciding simultaneously to withdraw and then carrying out their withdrawals at the same rate, we would predict that output would fall to zero in the long run. This is hardly a prediction of movement toward long-run equilibrium. We will therefore assume that some firms can move faster than others and, of course, recognize that this would be most likely where real firms are involved.

As a few firms complete their withdrawal, the industry supply will be reduced. The total quantity supplied by the remaining firms will be smaller at every price. This is indicated in Figure 13–6 by the shift from

FIGURE 13–6

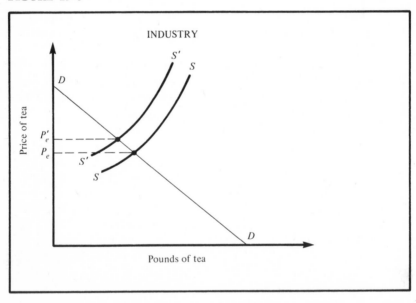

SS to S'S'. As the supply curve shifts, the equilibrium price gets higher. Once it gets high enough (P'_e) to cover the average total costs of the remaining firms as at A in Figure 13–7, then the losses are eliminated and the incentive to withdraw is gone. We are thus predicting that the withdrawal decision will move the industry in the direction of an equilibrium in which losses no longer occur (nor are returns above normal). It is an equilibrium because no firm in (or out) of the industry would be motivated to make further changes.

This equilibrium has a number of interesting characteristics. The fact that these are optimum-sized firms means that the price will be just

FIGURE 13–7

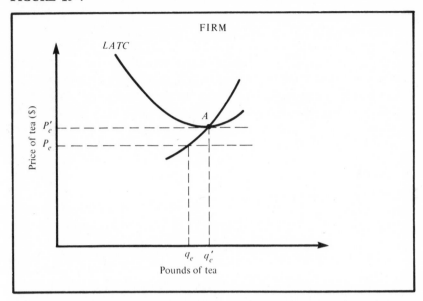

FIRM

FIGURE 13–8

high enough to touch both long-run and short-run average cost curves at their lowest points, as in Figure 13–8. Of course, the long- and short-run marginal cost curves will each go through the lowest point on the corresponding average cost curve. And since the price equals the

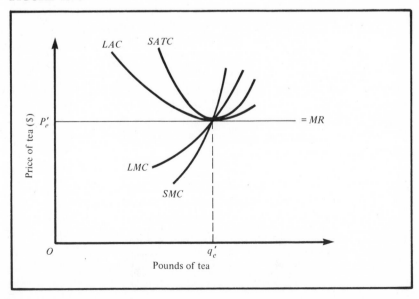

marginal revenue under competition, we get the following set of equalities:

$$P = MR = SMC = LMC = SATC = LAC.$$

This certainly will appeal to those who like things tidy (and that includes most economic theorists), but it also is appealing on normative grounds. Many have said, "We ought to have competition because in the long run, prices will be no higher than necessary to cover the minimum average costs of production." This statement is open to a number of objections, not the least of which is that the conditions of technology, preferences, and factor supplies that underlie these curves are constantly changing. The long run may never come. Nevertheless, Figure 13–8 reveals what has historically been one of the strong arguments in support of the view that perfect competition is a good policy goal.

INCREASING COST INDUSTRIES

We have already discussed long-run cost conditions for individual firms in Chapter 10. You will recall that a firm may experience decreasing average costs at low outputs because of economies of scale, and the opposite for other reasons at larger outputs. However, it is possible for whole industries to experience a similar cost situation. The reason is that expansion by an industry may cause the price of inputs to rise, fall, or remain unchanged. It is not hard to see that as an industry expands, the cost of those inputs that are highly specialized to it may be bid up. The results are shown in Figures 13–9 and 13–10.

Suppose that the industry is in long-run equilibrium at A on both figures, as shown by the fact that the price (P_e) is just high enough to cover the lowest point on the LAC. (We have shown only some of the curves from Figure 13–8 in order to keep the diagram simple.) Now, imagine an increase in demand from DD to $D'D'$ in Figure 13–9. In the short run the price will rise to P_1, and each firm will expand along its short-run marginal cost curve (SMC) to an output of q_1, as in Figure 13–10. Thus the existing firms have expanded output in the short run in response to a rise in demand. It is the rise in price that induces them to expand and, in fact, gives them their information about the rise in demand. The new short-run equilibrium is at B in both figures.

The price of tea now exceeds average total cost, so above-normal profits are being made. We can expect these profits to stimulate the entry of new firms and set off a second round of adjustments to the change in demand. The immediate effect of the entry of new firms will be to increase the quantity supplied at every price. We can show this effect as a shift of the industry supply curve SS to the right. If this were

FIGURE 13–9 **FIGURE 13–10**

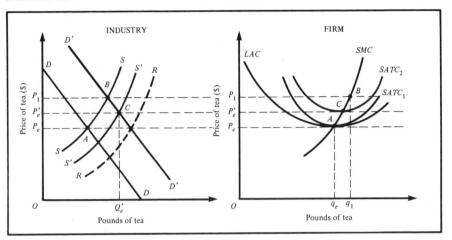

the only result, it would shift as far as *RR*, where the industry equilibrium price is back down to P_e and every firm is just covering its average total costs at output q_e.

Suppose, however, that the situation is somewhat more complex and that we must deal with a third round of adjustments. Suppose that as new firms enter and as existing firms expand, they bid up the cost (price) of some inputs. This is likely in the case of any input that is specialized to this industry. The increased demand for the input will move its supplier along his positively sloped supply curve. He will have to be paid more if he is to make and sell more. The average cost curve in Figure 13–10 will rise from $SATC_1$ to $SATC_2$.[6] This change eliminates some of the short-run profits.

Thus the entry of new firms not only pushes price down from P_1 by increasing the industry supply, it also pushes costs up. The two will meet each other where a price line higher than P_e (but lower than P_1) is tangent to the lowest point of a new short-run cost curve ($SATC_2$). When this point (C) is reached, the adjustment is over. The final price (P_e') is just high enough to cover the average costs ($SATC_2$) of the firms in the industry. (The exact output of each of these firms depends on the way in which the change in costs shifts its marginal cost curve. We have left the new MC curve off the diagram to keep it from getting too cluttered, but the sum of the outputs of all firms would of course equal Q_e' in Figure 13–9). The new equilibrium C involves a new supply curve $S'S'$. This curve is to the right of SS because of the entry of new

---

[6] The LAC curve and the corresponding marginal cost curves will rise too, but we have not shown that change because the figure is too cluttered as it is.

firms. It is, however, not far enough to the right to bring the price back to P_e because of the rise in input costs.

This has been an example of an industry with increasing costs. Expansion of the industry bid up the prices of some inputs. Expansion may lead to a fall in the price of some inputs as well. Expansion of the automobile industry probably led at one time to large economies of scale for the firms that supplied parts. As the cost of the parts to auto producers went down, the average cost of making cars went down. The *SATC* curve would shift downward as the industry expanded. This shift would increase any above-normal profits and induce still more capital to enter the auto industry. The new equilibrium price would be lower than the old because the new industry supply curve would be to the right of *RR* in Figure 13–9. Here we have an industry experiencing decreasing costs.[7]

SOME NOTES ON EQUILIBRIUM

In the diagrams used in this chapter, demand and supply curves have always intersected. We have called the price at which they intersect the equilibrium price and observed that the quantity demanded at this price is equal to the quantity supplied. This last observation indicates what we in fact mean by equilibrium.

The existence of an equilibrium price is dependent on the shape of the supply and demand curve. The shapes of these curves, in turn, depend on the assumptions we have made about consumption and production sets, preference patterns, production functions, and optimizing behavior. This set of assumptions may or may not be consistent with the existence of an equilibrium. Some sets of assumptions lead to curves that do not intersect. Whether or not our model has equilibrium as one of its implications is essentially a logical problem, a problem of deduction from the assumptions. It is similar to the question of whether a set of equations has a solution. Indeed, the equilibrium price is sometimes described as the solution of a set of simultaneous supply and demand equations. Even when we do not specify the actual quantities supplied and demanded at each price along the supply and demand curves, we may still be able to state that any pair of curves having certain general shapes will have an equilibrium price. We may thus be able to make a general statement about the existence of equilibrium under our assumptions.

This whole question is very important because economic analysis usually proceeds by comparing one equilibrium with another. The

---

[7] It should be noted that if suppliers of some input realize economies of scale, then the input industry is not made up of optimum-sized firms. It is not in a position of long-run competitive equilibrium.

economist asks, "How will the output and price of tea be different if the supply of bakers is larger?" The answer involves the use of "comparative statics." Each equilibrium is viewed as a static state that results from a different set of conditions. We can vary one factor at a time and compare the equilibrium after the variation with the previous equilibrium. In this way we can discover the importance of each assumption or condition that is part of the model.

If we can say of some particular model, "Yes, an equilibrium exists," we can then ask a second question. "Can this equilibrium be achieved and will it be stable once achieved?" A "yes" answer to this question requires some assumption about the way buyers and sellers respond to disequilibrium. Disequilibrium means that the quantity demanded is not equal to the quantity supplied. There is either excess demand or excess supply. A simple assumption that will usually lead to equilibrium is that buyers will offer a higher price for a good that is in excess demand and that suppliers will lower the price of a good that is in excess supply. We think real buyers and sellers often behave this way.

In Figure 13–11, this means that when price is P_0 we can count on sellers to cut the price. The cut then reduces the quantity producers are willing to produce and increases the quantity that buyers want to buy. This moves the market toward the equilibrium price P_e. The equilibrium represented by price P_e and quantity Q_e seems to be stable in the sense that any departure from this price and quantity sets off a reaction by buyers or sellers that pushes the market back to equilibrium.

FIGURE 13–11

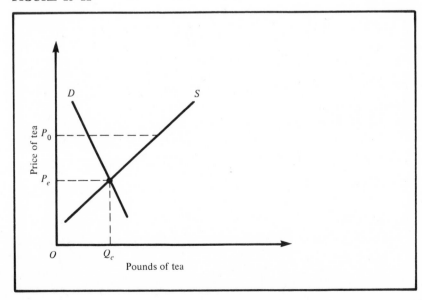

One can, however, point to a very simple situation in which this mechanism does not work properly and the equilibrium is not stable. In Figure 13–12, we present supply and demand curves that cross so that equilibrium still exists at the price P_e. The negative slope of the supply curve suggests that these firms are experiencing decreasing costs as the industry expands. However, if the price happens to be at P_0 then quantity supplied (Q_S) is greater than quantity demanded (Q_D), and there is excess supply. With excess supply, we expect sellers to lower their price in an effort to sell the excess. However, lowering the price

FIGURE 13–12

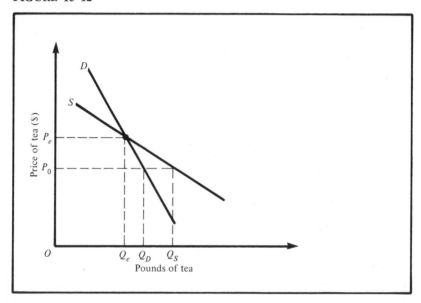

merely increases the amount of excess supply and moves the market further from equilibrium. This market is unstable. The condition for stability here is that the supply curves have a positive slope, so that a price *above* equilibrium means excess supply and a price *below* equilibrium means excess demand.[8]

Economists frequently formalize the assumption about the way buyers and sellers respond to disequilibrium in a market "game." The players are buyers and sellers and an umpire announces the prices. The game begins when the umpire announces the first set of prices for all

---

[8] It is worth noting in this chapter on competitive equilibrium that a supply curve with negative slope will not occur under competition. Each firm is small relative to demanded quantities and it can and will, therefore, move along its marginal cost curve to the rising portion. Since each firm is on the rising portion of its supply (marginal cost) curve, the industry curve must also rise. For further explanation, see Chapter 10.

goods. These prices may be chosen at random and each player then indicates the quantities he wishes to buy or sell at those prices. No buying or selling takes place as yet, but the umpire applies a rule that says, "Raise the price of any good that is in excess demand and lower the price of any that is in excess supply." Now the players respond to the new set of prices with new offers to buy or to sell. The game continues with the umpire adjusting prices until all excess demands and supplies have been eliminated, that is, until the equilibrium prices have been announced. Then exchange actually takes place.

This is, of course, an artificial game, but it does make clear the importance of the assumption about response to disequilibrium. The game has another function as well, however. It enables the economist to compare two equilibrium positions without introducing consideration of the paths by which a real market might move from one to another. These paths are complex. They may differ from the game in that real buyers and sellers may not adjust their prices as was assumed. Even where the adjustment is in the direction assumed, it may be too large or it may come at the wrong time.

It is worth looking at a famous example of this problem, the cobweb model. Suppose we assume that producers make their decisions on output on the basis of current prices, but that it takes some time for those decisions to affect the rate of output. The usual examples come from agriculture. A farmer may decide how many pigs to raise on the basis of the current price for pork. He must then wait for the pigs to grow to marketable size. Hence in Figure 13–13 the current price P_0 leads to the

FIGURE 13–13

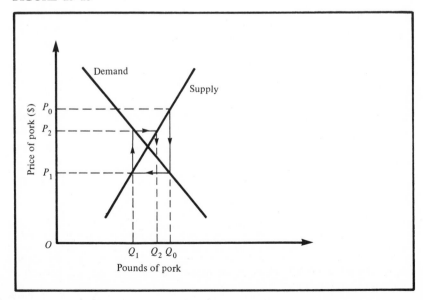

production of output Q_0. When the pigs are grown and come on the market, they will be sold for as much as they will bring and the demand curve indicates that this is the price P_1. The price P_1 now becomes the guide to producers for the next crop of pigs. At price P_1 the supply curve indicates the decision to produce the quantity Q_1. When Q_1 is finally ready for the market, it can be sold at the price P_2, as indicated by the demand curve. This, in turn, leads to the new quantity decision Q_2, and so on. Price and quantity keep adjusting along a path that gradually converges on the equilibrium price and whose cobweb shape gives this model its name.

FIGURE 13–14

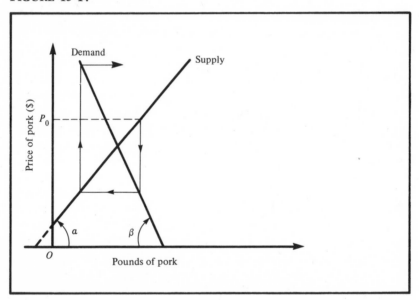

The cobweb-shaped path to equilibrium is entirely the result of a time lag between the production decision based on current prices and the time when the pork is ready for market. A further but slight change in the shape of the demand and supply curves is enough to introduce still another complication. In Figure 13–14, we have changed the relative slopes of the two curves with the result that the price moves away from the equilibrium with each adjustment instead of toward it. Convergence requires that the absolute slope of the demand curve be less than the absolute slope of the supply curve.[9]

---

[9] The slope of the demand curve is, of course, negative, while the supply curve has positive slope. What we must compare, however, is the slope without regard to sign. In Figure 13–14 this means that the angle α must be larger than the angle β if the market is to converge.

Thus equilibrium, like true love, may come—if at all—only at the end of a rocky path, and in spite of the importance of such paths in real markets, economists do rather badly at describing them.

There is one other aspect of the relationship between equilibrium theory and real markets that should be kept in mind. The predicted equilibrium price of tea depends on the conditions of supply and demand, and in the real world these are continuously changing. Thus, the market price may move toward the equilibrium price in the same way a dog runs after a rabbit. He runs towards the spot where the rabbit is now, but by the time he gets there the rabbit has moved. He may never catch the rabbit, and the market price may never equal the equilibrium price. However, as Boulding has said (he is responsible for the analogy of the dog and rabbit), "The fact that the equilibrium price may never be the actual price does not mean it is unimportant. The rabbit is absolutely necessary for the explanation of the dog's behavior even if it is never caught."[10]

This is true even (or perhaps especially) of long-run competitive equilibrium. Long-run equilibrium exists in economic theory as the logical implication of a set of optimizing choices made under a set of given conditions. It can in a theoretical discussion be imagined to have arrived, but it is clear that long before any real firm could enjoy the results of its long-run choices, some of the given conditions would likely be changed. It therefore has its value in indicating the direction in which the economy will be pushed, not in describing the character of that economy at some time in the future.

And if one is tempted to view a long-run competitive equilibrium as a desirable state of things, it is well to remember that we know all too little about an economy that may move continuously toward that equilibrium but never get there.

SUMMARY

In this chapter we have described the most important market model available to economists. Perfect competition is important, not because it is good, but because it leads to more testable hypotheses than any other model.

Using the assumption of perfect competition, it is possible to describe a long-run equilibrium with the characteristic that the price of each good will be just high enough to cover the average total cost of producing that good. If perfect competition exists in all markets, then the average total cost of each good will reflect the opportunity costs of the resources used to produce it.

---

[10] K. E. Boulding, *Economic Analysis:* vol. 1, *Microeconomics* (New York: Harper and Row, 1966), pp. 50–51.

This long-run competitive equilibrium has proved so attractive that many people have argued that perfect competition is a good thing and that it ought to be our policy goal. This is a possible but not a necessary conclusion, and it need not be accepted even though the assumption of perfect competition is to be used in an analysis.

The other important concept introduced in this chapter is "equilibrium." An equilibrium describes the logical implications of a particular set of assumptions and conditions. We generally proceed as economists by comparing equilibriums before and after some change in the assumptions or initial conditions. This is the way we come to understand the significance and meaning of different sets of assumptions. An equilibrium is not, however, a description of the way the world will look at some point in time for the conditions are constantly changing in the real world, and the equilibrium will not have a chance to appear.

There have been at least two very important attacks on the proposal that perfect competition should be our policy goal. One of these comes from the admitted existence of the externalities we have sought to assume away up to this point. We will therefore consider them carefully in the next chapter. The other comes from the analysis of monopoly, which we will take up in Chapter 15.

SELECTED READINGS

See list at end of Chapter 15.

Chapter 14

Externalities

INTRODUCTION

Very early in this book we described consumers choosing among alternate baskets of consumer goods on the basis of their preferences. A specific constraint was placed on this choice, namely, that the preference for any basket of goods depends solely on the goods contained in the basket.[1] We thus did not permit the desirability of a house to depend on the neighborhood in which it is located. As this example makes clear, something very important was assumed away. When we consider buying a house, the neighborhood is as important to many of us as the number of rooms or the state of repair.

It is common to call effects of this kind "externalities" or "spillovers." What goes on in the surrounding area spills over onto the house and land that you might choose to buy. The family that repairs cars in the front yard may produce, as a by-product, noise and oil that spill over on to the surrounding property. The *effects* of noise and oil are external to the basic activity, car repair. In this case they affect the consumption possibilities of nearby individuals with respect to housing. Clearly, some external effects can make a house in the neighborhood more desirable. The terms spillovers and externalities (which are used interchangeably) are intended to cover both desirable and undesirable effects.

The consumption example used above is one in which the spillover

---

[1] Chapter 3.

is obviously very important, but it does not reveal the pervasiveness of these effects. We assumed them away in Chapter 7 as well when considering production choices.[2] We made output along each production function independent of other productions carried on in its neighborhood. In Chapter 11, where choices among production processes are considered, there was again an assumption that no externalities appear.[3] Finally, though there has as yet been no specific mention, we have assumed that production does not spill over on to consumption and vice versa: factories do not produce smoke that falls on homes and vacationers do not clog the highways and slow down the transport of goods to market. It is not difficult to be convinced that these assumptions, all of them, are highly unrealistic and that spillovers impose constraints on choice of such importance as to warrant a careful examination of the whole subject.

THE CHARACTERISTICS OF A SPILLOVER

To begin with, spillovers are unintentional effects of some activity. The smoking steel mill does not produce smoke in the sense that its management makes choices based on the output of smoke. Choice depends on the output of steel, the costs of inputs, and the technologies available for making steel. The output of smoke becomes merely whatever it is when the choice about steel has been made.

It is hard to imagine that the manager of a steel mill would be unaware of the smoke he produces as a by-product, but in other situations, management may not be aware of some of the external effects of its activities. Awareness, however, is not relevant. What is important is that the externality does not affect the decisions of the individuals engaged in the activity that produces it.

The examples used so far suggest that spillovers affect either consumption or output choices. This is correct but there is more. The effects must be produced through changes in the relationship between inputs and output or in the qualities of consumer goods that make them desirable. A spillover occurs when pollution of a river by one industry alters the production function of the fishing industry in that river, or when deterioration of a neighborhood alters the capacity of its houses to produce housing services for individuals.

On the other hand, we do not include among spillovers changes in production or consumption that are brought about by changes in prices. If, for instance, a new, rich deposit of iron ore is discovered, it is obvious that the prices of steel and products made with steel are likely to

---

[2] See Chapter 7, footnote 1.
[3] See Chapter 11, footnote 5.

decline. Consumers are likely to increase their consumption of such goods at the expense of substitutes made from other materials. The change in consumption is brought about by the change in relative price of steel. Such a change will be viewed as desirable. The resulting readjustment of consumption patterns is consistent with an optimum allocation of resources in the economy. Spillovers cannot be defended on this ground and we will shortly argue that they make the achievement of such an optimum impossible.

EXTERNALITIES AND THE OPTIMUM

At the end of Chapter 13 we have the attractive picture of a competitive industry adjusted to a long-run equilibrium. This picture is attractive because it makes the prediction that under perfect competition, each price will be just high enough to cover average total costs of production, where total cost is the sum of the minimum payments necessary to induce the marginal unit of each input to enter this production. A particular output is determined, and the argument can be extended to prove that when all other industries are in this position then we will have an optimum allocation of resources. By "optimum" we mean that production cannot be rearranged in any way that will put someone on a higher indifference curve and no one on a lower curve. This is the notion of a Pareto optimum that was first introduced in Chapter 6 on exchange and that will be discussed again in Chapters 18 and 19.

The importance of externalities is that they make the achievement of an optimum under perfect competition impossible. It should be added that they present similar obstacles to the achievement of an optimum in a planned economy.[4] An externality leads the competitive firm (and perhaps the planning commission as well) to select a nonoptimum level of output. A competitive firm selects the output level for which marginal cost equals price because this maximizes its profits. The community within which that firm operates will want output adjusted until marginal "social" cost equals price. Marginal social cost will be larger than the marginal cost of the firm whenever the externality imposes a cost on society that is not borne by the firm. When the firm adjusts output so as to make marginal cost equal to price, it picks an output for which marginal social cost is greater than price. The value of the resources used to produce this good, as measured by the price people are paying for it, will then be less than its costs in terms of total resources used to produce it. The cost of the total resources used is determined by the value of those resources in the *other* uses to which they could be put. Hence,

---

[4] In the next chapter we will discuss monopoly as an obstacle to the achievement of the optimum. Externalities are at least as important as monopoly.

this production uses resources whose value elsewhere exceeds the price people pay for them here.

In the production of electricity for example, the marginal social cost per kilowatt-hour will include the coal, labor, and many other inputs plus the cost of cleaning the curtains made dirty by smoke when the coal is burned. The last of these will not be considered a cost by the firm itself. The firm will have a marginal cost curve represented by MC_F in Figure 14–1, and it will pick the output Q_F. Society, however, will

FIGURE 14–1

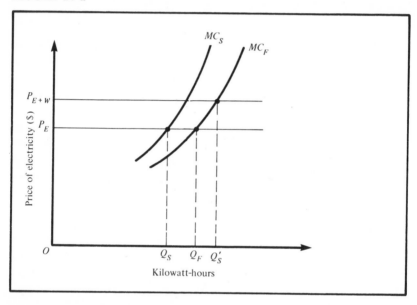

have a marginal social cost curve (MC_S) that lies above MC_F by the marginal costs of laundering the drapes as output expands and more smoke is produced. The optimum output for society at price P_E is Q_S, a smaller amount. In a competitive situation, electricity will be over-produced because the firms that make the choices ignore some of the costs. This is a situation in which marginal social costs are higher than marginal private costs.

This argument can be adapted to the situation in which the externality is a good, not an ill. Suppose that electricity production used much water and in the process purified that water. This pure water may have value to the community so that the electric company ought to be paid not only the price of electricity (P_E in Figure 14–1) but something in addition for the pure water. This higher price is represented by the line P_{E+W}. If the extra payment is not made, the firm will produce Q_F

whereas it should produce Q'_S, a larger amount. At the output Q_S' marginal (private) cost is equal to the marginal *social value* (P_{E+W}) of both the electricity and the water.

In the past 20 years, economists have become very interested in externalities. This interest reflects a growing public awareness. It is an awareness that could hardly be avoided because modern spillovers like the smog in Los Angeles have serious consequences for very large numbers of people. The economist has asked, "What can be done about spillovers?", and he has found some answers.

PLACING THE BLAME

Before we look at some of these answers, however, we need to consider whether someone can be blamed for a particular spillover. The spillovers that most insistently demand public attention are ones whose effects are undesirable. We don't like the smoke that darkens the sun over our homes, and we blame the power plant for polluting the air. This is not, however, a useful way to look at these problems. To begin with, spillover effects can be favorable as well as unfavorable. The production of hydroelectric power often produces a lakeside recreational area as its unintended by-product. We tend to be much less conscious of favorable spillovers, and this leads us to think only in terms of placing the blame.

The truth, however, is that the blame should not be placed at all. A spillover merely means that one process has interfered with another. The smoke from the power plant interferes with the capacity of houses to provide enjoyment to their owners. The spillover would disappear if the power plant were moved away from the city, but it would also disappear if the city were moved away from the power plant. The production of electricity from coal and the production of enjoyment from houses—these two production processes—must be carried on side by side if there is to be a spillover. If a new airport is built in a residential area, it is easy to blame the airport for noise pollution, but the noise pollution requires that the residents be near the airport. Often the new airport is built in open country on the outskirts of the city and then the residents move into the area around the airport. In the economic sense that noise affects welfare, the new residents, not the airport, have created the pollution—the spillover. In the end, there will not be much point in trying to place blame. It always "takes two to tango."

PROHIBITION OF SPILLOVERS

Economists have considered a number of ways of dealing with spillovers. The most obvious suggestion is that the spillover be prohibited, but the naive notion of complete prohibition has little attraction for the economist. This is because he views the problem as one of maximizing by equating marginal costs and marginal benefits. Noise may be added to the marginal social costs of an airport, but the airport yields a stream of social benefits as well. Maximizing welfare requires that the number of flights per day be expanded until the marginal social benefit of a flight is approximately equal to the marginal social cost, a cost that includes the noise spillover. This level of activity of the airport will not normally be zero, meaning that at the optimum there will be some noise. Moreover, people would be worse off if the number of flights were reduced below this level since the marginal social benefit would then exceed marginal social cost. In other words, given individual tastes and preferences people can be better off if they absorb some noise as one of the costs of other goods that confer positive benefits.

However, there may be situations in which we want to prohibit the spillover anyway. These arise where we find it very expensive to determine the optimum level of the activity or very expensive to enforce that level. There are pollutants whose effects are not precisely known but appear likely to be harmful. The use of fluorocarbons as propellent in spray cans is a good example. Fluorocarbons may affect the atmosphere and hence the quality of life on earth, but we do not know for sure. It will take much expensive research and some time before the question can be answered. We cannot, therefore, estimate the optimum level for the process that produces them. We will have to decide whether to prohibit the process or leave the pollution unregulated. We may choose the former.

This argument for prohibition should not be defeated by a simplistic view of the word "prohibit." We do not mean to imply that every trace of a pollutant be eliminated. "Pure" air or "pure" water will always prove to be prohibitively expensive. All we propose is that the pollutant be kept at a low level by prohibition of those processes most likely to raise the level.

VOLUNTARY AGREEMENT

When there is a spillover that brings about a level of output different from the optimum, there is a basis for a mutually advantageous bargain between the producers and the consumers of this spillover. The noisy airport will expand its operations until the marginal revenue from one more flight per day is just equal to the marginal costs it incurs as a result of that flight. It will expand beyond the optimum because its calculation of the costs does not include the noise that reduces the welfare of people who live near the airport. These people could afford to pay the airport to reduce noise by reducing the number of flights. The noise reduction will increase their welfare, and they should be willing to pay some price for that increase.

We can treat this possible payment as a change in the cost conditions of the airport. The marginal cost of one more flight per day must now include the loss of some payment from surrounding residents. Consequently, the marginal cost curve will shift from MC_F to MC_S in Figure 14–1. The difference is the size of the payment that can be collected from residents if the flight is cancelled. The firm will use MC_S as its supply curve, and output at the airport will be lower. If the homeowners find a way to pay the airport an amount exactly equal to the value of the increased welfare gained, then the new output will be an optimum.

It should be remembered of course that the homeowners can also move away from the airport and would be expected to do so if the moving costs were less than the necessary noise payment.

A voluntary agreement is not likely, however, to solve very many spillover problems. The trouble is that what are called the "transactions costs" are usually quite high. Transaction costs include the costs of negotiating an agreement and of enforcing that agreement and may include some capital investments necessary to implement the agreement. A look at negotiating costs will make clear at least some of the reasons to expect these costs to be high.

In the first place, the victims of the spillover will have to be discovered. This means that the pattern of noise pollution around an airport will have to be mapped. There will be some boundary beyond which the noise level is not perceived by individuals as an irritant. The people inside that boundary must be identified.

Next, these people will have to be persuaded to make a joint offer to the airport. They must reach an agreement on the character of that offer, and they must decide how much each person will contribute to the necessary payment. With large numbers of persons and democratic processes, this will be neither cheap nor easy to accomplish.

Finally, there will be costs in negotiating the agreement with the airport itself. The agreement is of course possible on the assumptions with which we began this section, but it may take some time and research before both sides can agree on the actual costs and corresponding payments involved. Some of these costs will be lower if the initiative is taken by the single polluter, the airport. They will nevertheless remain quite high.

One thing that becomes clear here is that all these costs rise rapidly as the number of parties on each side of the bargain expands. Spillovers that impinge on large numbers of people become virtually impossible to handle by voluntary agreements even if the effect is quite important to each individual. We can rely on voluntary agreement only where the spillover is generated by one or a few firms and falls on another small group of firms or individuals.

Clearly the government can facilitate voluntary agreements. Its police powers may make enforcement of an agreement cheaper than it would be for the private parties. It may also be able to assemble information on the extent of the welfare loss experienced by the victims, more cheaply and in a form more acceptable to both parties.

Probably more important than either of these is the power the government has to determine the property rights of firms and individuals. If, for instance, home owners have the right to a relatively noise-free home and the power to sell that right, then a new airport will not be built near private homes until those rights have been bought. If the welfare effects of noise are very large and the right to pollute therefore very expensive, the airport will be built somewhere else where the noise spillover is smaller.

INTERNALIZING A SPILLOVER

In fact, faced with the need to buy pollution rights, the airport firm may decide to internalize the pollution costs. They can do this by buying land around their new airport and then renting this land, perhaps to firms that find it convenient to be near the airport. The result is that the airport firm now regulates the output of noise in such a way as to maximize profits from running the airport *and* renting the land around it. Its marginal revenue must include the marginal rents from land and any expansion of noise will reduce those rents. Ignoring all other costs of both activities, it will expand activity at the airport until its marginal profit from additional flights is exactly equal to its marginal loss from noise-depressed rents.

Take another simple example of internalizing a spillover. Suppose that one firm pollutes the river and thereby reduces the catch of another firm that fishes downstream. The upstream polluter will not count the loss of fish as one of its costs and will expand its output beyond the optimum. If, however, the fishing firm has a legal right to some degree of purity in its water, then two outcomes are possible:

1. The two firms may reach a voluntary agreement that involves some compensation of the fishing firm for the fall in its output. The upstream firm will want to buy the right to pollute up to the point where the marginal cost of a little more pollution in terms of lost fish is just equal to the marginal cost of preventing that pollution either by reducing output or increasing the filtration of the water returned to the river.

2. The two firms may be merged so that the firm has two outputs. The new firm will balance production at both plants in such a way as to maximize total profits. It will reduce pollution and expand fishing until the marginal revenue lost by producing less at the upstream plant is just offset by the marginal revenue of the additional fish output (ignoring of course all the other costs of both processes).

The thing to keep in mind is that a difference between the marginal private cost (of the firm) and marginal social cost or a difference between marginal revenue (of the firm) and marginal social benefit will create a situation in which voluntary agreements or internalizations are possible. They are possible in the sense that both parties to the spillover can be made better off by a change in the level of output. If an agreement or a merger is reached, the resulting output level can be optimum, meaning that marginal social cost will equal marginal social benefit. The government may facilitate these arrangements by wise policies but in many very important cases the number of parties is much too large to make such arrangements possible.

TAXES AND SUBSIDIES

The classic solution to the output problem of an industry that produces undesirable esternality is a specially designed tax. This approach will also call for a special subsidy if the spillover is considered desirable. It was first carefully formulated by the English economist Pigou in the 1930s.[5] It has been the subject of much controversy since but is still viewed by the economist as the most important among techniques for dealing with these problems.

We will assume that an industry produces some good and a spillover as the joint outputs of a particular production process—say, the airport and the noise. We will treat the spillover as if it is undesirable, but with small reversals of language in what follows we could make it an analysis of one that is desirable.

Earlier in this chapter we made such spillovers very simple functions of output. Noise was assumed to expand with the number of flights, and thus the costs imposed on others by the noise expands with output as well. A number of more complicated hypotheses about the relationships of both noise and its costs to the level of output could be introduced here. No doubt at one extreme, there are cases in which the effects are the same at all levels of output. An ugly building is an eyesore no matter what volume of business is done inside. On the other hand, we can suppose that in some cases like the airport case, transportation and noise may be produced in fixed proportion to each other (or increasing or de-

---

[5] A. C. Pigou, *The Economics of Welfare* (London: Macmillan, 1938).

creasing proportions depending on technologies available). Moreover, the costs of noise measured by the welfare loss of people who live near the airport may not expand in fixed proportion to the noise increase measured in decibels. Each of these hypotheses can be represented by a marginal spillover cost curve that describes the change in cost as a function of the level of output.

We will assume a fairly simple shape for this curve, as shown in Figure 14–2. The curve labeled *MSC* suggests that the marginal cost of

FIGURE 14–2

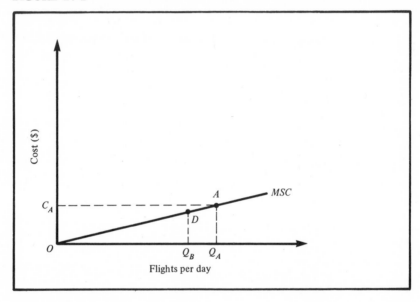

noise, in the form of the dollar value of welfare lost, rises as the number of flights per day rises. What we now have to say about this curve could be extended to most of the other curve shapes suggested above with very little change.

In most real cases, however, the cost conditions are somewhat more complex. If we take any particular output, Q_A flights per day, for instance, we can consider the possibility that there are techniques for varying the amount of noise, and hence costs, associated with that output level. There will be devices for muffling the noise of each aircraft. Very likely these devices will involve costs that rise as noise is reduced and rise very rapidly in the neighborhood of zero noise. What we want to assume now is that the cost C_A on Figure 14–2 actually involves an appropriate use of these devices. What would be appropriate?

Since we are now considering the imposition of a tax on the producer of noise that is determined by the noise cost, we can assume that the firm will be motivated to reduce that cost as long as the marginal noise cost (the marginal tax it will have to pay) is greater than the marginal cost of increasingly effective mufflers. Therefore, we will assume that at each level of output in Figure 14–2 the airport has also adjusted its noise output until the reduction of noise by one more decibel would cost more in terms of muffler refinement than it would save in the tax liability for noise damage. The curve *MSC* therefore represents the results of this adjustment at every level of output.

Let us now make the rather unrealistic assumption that the airport

FIGURE 14–3

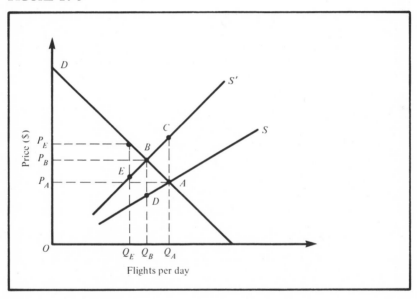

operates as a competitive seller of the right to fly in and out. We could assume many small airports or many small firms at one airport, each of which sells landing and take-off services. This is not the way airports are currently run and so this assumption is unfortunate. We have run into one of the hazards of spillover pedagogy. No single example seems to work well all the way through the argument. We do, however, want to consider a competitive case and so we will stick with the assumption.

The competitive assumption will permit us to draw the supply curve (*S*) in Figure 14–3. It is the horizontal sum of the marginal cost curves of all the firms. We can also put in the demand curve (*D*) of airlines that want to fly in and out. We will assume quite a number of these so that we have competition on the buying side as well. The analysis of competitive markets in Chapter 13 concluded that the equilibrium price will be P_A and the output (number of flights per day) will be Q_A. Each firm will have pushed its own output to the level at which its marginal cost is equal to the price, and the sum of all the individual firm outputs at that price is equal to Q_A.[6] The spillover did not influence this adjustment process. It is as if the spillover did not exist, though the truth is that it exists but its costs do not affect the supply and demand conditions of the choice makers in this market. The spillover costs are borne by third parties.

Now, suppose that study of the area around the airport establishes a marginal spillover cost curve like MSC in Figure 14–2. From a social point of view these costs must be added to all other flight costs. We should put this curve on Figure 14–3 in such a way as to indicate that for each firm the marginal cost of expanding the number of flights includes the marginal costs imposed by the added noise. Every individual marginal cost curve will be shifted upward, and hence their horizontal sum on Figure 14–3 will also be shifted upward to S'. At each level of output (flights per day) the vertical distance between S and S' on Figure 14–3 is equal to the cost of that output on Figure 14–2. For instance, AC on Figure 14–3 is equal to C_A on Figure 14–2.

Clearly, the output Q_A on Figure 14–3 exceeds the optimum by the amount $Q_A - Q_B$. The optimum requires a lower level of output, meaning, of course, that there will be less noise as well, and will imply a somewhat higher price for flight services (P_B). This last is not at all surprising since under competition the lower quantity supplied will have to be price-rationed among demanders. How can we achieve this new optimum? The answer is to impose on these firms a tax that will add to their costs in such a way that S' becomes the industry supply curve rather than S. The tax can be T dollars per flight. Thus the firm must add T to its marginal cost of every output. Moreover, T will have to be equal to the marginal social cost of the optimum output Q_B. That is, $T = DB$ in Figure 14–3, which in turn is equal to $Q_B D$ in Figure 14–2. If such a tax can be discovered and successfully levied, then the competitive industry with a spillover will adjust to a competitive optimum, an optimum that has all of the characteristics that perfect competition would have in the absence of any spillovers at all.[7]

---

[6] See Chapter 13 for adjustment to competitive equilibrium.

[7] It has been argued that once the optimum Q_B has been reached, there is still some noise. This noise will impose costs on people who live near the airport, and so there is still the potential for a voluntary agreement between polluters and pollutees for further reduction. This agreement would take the industry away from the optimum, meaning that at any output less than Q_B, Q_E for example, a price (P_E) would be above marginal social cost measured at E on the supply curve S'. This result is possible, but very unlikely. If voluntary agreement is possible, it is likely to be achieved before the tax is imposed as the incentives (noise costs) are even greater.

NOW FOR THE BAD NEWS

The biggest obstacle to this solution of the spillover problem is the need for information. One must find some way to estimate the welfare loss experienced by individuals who have to live with the spillover. This has obvious difficulties in the case of noise. We are tempted to say that an increase in noise will shift an individual to a lower indifference curve, but we will not be able to observe that shift, nor will we be able to ask the individual to tell us what has happened to him. Real individuals do not have cardinal utility functions that enable them to tell us how much the noise costs them, even if they are willing to tell the truth. The information must be approached indirectly. Perhaps we can find a situation in which individuals choose between two goods with different noise levels but otherwise similar characteristics. Maybe two similar automobiles with different interior noise levels will permit estimation of the value of a decibel. One can see immediately that indirect approaches are likely to give only rough guesses.

Moreover, the large numbers of pollutees involved will add its own problems. Usually their losses will be a function of one or more other variables such as their distance from the airport, direction of the prevailing wind over their houses, and their position relative to the main runway. This means that fairly substantial data must be assembled for each of the many victims.

These problems are not impossible to deal with. There are examples of successful studies in the literature. However, the most important pollution cases tend to be those in which numbers are large—smog in Los Angeles. Therefore voluntary agreements are unlikely and taxes are called for, and then one discovers that estimation of the size of those taxes is prohibitively expensive if it is possible at all. When we need them most, taxes are most likely to be unworkable. A way out of this dilemma has recently been suggested by Professor Baumol, but before we go into that, we will take a look at óne more alternative approach to spillovers.

REGULATION

The object of regulation would be to reduce the level of output, in the case of an adverse spillover, to the optimum level described as Q_B in Figure 14–3. It therefore runs into the same problems of information as the tax solution does. The information is needed in order to discover Q_B, and obtaining that information runs into all of the difficulties just described. For the most part, regulation offers no easier solution than taxation. If in some particular case the necessary information can be obtained, however, then one might want to compare the relative advantages of taxes versus regulation. It has been vigorously argued that regulation is likely to be a more expensive way to reach the optimum than taxation. We will not examine this question except to note that the relative costs of using those two techniques is likely to depend very much on the characteristics of the particular spillover being dealt with.

A REASONABLE PROPOSAL

If the society is willing to relax its demand for an optimum, then it may in fact be able to achieve some acceptable minimum standards with regard to undesirable externalities. The first step is to decide on an acceptable minimum. In the case of polluted streams, this means a minimum standard of purity. We must set a maximum proportion of any impurity, such as sulfuric acid, that will be permitted. This is the kind of definition now used by city water plants to determine whether their filtration processes are adequate.

Once the standard is set, a tax is then imposed on the polluters of the stream, that is proportional to the acid content of the water they return to the river. It is not suggested that we could determine in advance the size of this tax the way we were supposed to do in the optimizing case discussed above. An inadequate tax soon reveals itself, however, in that the desired purity is not achieved. A cut-and-try process is possible, with taxes being adjusted over time until the standard is reached and with analysis of the water always indicating the direction of the next adjustment (though not its magnitude).

This proposal[8] has the additional advantage that it minimizes the real costs of achieving a given target. If there are many polluters of a given stream, they may have differing costs of reducing their contributions to the pollutions. Nevertheless, each will be encouraged to make reductions as long as the marginal cost of a unit reduction is less than the unit tax. Those who find reduction cheap, meaning that the marginal cost of increasing purification of their effluent water rises slowly, will make the largest reduction. The result will be minimization of the resource cost of achieving any given standard.

This proposal also has some limits. Setting minimum standards may be difficult. The necessary technical knowledge may not be available. The recent controversy over saccharin is probably a case in point. Saccharin intake is believed to cause cancer, with the probability of cancer rising as the intake of saccharin rises. We are not, however, able to indicate the size of those probabilities for different levels of saccharin use. What can we do? We may be able to make the very rough guess that reducing total saccharin use by half will move us in the direction of the optimum without pushing us beyond it. This kind of guess or es-

---

[8] William J. Baumol, "On Taxation and Control of Externalities," *American Economic Review*, vol. 62, no. 3 (June 1972), pp. 307–22.

timate requires very much less information than the achievement of an optimum would require. There will be many more situations in which this much information can be had. When we have it, then the tax produces a situation preferred on welfare grounds to the existing situation. If over time more information becomes available, then the standards and the taxes can be revised. This argument should not obscure the fact that even this much information may be missing, but then, of course, all other techniques except possibly outright prohibition (discussed above) are also ruled out.

A FINAL DIFFICULTY

The argument so far has implied the use of resources to limit only one spillover. We still need to face the allocation of resources to the reduction of a number of spillovers simultaneously. We need to know which among many possible improvements in the environment is in fact most important to us and use that information to set the minimum standards. We may then find that reductions of some kinds of pollution are very expensive in resources used, even though they are also very important to welfare. Allocating resources among antipollution uses can be organized as an exercise in getting the maximum increase in welfare from a given set of resources, but the information necessary for a maximum is unlikely to be available. In fact, if it were available, we would be able to estimate the necessary Pigouvian optimizing tax and not need to consider this last procedure.

SUMMARY

Externalities are the unintended by-products of many consumption and production processes. They are important because they alter the conditions under which other consumption and production processes can be carried out. Some may be viewed as desirable and others are viewed as disastrous, but it is not useful to try to deal with them by searching for someone to blame.

Spillovers create either costs or benefits, but their producers do not generally recognize them as explicit inputs or outputs of the process. The result is that competitive markets will underprice an output from which spillover costs are excluded and overprice an output from which spillover benefits are excluded. This leads to an allocation of resources that can depart radically from the competitive optimum.

Prohibition of spillovers is generally rejected by economists simply because it is not consistent with the achievement of an optimum. Voluntary agreements between polluters and pollutees can lead to an optimum, but are very difficult to arrange when both groups have many members. A spillover may be internalized by a producer if those who experience the spillover are in a position to sell their rights to that experience. Taxes, subsidies, and regulations can handle a spillover in such a way as to produce the optimum. Nevertheless, they are not often used because they demand impossible amounts of information about the impact of the spillover.

The most likely solution requires that we set a minimum standard for the spillover and cease to search for the optimum allocation of resources. In many cases this will economize on the need for information to the point where an adjustment of the offending consumption or production process becomes practicable.

It is now time we had a look at that other great interference with an optimum allocation of resources, namely, monopoly.

SELECTED READINGS

Bator, Francis M.   "The Anatomy of Market Failure," *Quarterly Journal of Economists,* vol. 72 (1958), pp. 351–79.

Coase, R. H.   "The Problem of Social Cost," *Journal of Law and Economics,* vol. 3 (October 1960), pp. 1–43.

Makin, John H.   "Pollution as a Domestic Distortion in Welfare Theory," *Land Economics,* vol. 47 (May 1971), pp. 185–88.

Chapter 15

Partial Equilibrium: Monopoly

INTRODUCTION

If a perfect competitor is a price taker, then a monopolist is not. However we define the commodity, we now want to consider the case in which it is sold by only one firm. We are talking about the case in which the demand curve for the output of this firm is the market demand curve for the commodity. The market demand curve has negative slope, and the perfect monopolist is presumed to act in full consciousness of the effect of his output decisions on price. This is, of course, an analytic definition. It is the basis for the deduction of a set of predictions about prices and quantities, and we will examine these shortly.

This definition does not, however, enable us to name some particular real industry a monopoly. We will want to call a firm a monopoly only if we can predict its behavior using this model. It will be the success of the theory that assigns some industry to the monopoly category. Those industries in which this model is useful are likely to have some common characteristics. If we can identify these characteristics, we may be able to suggest industries, firms, or problems to which the monopoly model can be applied. In sum, we not only want a model that leads to hypotheses about reality, we also want to know enough about reality so that we know when and where to use the model.

BARRIERS

We all expect monopolies to make large profits. As we shall see, they sometimes do not, but wherever they do, we must explain why the industry remains a monopoly. What prevents the entry of new firms attracted by the monopoly profits?

Certain barriers to entry come to mind quickly. The existing firm may own the entire supply of some essential resource, such as a raw material deposit or the site for a hydroelectric dam. The firm can use its property rights to prevent entry and protect its monopoly. Patent rights generate a very similar situation. The firm that owns the first patents in some field has a monopoly during the life of those patents. It may then find that long before its first patents run out it has secured many new ones from its own research. Its monopoly may thus be protected for a very long time. Trademarks and copyrights are similar, but probably less important, devices for protecting monopoly. Note that each of the devices mentioned in this paragraph depends on the grant of an exclusive property right by the state.

To this list we should add government grants of another type, the exclusive franchise. One electric company may be designated the only seller in a city. Or a growers' association may be made the only seller of some agricultural commodity. Or a union may get state help in enforcement of a union shop clause in its contract.

An interesting special case arises when the government requires members of some profession to obtain a license. Licenses are generally issued by a licensing board after a candidate has passed a test of some sort. Economists have studied the effects of these licenses and tests, and it is possible to see how they are used to protect a monopoly. For instance, in some professions the "pass rate" on the test is found to be inversely related to an increase in the demand for the service.[1] In particular, a 10 percent rise in excess demand generates a 1 percent to 10 percent decrease in the pass rate. The licensing board, which is often dominated by the professionals it licenses, is restricting entry to the profession and doing so with greater vigor when excess demand increases the prospect of professional gains. The license is a government requirement and thus a government-enforced barrier to entry.

This brief list of barriers has revealed the state as a major protector of monopoly and rightly so. It is only fair to add, however, that many government-established barriers have wide public support. Patents and union shop agreements are believed by many, if not most, people to be good things. Licensing in many professions is believed to be in the public interest. Popular or not, these measures create and protect monopoly.

---

[1] Alex Manrizi, "Occupational Licensing and the Public Interest," *Journal of Political Economy,* vol. 82, no. 2 (March–April 1974), p. 399.

It may seem that the really crucial and interesting cases have so far been ignored. These are the private and often illegal tactics that existing firms use to prevent entry of new firms. Prices may be manipulated to the detriment of a new firm in one part of the country if the existing firm sells nationwide. Or special prices may be used against a new firm that enters one stage of production where the existing firm has integrated many stages. Essential suppliers or customers of the new firm may be bribed or intimidated to prevent their dealings with the new firm. The list is endless, and it should be added that when bribery, intimidation, and fraud can do the job, it is often government officials who are most likely to be threatened or offered the bribes. This is because the power of the state is great enough to offer a protection that cannot usually be had from private sources. Monopoly without state support tends to be weak and short-lived. This last point is developed somewhat further in Chapter 16, where collusion among oligopolies is considered.

There is one very important kind of monopoly that does not have its roots in government protection but depends instead on the economies of mass production. These in turn can form a barrier to the entry of new firms. The economist calls this kind natural monopolies and we will discuss them in some detail later in this chapter. At this point, however, we might explain how economies of scale can prevent the entry of new firms.

A firm that realizes economies of large-scale production may find that it must be very large relative to its market to gain all of those economies. Any new firm that chooses to enter will also have to be very large if it is to realize the economies. If it enters the industry on a small scale and does not succeed in growing quickly, its average costs will be higher than those of the existing firm. Thus, when a large new firm enters, the supply will be significantly increased, and this will have an important effect on the selling price. Even if the pre-entry price, the price before entry of the new firm, was high enough to provide the first firm with monopoly profits, the post-entry price may be so low as to impose losses on both firms. It is the post-entry price that influences the decision of the new firm. Unless this price provides for normal or above-normal returns on investment, the new firm will stay out, and the monopoly profits of the existing firm will continue.

This description of the barriers to entry is very brief. It rightly suggests, however, that economies of scale are an important source of monopoly. It also suggests that monopolies that are not based on economies of scale are likely to require some form of government support. Finally, it is probably true that monopolies that do not have some form of government support tend to be fragile and short-lived.

SHORT-RUN MONOPOLY EQUILIBRIUM

The shape of the demand curve for a good has nothing to do with the number of sellers of that good.[2] In Chapters 3 and 4 we examined the determinants of demand, and no mention was made of the way in which the seller's side of the market was organized. We can, therefore, start with the usual negatively sloped industry demand curve as in Figure 15–1.

FIGURE 15–1

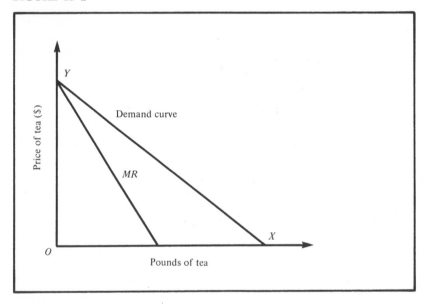

Keep in mind that there are other goods people can buy with their money. There may be no really good substitute for a telephone call, but still as its price gets higher, we reduce the number of calls we make. We spend our money on other goods, ice cream perhaps, not because they are substitutes, but because we prefer them to telephone calls at current prices. What we are saying in economic language is that there is a substitution effect when prices change, even for goods with no close substitutes. This effect guarantees that the demand curve will have negative slope.

Actually negative slope turns out to be very important when the

---

[2] It is, of course, possible that once a monopoly is formed it can alter the shape of its demand curve through advertising. The precise affect of advertising is by no means clear, however.

seller is a monopolist because it means that for every output level marginal revenue will be less than price. You will recall from the discussion in Chapter 5 that when the firm tries to sell one more unit of output per week, it will have to lower price slightly. Its total revenue for the week will be increased by the selling price of the additional unit sold. However, total revenue will also be reduced because all units sold that week must be sold at the new, slightly lower price with the result that marginal revnue will always be less than the selling pirce.

We will assume that the monopolist, like the competitor, tries to maximize profits by choosing the output for which marginal cost is

FIGURE 15–2

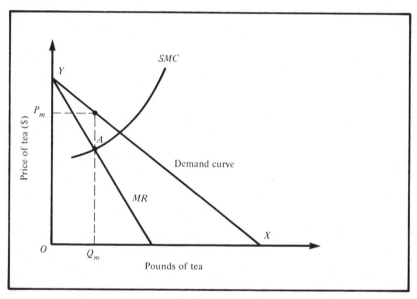

equal to marginal revenue.[3] This means, of course, that the marginal cost curve of the monopoly firm determines its output at each possible value for the marginal revenue. It also means that the output of the monopoly firm is the output of the industry since we have assumed a single firm in the industry. We can therefore put a short-run marginal cost curve (SMC) on the same diagram with the industry demand curve, as in Figure 15–2.

Marginal cost is equal to marginal revenue at A, and the monopolist

---

[3] The argument that makes $MC = MR$ the profit-maximizing rule is exactly the same for both types of firms. See Chapter 9.

will choose Q_m as his profit maximizing output. He will then set his price by asking, "What is the highest price I can charge and still be able to sell all of Q_m?" This information is, of course, provided by the demand curve and P_m is the price. If he does not know the demand curve well enough to pick out P_m, he can still count on the usual market forces to establish that price. P_m is, after all, the equilibrium price as long as he supplies the quantity Q_m. At any price below P_m there will be excess demand and frustrated demanders will push it up to P_m. At any price above P_m he will be aware of excess supply and motivated to lower the price until P_m is reached.

The monopoly firm is thus constrained by the profit-maximizing motive to sell at a single price. He cannot set any price he wishes and still maximize. The power to set any price is often what the layman means by "monopoly power," but this is not an option open to the monopolist we have described. His options under these constraints are no different from those of the competitive firm; namely, that his profits will not be a maximum unless he produces and sells the quantity for which $MC = MR$. He will then pick a price that exceeds his marginal cost, and the economist will call this monopoly power. It gives the term "monopoly power" a quite different meaning. The monopoly firm may also misallocate resources. This possibility must soon be discussed, but first we will ask a crucial question.

MONOPOLY PROFITS

"Will the monopoly firm make monopoly profits?" Monopolies are certainly supposed to! Nevertheless, whether they do or do not depends on the relationship of average revenue and average cost, just as it did in the competitive case. When average revenue exceeds average costs (and we include in the latter the normal return on investment), then returns will be above normal and we will call them monopoly profits. Since the demand curve is, of course, an average revenue curve, we need only to add an average cost curve to the diagram and compare. We have added a short-run average total cost curve ($SATC$) in Figure 15–3. At output Q_m and price P_m, this firm is realizing profits. Average revenue exceeds average total cost by an amount represented by the distance BG. This is the profit per unit of output, and total monopoly profit is represented by the area of the shaded rectangle.

Such profits are not, however, necessary. They depend on the location of the short-run average total cost curve. If it happened to be higher and go through G, as $SATC'$ does in Figure 15–3, then the firm would make no monopoly profits at all. It would only earn the "normal" return on its investment, which would be no larger than it could earn in

FIGURE 15–3

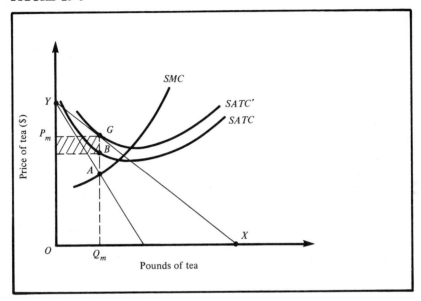

a competitive industry involving similar investment risks. The average cost curve may even lie above $SATC'$, in which case even a monopoly will suffer short-run losses and will consider what long-run choice can eliminate those losses.

LONG-RUN MONOPOLY EQUILIBRIUM

Whatever its short-run profit position, the monopolist will have long-run choices to consider. If it incurs loss, it must consider a change in scale or exit from the industry. If it makes profits in the short run, it need not worry that they will disappear, but it will still want to look for the optimum scale. We can consider this last choice first.

The optimum long-run scale of production is indicated by the shape of the long-run average total cost curve (LAC) as in Figure 15–4. For any given demand conditions, profits will be maximized in the long run where marginal revenue equals long-run marginal cost, as at A. This indicates an output of Q_m at price P_m. This firm will therefore plan to build a plant that will produce Q_m at least cost. We can represent such a plant on Figure 15–5 by $SATC$ and SMC curves, the short-run average and marginal cost curves.[4] Note that the optimum scale for this

---

[4] It is interesting to note that both short-run marginal cost and long-run marginal cost are equal to marginal revenue at A. This result is made necessary by

FIGURE 15-4

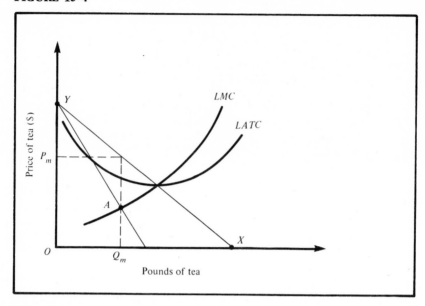

the geometry of the curves we are using. At the output Q_m short-run average cost is tangent to long-run average cost as in Figure 15–5.

Thus at Q_m, $SATC = LAC$, and since total cost is equal to average cost multiplied by output (Q_m):

$$SATC \cdot Q_m = LAC \cdot Q_m,$$

and

$$STC = LTC$$

at Q_m. If we put both total cost curves on the same figure they must have the same value when output is Q_m. They will be tangent at Q_m as shown. Since they

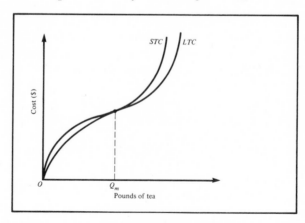

are tangent, they have the same slope at Q_m, and since the slope of a total cost curve is marginal cost, then $SMC = LMC$.

FIGURE 15–5

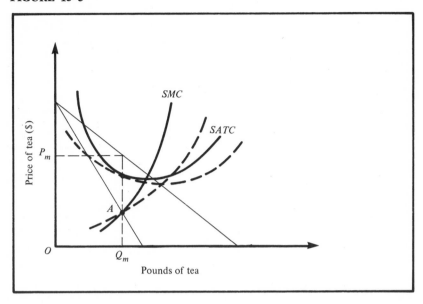

monopoly firm does not fall at the bottom of its long-run average cost curve. In a long-run monopoly equilibrium, production will not necessarily take place at the long-run competitive equilibrium position.

If the adjustment to optimum size still does not eliminate the losses, then the firm will withdraw. This is a monopoly that will not make even normal returns. It hardly matches the popular view of monopoly, but it is really very common. The patent office has granted uncountable monopolies of this sort. It does not matter how humane and efficient your electronic solid-state mouse trap turns out to be; if you can't produce it at a price people are willing to pay, they will go right on buying that little wooden two-bit Last Supper machine and no one will beat a path to your door.

NATURAL MONOPOLY

Some monopolies are called natural monopolies because the monopoly will arise "naturally" out of the supply and demand conditions existing in the market. The necessary condition is that the optimum scale of production for the firm, that is, the scale at which long-run average cost is a minimum, must be large relative to the quantity demanded at a price that will cover average total cost.[5] In Figure 15–6,

---

[5] The term "technical monopoly" is also used because it is the technology used that gives the long-run average cost curve its shape.

the optimum scale of production is at output Q_o. We will refer to any firm that produces at a point like Q_o at the bottom of its long-run average total cost curve as an optimum-sized firm. The price P_o is just high enough to cover the average total cost of this optimum-sized firm. The demand curve (YX) and other demand curves that lie to the left of it and still others that do not lie too far to the right will lead to monopoly. If the demand curve is far enough to the right, then it will take two or more optimum-sized firms to supply the quantity demanded at price P_o, and the industry will no longer be a monopoly.

Suppose for a moment that two (or more) firms exist in the industry represented by the demand curve of Figure 15–6 and that they each sell

FIGURE 15–6

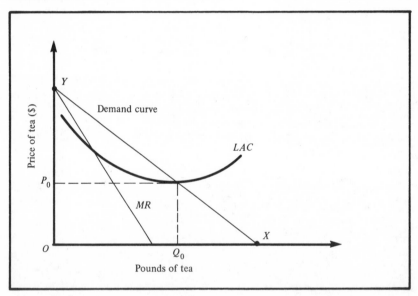

part of the demand. They would each be operating at lower output levels than Q_o and, hence, somewhere to the left on the long-run average cost curve. If either could expand its output and sales, it could (in the long run) move down the LAC curve. With the lower average costs that resulted, it could undersell its rival. Among the rivals, the one with the largest scale of output will have the lowest average costs. That firm can and will finally drive the other (or others) out of the industry by setting a price high enough to cover its own costs, but not high enough to cover those of its rivals.

In fact, if these firms clearly realize their position, they may engage in vigorous price wars and suffer substantial losses in the effort to be the one firm that expands fast enough to be the survivor. Or, recognizing the cost of such wars that only one can win, they may negotiate a merger so that the merged firm can then make long-run plans for the optimum scale of production indicated in Figure 15–6.

What should we do about a natural monopoly? It appears unlikely that society will want to break up such a monopoly into a number of smaller firms. Each of the post–break-up firms would have higher average costs than the monopoly, and society would lose any chance to enjoy the benefits of economies of scale. Consequently, the usual solution to the problem has been public ownership or at least public regulation.

This solution has often been applied in the electric power generation industry. Many cities own their own electric power plants and those that do not tend to make exclusive agreements with a single private firm to buy electricity at regulated rates. The rates are likely to be set by a government agency. The avowed purpose of government regulation in such a situation is to prevent exploitation of consumers by the monopoly.

This intent has led to a "consumer-protection" hypothesis about public regulation, which implies that regulation will result in lower prices, prices that equal marginal costs, and reduced industry profits, among other things. These are hypotheses that can be tested. In a summary of existing empirical evidence, William Jordan has concluded that "the implications of the consumer protection hypothesis . . . are simply not supported by most of the existing evidence."[6] Unfortunately, the implications of a producer protection hypothesis *do* turn out to be consistent with much of the available evidence.

It is therefore interesting to look at a recent study that challenges the basic premise on which the consumer-protection hypothesis rests.[7] This premise is that the point Q_o on Figure 15–6, where long-run average cost is lowest, represents a very large output by the firm. It is argued that dividing the market between two or more firms will mean that each firm operates to the left of Q_o, where its average costs will necessarily be much higher.

The study referred to has concluded that the average cost curve of electric utilities was shaped as in Figure 15–7 in 1970. It is argued that economies and/or diseconomies of scale are not significant between points A and B. This means that a firm using 1970 technologies could expand from about 20 billion kilowatt-hours (KWH) output to about

---

[6] William A. Jordan, "Producer Protection, Prior Market Structure and the Effects of Government Regulation," *Journal of Law and Economics,* vol. 15, no. 1 (April 1972), p. 151.

[7] L. R. Christensen, and W. H. Greene, "Economies of Scale in U.S. Electric Power Generation," *Journal of Political Economy,* vol. 84, no. 4 (August 1976), p. 655.

65 billion KWH without appreciable change in its average cost. Further-more, it is argued that almost half (44.6 percent) of the power used in the United States is generated by firms of this size. This means that the introduction of competition for these large firms could lead to substan-tial changes in the output of each firm without having a significant effect on its average cost, hence on rates.

Perhaps even more interesting is the conclusion that this statement made concerning 1970 could not have been made of 1955, when "there were significant scale economies available to nearly all firms." This is

FIGURE 15–7

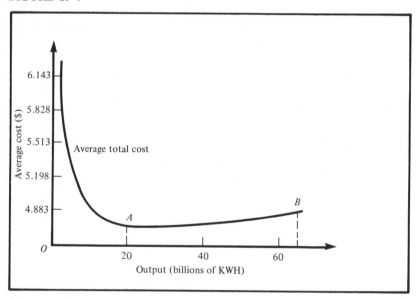

true because the shape of the cost curve changed little between 1955 and 1970, but the size of the market increased sharply. By 1970 a great many firms found themselves large enough to be on the nearly horizon-tal portion of the curve between *A* and *B*. Thus, a policy of public regu-lation based on economies of scale as perceived in 1955 was getting out of date as early as 1970, only 15 years later.

ANOTHER PROPOSAL

Natural monopoly depends, as we said earlier, on the relationship between the output of the firm at Q_o in Figure 15–6 and the size of the market it sells in. The study we have just mentioned suggests what happens when the size of the market increases rapidly while the cost curve remains fairly stable. The shape of the cost curve depends mainly on the technology used, however, and it is obvious that rapid change in technology is one of the most obvious characteristics of our economy. Thus, natural monopoly may be made more or less likely in any given industry by a change in technology that shifts the optimum size for a firm relative to the size of the market. In fact, it has been argued that we ought not to regulate a natural monopoly at all; that we ought instead to let it realize monopoly profits, as these will be a powerful stimulus to the invention of new technologies that will make the optimum-sized firm smaller and thus destroy the monopoly. If this position appears attractive, one should remember that technological change can either increase or decrease the size of an optimum firm. It can either create or destroy natural monopoly, and there seems no reason to believe that one of these is more likely than the other.

MONOPSONY AND BILATERAL MONOPOLY

It is possible to extend monopoly analysis to the case in which the buyer, not the seller, is the monopolist. We are thus proposing the situation in which a single buyer of some good recognizes that he faces the industry supply curve for that good. He thus recognizes that as he buys larger quantities he will move up the usual positively sloped supply curve, bringing about a rise in the price of the good. He is not, therefore, a "price taker." His decisions about quantity demanded will have an effect on price. A firm in this situation is called a monopsonist.

A coal-mining company buying labor in a one-company town is the common example of a monopsonist. In this example, labor is an input to coal production and we have not yet examined input markets. It is an important topic whose monopoly aspects are covered in Chapter 17. Since monopsony is often an input market problem, we have put its analysis in that chapter, but it should be added that the analysis will be the same if the good being bought is not an input. The student may want to look at Chapter 17.[8]

At this point, some student is sure to suggest that if monopoly can occur on either side of the market, then perhaps it can occur on both sides at once. Economists call this the case of bilateral monopoly. It is uncommon in the real world, but again we tend to draw examples from input markets. For instance, it may occur when a labor union sells the services of its members to an employers association representing the firms. We have therefore put off this analysis as well to Chapter 17.

---

[8] The student should also look at the discussion of the special problems connected with the supply curve of the input labor. This can be found in Chapter 17.

PRICE DISCRIMINATION

Sometimes a monopolist finds that his customers buy in two separate markets and that there is no real possibility of resale between them. An electric utility company selling to commercial users on the one hand and residential users on the other is in this position. So is a small-town surgeon selling appendectomies to the rich and the poor. The key to these cases is the impossibility of buying in one market and reselling in the other. In these cases, the monopolist may find it profitable to charge a different price in each market, and we will call him a discriminating monopolist. Consider the two markets shown in Figures 15–8 and 15–9, for instance.

We have shown the demand and marginal revenue curves in each. Now notice that if the monopolist sets the price at P_A in both, the marginal revenue is larger in one market than in the other ($MR_{A2} > MR_{A1}$). Since the goods sold in both markets are being produced by one firm, the cost conditions are the same no matter which market the goods are sold in. Therefore he could increase his profits on the output ($Q_{A1} + Q_{A2}$) by selling less in market 1, where marginal revenue is lower, and more in market 2. For each unit shifted, he gains an amount equal to $MR_{A2} - MR_{A1}$. This means, of course, lowering the price in the second market, raising it in the first, and shifting output until *mar-*

FIGURE 15–8   **FIGURE 15–9**

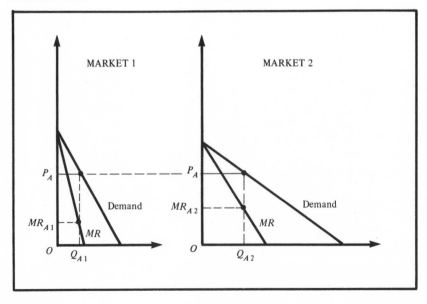

ginal revenue is the same in both. This last statement is a condition for
maximizing profit. It is the profit-maximizing rule for dividing any *given*
total output between the two markets.

We now need to determine what the total output ought to be by
deriving a marginal revenue curve for both markets together and finding
the output that equates marginal cost and this combined marginal
revenue curve.

From Figure 15–10, it is clear that when Q_{B1} is being sold in market
1 then the marginal revenue will be MR_B. When the quantity Q_{B2} is
sold in the second market (Figure 15–11), then the marginal revenue
will also be MR_B. Thus, total sales of $Q_{B1} + Q_{B2}$ can be sold in such a
way that the marginal revenue is the same in both markets and equal to
MR_B. We can plot this situation on Figure 15–12 as a point (B) on
the combined marginal revenue curve. MR_B is the marginal revenue
when $Q_{B1} + Q_{B2} = Q_B$ is being sold. Repeating this process will provide
other points on the curve, and ultimately give us the whole curve.

We will now add a marginal cost curve to Figure 15–12 so that we
can find the total output (Q_C) that maximizes profits to the firm. At
this output, the marginal revenue will be MR_C. We can then look back
at Figures 15–10 and 15–11 to see how to divide that total output between the two markets so that both have the same marginal revenue
(MR_C). Note finally that the separate market demand curves indicate

FIGURE 15–10   **FIGURE 15–11**

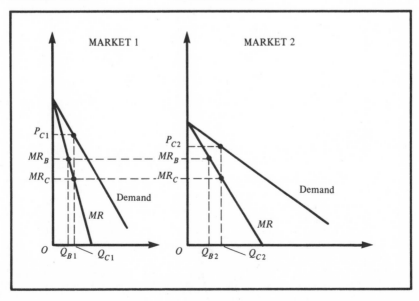

FIGURE 15–12

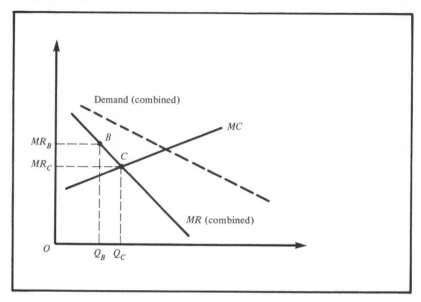

that in order to sell Q_{C1} in the first market, the price will have to be P_{C1}, but that the price will have to be lower (P_{C2}) in the second market in order that Q_{C2} can be sold. The quantity to be sold is thus chosen in such a way as to maximize profits, and the price in each market is then set in such a way that marginal revenue is the same and total output can be sold. Since the price will be higher in one market than in the other, the firm is said to practice price discrimination.

MONOPOLY VERSUS COMPETITION

We will now try to make a comparison of competition and monopoly by analyzing a given industry that is first competitive and then a monopoly. The demand conditions have nothing to do with the way in which the industry is organized, consequently we can use a single demand curve, as in Figure 15–13, for both competitive and monopolistic cases.

If we add an industry supply curve that is the sum of the marginal cost curves of the *competitive* firms, we know there will be a competitive equilibrium price, P_c, and an equilibrium quantity, Q_c. The first important question is, what happens to the supply conditions if all the firms are merged into a single monopoly firm?[9] If all of these firms

---

[9] It is sometimes argued that a monopoly firm does not really have a supply curve. A supply curve is supposed to relate quantity supplied to price. The

FIGURE 15–13

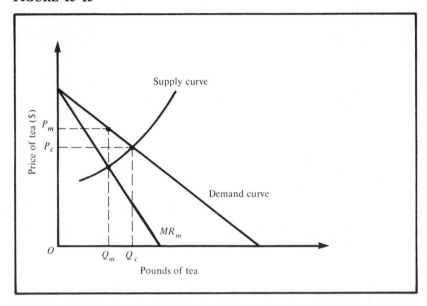

marginal cost curve of a monopoly indicates the quantity that will be supplied at every possible marginal revenue, but marginal revenue is not equal in price. In fact, if the demand curve shifts, then one price may correspond to two different marginal revenues and hence two different quantities supplied, as in the accompanying figure. This can happen even though the marginal cost curve has

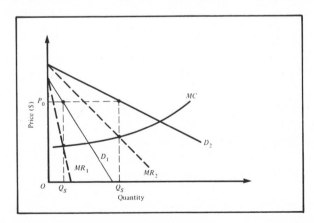

not shifted. Quantity supplied is not uniquely related to price along the marginal cost curve, and many economists are therefore reluctant to call the marginal cost curve a supply curve. However, the marginal cost curve summarizes the supply conditions faced by the firm no matter what it is called and can therefore be used as we have used it, to determine the appropriate level of output.

are of optimum size, then there can be no economies of scale from merging them. There may be some diseconomies, however, as a single management tries to control them all. Thus the long-run marginal cost curve is likely to be higher. This argument suggests that the monoply firm now exceeds optimum size.

The case against monopoly, however, does not rest on the possibility that it may be less effectively managed because it is too large. We will continue to use the supply curve shown in Figure 15–13 but interpret it now as the marginal cost curve of the monopoly. We are picking a special case to facilitate the comparison between monopoly and competition. This is the case in which a competitive industry composed of optimum-sized firms is simply merged into a single monopoly firm with no economies or diseconomies of scale resulting from the merger. We are treating a single supply curve as the sum of the supply curves of the competitive firms or as the marginal cost curve of the monopoly firm.

The case against monopoly rests on the fact that marginal revenue, which still determines the profit-maximizing output, is not the same in both cases. In the competitive case, marginal revenue is equal to price and thus appears at each output as a point on the demand curve. Marginal revenue for the monopolist is, however, always less than price and is shown as the curve MR_m on Figure 15–13. Output for the monopoly will therefore be limited to Q_m instead of Q_c and will be sold at a price P_m. Thus, monopoly means a lower output and a higher price.

If marginal cost reasonably measures the opportunity costs of using additional resources in the monopoly firm, then the firm is forcing its customers to pay more for resources used here than elsewhere. The customer who buys one more unit of the monopolist's output pays more for the resources used to produce it than they are worth in other industries because $P_m > MC$. The monopoly price is a false measure of the opportunity cost of the monopoly good. The consumer who allocates his income on the basis of this "false" price misallocates it.

Another way of looking at the problem is this. When a consumer pays the monopoly price he indicates the value he puts on the resources used. Since this price exceeds their value in other uses (their opportunity cost), he is indicating that they are more valuable to him when used to make the monopoly good. He would be better off if more resources were moved into production of the monopoly good and out of other uses. Too few resources are used to make the monopoly good and its output is too low. Thus we say that monopoly leads to misallocation of resources.

REGULATION

We can ask one final question: "Is it possible to regulate a monopoly in such a way that some of its social disadvantages are eliminated?" One simple proposal is to set price. Suppose in Figure 15–14 that a public utility commission imposes a ceiling price (P_1). This action will change the effective demand curve since the firm can sell any quantity up to Q_1 at the price P_1. P_1AD is the new demand curve, and marginal revenue is now equal to price between P_1 and A. At A there is a break in the new marginal revenue curve as it drops to B and continues along the old curve to the right of B. Marginal revenue is now equal to marginal cost at A, and the firm will choose the output Q_1, which is larger than the monopoly output Q_m.[10]

FIGURE 15–14

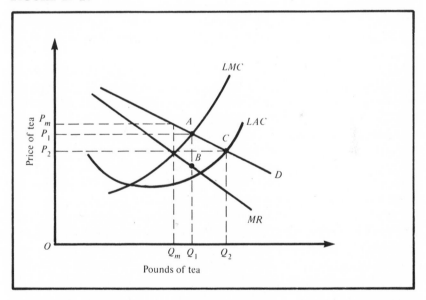

Pursuit of such a policy requires substantial information about cost and demand conditions. It is probably not possible to get really satisfactory data. Nevertheless, a regulatory body might feel justified in trying to set a price in the neighborhood of P_1 as long as that price seemed to be at least high enough to cover average total cost.

Sometimes a commission will try to set the price just high enough

---

[10] This outcome requires that the cost curves slope up to the right, that is, that this is an increasing-cost industry.

to cover average total cost. In Figure 15–14, P_2 is such a price; output would also need to be regulated at Q_2 since marginal cost exceeds marginal revenue at C. These alternatives have generated an elaborate controversy in economic literature that would be interesting to most students.[11]

SUMMARY

The appearance of monopoly in a market will distort the allocation of resources. It will no longer be possible to achieve the optimum allocation that appears in a long-run competitive equilibrium.

This result follows from the fact that a monopoly will sell its output at a price that exceeds its marginal revenue in order to maximize profits. For the same reason it will produce the quantity for which marginal revenue equals marginal cost. When there is competition in all markets but this one, marginal cost measures the opportunity cost of resources used to make the monopoly good. Buyers of the monopoly good obviously place a value on those resources that exceeds opportunity cost because they pay the monopoly price. These resources have greater value to consumers when used to produce the monopoly good than they do in other uses. A shift of resources into the production of this good would therefore make consumers better off.

Much monopoly in our economy is the product of government policies. It is therefore possible to reduce monopoly significantly by changing those policies. This does not happen because those policies are generally believed to be in the best interests of public even though they create and protect monopoly.

Natural monopoly is another important source in our economy. It is dependent on technological conditions and thus subject to continuous change in importance as technology changes. It is usual to deal with natural monopoly through public ownership or regulation. Both of these techniques tend to outlive the existence of the monopoly itself.

This brings to an end our discussion of the model of perfect monopoly. It is the soul mate of perfect competition. Together they have made an almost unbeatable team that has not been loved for its victories. We will now consider a couple of alternatives that have proved delightful but incompetent.

SELECTED READINGS

Coase, R. H. "Some Notes on Monopoly Price," *Review of Economic Studies,* vol. 5 (1937–38), pp. 17–31.

[11] See Nancy Ruggles, "Recent Developments in the Theory of Marginal Cost Pricing," *Review of Economic Studies,* vol. 17 (1949–50), pp. 107–126.

Harberger, A. C. "Monopoly and Resource Allocation," *American Economic Review,* vol. 44 (May 1954), p. 77.

McNulty, P. J. "Economic Theory and the Meaning of Competition," *Quarterly Journal of Economics,* vol. 82 (1968), pp. 639–56.

Smith, Vernon. "An Experimental Study of Competitive Market Behavior," *Journal of Political Economy,* vol. 70 (1972), pp. 111–37.

Stigler, George. "Perfect Competition Historically Contemplated," *Journal of Political Economy,* vol. 65 (1957), pp. 1–17.

Swartzman, D. "The Effect of Monopoly on Price," *Journal of Political Economy,* vol. 67 (1959), pp. 352–62.

Chapter 16

Imperfect Competition

INTRODUCTION

Some economists argue that the model of perfect competition should be used in the analysis of any and all situations where it can be made to work and should be supplemented sometimes by the model of perfect monopoly on the same grounds. This approach is said to lead to the successful prediction of events in a wide variety of circumstances. This position has been strongly associated with economists at the University of Chicago. They point out that the alternative models of monopolistic competition and oligopoly seldom lead to unambiguous predictions. The ambiguity extends to the amount by which some variable, price perhaps, may increase in certain circumstances, and even to the direction of the change in price. Competition and monopoly models are usually unambiguous about the direction of a change and occasionally indicate the size as well.

The Chicago position has not been satisfactory to many other economists. Chicago is not wrong about the ambiguity in the predictions made with the alternative models. The real world, however, displays "a variety of behavior" not permitted by the assumption of perfect competition. The alternative theories are seen as necessary for "handling genuine empirical deviations from perfect competition."[1] Readers will,

---

[1] P. A. Samuelson, "The Monopolistic Competition Revolution." In *Monopolistic Competition Theory,* edited by Robert Kuenne (New York: John Wiley & Sons, 1965).

in fact, discover in this chapter the attractiveness of these theories as descriptions of reality. They seem to lie closer to the real firms and industries we all can observe than any of the earlier materials in this book. Indeed, when Professor Friedman argues that a tax on cigarettes will have the incidence that we would predict if we assumed the cigarette industry to be competitive, one is likely to feel uneasy.[2] Even if Friedman is right about the tax, the cigarette industry does not *look* to be competitive. We are thus tempted to investigate the alternative models, monopolistic competition and oligopoly. While such an investigation is undoubtedly worthwhile, one probably should add that until these alternative theories begin to make more testable predictions of real events, even their pronounced likeness for real firms and real industries will not help them replace perfect competition as a central concept of microeconomic theory.

We can begin the discussion with a few general comments on the meaning of imperfect competition. To be consistent with our definition of perfect competition, we will argue that firms in imperfect competition are not price takers. They have some power to influence price by controlling their own output. We will present their demand curves as less than perfectly elastic. These economic firms will, however, differ from the monopolies of earlier chapters in that any acceptable definition of "commodity" or "industry" must permit more than one firm in the industry.

Industries that meet these conditions are usually divided into two groups. In the first group we put firms whose behavior has a minor impact on any other firm in the same industry. Their decisions, therefore, are not conditioned by anticipation of the response of others. Firms in this industry are "nonrivalrous," and are engaged in what we call monopolistic competition.[3] In the other group, the reaction of rivals is the essence of each firm's problem. We will have occasion to talk about the types of reactions that appear, product differentiation, price cutting, and so on. We should avoid using the term competition in this connection, as in "competitive price cutting," because competition as economists define it excludes rivalry. We are better advised to use the term "rivalrous" in place of "competitive" and call this rivalrous group an oligopoly.

As a final general comment on both groups, we should indicate that the theories to be discussed will all make the standard assumption that these firms seek to maximize profits.

---

[2] Milton Friedman, *Essays in Positive Economics* (Chicago: The University of Chicago Press, 1953), pp. 36–37.

[3] The terms *rivalrous* and *nonrivalrous* were introduced in this context by Robert Kuenne, *The Micro-economic Theory of the Market Mechanism* (New York: Macmillan, 1968).

MONOPOLISTIC COMPETITION

On a descriptive level, there seem to be a number of real industries in the category of monopolistic competition. We have in mind industries in which the number of firms is large. The output of each of the firms is similar enough to belong to the same "product group," but it is differentiated in minor ways among firms. Because we have in mind a large number of firms, we feel justified in making the assumption that the behavior of any one firm impinges very little on any one of the other firms. One firm can therefore act without taking account of possible reactions by the other firms. Moreover, there is enough product differentiation so that we feel justified in assuming that the demand curve for the individual firm has some negative slope. Buyers have enough loyalty to brand so that a small rise in price will not cause the quantity demanded to fall precipitously to zero.

There is a serious problem here. The more successfully these firms differentiate their products, the harder it is to decide that they belong to a single industry. Are Nikon and Kodak both in the same camera industry? Are Instamatic cameras a separate industry? Product differentiation is essential to separate this model from the model of perfect competition, but it also threatens to define the industry so narrowly as to suggest a group of monopolies. Economists do not yet have a satisfactory definition of "product group" as distinguished from "homogeneous commodity." One result is that we will analyze the individual firm and have little to say about the industry.

The analysis of the behavior of a monopolistically competitive firm is very much like the analysis of a monopoly. The demand curve will have negative slope as in Figure 16–1. Its negative slope requires that marginal revenue for any level of sales be less than price so that the *MR* curve will lie below the demand curve. Since we are assuming profit maximization, the firm will produce the quantity for which $MR = MC$. Thus in Figure 16–1, it will produce Q_1 and sell this output at price P_1.

It is almost explicit in our definition of this industry that entry is rather easy. The industries where we expect to apply this model have many small firms producing somewhat different products. It is reasonable to assume that another firm could enter and produce a still different variety without difficulty. With ease of entry, any monopoly profits are likely to vanish in the long run. If monopoly profits exist, then the industry will attract new firms. These new firms will lure some customers away from the old firms, shifting their demand curves to the left. The new firms may also bid up the prices of some inputs, causing average cost curves to rise. In the long run, the average total cost curve is likely to appear as it is represented in Figure 16–1 so that at the price P_1, long-run average costs are likely to be equal to average

FIGURE 16-1

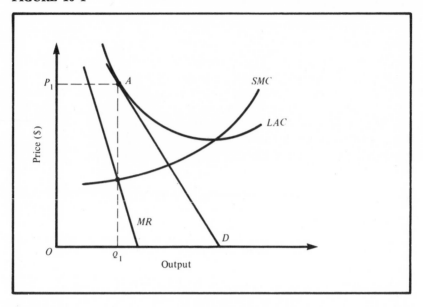

revenues indicated by the demand curve, and profits are zero. (Remember that for economists, average total costs include a "normal" return on investment.) It is obvious that the firm is not operating at the lowest point on its long-run average cost curve. If it could expand along that curve, it could produce additional output at lower average costs, an advantage from the point of view of society. It has, in this sense, an excess capacity at its profit-maximizing output, and this is sometimes called "the excess capacity theorem" of monopolistic competition.

In the course of this analysis, we have acted as if the demand curve is a given for each firm. However, sometimes the forces that cause this firm to move along its demand curve toward point A of Figure 16-1 will push other firms along their demand curves too. Their moves are not in any sense a rivalrous response to each other. They are, instead, a profit-maximizing response to changing cost and demand conditions that hit all firms in the product group. Since these firms produce very similar commodities, however, we cannot assume that the demand curve of one of them will remain constant as all others adjust their prices. Therefore, as one firm tries to move along its demand curve toward a point like A, it may find that the whole curve is shifting because other firms are also altering their prices. Hence the demand curve will not accurately predict what will happen to quantity demanded when a price change results from factors that affect other firms in the industry as well.

A FEW MORE COMMENTS

Under monopolistic competition we can find a motive for a behavior that is very common in the real world but not usually logical for competitive or monopolistic firms. A firm in monopolistic competition has a reason to advertise and incur other selling costs. Two outcomes are possible if the advertising is successful. The demand curve may become less elastic and it may shift to the right. As it becomes less elastic, the degree of monopoly power (customer loyalty) is increased. Customers are convinced that the special features of this commodity are very important, and they are thus willing to buy almost as much at a somewhat higher price. They may also become convinced that this commodity is really better than the others in the same product group and be willing to buy larger quantities at every price. This we would represent by shifting the entire demand curve to the right. It also helps the firm in that a shift to the right will reduce the elasticity at each price.

The most important thing to be said on behalf of the theory of monopolistic competition is that it attempts to deal with another very widespread phenomenon, namely, product differentiation. Perfectly competitive firms with their horizontal demand curves have no need to differentiate their products. They can sell all they want at the market price and so the competitive model makes no comments on differentiation. The monopolistic competitor, however, searches continuously for a successful differentiation, one that will make his demand curve less elastic, an innovation so attractive that it makes his firm a monopoly. When customers are not well informed, a firm may actually use a price difference as a means of differentiating its product. The firm takes advantage of the belief we all exercise at one time or another, that what costs more is worth more. Both innovations and price differentials usually fail in the long run to create a monopoly. The innovation is imitated by rivals or proves uninteresting to customers. The most a firm can usually hope for is a temporary advantage, but that will often be important enough to warrant the effort.

OLIGOPOLY

We have already argued that oligopoly firms are not price takers. Their demand curves have negative slope and their position is similar to that of a monopoly, but with an important difference. The industry contains more than one firm, though the number is still small. Small numbers mean that they act with explicit consciousness of their rivalry with each other. In fact, each model of oligopoly behavior can be characterized by the assumption it makes about the reactive behavior of rivals. It should be added that if we are asked to explain the causes of an industry with a small number of large firms, we will refer to those factors used to explain monopoly itself and, especially, to the notion of natural monopoly (see Chapter 15).

The statements above are meant as an initial definition of oligopoly. They are descriptive of some characteristics of a number of industries. The automobile industry in the United States is often cited as an example. One would not be surprised to find that the demand curves of Ford, General Motors, and Chrysler are less than infinitely elastic. Their rivalry over design, price, and advertising often makes news.[4] Nevertheless, the object of the definition is not to describe an industry but to predict behavior. In the end, an oligopoly is an industry in which the theory of oligopoly can be successfully used. We have expressed the same view with regard to both competition and monopoly earlier in these chapters.

EARLY MODELS

The analysis of oligopoly behavior dates at least from the French economist, Cournot, in the 19th century.[5] The essential feature of his model was the proposal that each firm in a simple two-firm industry assumes that the other firm will not change its existing level of output. Firm A could then choose a profit-maximizing output given the existing output of B. Once Firm A has chosen, then Firm B is presumed to make the same assumption about the fixity of Firm A's output and pick for itself a profit-maximizing output. As each firm is imagined to readjust to the previous decision of the other, a series of steps is laid out that lead to an equilibrium output for each firm. This output is smaller than the competitive output and larger than the monopoly output for the same cost and demand conditions. It was the very fact that this simple assumption led to a stable equilibrium position that made this model interesting to economists.

Edgeworth offered a criticism of this model in the form of a proposal that each firm assumes that the other will hold price constant, not quantity.[6] With this slight change in the assumption, however, no stable equilibrium will ever be reached and the Cournot approach becomes much less interesting. Also important is the fact that both models

---

[4] These firms confuse their rivalry with competition. They like to refer to their industry as competitive because of the favorable connotations of that word. It is not, however, competitive in the economic meaning because, in fact, it is rivalrous and competition is not.

[5] Augustin Cournot, *Recherches sur les Principes Mathematiques de la Theorie des Riches,* trans. Nathaniel Bacon (New York: Macmillan, 1897).

[6] F. Edgeworth, "Lo Teoria Pura del Monopolio", *Giornale degli Economisti* (1897).

depend on the willingness of the two rivals to go on making the same mistake about each other over and over again. Each one must assume repeatedly that the other will not alter his price (or output) immediately after he has done so. While this is not at all realistic, we might be willing to overlook that and use the device if it were more successful in making predictions.

In 1933, Chamberlain suggested an improvement.[7] He proposed that after each firm has had some experience with the behavior of the other, one of them might decide to set the monopoly price for the whole industry and then to sell half of the total demanded at that price, hoping that the other firm would also see the wisdom of this policy and be willing to cooperate without explicit collusion. The two firms would thus split the monopoly profit and prices would be relatively stable.

In those real industries that we feel are most likely to be oligopolies, great rigidity of prices has been noted. Chamberlain's model offers some explanation of this observation, but so does one advanced in 1939 by Paul Sweezy.[8] He suggested that any price cut by Firm A is likely to be matched by other firms in the industry, but a price rise is not so likely to be matched. Thus the demand curve for Firm A is more elastic at prices above the existing price than at prices below it. The demand curve is kinked as in Figure 16–2 at E. As a result, the marginal revenue curve has a discontinuity between A and B. The marginal cost curve (SMC) can shift considerably, but as long as it crosses the marginal revenue curve between A and B, P_1 will remain the most profitable price.

Economists, however, have not found this an adequate model of oligopoly pricing. There is, for instance, evidence that price rises are matched by rival firms. This evidence first appeared in an article by George Stigler in 1947.[9] It was supported more recently in a study of the drug industry.[10] In that industry, price increases and decreases for oligopoly products from 1964 to 1973 were found to be *in*consistent with the predictions of the kinky demand curve in 76 percent of the cases. This means that rival firms either matched each other's price rises, or did not follow one another's price cuts, or made price changes in the opposite direction from a rival's change. In fact, an examination

[7] Edward Chamberlain, *The Theory of Monopolistic Competition* (Cambridge, Mass.: Harvard University Press, 1933).

[8] Paul Sweezy, "Demand Under Conditions of Oligopoly," *Journal of Political Economy*, vol. 67 (August 1939), p. 568.

[9] G. Stigler, "The Kinky Oligopoly Demand Curve and Rigid Prices," *Journal of Political Economy*, 1947.

[10] Walter J. Primeaux, Jr., and Mark R. Bomball. "A Reexamination of the Kinky Oligopoly Demand Curve," *Journal of Political Economy*, vol. 82, no. 4 (July–August 1974), p. 851.

FIGURE 16-2

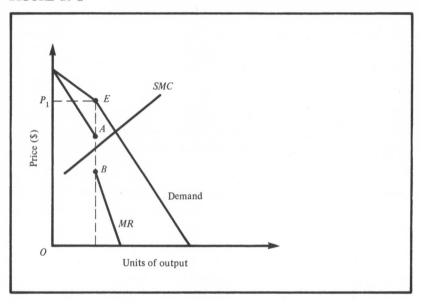

of all evidence available up to 1974[11] led to the conclusion that, "There have been no empirical studies confirming the pricing behavior predicted by the [kinky demand curve] hypothesis."

Finally, it should be added that a kink in the demand curve might explain rigidity at the price P_1 in Figure 16–2, but it does not offer any explanation of the size of P_1 itself.

GAME THEORIES

The most recent oligopoly models involve application of the theory of games. This is not surprising since the key characteristic of the theory of oligopoly is the existence of rivals and the need of each rival to take account of the behavior of others. This is a key characteristic of most of the games we play. One can get a feeling for the game-theory approach by examining a two-person zero-sum game. This is one of the simplest models, but it has most of the essential characteristics.

Our "two persons" will be two firms. Each firm is considering perhaps three alternative actions, which we will call strategies. We might have in mind three levels of advertising budget, or three different output levels, or a set of alternative proposals for adding new products and

[11] Walter J. Primeaux, Jr., and Mickey C. Smith, "Pricing Patterns and the Kinky Demand Curve," *Journal of Law and Economics*, vol. 19 (April 1976), p. 189.

dropping old ones from the product line. The number of alternatives is not important, but three will keep the problem simple. "Zero sum" means that we are going to imagine these firms to be *very* close rivals, so that whatever one gains the other loses. We can then set up a payoff matrix, as in Table 16–1. In each box is written the profit of Firm *A* that would result if each firm chose the indicated strategies. Thus if Firm *A* chose strategy number one and *B* also chose number one, then Firm *A* would make a profit of three and Firm *B* would lose three. *A*'s profits are *B*'s losses, and the table can be read either way.

TABLE 16–1

Firm A *strategies*	*Firm B strategies*			*Row* *minimums*
	1	2	3	
1	3	2	4	2 (maximin)
2	−1	1	2	−1
3	+1	2	4	+1
Column *maximums*	3	2 (minimax)	4	

Which is the best strategy for each firm? Firm *A* can assume that if it chooses strategy 1, then Firm *B* will choose strategy 2. Firm *B* would thus minimize its losses. In fact, Firm *B* can be assumed to behave this way, no matter what choice is made by *A*. This is the essential assumption! *A* will assume that no matter how he chooses, *B* will try to minimize *A*'s profits. Consequently, Firm *A* will want to know the minimum for each strategy. It can then pick the strategy with the largest minimum. The minimums are shown in the column on the right, labeled "row minimums." Clearly Firm *A* should choose strategy 1 because the worst it can do is realize a profit of 2. The other two strategies would result in smaller profits or actual losses.

Meanwhile Firm *B* follows a similar line of reasoning. It wants to pick the strategy that gives *A* the smallest profit and, therefore, gives *B* the smallest loss. It looks for the maximum in each column. These maximums are listed in the bottom row of Table 16–1. Clearly if Firm *B* chooses strategy 2, then the profits of Firm *A* cannot exceed 2 no matter what choice is made by *A*. Either of the other strategies promise larger profits to *A*, which means larger losses to Firm *B*. Firm *B* picks the smallest of maximums, the "minimax," from the bottom row. Firm *A*, as noted above, picks the largest minimum from the last column, the "maximin." Firm *A* chooses strategy 1 and *B* chooses 2. The two choices constitute an equilibrium combination of strategies. Neither firm can benefit from a further change as long as the other sits tight.

Slight changes in the payoffs in this matrix, however, may create a game that is not stable. It will not have a "saddle point" as the one above. Then the firms must shift from single strategies to mixed strategies. That is, instead of choosing a given strategy and sticking with it, they must switch from one to another and decide what proportion of the time to spend with each.

Economists have explored much more complex games than the zero-sum game. For a while it appeared that once we understood the mathematics of complex games we would have useful models of reality. Not so. Reality has remained still more complex. Moreover, economists have begun to have doubts about the "conservatism" of behavior in game theories. The minimax principle, which underlies most of these theories, requires that rivals expect the worst from each other and try to minimize the damage it can do. Real entrepreneurs often take much more optimistic views and make their decisions in expectation of favorable conditions.

Each of the models we have described results from a particular assumption about the type of reaction a firm can expect of its rivals. We have not considered all possible assumptions. The list is much longer. The core of the problem is that we lack information. In spite of substantial study of industries, we do not know which assumptions or perhaps combinations of assumptions are empirically important. Nor do we know the circumstances in which one rather than another may be important. When we can answer those questions, we should be able to simplify what now appears to be a very large variety of noncompetitive situations.

A FEW MORE NOTES ON OLIGOPOLY

We have noted several times the tendency for oligopoly prices to be relatively stable. The small number of firms and their close rivalry suggest that price cutting is likely to be painful.[12] This has most certainly been the conclusion of firms that have experienced price wars. It would not be surprising if attempts were made in some industries to prevent these wars through the establishment of a price leader. Price leadership does not imply collusion. Quite the contrary. It appears where collusion is illegal or difficult. It means merely that most firms in the industry set the same price as the leader and change when he does.

Who is the leader? Economists describe two types. The first is called a "dominant firm." If the industry has one very large firm and a num-

---

[12] It is possible that the danger of price wars decreases as the differentiation of products increases. Customer loyalty reduces the effect on demand of a change in the rival's price.

ber of smaller ones, the large firm may set its own price and let the smaller firms sell all they want at that price. This price is assumed to be profit-maximizing for the large firm. In Figure 16–3 we have drawn the industry demand curve and labeled it *ID*. This curve shows the total amounts that can be sold at each price, no matter how the industry is organized. We assume in this model that the small firms will take as given any price set by the dominant firm. They will therefore act like the usual competitive firm. Each will determine its output by setting its marginal cost equal to the given price. Thus, the marginal cost curve is the supply curve of each individual firm and these can be added to give the small firm supply curve (*SFS*) on Figure 16–3.

We can now find the demand curve for the dominant firm alone. By assumption, it will let the small firms sell all they want at each price and sell whatever remains of the total demand itself. For instance, at a price P_0, the small firms will sell Q_A out of a total industry demand of Q_B leaving $Q_C = Q_B - Q_A$ to be sold by the dominant firm. Thus, at a price of P_0 the dominant firm faces a demand for Q_C, and so the point C is one point on its demand curve. By making the same subtraction $ID - SFS = DFD$ at every price, we can develop the dominant firm demand curve (*DFD*) as shown on Figure 16–3.

Since the dominant firm is presumed to maximize profits, it will want to produce the quantity for which marginal cost and marginal revenue are equal. We can find its marginal revenue curve from its

FIGURE 16–3

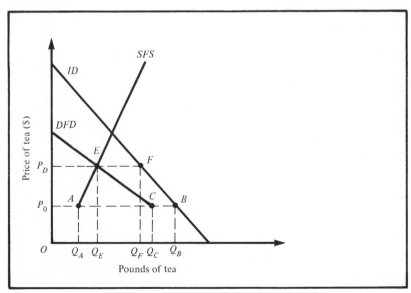

FIGURE 16–4

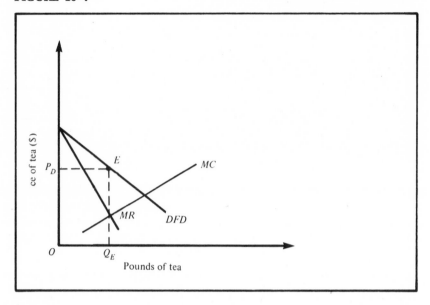

demand curve,[13] and both are shown in Figure 16–4. Adding the marginal cost curve of the dominant firm to Figure 16–4, we can determine its profit maximizing price P_D and output Q_E. Going back to Figure 16–3 we find that at the price P_D, total demand will be Q_F, of which Q_E will be supplied by the dominant firm and the rest $(Q_F - Q_E)$ by the small firms.

It was noted earlier in this chapter that each oligopoly model can be characterized by the assumption it makes about the behavior of rivals. In this case, the assumption is that all the small firms will take the price as given and respond like perfect competitors. It is this assumption that leads to the fairly simple equilibrium solution outlined above, although it is probably not really useful to call all the small firms "rivals."

The other type of price leader is called a "barometric firm." The name is meant to imply that this firm is especially sensitive to those changes in supply or demand conditions that will require a change in price. Other firms in the industry therefore watch this firm and follow its lead in pricing. The firm is believed to have especially good management, and hence some prestige may attach to being the price leader. If a struggle for leadership develops, it will lead to price fluctuations that are unwanted and prevent the leader from performing his basic function, namely, providing price stability.

---

[13] Any student who has forgotten the relationship between demand and marginal revenue curves should look back at Chapter 5.

OTHER FORMS OF RIVALRY

Price leadership does not, however, eliminate rivalry among the firms in the industry. Price changes are merely the most obvious manifestation of such a rivalry. Because they are obvious to rivals and customers as well, they bring quick retaliation and the threat of instability and price wars. However, if they can be controlled, then the rivalry will turn in other directions. Firms will differentiate their products, advertise vigorously, spend large sums on product design and packaging, offer credit and service facilities to their customers, and so on. These actions are less disruptive. The results of advertising or packaging or a particular innovation are not immediately obvious. Special credit terms can often be kept secret. Immediate retaliation is less likely and life in the industry more comfortable because the effects of these kinds of changes are much harder to evaluate. Of course, if they are harder for rivals to evaluate, then they are also likely to be harder for customers to evaluate. If so, they are not likely to be very attractive to customers and so may give little advantage to the firm that uses them.

CARTELS

The fear of destructive behavior may also lead rivals to collude. The firms in an industry may try by agreement to set prices, keep them stable, and regulate the timing of any necessary changes. A group of firms that reaches such an agreement is called a cartel. In the United States, collusion is illegal in almost all cases. The agreements must be made in secret and kept secret. There are, however, some exceptions. We permit some professions to set minimum-fee schedules and to discipline members who charge lower prices. We permit some producers' associations, like the orange growers, to set prices and control marketing. Other examples could also be found.

Firms that enter into secret agreements have two important objectives. They want to make larger profits and they want to stabilize the market in which they sell. Though we tend to think of profits as the main reason for collusion, it is true that stability is often more important. What the firm wants is some protection against actions by its rivals that abruptly alter its demand curve. Price cutting by a rival is merely the most obvious of such threatening behaviors. Studies of the behavior of businessmen are replete with examples of efforts to insulate the firm from the actions of rivals.

A cartel agreement will almost always include a clause that sets the price of the jointly produced good. One reason is that the price may then be set in such a way as to increase the total profits of the industry. If the cartel is strong enough, it can treat the industry as a single-firm monopoly. For reasons we will soon discuss, cartels are not usually this well organized. Nevertheless, if the price is to be raised at all, then the negative slope of the demand curve tells us that quantity sold will have to be smaller, and the positive slope of the supply curve tells us that individual firms will want to increase their outputs. The cartel must, therefore, control output as well as price. It must have some technique for rationing the quantity demanded (at the cartel price) among suppliers. Control of output will also be used to stabilize the market by giving each cartel member some guaranteed share. Moreover, the cartel may try to regulate still other behaviors that give special advantage to one firm. The techniques that the cartels have used are very numerous and fascinating. In summary, they are a testimony to human ingenuity, but rather than describe them here, we will look at the conditions under which they are likely to appear and then some of the reasons they are likely to be unsuccessful.

The Department of Justice investigates a number of complaints about price fixing every year. These investigations assemble information about firms and the markets in which they operate. This information becomes a report that is used to decide whether to file a case. Some 50 to 60 such reports were recently analyzed to determine which characteristics price fixing cases have in common.[14]

It was found that most price-fixing agreements cover some product or market in which the number of firms is small. Seventy-nine percent of these agreements involve ten or fewer firms. It was also found that there was a high degree of industrial concentration in most of these cases. The four largest firms sold more than 50 percent of the output in 38 out of 50 cases. One other characteristic also seems important, and that is geographic location. Conspiracies are more likely to develop if the firms are all located in the same geographic area. These three findings are somewhat surprising as they run counter to the argument that small, concentrated industries do not need explicit conspiracy agreements. Presumably, they find it easy to engage in various forms of tacit collusion, and meetings and formal agreements need be used only where the group of firms involved is large. Such is not the case, however, and this suggests that the low cost of organization and the reduced chance of being caught that go with small numbers and concentrated production are important stimulants to conspiracy.

INSTABILITY OF CARTELS

Against this must be set some of the problems of a conspiracy, and the most important of these is the need for secrecy because the agree-

---

[14] George A. Hay and Daniel Kelley, "An Empirical Survey of Price Fixing Conspiracies," *Journal of Law and Economics,* vol. 17 (April 1974), p. 13.

ment is illegal. Every cartel action is hindered by this need. For instance, the cartel must be able to detect a violation by one of its members. The incentives for any one firm to be a "chiseler" are very strong. It can make a secret price agreement with one or a few special customers. Such an agreement can be made attractive to both parties, so that the customer helps to keep it secret. The cartel cannot count on any government statistical agency for information about member behavior. It has no recourse to the courts to force disclosure by the firms involved. What this effectively means is that detection of a violation of the agreement is likely to be very expensive.

Both detection and enforcement problems are, of course, magnified if there are many firms in the industry and entry of new firms is easy. Restriction of entry usually requires the support by the government in some way. We have already discussed this problem in connection with monopoly in Chapter 15. The cartel certainly cannot expect direct government help in keeping new firms out, although it may be able to use some of the standard devices like patents. It may, therefore, be very expensive for existing firms to keep out new firms. It is easy to see that the cost of a cartel agreement could easily exceed any benefit that could be gained.

Testimony in the 1960s at the trial of a cartel in the electrical equipment industry confirms these problems. In the 25 years before 1960, the industry tried repeatedly to reach an agreement that would survive, but none lasted more than 18 months. Contracts in this industry are awarded by secret bid. The cartel sought to designate which member firm should be low bidder on each major contract. The others were then supposed to bring in higher bids, and thus the available demand would be rationed among member firms at a price (the bid) that provided adequate profits. At least one member, however, always seemed to be in such financial straits that the temptation to underbid the designated firm and get an extra contract was not resisted.[15]

This discussion is much too brief for such a colorful and complex topic. An interested student might want to look further at the literature.[16]

SUMMARY

Firms in imperfect competition find that the price at which they can sell their output depends in part on the size of that output. Some firms in this position must be concerned about the behavior of their rivals in

---

[15] *The Wall Street Journal:* January 10–12, 1962.

[16] George W. Stocking and Myron W. Watkins, *Cartels in Action* (New York: Twentieth Century Fund, 1946).

the same industry, and these firms are called oligopolies. Others, called monopolistic competitors, need have no such concern.

Analysis of the behavior of monopolistic competitors is much like the analysis of single-firm monopoly. Where it can be used, it makes much the same predictions.

Oligopolies are explained by a very large number of models, which is the equivalent of saying that none of these models is very good. Collusion as a substitute for rivalry turns out to be very difficult unless the government can somehow be induced to support it.

Thus the argument made at the beginning of this lecture should by now be clear. Models of imperfect competition have nothing like the range of testable implications that one can draw out of the competitive assumption. This is a serious, and in the long run, fatal failing. On the other hand, they have descriptive attractiveness. They talk about advertising, product differentiation, price leadership and other things that are very familiar parts of the real world. We are therefore reluctant to give them up and, instead, keep looking for ways to make them more useful in the predictive sense.

SELECTED READINGS

Harrod, R. F. "The Theory of Imperfect Competition Revised." In Harrod, R. F., *Economic Essays* (New York: Harcourt Brace, 1952), pp. 139–87.

Modigliani, Franco. "New Developments on the Oligopoly Front," *Journal of Political Economy*, vol. 66 (1958), pp. 215–32.

Stigler, George J. *Five Essays on Economic Problems* (New York: Macmillan, 1950), pp. 12–24.

Chapter 17

Input Markets

INTRODUCTION

As firms produce goods to sell to consumers, they create markets for inputs. Thus the demand for inputs (or factors of production or productive resources, to use other names) is a "derived demand." The most important thing to say about input markets is that economic theory treats them in the same way it treats output or final-good markets. Economists use all the techniques we have developed in earlier chapters in their analysis. Since we have already examined these techniques at length, we are well equipped for a look at input markets.

The next most important thing to note is that the two sets of markets *must* be completely interdependent. The prices of inputs influence costs in the output markets. The price of output influences demand in the input market. As each market seeks its own equilibrium price, it is constrained in certain ways by the other. For instance, the equilibrium price of the final good must be high enough to cover the cost of enough inputs to produce the equilibrium supply of the final good, and the prices of the inputs must be high enough to get suppliers to produce the needed amounts. Therefore, we should not be surprised if the analysis of the way a firm decides on the scale of output and the proportion among inputs can now be used to explain the way it decides to hire certain quantities of each input.

Before starting the discussion of input markets, it should be noted that one of the hazards of a discussion of input markets is the tendency to think of labor as if it were *the* input. To many of us, it is the most

341

significant input because it is our own labor that is "put in." Even text-books sometimes analyze the determination of input prices as if they were analyzing the determination of wage rates. If wage rates are analyzed with the techniques used earlier in this book, the result is a "Marginal Productivity Theory of Wages." This theory reaches the conclusion the wage will be just equal to the value added to total output by the marginal unit of labor. Historically this has been one of the most important explanations of wages. The same model is used for the explanation of other input prices and will be developed below. As applied to labor, however, it has been one of the most controversial parts of economic theory.

Labor is, after all, supplied by human beings. Its employment is surrounded by elaborate legal regulations, ancient customs and traditions and special forms of discrimination and prejudice. These factors are frequently inconsistent with behavior designed to maximize; that is, with economic behavior. They make analysis of labor markets more complex and different in substance from other markets. Therefore, we will deal systematically only with markets in which the input is a commodity. There is some further discussion of labor-market peculiarities later in this chapter, but it is clear that the determination of wage rates is a study in itself and ought not to be stuffed into one corner of a general treatment of micro-theory.

The analysis of input markets starts with a couple of assumptions that will startle no one. The first is the assumption that firms try to maximize profits in input markets as elsewhere. Since the production choices analyzed earlier involved the decision to produce a profit-maximizing output after buying a bundle of inputs, we can hardly let motives change now without destroying the interdependence of input and output markets. As a second assumption, let us assert perfectly competitive conditions in input markets. This is a big help in simplifying the argument. We will stick to it through the first part of this chapter, but later we will explore what happens if we relax the competitive assumption in a number of ways.

MAXIMIZING IN OUTPUT MARKETS: A REVIEW

Firms want inputs because they cannot produce without them. The quantity demanded is closely related to the level of output chosen by the firm. In the long run, the firm will choose the profit-maximizing output level; that is, the level for which

$$LMC = MR.$$

We can think of this as the criterion that determines the scale of operations. The quantity demanded of any one input depends as well on the proportions among inputs. Profit-maximizing also sets the criterion for proportions by laying down the rule that:

$$\frac{MP_A}{P_A} = \frac{MP_B}{P_B} = \cdot \cdot \cdot = \frac{MP_Z}{P_Z},$$

where A through Z are all possible inputs to the process. These two criteria appeared in earlier chapters, when only final good markets were discussed. We must now adapt them to input markets.

Suppose the firm is considering larger and larger outputs of apple pie using more and more apples and other inputs. We will assume that apples are a "normal" input, because it seems reasonable that more apple pie will require more apples, though pie output and apple inputs need not increase at the same rate. The decision to make more and more pie is the decision to move to higher and higher isoquants on the production surface or hill, as in Figure 17–1. On each level, the firm will want to satisfy the criterion about proportions. It will thus move around the hill along each isoquant until

$$\frac{MP_A}{P_A} = \frac{MP_B}{P_B} = \cdot \cdot \cdot = \frac{MP_Z}{P_Z},$$

where we are letting MP_A be the marginal product of apples and P_A the price of apples. For long-run decisions about output, all inputs will be variable and this criterion can be completely met. Any point on the isoquant *can* be chosen, and the least-cost point will be chosen. In the short run, at least one input is not variable, and for many short-run choices more than one input will be fixed. Nevertheless, the firm will

FIGURE 17–1

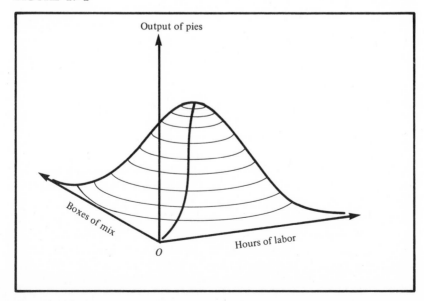

use this criterion to determine the proportions among all of the variable inputs during each possible short-run period.

As the firm moves up the hill from the least-cost point on one isoquant to the least-cost point on the next isoquant, it will be seeking the scale for which

$$LMC_\pi = MR_\pi,$$

where LMC_π is the long-run marginal cost of apple pie and MR_π its marginal revenue. In dealing with a single firm, our competitive assumption will let us equate the marginal revenue of another apple pie to the price of pie. Hence

$$LMC_\pi = MR_\pi = P_\pi.$$

MAXIMIZING IN INPUT MARKETS

Now we can relate these profit-maximizing criteria to their equivalents in the input market. If the price of apples is P_A per bushel, then we would expect the firm to buy apples until

$$P_A = VMP_A,$$

where VMP_A is the value of the marginal product of a bushel of apples. If one more bushel of apples is bought and put into the production process, then VMP_A is the revenue from selling the additional pies. It is thus

$$VMP = (MP_A)P_\pi.$$

That is to say, it is the marginal product, seven apple pies, perhaps, multiplied by the market price for those pies. The firm will want to buy more apples and make more pie whenever

$$P_A < VMP_A$$

and to reduce its purchases of apples and make fewer pies whenever

$$P_A > VMP_A.$$

This is another application of the logic used in Chapter 9 to argue that profits will be maximized at the output for which marginal cost equals marginal revenue. In the apple case VMP_A is the addition to total revenue from selling the output of one more bushel of apples, and P_A is the addition to costs. As long as $P_A < VMP_A$, the firm expands because it thereby increases its revenues more than its costs, and is made better off by the difference.

We have, therefore, a profit-maximizing criterion for hiring inputs and thus determining the scale of output. The quantity of apples bought also determines the amount of pie made, so we appear to have two criteria for choosing the right scale of output. They are that

$$LMC_\pi = MR_\pi = P_\pi \text{ (in the final-goods market)}$$

and

$$P_A = VMP_A \text{ (in the input market).}$$

Presumably these two criteria will specify the same scale when the firm is in equilibrium, for the firm can produce only one output at a time. We can, in fact, convert one of these criteria into the other very easily by noting that

$$MC_\pi = \frac{P_A}{MP_A} \cdot {}^1$$

This means that if, for example, another bushel of apples will cost \$3 (P_A) and will add ten pies (MP_A) to output, then the added cost, the marginal cost of one pie (MC_π), is

$$\frac{P_A}{MP_A} = \frac{\$3}{10} = 30\text{¢} = MC_\pi.$$

If we now rewrite the criterion for scale in the final-goods market by putting in this information, we get

$$LMC_\pi = \frac{P_A}{MP_A} = MR_\pi = P_\pi,$$

and multiplying the second and fourth of these equal quantities by MP_A, we get

$$MP_A \frac{P_A}{MP_A} = P_\pi \cdot MP_A,$$

which reduces to

$$P_A = VMP_A.$$

This last expression is the scale criterion in the input market introduced above. Thus, when there is equilibrium in both markets, which includes an equilibrium price for pie (P_π), an equilibrium price for apples (P_A), and a particular marginal product for apples (MP_A) determined by the quantity of apples actually used, the two criteria for determining scale of operations are equivalent to each other. It is worth adding that even though we have considered only the input of apples in arriving at these conclusions, we could have used any of the variable inputs because of the requirements of profit-maximizing at equilibrium. We started this argument with the expression

$$MC_\pi = \frac{P_A}{MP_A},$$

---

[1] The reciprocal relationship between marginal cost and marginal product was first introduced in Chapter 10.

which can be rewritten

$$\frac{1}{MC_\pi} = \frac{MP_A}{P_A}.$$

Equilibrium requires that

$$\frac{MP_A}{P_A} = \frac{MP_B}{P_B} = \cdots = \frac{MP_Z}{P_Z},$$

and therefore we can write

$$\frac{1}{MC\pi} = \frac{MP_B}{P_B} \quad \text{or} \quad MC_\pi = \frac{P_B}{MP_B}$$

for any input from A to Z.

Thus both input and output markets precribe the same profit-maximizing level of output for equilibrium, and this is true no matter which input market we consider.

THE INPUT DEMAND CURVE

We can now switch attention to the input market for apples with complete confidence that we are dealing with the same choice problem dealt with earlier in output markets. What we want is a demand (and later a supply) curve for bushels of apples. Firms want apples because their marginal product has value. As noted above, they want to buy apples until

$$VMP_A = P_A.$$

If we can find the value of the marginal product of every quantity of apples, we can determine the quantity that will be demanded at each price.

The value of the marginal product depends on the size of the marginal product iself (MP_A) and on the price at which apple pie is sold (P_π). The marginal product curve is derived from the production function and the student may want to look back at Chapter 10, and especially Figure 10–5, where we have derived the marginal product curve for an input. The graph of this curve is reproduced in Figure 17–2 and indicates that marginal product may rise at first, but it *will* ultimate decline. In the short run it declines because of the law of variable proportions, and in the long run because the firm faces decreasing returns to scale.[2]

---

[2] In many textbooks, the marginal product curve for an input is prepared on the assumption that quantities of all *other* inputs are held constant along it. If for any reason a change in the proportions among inputs is necessary (the firm decides to increase its scale of operations, for instance), then a new marginal product curve is necessary. In this book, however, we have assumed that the

FIGURE 17–2

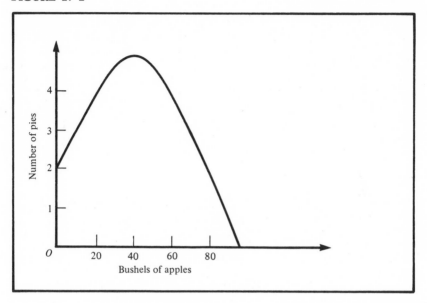

We can convert this marginal-product curve into a value-of-the-marginal-product curve (*VMP*) by multiplying the physical amounts shown in Figure 17–2 by some price for apple pie. We have to change the verticle axis from number of apple pies to dollars' worth of apple pies. Suppose pies are selling for $1 each, then the value of the marginal product starts at about $2 (two pies on Figure 17–2 at $1 each), appears to rise to about $5, and then falls to zero when 90 bushels of apples are used. This curve is shown in Figure 17–3. The positively sloped portion is drawn as a dashed line because a profit-maximizing firm would not operate on this portion.[3] If the price of apples is P_A, the firm will *not* want to limit its purchases to 20 bushels because

$$VMP_A > P_A$$

for the 21st bushel and all additional bushels until B (Q_B equals about 60 bushels) is reached.

The curve in Figure 17–3 is drawn on the assumption that apple pies are selling for $1 each. We can obviously get a whole family of *VMP*

proportion among variable inputs is a least-cost proportion at every output. Consequently there is only one marginal product curve, along which proportions among variable factors are permitted to change as necessary to provide for least cost.

[3] There is a possible exception to this rule when the firm is a monopoly that finds marginal cost equal to marginal revenue along the declining portion of its marginal cost curve.

FIGURE 17–3

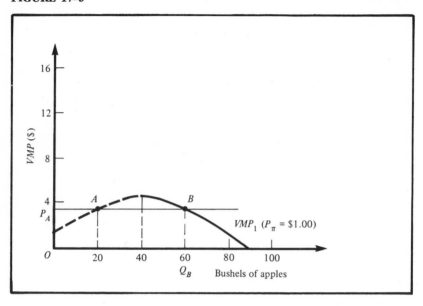

curves by considering other pie prices as in Figure 17–4. VMP_2 represents the value of the marginal product of apples when apple pies sell for \$2 each, and so on.

Now consider some particular price for apples represented by the horizontal line $P_A = 5$ on Figure 17–4. This horizontal line crosses the family of VMP curves. At each intersection the price of apples (P_A) is equal to the value of their marginal product, and at each intersection apple pie has a different price. At B, for instance,

$$P_A = 5, P_\pi = 2, \text{ and } MP_A = 2.5.$$

Therefore

$$P_A = 5 = VMP_A = MP_A \cdot P_\pi = 2.5 \cdot 2 = 5.$$

Thus the firm will want to buy about 70 bushels of apples in order to maximize its profits when it can sell apple pies for \$2 each and apples cost \$5 per bushel. Since the firm is a competitive buyer of apples, $P_A = 5$ is a supply curve for bushels of apples. It can buy as many bushels as it wants at \$5 per bushel. The curve VMP_2 is the demand curve for apples (when $P_\pi = \$2$), and so the point B is an equilibrium point in the input market. Every intersection like B is a possible input market equilibrium when $P_A = 5$. The intersections differ only with regard to the price of the output, pie.

However, only one of these pie prices is consistent with equilibrium in the output market, the apple pie market. At one of these output prices, the demand for pie is equal to the supply of it. If we can find

FIGURE 17–4

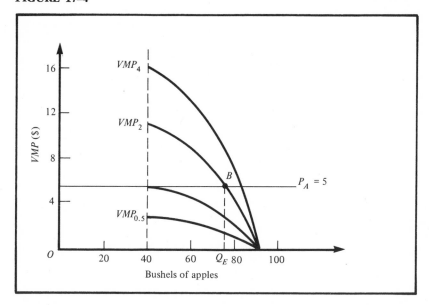

that price, we will know the demand for apples when equilibrium exists in both markets at once. In the analysis just above we discovered that when $2 is the equilibrium price of pie in the output market, then the firm will move to B in the input market and demand 70 bushels of apples. B is therefore a point on a demand curve for apples that is consistent with simultaneous equilibrium in both markets.

Now suppose the price of apples goes up, perhaps to $10 per bushel ($P_A = 10$), as shown in Figure 17–5. How will the individual firm respond to higher input prices? It will, of course, reduce its use of apples, moving back along the value of the marginal product curve toward B' where once again $VMP_A = P_A$. This is because $VMP_A = P_A$ is the condition for maximizing profits in the input market. The adjustment, however, is not quite that simple. As this firm and other firms in the industry respond to the higher apple price by buying fewer apples, they reduce the supply of apple *pies*. The price of pie in the output market must rise to restore the output market equilibrium. The firm that decided to move along VMP_2 on Figure 17–5 from B to B' finds that it is being shifted to a new value of the marginal-product curve by the rise in the price of pie. Instead of coming to rest at B', it will come to rest at some point like C, where

$$VMP_{2.5} = P_A = 10.$$

This is another profit-maximizing point for the firm. It maximizes profit when the price of apple pie is higher and the amount of apple pie being sold in the final goods market is smaller. It indicates a demand

FIGURE 17–5

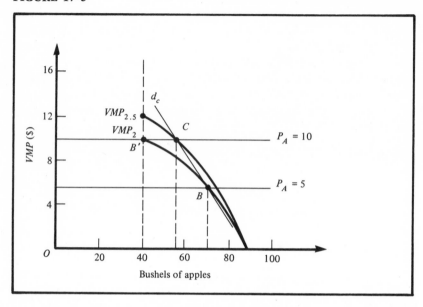

for fewer apples (about 55 bushels) because their price (P_A) is higher. The firm makes fewer pies with fewer apples and sells the pies at a higher price ($P_\pi = 2.5$). Thus point C becomes another point on a demand curve for apples that involves equilibrium in both input and output markets at once. By considering still more prices for apples, we could derive a whole curve labeled dc in Figure 17–5. (We are using a small d to indicate a single firm and c to indicate competition; dc is the apple demand curve of the individual firm under competition.)

So far we have assumed that points like B and C exist. Thus we assume that there are pairs of prices P_A and P_π) that are consistent with equilibrium in both markets at once. A particular price P_A must lead to the purchase of enough apples to make enough pies to provide the equilibrium supply quantity of pies at some price P_π. Whether such pairs exist for our model is a question answered by careful deduction from the assumptions we have already built into this model. The model presented in these chapters does have as one of its implications simultaneous equilibrium in input and output markets, but we have neither the space nor the logical tools to prove this statement.

THE MARKET DEMAND FOR APPLES

The curve dc is the demand curve we sought, and the remaining task is to combine the curves of all firms into an industry curve (Dc) for apples in Figure 17–6. We will engage, as we have before, in a simple summation of all individual curves, but again the problem is not quite that simple. We are now, more than ever, dependent on the assumption that all firms are alike. When one moves along its demand curve, all must do the same because every point on the individual curve assumes that output of pie adjusts to an equilibrium level in the output market. This we must keep in mind. It may make this analysis seem somewhat contrived, but it can be justified because the resulting demand curve (*Dc*) brings out so clearly the interdependence of input and output markets.

FIGURE 17–6

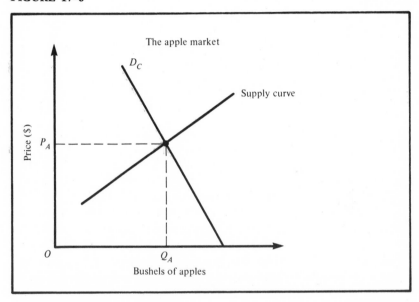

By now some student will have recognized that when we introduced demand (for final goods) in Chapter 5, we did not reveal the dependence of final-goods markets on input markets. We covered up the whole problem by taking all prices including input prices as given, which suggested to the wary that these markets somehow got to equilibrium on their own hook. They did not, and we now know more about their dependence on output markets. With this in mind, we will go on to consider the supply of apples.

THE INPUT SUPPLY CURVE

Apples grow in orchards. They have to be produced by some firm. This is true of every input except labor and partly true of labor as well. What this means is that each apple grower has a marginal cost curve that is his supply curve. This curve has the usual positive slope because

he must face decreasing returns to scale (or the law of diminishing returns in the short run), like any other firm. Hence, on Figure 17–6, we
have a very familiar picture. The demand curve (Dc) is the sum of the
individual demand curves of all pie makers, and the supply curve is
the sum of the marginal cost curves of all apple growers. There is an
equilibrium price, P_A, and an equilibrium quantity, Q_A. Each competitive pie maker will take this price as given and hence treat his
apple supply curve as a horizontal straight line at P_A, as in Figure 17–7.[4]

FIGURE 17–7

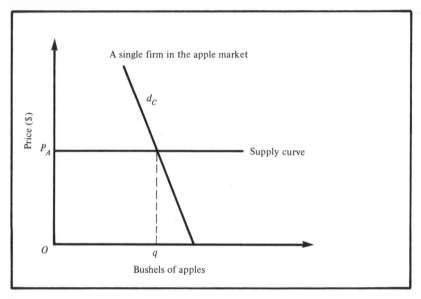

He will demand the quantity q because at q the value of the marginal
product of apples is just equal to the market price of apples.

Once again, it must be quite clear that the tools we have used in the
current project, the analysis of input markets, are similar to the ones
we used earlier in output markets. If we leave out the special case of
labor, input markets are nothing special.

LABOR

Labor *is* something special. In the first place, we get very little help
from a consideration of the supply of labor as a function of the costs of

---

[4] Note that competitive conditions in the output market lead the individual firm
to view its *demand* curve as horizontal, but in the input market it is the *supply*
curve that appears horizontal.

producing labor. Most labor, of course, has some skills, and the acquisition of those skills requires time and resources. There are inputs to training and education, and probably decreasing returns to scale.[5] Still, educational institutions do not sell their product. The educated individual sells it himself, so the connection between costs borne by the public through the institution are separated from the revenues derived from selling the product.

In addition, the nonpecuniary advantages and disadvantages of a particular use mean nothing to apples. They are often crucial to labor. "Do you like your work?" is a common and very serious question. The nonpecuniary factors are not easy for economists to handle. Our discipline has gotten as far as it has at least partly because so many of the things that interest us can be measured by money.

Finally, we should point out that there is no eight-hour day for apples, but the supply of labor is constrained in a myriad of ways. There are child labor laws, union rules, licenses, safety rules, and so on. Apples do not escape all such prescriptions, but their lot is small by comparison.

LEISURE AND INCOME

It is tempting to end these comments on the supply of labor with an application of indifference curve analysis. The result will be a better understanding of indifference curves and some additional information about labor, but this argument will not give an adequate picture of the supply of labor.

Suppose we think of the individual who makes a choice between income earned by working and leisure enjoyed by not working. He can allocate his available time between these two uses. There must be some maximum time available, however, since there are only 24 hours in a day and he cannot work all of those. Suppose the maximum number of hours available for work or leisure to be J in Figure 17–8. This then becomes the constraint that locates one end of a line of attainable combinations. He can start from J and trade hours of leisure for income at a rate determined by the wage rate. Let H represent his income if he gives up all his leisure and works "all" the time. The line HJ then represents all possible combinations of work and leisure that use up his time.

Somewhere along HJ there will be a combination he prefers. Leisure is being treated like one good and income is used to represent all others. He is thus choosing among baskets of goods that contain different combinations of leisure and all other goods and may choose A. Now, suppose the wage rate rises. The point J will be unaffected, but if he works

---

[5] One may suspect that at some large state universities the scale is such that the marginal educational product has dropped below zero.

FIGURE 17–8

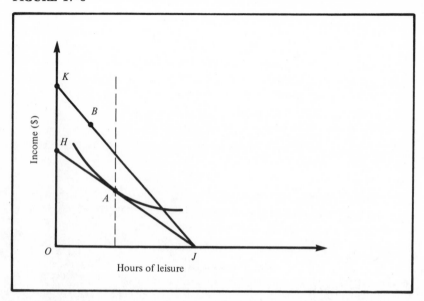

every hour his income will now be larger (K). The new line of attainable combinations will be KJ. Where will the new optimum be?

We would expect a substitution effect on leisure. The rise in the wage rate has made leisure more expensive. He must give up more income, meaning more of all other goods, for an hour of leisure. The substitution effect always changes consumption in a direction opposite from the change in price. Leisure, which has gone up in cost, will therefore be reduced in consumption, and we can say that the substitution effect *by itself* will push him from A towards B.

But it is also clear that the rising wage has produced an income effect. He can now be on a higher indifference curve. The direction of the income effect is not obvious. If leisure is a normal good, then its consumption will rise with income. If it is inferior, then its consumption will fall as income rises. It seems very likely that leisure is a normal good. To most of us, leisure seems like many other "luxury" goods that we buy more of as income rises. If so, the income and substitution effects work in opposite directions and it is not certain that a point like B will be the final point.

As long as the substitution effect is stronger than the income effect, the final point will be to the left of the vertical dashed line through A. We can conclude that with the rise in wages less leisure is consumed, more labor is offered, and this individual labor supply curve has positive slope. On the other hand, if the income effect is the stronger effect, then a rise in wages increases the consumption of leisure, meaning less work and a *negatively* sloped supply curve for labor results.

Economists sometimes speculate that the substitution effect is strongest at low incomes (low wage rates) and that the supply curve is positively sloped. As wages rise, however, the income effect becomes more important until it dominates, and the supply curve has positive slope as in Figure 17–9. This is called the backward bending supply curve of labor.

There is some tentative evidence in support of this shape in a study of the income of physicians, an upper-income group.[6] It appears that

FIGURE 17–9

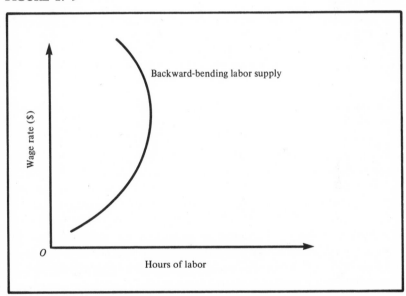

they "reduce the quantity of services provided when fees rise." Thus the income effect appears to be stronger than the substitution effect and the consumption of leisure increases as its price rises. This suggests that efforts by the government to hold down medical fees may actually increase the supplied quantity of physicians' services, at least in the short run.

Nevertheless, the backward-bending labor supply curve does not represent a full answer to the question of the supply of labor. It is included here because of the way it uses indifference curves, but the in-

---

[6] Martin Feldstein, "The Rising Price of Physicians' Services," *Review of Economics and Statistics,* vol. 52, no. 2 (May 1970), pp. 121–33.

terested student should proceed to some of the specialized literature on labor markets.[7]

MONOPOLY IN INPUT MARKETS

It is now time to drop the competitive assumptions and let monopoly rear its ugly head. We will look at three types of monopolies:

First: A firm may be the monopoly seller of the final good but buy inputs in competitive markets. We considered this case in Chapter 15 but ignored any affects it might have in input markets.

Second: A firm may be a monopoly buyer of one of its inputs. It is then called a "monopsonist."

Third: A firm may be the monopoly seller of a good that is an input for other firms. This analysis will be quite similar to the examination of monopoly sellers of output in Chapter 15.

We will take up each of these separately because it simplifies the analysis, but there is no reason why they might not appear in various combinations. We will therefore look at one combination, bilateral monopoly, as well, but we will not consider in any detail the occurrence of these types of monopoly in labor markets for the reasons given earlier. Labor markets are special in their character and complexity.

THE MONOPOLY SELLER

Surely we can count on the monopolist to try to maximize his profits. We already know that a competitive profit-maximizer will buy apples right up to the point where he can sell their marginal product for just enough to cover their price. He buys until

$$VMP_A = MP_A \cdot P_\pi = P_A.$$

A monopolist will do almost the same thing. The only difference arises because the monopolist finds his marginal revenue less than the price of pie. The monopolist is the industry, and he must sell to the industry demand curve. He must face the fact that the selling price of pie will fall as he expands his output. Instead of using the price of pie (P_π) to calculate the value of the marginal product, he must use the marginal revenue (MR_π). This new value gets a new name, marginal revenue product (MRP_π), and he expands until

$$MRP_\pi = MP_A \cdot MR_\pi = P_A.$$

---

[7] See Albert Rees, *Economics of Work and Pay* (New York: Harper & Row, 1973); and Richard Perlman, *Labor Theory* (New York: John Wiley & Sons, 1969).

It can be deduced from the argument above that at each level of output:

$$MRP_\pi < VMP_\pi \text{ because } MR_\pi < P_\pi$$

As shown in Figure 17–10, the marginal revenue product curve will lie below the value of the marginal product curve, even when both describe the demand for apples at a single price of pie, $P_\pi = \$1$, for example.

Obviously a whole family of marginal revenue product curves exists, one for every price of pie. Two examples are presented in Figure 17–11, which looks very much like the analogous competitive "picture" shown

FIGURE 17–10

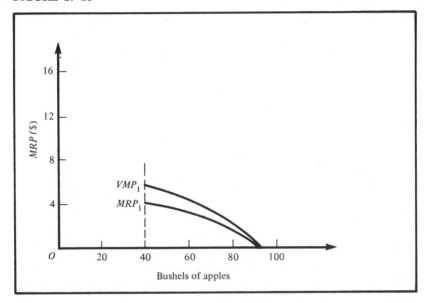

in Figure 17–4. We can now derive the monopolist's apple demand curve by exactly the same method used earlier in this chapter to get the competitive curve (dc). Somewhere along the line $P_A = 5$ in Figure 17–11, we presume that the output (pie) market will be in equilibrium. Suppose B is the point that corresponds to equilibrium in the output market. Since this monopoly seller of pies is, however, a competitive buyer of apples, we can treat the line P_A as his supply curve. B is, therefore, an equilibrium in the input market too. Thus Q_B is the equilibrium demand for apples when *both* markets are in equilibrium. Point B is a point on the apple demand curve that meets this double equilibrium condition. Other points can be found by considering other prices for apples ($P_A = 10$) and proceeding in the same way to find point C, which also meets the double equilibrium condition. The result is the demand curve *Dm,* which indicates the quantity of apples demanded at each price of apples on the condition that the market for apple pie is in equilibrium.

The firm we are considering is the only maker of apple pies, but it is not the only buyer of apples. Other firms making jellies, ciders, and strudels are also in the input market. The assumption of competition here means that the supply curve of apples looks horizontal to the pie maker at the market price P_A. It is shown in Figure 17–12 along with

FIGURE 17–11

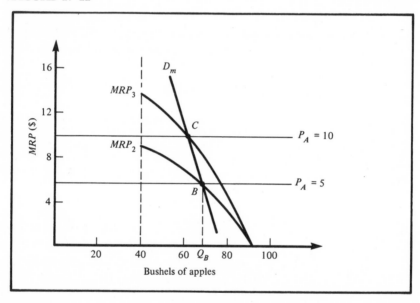

his demand curve (*Dm*), and together they indicate the quantity demanded by this one firm, which buys inputs competitively but sells output monopolistically. Note that monopoly in this market has had its impact entirely through its effect on the position of the apple demand curve. This curve is shifted because

$$MRP_A < VMP_A$$

at every output market equilibrium, and this, in turn, results from the fact that

$$MR_\pi < P_\pi$$

at every output.

FIGURE 17–12

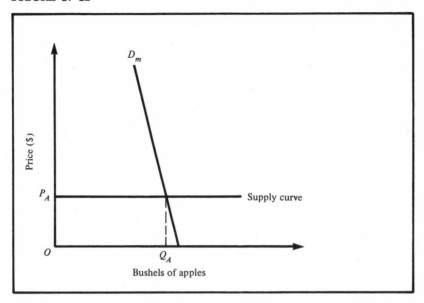

COMPETITION VERSUS MONOPOLY

It is tempting to take time out here to give a simple demonstration of what economists mean when they say monopoly leads to a misallocation of resources. We will need two industries, the pie industry—consisting of one pie maker—and a "hard" cider industry with many (hurrah!) firms. Together they buy in a competitive market for apples. Each of them takes the price of apples as given and adjusts his purchases until

$$P_A = VMP_A \text{ (for the competitor)}$$

and

$$P_A = MRP_A \text{ (for the monopolist).}$$

Pie will sell for a price P_π, and cider a P_c per quart.

We can now expand the profit-maximizing equations above as follows:

$$P_A = VMP_A = MP_{Ac} \cdot P_c \text{ (for the competitor)}$$
$$P_A = MRP_A = MP_{A\pi} \cdot MR_\pi < MP_{A\pi} \cdot P_\pi \text{ (for the monopolist),}$$

where MP_{Ac} is the marginal product of apples used to make cider and $MP_{A\pi}$ is the marginal product of apples used to make pie. If we simplify we get:

$$P_A = MP_{Ac} \cdot P_c \text{ (for the competitor)}$$

and

$$P_A < MP_{A\pi} \cdot P_\pi \text{ (for the monopolist).}$$

Combining the two, we get:

$$MP_{Ac} \cdot P_c < MP_{A\pi} \cdot P_\pi.$$

There it is! This expression makes the statement we need to understand "misallocation." It tells us that we place a higher value on the marginal product of a bushel of apples if it is used to make pie, the monopoly good. We should shift bushels of apples from cider making to pie making until the marginal product is worth the same to us in both uses. If this shift has a trivial effect on the distribution of income among us, then we can say that the result will be a rise in real income. One of our predictions made in Chapter 13 is that this shift is exactly what will occur under competition and is here prevented by whatever forces defend this monopoly.

THE MONOPSONIST

Now for a look at monopoly in a different guise, as a single buyer of some input. To keep it simple we will assume this monopolist buys from many sellers and sells to many buyers. Real examples are hard to come by, but the common textbook example is the coal mine company town. In this example, there is only one important employer but many sellers of labor, and, of course, the coal is shipped to many buyers in other parts of the country. Shipping is important here. It is the mobility of the coal that forces a competitive output price on the coal company even in its own locale. A similar mobility of coal miners would prevent the coal company from acting as the monopoly buyer of labor in its own company town. Labor, unfortunately, is often immobile for reasons that all of us can understand.

We cannot use this example, however, without getting tied up with labor markets, so we will stick with apples and pies. It is a little hard to imagine how a competitive seller of apple pie can be the only buyer of apples, but perhaps all other pie makers use synthetic apples. The demand curve for real apples is the demand curve of one firm, hence it is *dc* from Figure 17–5 and appears below in Figure 17–13. On the supply side, each apple grower has costs of production and a marginal cost curve. These can be combined into a supply-of-apples curve for all growers. This market supply curve is also shown in Figure 17–13. Now the plot changes.

The monopsonist knows that as he buys more and more apples, he moves along this supply curve. He must pay more for every bushel when he buys more bushels. If he wants 100 bushels per week (Q_A), he may

FIGURE 17–13

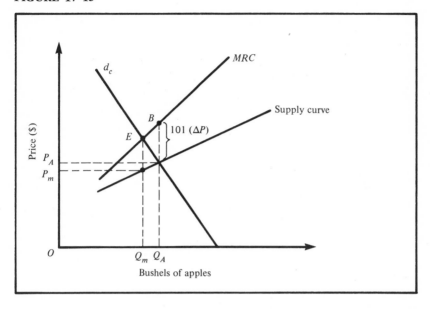

get them at a price P_A and pay $100\,P_A$ dollars. But if he wants 101, he will find the price to be $(P_A + \Delta P)$, where ΔP is a small rise in price. The added cost of a bushel of apples will be the difference between the total cost of 101 bushels and the total cost of 100. It is called the marginal resource cost (MRC_A) and appears as follows:

$$
\begin{aligned}
MRC_A &= 101\,(P_A + \Delta P) - 100\,P_A \\
&= 101\,P_A + 101\,\Delta P - 100\,P_A \\
&= P_A + 101\,\Delta P.
\end{aligned}
$$

Thus at the output Q_A, the cost of increasing his rate of use by one bushel will exceed the price of that bushel (P_A) by the rise in the price for all bushels $(101\,\Delta P)$. This result is indicated at B on Figure 17–13. This is true of every output, and so the marginal resource cost curve (MRC) lies everywhere above the supply curve.

The profit-maximizing rule is the same here as elsewhere. Buy apples until the value of their marginal product (VMP_A), shown by curve dc, is just equal to the marginal cost of the additional bushel of apples (MRC). This turns out to be at E on Figure 17–13. The quantity thus determined is labeled Q_m. Once quantity is determined, the supply curve will indicate the price P_m that must be paid to get that quantity (Q_m). As we noted earlier in this chapter, the competitive price would be P_A and quantity Q_A. So once again we predict that monopoly will restrict output. In the output market, monopoly leads to higher prices for pie,

but here in the input market it leads to lower prices for apples.[8] It leads
to the misallocation of resources no matter where it occurs.

THE MONOPOLY INPUT SELLER

The total supply of some input can be in the hands of a single seller,
and this will give yet another view of monopoly. This situation is most
likely to result from individual ownership of some natural resource, but
it may also result from any of the other sources discussed in Chapter 15.

FIGURE 17–14

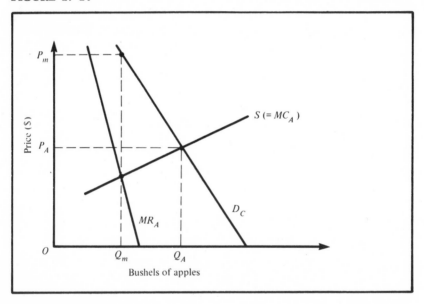

The monopoly seller of an input will behave, given our assumptions of
course, like the monopoly seller of output in Chapter 15. He will supply
quantities as indicated along his marginal cost curve, which is positively
sloped as in Figure 17–14, because of the shape of the production
function. As the only seller, he faces the combined demand curve (Dc)
of a set of competitive firms. This curve has negative slope, and so he
finds that the marginal revenue from selling a bushel of apples (MR_A)
is less than their price at every quantity. He picks Q_m where

$$MC_A = MR_A$$

---

[8] When an input receives less than the value of its marginal product, as on
Figure 17–13 where $P_m < VMP_A$ at the chosen output, it is sometimes said to be
"exploited." This use of the term was introduced by Joan Robinson in *Economics
of Imperfect Competition* (London: Macmillan, 1933), pp. 281–91.

and then sells at the price P_m. His price is above the competitive price, and he produces fewer apples than would a group of competitive sellers. A higher price for apples means a higher price for pie in the output market. In addition, misallocation of resources occurs as usual.

BILATERAL MONOPOLY

Our last look at monopoly is a double feature. We will introduce monopoly on both sides of the input market at once. We will suppose a single apple grower who sells to the only pie maker.[9] We can start with the single seller of Figure 17–14. We know what quantity he wants to sell and what price he wants to charge. This is laid out again in Figure 17–15, but we will now label the price "P_s", and the quantity "Q_s", for

FIGURE 17–15

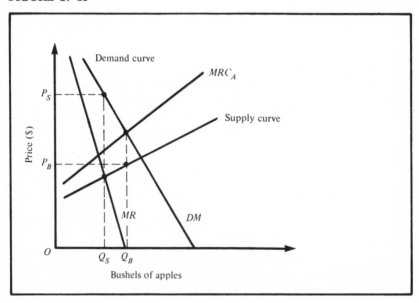

"seller." The desires of a monopoly buyer, a monopsonist, can be taken over from Figure 17–13. As you remember, the distinctive feature is the marginal resource cost curve (MRC_A in Figure 17–15), which leads to a demand for Q_B at a price P_B, where the B indicates that this is the buyer's profit-maximizing point. The problem is now clear. $P_s \neq P_B$ and $Q_s \neq Q_B$. The buyer and seller are not in agreement.

This model does not have a unique solution. Even though our as-

---

[9] The more common textbook example is that of the labor union selling to the employees' association, but labor markets are special.

sumptions have provided single equilibrium positions in all earlier analyses, they fail to do so here. Bilateral monopolies, however, do business, so they must in fact agree on a price and quantity, but we have no logical way of deciding what the price and quantity will be. We sometimes talk about a "bargaining" skill or power that presumably helps either buyer or seller get close to his profit-maximizing price. We do not have a precise meaning for these terms, however, and so they are mainly names for ignorance.

If these two firms collude, however, they can find a single quantity that will maximize their joint profits. Suppose that at first the quantity exchanged is Q_S in Figure 17–15. The seller will maximize his profits and the buyer will not. The buyer will want to move toward the larger quantity Q_B. A move toward Q_B will reduce the seller's profit and increase the buyer's profit. If the increase exceeds the reduction, then the move will increase joint profits. There will be a quantity somewhere between Q_s and Q_B where joint profits are maximized. Just what quantity this is depends on the elasticities of the supply curve and the demand curve. It could be anywhere between Q_s and Q_B, including the end points themselves, but it cannot be larger than Q_B nor smaller than Q_s. Any move outside this range reduces the profits of both firms and must therefore lead away from the joint maximum.

Thus collusion will eliminate the indeterminacy and provide a unique solution in terms of joint profits. This is important because collusion seems extremely likely. To begin with, the two firms must get together to discuss price and quantity if there is to be any trade at all. If they initially pick a point of less than maximum joint profit, then one of them will be interested in a change and he will be able to offer the other some of the increased profit as an inducement to change. The new distribution of profits between them can be brought about by an adjustment of the price paid by buyer to seller. Thus quantity can be adjusted until joint profits are maximized and then these profits divided by setting the price. And from outside we have no way of judging whether the outcome involves collusion or bargaining. Our notion of "bargaining" tells us absolutely nothing about what price and quantity to expect. A "bargain" may be struck anywhere between Q_s and Q_B and *may* even coincide with the quantity that maximizes joint profits. In this situation, we can expect either collusion or foolishness.

RENTS

We have generally dealt with goods that have positively sloped supply curves. The quantity supplied is thus affected by price, and a rise in price will bring about an increase. There are some goods, however, whose supply is fixed. Agricultural land is often used as an example. This land will be offered for use no matter what the price. The price is determined as in Figure 17–16 by the demand at R_0.

Since this supply is available at any price, does the price have any function? It does, of course. It rations the available supply among demanders. It ensures that only those who can make the most effective use of this input and therefore who can pay the highest price for it will get it. We have adopted the convention of calling a price that rations supply but does not affect quantity supplied, a *rent*. This term is used because of the early application of this notion in agriculture, but it should be used for the price of any good that is fixed in supply.

FIGURE 17–16

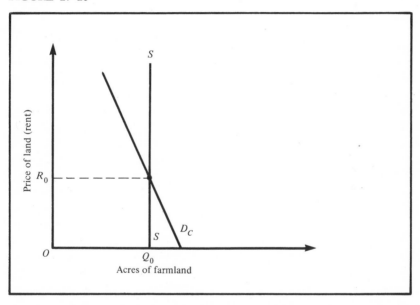

Simple examples are hard to find. Even the supply of arable land will increase some as its rent rises. At higher rents it will pay to drain or level or otherwise improve land that was not previously arable. Arable land will also be withdrawn from residential uses if the rent is high enough. Despite the absence of perfect examples, the concept is important. This is because a reduction in rent has little effect on supply. The government could tax rents without affecting supply. It has been argued, in fact, that the government should tax away all rents since this would provide the government with revenues and yet leave the allocation of resources unaffected. As long as the supply curve of the taxed item is completely unelastic and as long as the tax does not interfere with the rationing function of rents, this is correct.

There are also situations in which the supply of some good or input is temporarily fixed. An increase in the demand for medical services will at first cause an increase in the incomes of existing doctors because it takes some time to expand the supply. This income increase is a short-run rent and is called a *quasi-rent*. The same term can be used for any payments made to specialized fixed inputs in the short run. Being specialized means that they cannot readily leave the firm if they are not paid, and in the short run they cannot be increased even if well paid. What they are paid, if anything, is a quasi-rent. Goods that earn quasi-rents in the short run will, of course, be increased in supply in the long run.

SUMMARY

It is the purpose of this chapter to establish the interdependence of input and output markets. This interdependence expresses itself primarily in the requirement that equilibrium be possible in both markets simultaneously, even though the equilibrium price in the input market impinges on the supply curve for output, and the equilibrium price in the output market impinges on the demand for inputs.

The interdependence of these two markets has been established by using exactly the same techniques that are used to analyze either market separately. It turns out that the assumption of profit maximization leads to the determination of an output level that is the same no matter which market the assumption is applied to.

Monopoly in the input markets turns out to have the same effect discovered earlier in output markets. It leads to an output that is below the competitive output. This output level involves a misallocation of resources. It also leads to a final-good price that is above the competitive price and an input price that is below the competitive price.

This ends our consideration of partial equilibrium. We now turn to the consideration of general equilibrium in Chapter 18.

SELECTED READINGS

Ferguson, C. E. *Microeconomic Theory*, 3d ed. (Homewood, Ill.: R. D. Irwin, 1972), Chapter 13. © 1972 by Richard D. Irwin, Inc.

Friedman, Milton. *Price Theory* (Chicago: Aldine Publishing Co., 1976), Chapter 9.

Rees, Albert. *The Economies of Work and Pay* (New York: Harper & Row, 1973).

Russell, R. R. "On the Demand Curve for a Factor of Production," *American Economic Review*, vol. 4 (1964), pp. 726–33.

Chapter 18

General Equilibrium

The time has come, Walras said,
To speak of many things.

INTRODUCTION

It is time to consider some very general aspects of economic theory. Up to this point every equilibrium we have considered was partial in some way. For instance, we considered the allocation of consumer income among commodities without reference to production. We analyzed efficient production as if prices were given, so that we could ignore demand. We studied equilibrium in the market for one good while assuming all other markets already in equilibrium. We looked at an output market without reference to its impact on input markets.

In each of these cases, we had to take some things as given from outside in order to complete the analysis. Some of those givens, however, are in fact quantities whose value we want economic theory to help us predict. The most important of these is the quantity of each input and output that will be produced and consumed. It will be most interesting to know whether economic theory can predict a set of equilibrium quantities of all goods at once. Almost as important as quantities are prices. The partial equilibriums already considered all involved some given prices. If we apply these theories to market economies, then it is clearly important that we be able to predict prices. Even a centrally planned economy may want to find a set of equilibrium prices and use them to guide the organization of production.

We will, therefore, take all prices and quantities out of *ceteris paribus* at this point and try a model in which they are the dependent variables. This move will not leave *ceteris paribus* empty, however. It will still include among the given conditions, a state of technology, a pattern of tastes and preferences, some information about the supply of inputs, and a few other things to be mentioned as we go along. Thus it is clear that we are still dealing with statics, that is, with the characteristics of the particular state of the economy that is implied by a particular set of given conditions. We hold constant those things that change over time. Even general equilibrium theory does not describe very well the paths along which economies move as time passes.

The most satisfactory way to handle general equilibrium analysis is to use algebra. This is because the number of variables immediately exceeds the limits of three-dimensional geometry. Economists, however, have a long habit of explaining complicated problems with simple diagrams, so you will not be surprised to find that even for general equilibrium there is a set of geometric techniques at hand. They were carefully put together by Francis Bator in a 1957 journal article, and we will make extensive use of that article.[1]

PRODUCTION FIRST

Suppose there is some finite set of commodities, a set of m commodities that we can label $\{x_1, x_2, \ldots, x_m\}$ where m merely means a large but finite number. Some of these we think of as consumer goods: pie, tea, and so on, but some will be inputs like labor, and some will be used both ways, like apples. Every producer will use some quantities of these goods in his production process and produce some other quantities as his outputs. For any particular producer, the quantity used and the quantity produced of many of them will be zero because he will limit himself to certain outputs that require only certain inputs.

In order to make use of geometry, the number of commodities must be reduced from m to four. As you may already suspect, we will make pie and tea out of labor and mix. It is possible to imagine that labor has skills for making either output, but it is less believable that the mix has the raw materials out of which either pie or tea can be made. Disbelief must be suspended, however, in the interest of simplicity. To keep the symbols simple, we will use $\{\pi, T, L, M\}$ as the commodity set. Geometry also requires that we start with given quantities of labor and mix. This would not be done in a mathematical treatment. The supply of labor depends on a choice between work and leisure. That choice is an economic choice, dependent on individual tastes and a rate of exchange between the two, so the quantity of labor should be determined by a general equilibrium analysis, not assumed before it

---

[1] Francis Bator, "The Simple Analytics of Welfare Maximization," *American Economic Review*, vol. 47 (1957), pp. 22–59.

starts. However, that would require that a third output, leisure, be introduced to the model, and the number of variables would then get too large for geometry.

With these assumptions, we can present the entire production set in a simple way as in Figure 18–1. The technique is the same one used in Chapter 6 to analyze exchange. The total quantity of labor is marked on the horizontal axis as OL and the total mix on the vertical axis as OM. The Edgeworth box then contains all possible baskets of inputs that can be used for production. Any point (K) actually represents two

FIGURE 18–1

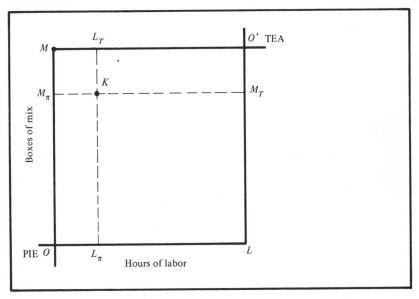

baskets of inputs. We can think of one of these being used to make pie and measure its contents from the origin (O) as L_π and M_π along the horizontal and vertical axes, respectively. All the rest of the labor and mix will be in the other basket from which tea is made, and we measure its contents from O' as L_T of labor and M_T of mix. Choosing among points like K is the economic problem of production.

Each basket has some output, hence at K we can talk about some output of both pie and tea. Suppose K will produce 1,000 apple pies. We can then find all other baskets that will produce 1000_π and draw an isoquant through them. In Chapter 7, we made certain assumptions that give a negatively sloped convex isoquant like π_{10} in Figure 18–2. There is also an isoquant through K that indicates the output of tea. It is labeled T_8 and drawn convex to the origin O'. These isoquants are

FIGURE 18–2

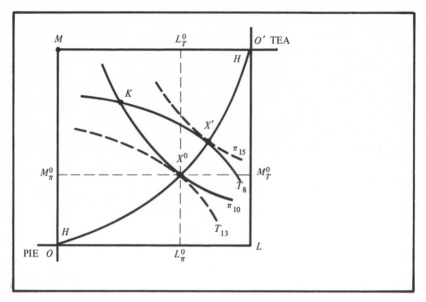

everywhere negatively sloped (each in relation to its own origin), meaning that any kind of satiation is assumed to be impossible. This will make the argument simpler, but it is not necessary to the outcome. Once the isoquants have been added, then every point on Figure 18–2 indicates a value for each of six variables $(L_\pi, L_T, M_\pi, M_T, \pi, T)$. As long as we stay on this diagram, the relationship among them depends on the production function.

PRODUCTION POSSIBILITIES

It is clear from Figure 18–2 that K is not an efficient allocation of the two inputs to production. Any allocation lying between isoquants π_{10} and T_8 will produce larger quantities of both pie and tea, meaning that it will lie on higher isoquants. K is "inefficient" in the economic sense that more of at least one output is possible without any reduction in the other and with no increase in the quantity of inputs. We will have an efficient allocation when neither output can be increased without decreasing the other. All of the efficient allocations in Figure 18–2 lie on the line HH. This line has been drawn through the points where a pie isoquant is tangent to a tea isoquant. If we look at X^0, a point on this line, it is easy to see that any move away from X^0 must take us to lower isoquants for either pie or tea or both.

At the point X^0 we can read a set of quantities. The amount of labor used to make pie is $L\pi^0$, and the rest L_T^0 is used to make tea. Similarly, mix is divided with $M\pi^0$ pie making and M_T^0 to tea. The output of pie is indicated by the isoquant π_{10} through X^0 and the output of tea by isoquant T_{13}. This set of values is one of an infinite number of efficient production patterns, each represented by a point on HH. Any other point in the space that is not on the line HH is inefficient. To organize production efficiently means to move to the line HH from any point not already on the line.

It is very convenient at this point to shift some of this information to a new diagram. We leave behind information about the exact amounts

FIGURE 18–3

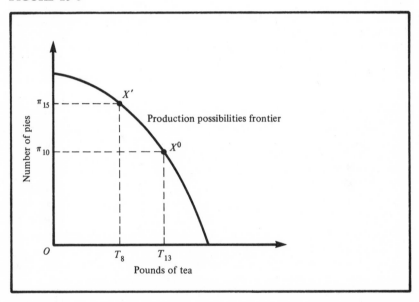

of labor and mix used in tea and pie production at each efficient point. We take with us only the amount of pie and tea produced. The point X^0 can be plotted on Figure 18–3 by measuring the amount of pie (π_{10}) on the vertical axis and the amount of tea (T_{13}) on the horizontal axis. The point X^0, therefore, represents a basket of the two outputs. Other efficient output points can be transferred from Figure 18–2 to Figure 18–3 in the same way until all points on the line HH appear in the new figure. The resulting curve is called the production possibilities "frontier."[2]

The term "frontier" is deliberately used to imply that these outputs are the maximum outputs that can be achieved with given input supplies

---

[2] This curve was first introduced in Chapter 8.

and the existing technology. Point X^0 represents the highest isoquant for tea production (T_{13}) when pie is produced along isoquant π_{10}. Every reallocation of resources that would increase output of one good without reducing the output of the other has been accomplished. We have shifted along π_{10} on Figure 18–2 until we reached the highest output of tea at X^0.

OPTIMUM CONDITIONS

All the points on the frontier of Figure 18–3 (and along HH in Figure 18–2) are called efficient because they call for the maximum output of tea with any given output of pie, and vice versa. We mean that every change in production that would increase one output without reducing the other has been made. Our interest in the frontier as a set of optimum, or efficient, productions is part of our general economic concern with maximizing. We are trying to describe the general character of optimums and to do so without regard to who is maximizer or how maximization is accomplished. This general description is useful in the analysis of many institutional arrangements from market competition to central planning.

Economists have adopted a particular way of stating the conditions for an optimum. Each efficient point is a point of tangency of isoquants (see Figure 18–2). Therefore, the pie and tea isoquants have the same slope at any efficient point, and the slope of an isoquant at a point is called the rate of technical substitution. This is the basis for a statement of what we will call "the optimal condition for production." It can be stated thus:

> *An optimal allocation of resources to the production of goods requires that the rate of technical substitution between any two inputs be the same for every output that uses some of both. In our example the $\mathrm{RTS_{LM}}$ in the production of tea must equal the $\mathrm{RTS_{LM}}$ in the production of pie.*

This is the first of three optimality conditions. Taken together they are sufficient conditions for an optimal allocation of resources in the production and consumption of all goods. The other two will soon appear.

CONSUMPTION NEXT

The next step is to add a group of consumers to our model. Suppose we have n consumers as follows: $\{c_1, c_2, \ldots, c_n\}$. The output of goods must somehow be divided among them so that each consumer gets a basket containing $(x_1, x_2, \ldots, x_m)$. Each x represents a certain quantity of one of the goods that goes to a particular consumer.[3]

---

[3] Remember, it is a rate of consumption that is intended here and a rate of production that was intended in the similar expression earlier in this chapter.

We want to know how an optimum basket can be assigned to each consumer.

To handle this question geometrically, we will once again limit ourselves to two goods, pie and tea. We will use the set $\{\pi, T\}$ instead of the set $\{x_1, x_2, \ldots x_m\}$.[4] And similarly we will consider only two consumers, old friends Archer and Bascomb, so that

$$\{A, B\} \quad \text{replaces} \quad \{c_1, c_2, \ldots, c_n\}.$$

We will use (π_A, T_A) to indicate the basket of goods that goes to Archer and (π_B, T_B) for the basket that goes to Bascomb.

Look at X^0 on Figure 18–4. It is one of the efficient production pos-

FIGURE 18–4

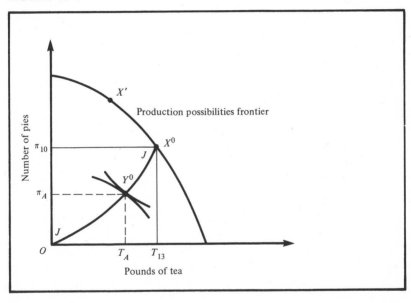

sibilities that lie on the frontier. It yields certain quantities of pie (π_{10}) and tea (T_{13}). These are the total quantities available for consumption by Archer and Bascomb. In fact, the box $O\pi_{10}XT_{13}$ contains all possible distributions of the two goods when X^0 is the production chosen. The problem of distributing these goods is now set up in the way it was in Chapter 6 on exchange, and the analysis will proceed in the same way.

We are interested in the set of efficient exchanges that lies along the

---

[4] In the basket $\{x_1 \; x_2, \ldots, x_m\}$ we have included inputs as well as outputs. Each consumer sells some inputs and buys some outputs. However, in this example the basket does not include the two inputs labor and mix because we have not assigned ownership of these to our consumers. The reasons for this are discussed at the end of this chapter.

line *JJ*. Line *JJ* goes through the points of tangency of Archer and Bascomb's indifference curves. Each point on it is efficient in the sense that any move away from such a point must put one or both individuals on a lower curve. Y^0 is one such point. It gives a certain amount of pie and tea to Archer, whose quantities we will measure from the origin O. He gets a basket (π_A, T_A) associated with Y^0, and Bascomb gets the rest. Each efficient point like Y^0 indicates the highest indifference curve that Archer can attain for any given curve for Bascomb with the given supplies of goods.

Since indifference curves are tangent at Y^0, they have the same slope at that point. The slope of an indifference curve represents the rate of substitution of one good for the other, so Archer and Bascomb have the same rate of substitution of pie for tea $(RS_{\pi T})$ at Y^0. This is true at every efficient trade along the line *JJ*, and we can state the second optimality condition as follows:

> *An optimal distribution of commodities among individuals requires that the rate of substitution between any two commodities must be the same for every consumer who gets some of both. The* $RS_{\pi T}$ *for Archer must be equal to the* $RS_{\pi T}$ *for Bascomb.*

THE THIRD CONDITION

At this point we have identified an infinite number of efficient production possibilities shown on the frontier in Figure 18–4. The point X^0 is only one of them. Other points on the frontier like X^1 also have a box associated with them that shows all of the consumption possibilities, and in each such box are an infinite number of efficient exchanges. For X^0 these are shown as the line *JJ*, and Y^0 is one of them. This is a double infinity of optimums, and we do not seem to be getting much closer to a simple, perhaps single, optimum. We have, however, overlooked one bit of logic that will help. The rate at which producers can transform pie into tea by manufacturing less pie and more tea must be equal the rate at which Archer and Bascomb are willing to substitute pie for tea at some point on their indifference curves.

Notice what can happen when these rates are not equal. Suppose Archer can trade two pies for one pound of tea and stay on the same indifference curve. He is willing to substitute 2π for $1T$ because the substitution will not make him worse off. Suppose also that producers can make three pies if they reduce production of tea by one pound. This means the resources used to make one pound of tea can make three apple pies if shifted. Producers can then make one fewer pound of tea, use the resources to make three pies, give two of the pies to Archer to compensate him for the loss of one pound of tea, and then have one pie left over to divide between Archer and Bascomb. Both would be better off by some portion of the extra pie, meaning that both can be put on a higher indifference curve. If both are now better off, they were not at an optimum before this change. Therefore, a situation in which the rate of transformation in production and the rate of substitution in consumption are not equal cannot be an optimum. We can now state the third optimality condition as follows:

> *An optimal allocation of resources requires that the rate at which producers can transform any one good into any other must be equal to the rate at which any consumer is willing to substitute the one for the other in his consumption pattern. Thus:* $RT_{\pi T} = RS_{\pi T}$.

What does this mean on Figure 18–5? In the first place, we can represent the rate of transformation of pie for tea ($RT_{\pi T}$) by the slope

FIGURE 18–5

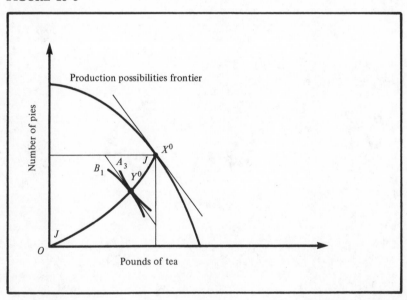

of a tangent to the frontier at X^0. Then the rate of substitution of pie for tea ($RS_{\pi T}$) can be represented by the slope of a tangent through a point where two indifference curves touch; that is, a point on JJ. If we can find a point on JJ where these two slopes are the same, we have found a point where

$$RT_{\pi T} = RS_{\pi T},$$

and the third optimality condition is met.

In Figure 18–5, we have drawn the point Y^0 as such a point; hence Y^0 meets all three optimality conditions. It is an optimum because:

1. RTS_{LM} (in pie making) is equal to RTS_{LM} (in tea making). This is how the point X^0 was discovered.
2. $RS_{\pi T}$ (for Archer) is equal to $RS_{\pi T}$ (for Bascomb). This is how the point Y^0 was discovered.
3. $RT_{\pi T}$ is equal to $RS_{\pi T}$. This means that X^0 (production) and Y^0 (consumption) are related to each other in an optimum way.

Once we have identified a point Y^0 that meets all the optimality conditions, it becomes convenient to take some of the information out of Figure 18–5 and display it in a simple way.

THE UTILITY FRONTIER

Figure 18–6 is a completely new type of diagram. What we wish to measure along each of its axes is movement to higher or lower indifference curves: to more preferred or less preferred situations. The diagram suggests that "more preferred" means more utility, but we have no intention at this late date of introducing a cardinal measure of preference. When Archer moves to a higher indifference curve, we will move him along the horizontal axis to the right, but we will attach no significance to the distance moved. We attach significance only to the direction.

The information we now want to carry forward to Figure 18–6 is the information about which indifference curve Archer and Bascomb enjoy at Y^0. Archer's curve is labeled A_3 just to establish its *order* relative to

FIGURE 18–6

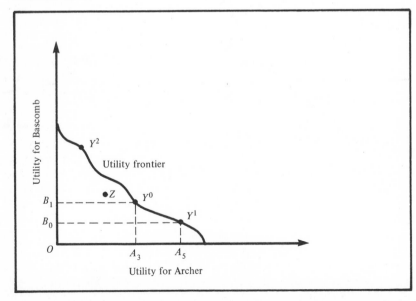

other Archer curves. We will plot A_3 somewhere on the horizontal axis of Figure 18–6 and Bascomb's curve, B_1, somewhere along the vertical. Exactly where is unimportant, but if we have to indicate any other indifference curves on this figure, we must be careful to put them on in proper order. The information we have left behind in Figure 18–5 is the exact quantity of each good that goes to Archer and Bascomb at Y^0.

The point Y^0 on Figure 18–6 now represents a distribution of utility (well-being) between Archer and Bascomb. It is a distribution made possible by meeting all three optimality conditions. That is, production is efficient, exchange is efficient, and production and exchange are efficiently adjusted to each other. Therefore, Y^0 is on the "utility frontier." It indicates the highest indifference curve that Archer can get to when Bascomb is on curve B_1 and all the optimality conditions are met. Are there any other points on this frontier? The answer is yes! Remember that X^0 was only one among an infinite set of efficient productions represented by the production possibilities frontier in Figure 18–4. For any other efficient production, X^1 for example, we can draw in an Edgeworth box and find a new set of efficient exchanges. We have done this in Figure 18–7. Again we can apply the third optimality condition to pick out an exchange in the new X^1 box where

$$RT_{\pi T} = RS_{\pi T}.$$

Call this point Y^1. It will lie on some pair of indifference curves. Archer may be on a higher or lower curve than before. Tastes did not change as we shifted from the X^0 box to the X^1 box, so the same Archer indif-

FIGURE 18–7

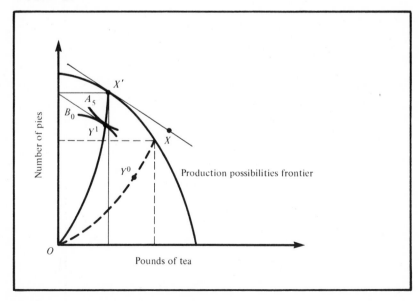

ference curves will be found in both and the new optimum indifference curve can be ordered in relation to A_3. Suppose Archer has moved to a higher curve, A_5 as shown on Figure 18–7. Bascomb must then be on a lower curve, B_0 perhaps. This is because each distribution of utility is on the frontier; it is the maximum Archer can have for any given amount going to Bascomb, and vice versa. If it were possible for both of them to move to a high curve at Y^1, it would mean that exchange, or perhaps production, at Y^0 had not been efficient after all.

Thus when we put the point Y^1 on Figure 18–6, it is below and to the right of Y^0. It is a second point on the utility frontier, and we are indicating that that frontier has negative slope. To move along it is to redistribute utility from one to the other of these two people. If one is to get more (move onto a higher indifference curve), the other must be pushed to a lower indifference curve. Though the utility frontier going through Y^0 and Y^1 has negative slope, we cannot say much more about its shape. We have not made enough assumptions to guarantee that it will be convex or straight or any other simple shape.

THE BEST

All the points on this utility frontier have fine properties because all of them meet the three optimality conditions. Archer and Bascomb should certainly approve of any economic system that organized production and exchange so well as to put them on this frontier. But they might withhold their praise until they were told where on the frontier they will be. Archer may think the whole argument a bit hollow if he finds himself at Y^2 on Figure 18–6. He might like Z better than Y^2, even though it is not on the frontier simply because it gives him a bigger share of what may be a smaller total. Thus the final and crucial question is this: "What share is mine?" When society asks this question, it becomes "What distribution of utility among individuals is best?"

The answers that economists have considered are complex, and all of them are quite unsatisfactory. We will postpone any consideration of them until Chapter 19. In the meantime, we will turn back into this analysis to look for prices. In carrying out the search for prices it will be convenient to assume that somehow society has been able to pick Y^0 as the ideal or best distribution of utility among individuals. We will, therefore, assume that production and consumption are organized in such a way as to move the economy to Y^0 on the utility frontier.

IMBEDDED PRICES

If this general equilibrium model is going to have applications to market economies, then it must have something to say about prices.

It is also true that a planned economy may want a set of optimum prices to use as guides for individual behavior. Therefore, we will look for a set of prices $\{P_1, P_2, \ldots, P_m\}$, one for each of the m commodities, that are in some sense consistent with the optimum general equilibrium, Y^0.

In the simplified model we have been using, this means that we must identify the price of each of the four commodities $\{P_\pi, P_T, P_L, P_M\}$, if possible. The first bit of information about them comes from inside the Edgeworth box of Figure 18–5, which is reproduced in Figure 18–8.

FIGURE 18–8

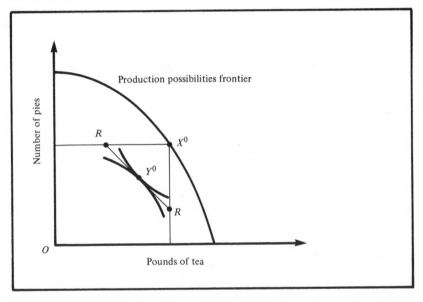

On the assumption made just above that Y^0 represents the "best" point on the frontier in Figure 18–6, then Y^0 inside the box in Figure 18–8 is the best distribution of pie and tea between the two consumers. The line RR goes through Y^0, and its slope is equal to the rate of substitution of pie for tea $(RS_{\pi T})$ for both consumers. It is the rate at which each of them is willing to exchange pie for tea; willing because a small substitution at that rate would leave them on the same indifference curve. Thus the optimum Y^0 implies a rate of exchange of pie for tea, an amount of tea that each would be willing to offer for a unit of pie. This rate of exchange can be expressed as a ratio of prices; a ratio of a price for tea to a price for pie (P_T/P_π). Its value at Y^0 is the slope of the line RR, which represents the rate of substitution. Hence

$$\frac{P_T}{P_\pi} = RS_{\pi T}!^{5}$$

Notice that we have not found P_T or P_π, but only a ratio between them. A particular rate of substitution of pie for tea is a characteristic of an optimum position. Y^0 implies a particular $RS_{\pi T}$, and, therefore, it implies a particular ratio of prices.

Similar information can now be obtained for input prices. The optimum Y^0 requires that production take place at X^0 in Figure 18–2, reproduced in Figure 18–9. Here the rate of technical substitution of

FIGURE 18–9

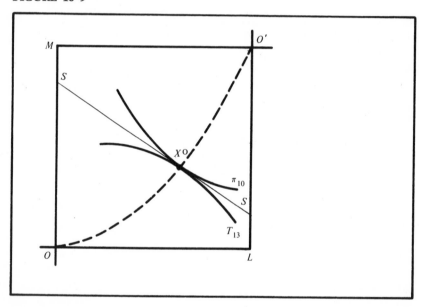

labor for mix (RTS_{LM}) is the same for the production of either good. It is represented by the slope of the line SS. If a small amount of mix were replaced by labor at this rate, output would remain the same. The producer would remain on the same isoquant. He would be willing to substitute one for the other if the ratio of their prices was the same as the technical rate of substitution.

There is a price ratio that corresponds to this rate of substitution. Any prices for labor and mix such that

$$\frac{P_M}{P_L} = RTS_{LM}$$

---

[5] This equation first appeared in Chapter 4, where a more elaborate explanation is offered.

will be consistent with the optimum production at X^0.[6] Again we have only a ratio of prices, not the individual prices themselves. Nevertheless, the rate of technical substitution has a particular value at X^0, and so the input price ratio will have a particular value there.

We now have a relationship between the two output prices and another between the two input prices, but no relationship between an input price and an output price. This third relationship does not appear in any simple way in the geometry we have used. It must be there, however. In Chapter 17, we described the large degree of interdependence between input and output markets. We can also find there a suggestion for a way to connect input and output prices. We can use the profit-maximizing rule; namely, that the input price must equal the value of the marginal product, for instance,

$$P_L = VMP_L = MP_L \cdot P_\pi$$

and

$$P_M = VMP_M = MP_M \cdot P_\pi.$$

Rewriting the first of these, we get

$$\frac{P_L}{P_\pi} = MP_L.$$

We could set out these same equations using the price of tea as well, but we would get no added information because at an optimum the value of the marginal product of labor must be the same in the production of every good that uses any labor.

This argument gives a third price ratio, but this time it relates an input price to an output price. It is on a little different footing than the other two. To get it, we had to add the motion of profit maximizing, whereas the first two relationships are characteristics of an optimum, no matter how it is achieved. This addition is made necessary by the simplicity of our model, however. With a mathematical treatment we could get the relationship as a characteristic of the optimum directly.

All four prices now appear in the following equations:

$$\frac{P_T}{P_\pi} = RS_{\pi T}; \tag{1}$$

$$\frac{P_M}{P_L} = RTS_{LM}; \tag{2}$$

$$\frac{P_L}{P_\pi} = MP_L \quad \text{or} \quad \frac{P_M}{P_\pi} = MP_M. \tag{3}$$

Since the rates of substitution ($RS_{\pi T}$, RTS_{LM}) and the marginal products (MP_L, MP_M) have specific values at the optimum, we can

---

[6] This equation was first presented in Chapter 7, where an explanation is offered.

determine a complete set of price *ratios*. Actually, it is the ratios that are important to us, not the absolute prices. Through this whole book it is relative prices, not absolute prices, that have guided the maximizing behavior of individuals and firms. The input price ratio (P_M/P_L) determined the slope of the isocost curve in Chapter 7 and the output price ratio (P_T/P_π) determined the slope of the budget line in Chapter 2.[7] We can count our search for an optimum set of prices a success.

INCOMES

As you may suspect, there are many ways that this model can be extended. Corner tangencies can be introduced, increasing and decreasing returns considered, and so on. We will not take the space to do these kinds of things here, but there is one more aspect that should be considered.

We know how much pie and how much tea should go to Archer at the optimum. These are indicated in Figure 18–4 as (π_A, T_A). How will he get this real income? In a market economy he would expect to exchange his money income for this real income. We can measure the size of the necessary money income. At the optimum Y^0 he will need

$$E_A{}^0 = P_\pi \pi_A + P_T T_A,$$

where $E_A{}^0$ is the necessary expenditure, at the prices determined at the optimum, to buy the quantities indicated at the optimum.

Where can Archer get enough money income? The obvious place is from selling any quantities of labor and mix that he owns to producers. We have not, however, assigned ownership in our simple model. We can do so, but the important point is that a particular ownership pattern is required. If $I_A{}^0$ is Archer's income from selling resources at optimum prices, then

$$E_A{}^0 = I_A{}^0 = P_M M_A + P_L L_A,$$

where M_A and L_A are the amounts of mix and labor owned by Archer. Only after the set of optimum prices is determined can we assign the ownership of inputs in a way consistent with the optimum.

In a more complex model, this problem would be solved simultaneously with the achievement of the optimum. The anaysis would start with some ownership pattern, and the supplies of inputs, instead of being given, would adjust to prices. A higher price for labor might

---

[7] We can get a set of absolute prices if we set one price, say $P_\pi = \$1$, and then solve the three equations for the other three prices. These prices are not, however, unique. We can multiply each of them by any positive number and get another set that is consistent with the same optimum. Only the price ratios are unique to a particular optimum.

induce individuals to reduce their consumption of leisure and offer more labor. The optimum would take account of a labor supply curve instead of a fixed quantity. We have not been able to do this sort of thing because it introduces additional goods (leisure, for instance) and therefore makes the use of geometry impossible. We would have to shift to mathematical techniques, so this would seem like a good place to end this discussion.

We are now reasonably well prepared for a discussion in Chapter 19 of the welfare implications of an optimum allocation of resources.

SELECTED READINGS

Bator, Francis M. "The Simple Analytics of Welfare Maximization," *American Economics Review,* vol. 47 (1957), pp. 22–59.

Baumol, William. *Economic Theory and Operations Analysis,* 3d ed. (Englewood Cliffs, N.J.: Prentice-Hall, 1972), Chap. 21.

PART V

WELFARE

Chapter 19

Welfare Economics

INTRODUCTION

The preceding chapter was concerned with general equilibrium. Thus it dealt with a situation that is the logical implication of a set of conditions and assumptions. No further change in this situation will occur unless the conditions themselves change. The allocation of resources to the production of different goods and the distribution of those goods among individuals are settled into fixed patterns.

This general equilibrium is described as an optimum under the given conditions. The optimum appears in the form of the grand utility frontier shown again in Figure 19–1. Any point on this frontier, C for instance, indicates the maximum utility that can go to Archer (U_A) when a given amount goes to Bascomb (U_B). This is a frontier in the sense that the constraints will not permit a point above the frontier. Calling the grand utility frontier a frontier is a way of saying that all changes that could make one individual better off without making any other individual worse off have already been made. In fact, it is the completion of all such changes that are possible within the constraints that produces the frontier. Each point on the frontier can therefore be called a Pareto optimum. We have mentioned Pareto before, and his proposal that an increase in welfare occurs when a change of some sort makes one individual better off without making any other individual worse off. By extension then, a Pareto optimum exists when no further changes can be made that will make one person better off without making someone worse off.

387

FIGURE 19-1

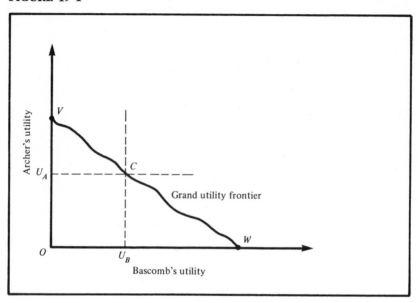

INTERPERSONAL UTILITY COMPARISONS

Point *C* is not, however, the only point on the frontier. There are an infinite number of them along the line between *V* and *W*. These points differ from each other in that they assign different utility levels to our two friends Archer and Bascomb. Remember that the word "utility" is *not* meant to suggest some desirable thing that can be divided between Archer and Bascomb in different ways. Instead, a movement along the frontier shifts one indiivdual to a higher indifference curve and the other to a lower curve. This is clear from the fact that the frontier has negative slope as well as from the fact that every change that would make one person better off (put him on a higher curve) without making the other worse off has already been made.

It is also important to remember that the effects on Archer and Bascomb of a move along the frontier cannot be directly compared. To say that Archer gets on a higher indifference curve is to say unequivocally that he gets to a position he prefers, and one can agree that this means he is better off. But one cannot compare his good fortune to the misfortune of Bascomb, who must go to a lower curve.

The indifference curves we are using do not permit us to say how much better off Archer becomes when he moves to a higher curve. There is no quantitative comparison between his old position and his new one. Furthermore, even if such a quantitative measure were available for both Archer and Bascomb, there is still no reason to assume that the units used to measure Archer's improvement would be comparable to the units used to measure Bascomb's loss. We have run into the problem of interpersonal comparisons of utility or well-being, and our entire analysis is built on the assumption that these kinds of comparisons are not to be made. They are not, of course, completely impossible. We often make statements about people we know well that require such comparisons. We may say for instance, "Alfred has had a better year than Stanley." If we know these people well, this statement is likely to be true. Nevertheless, economists are agreed that these statements cannot be made with sufficient precision to permit their use.[1]

THE GIVEN CONDITIONS

Before we go on, we should summarize the constraints or conditions that underlie the grand utility frontier. We included among them fixed quantities of inputs, but this was merely expedient. It permitted us to use geometry in the analysis. It is clear, however, that if we are willing to shift to more complicated techniques, we can make the supply of each input a function of its price. Given the choice between work and leisure that is open to each individual, it is clear that the supply of labor is likely to be some function of the price of labor. In fact there will be some own-price elasticity for almost all inputs.

The analysis also takes the pattern of tastes and preferences of each individual as given. This constraint appears in the form of the indifference maps attributed to Archer and Bascomb. There is nothing expedient about this constraint. It is basic. The analysis cannot proceed without this assumption or some substitute for it, and any shift in indifference maps will produce a whole new utility frontier. This assumption also reflects a value judgment that is quite commonly made. This is the judgment that it is individual preference patterns that *ought* to be taken as given. Other judgments are possible. One may believe that group preferences arrived at by some political process are more important. One may even argue that a king and his ministers ought to use their own judgments about the welfare of themselves and their subjects as the guide to production. No matter what the source of preference patterns, they are essential to the ranking of alternatives. Any preferences that lead to such a ranking can be made the basis of general equilibrium analysis.

---

[1] A full discussion of interpersonal comparisons can be found in I.M.D. Little, *A Critique of Welfare Economics*, 2d ed. (London: Oxford University Press, 1960), Chapter 4.

We also made the assumption that the state of technology was given in general equilibrium analysis. The state of technology expresses itself in the shape of isoquant maps. Equilibrium analysis is not equipped to handle a change in the shape of those maps in mid-analysis. This is unfortunate in a world in which technology is continuously changing and in which many resources are systematically engaged in the search for new technologies.

Finally, we have assumed that wherever a choice is possible, that choice will be made in such a way as to maximize something. Maximizing means that production choices are made so that the output of each good will be as large as possible, given the output of every other good, and consumption choices will be made so that every individual is on the highest possible indifference curve, given the curve that every other individual is on. These kinds of statements define efficiency at each step in the process of production and distribution of goods. Such efficiency is necessary if the points on the utility frontier are to be Pareto optima.

Once we get to the utility frontier, we have reached the limit of the Pareto definition of an increase in welfare. We need to pick out the point on the frontier that is the *grand* optimum when all the points are Pareto optima. Pareto does not tell us how to choose when each alternative makes one person better off and one worse off. We must look for a substitute criterion.

It will not help to ask which point on the frontier maximizes total utility, meaning the sum of Archer's utility and Bascomb's utility. This is because, as noted earlier, we have not measured the utility of either one. We do not have units of utility to attach to U_A and U_B on Figure 19–1, and even if we did, we would not be able to say that both U_A and U_B are measured in the same units and can be added.

KALDOR COMPENSATION

In the late 1930s, Nicholas Kaldor proposed a new criterion for an increase in welfare. He argued that any change that enabled the person who benefitted from the change to compensate the loser and still be better off increases welfare. This definition does not include the proviso that compensation actually be paid but only that it be possible. The situation to which this argument was usually applied is shown on Figure 19–2. The situation before any change is indicated by point D on the utility frontier VW. Suppose that some change is made in the way the economy is organized. This might involve the breakup of a monopoly or perhaps the end of some restraint on the mobility of a resource; there are many possibilities. Such a change may permit a move to a new point E. Archer is obviously a gainer, meaning that he moves from U_{AD} to U_{AE}, and Bascomb is obviously a loser. The change we are assuming also moves both of them to the new utility frontier $V'W'$, hence the change somehow increases the efficiency of the system.

It is of course obvious that Archer *can* compensate Bascomb simply by paying to Bascomb an amount necessary to shift the two of them from E to F. If Bascomb gets back to F after the change, he will be just as well off as he was before the change. Also at F, Archer will be better off. Therefore *if compensation is actually paid,* then the change

FIGURE 19–2

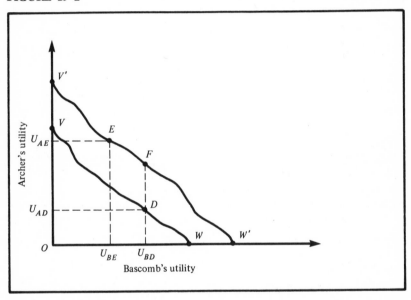

makes Archer better off without making Bascomb any worse off, and hence it represents an improvement in welfare on Pareto's grounds. But in many, if not most, situations of this kind, it is not possible to pay compensation. Both gainers and losers may include many people, and it may be impossible to discover exactly how much compensation to pay to each and precisely who should make the payment. This problem will arise even when it appears very clear that the total gains exceed the total losses.

For this reason Kaldor's proposal went beyond Pareto's and proposed that we treat the change from D to E as an increase in welfare even though compensation is not paid. In other words, the mere fact that Archer could compensate Bascomb, and still be better off after paying that compensation, is construed as sufficient evidence for the conclusion that total welfare is increased. This is obviously an attractive argument, as it would permit the economist to make many recommendations about policy that would otherwise be beyond the competence of his analysis. This proposal generated a great controversy and was in some technical respects modified by Scitovsky and others, but ultimately it was seen to have a fatal flaw.

Whether a particular change increases welfare or not depends in the end on whether compensation is paid. If it is not paid, we only know that Archer is better off and Bascomb is worse off. We still do not know whether Archer's gain in *well-being* exceeds Bascomb's loss of *well-being*. We may know that Archer could pay Bascomb enough to bring him back to his old level of well-being, but if Archer does not make this payment, then we must compare points D and E on Figure 19–2 directly to each other. We must ask whether the sum of Archer's utility at E (U_{AE}) plus Bascomb's utility at E (U_{BE}) exceeds the sum of their utilities at D ($U_{AD} + U_{BD}$).

This runs us abruptly into the difficulty that in fact generated the Kaldor proposal. We do not have any units for the measurement of a quantity like U_{AD}. We only know the ordinal relationship between U_{AE} and U_{AD}. Moreover, even if we could find units for measuring Archer's utility gain as he goes from D to E, we still could not compare them to a measure of Bascomb's loss as he goes from D to E. This requires an interpersonal comparison of well-being with a precision that exceeds the capacities of economic theory. It probably also exceeds the capacity of real people to judge the relative well-being even of their closest friends. We must therefore conclude that the Kaldor compensation principle will not solve our problem.

THE SOCIAL WELFARE FUNCTION

The final welfare criterion we will consider is associated with the economist Abram Bergson.[2] He argues that the only way to choose among alternative distributions of well-being among individuals is to formulate an explicit set of value judgments. These judgments must define what is meant by fairness or justice. Presumably the economist would then be able to discover their implications for particular distributions and be able to evaluate alternatives. On the utility frontier (VW) of Figure 19–3, this set of value judgments should tell us which point is best.

How can we formulate such a set of judgments? Each individual, including the economist, can probably work out his own set. Most of

---

[2] A. Bergson, "A Reformulation of Certain Aspects of Welfare Economics," *Quarterly Journal of Economics,* vol. 52 (1937–38), p. 310.

us have some ideas about the way we think things ought to be, and with enough careful thought we could probably convert these ideas into a fairly explicit and consistent set of statements. Nevertheless, such statements are individual statements and will differ widely among individuals. The economist, not wanting to impose his own judgments arbitrarily, may turn instead to some governmental authority or legislature and ask that he be provided with the necessary set.

This shifts the scene of action outside the usual boundaries of economics. We must now think about political processes for the

FIGURE 19–3

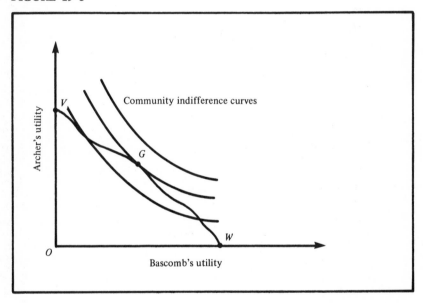

formulation of what is often called a social welfare function. This is a function that produces a preference-ordering of all alternative distributions of well-being based on some set of value judgments. One possible form for the social welfare function may be a set of "community" indifference curves as shown on Figure 19–3. This is an attractively simple form and will lead to the designation of G as the "best" alternative. A set of curves is, however, just a suggestion. Social welfare functions do not necessarily lend themselves to such simple geometric representation. In fact, economists have not proceeded very far in the analysis of the nature of social welfare functions. This is probably because there is no obvious set of value judgments with which they might begin.

PROBLEMS

We do, however, know some rather negative things about social welfare functions that require another look at the political processes that might generate one. Suppose that each individual has a welfare function that will order all possible distributions of welfare as represented, for instance, by the points along the utility frontier. We can then ask, "Is there any procedure that will reconcile these individual and differing rankings of the alternatives to produce a group ranking?" Kenneth Arrow has done the most important work in this area.[3] That is the question he posed, but he added a proviso that any procedure must meet certain conditions. The conditions are designed to impose certain reasonable and desirable constraints on the character of the procedure. They are value judgments about what is required of a good procedure. They are, however, widely held value judgments and hence very important constraints.

For instance, he suggests that the procedure must not permit anyone outside the group or any one person inside the group to dominate the group decision. This is a nondictatorship requirement and is certainly widely accepted in our culture. Secondly, the procedure must not lead to rejection of a particular choice just because some individuals in the group have come to view it *more* favorably. Thus, if some alternative moves up in the preference rankings of one or more members of the group, we would not want to find that it moves down in the group ranking of the same alternatives. Third, the group choice between any two alternatives must depend only on a comparison of those two alternatives by individuals. It must not be influenced by a change in the position of some third alternative. The final condition is one that will sound very familiar by now. It is the requirement that the group preference ranking be transitive. Thus, if alternative A is ranked higher than B and B is in turn ranked ahead of C, then alternative A must also be ranked ahead of C.

Reasonable and even attractive as these constraints seem to be, Arrow was ultimately forced to conclude that it is impossible to choose a procedure consistent with all four at once. If we think of voting as the procedure, we can describe a simple example of the way inconsistencies arise. Suppose that there are three alternative distributions of well-being under consideration. These could be represented by three points on the utility frontier. Now, suppose that Cloetta, Egbert, and Horatio are the group and vote their preferences among these three as follows:

---

[3] Kenneth Arrow, *Social Choice and Individual Values* (New York: John Wiley & Sons, 1951).

> for Cloetta, $A\rho B$ and $B\rho C;$
> for Egbert, $C\rho A$ and $B\rho C;$
> for Horatio, $A\rho B$ and $C\rho A$.

A majority, Cloetta and Horatio, prefer A to B, and a majority, Cloetta and Egbert, prefer B to C. Hence we would conclude using transitive reasoning that a majority prefers A to C. It is, however, immediately obvious that a majority, Egbert and Horatio, prefers C to A. Simple majority voting cannot satisfy the fourth condition.

Since Arrow published his small book we have become convinced the third condition, independence of third alternatives, is more restrictive than it ought to be. If it is modified, there may be some procedures that do not lead to immediate internal contradictions. This eases somewhat the pessimism of Arrow's conclusion, but it does not lead to optimism. It is still clear that certain simple and widely accepted procedures, like majority voting, may not be consistent with some simple, widely accepted criteria for democratic procedures. Arrow's argument has convinced us that it will not be easy to generate the social welfare function that Bergson has called for.

What then can we finally say about the role of economists in recommending policy for increasing the level of well-being in a community?

First: They can recommend any change that will make someone better off without making someone else worse off. This is the Pareto criterion. It is a prescription for economic efficiency, and, applied to all choices, it will lead to the grand utility frontier. It is the most useful criterion available to economists, though it must be obvious that there are many, many situations in which the economist cannot use it to make a recommendation simply because someone is made obviously worse off.

Second: The Kaldor overcompensation principle does not in fact increase the capacity of the economist to recommend. Its defect arises because compensation cannot actually be paid in many cases, even when overcompensation is quite clearly possible. If overcompensation is possible and compensation is actually paid, then the gainer is clearly better off and the loser no worse off, and the change can be recommended using the Pareto criterion. But if compensation is not paid, then an interpersonal comparison of gainers and losers, before and after change, is necessary. So far economists have not been able to make these comparisons with sufficient precision to permit them to recommend for or against the change.

Third: Bergson's quite sensible observation that the economist needs
              a social welfare function as a basis for his recommendation
              has likewise failed to expand the prescriptive powers of
              economics. A social welfare function would provide a prefer-
              ence order for all alternative states of the economy, but we
              are pessimistic about the possibility of obtaining such a func-
              tion if it must reflect in a democratic way the individual
              preferences of all members of a group.

The economist is therefore left with the Pareto criterion to use
wherever he can and without a great deal to say when Pareto cannot
be used.

COMPETITION AND THE OPTIMUM

It has been suggested many times in these chapters that perfect
competition will lead to an optimum allocation of resources. If we can
pick some point on the grand utility frontier as "best" on welfare
grounds, then perfect competition will lead to an allocation of resources that permits achievement of that best. Proof of this statement
requires an elaborate logical argument. Many parts of the argument
have been introduced in this book. For instance, we have described
the way in which each consumer maximizes his own well-being. We
have analyzed the way exchange enables individuals to reach an
"efficient" distribution of goods. We have shown how firms adjust
their production to reach the production-possibilities frontier and how
industries adjust to the long-run competitive equilibrium. These and
other examples indicate the nature of the argument, but we have not
been rigorous enough nor inclusive enough in these chapters to claim
that the proposition is proved. It is, however, one of the most important assets of the perfectly competitive model that the proposition
can be proved. This means that we know fully the implications of assuming perfect competition together with the other assumptions and
conditions of economic theory. We cannot say as much for the assumption of oligopoly, or monopolistic competition, or even perfect monopoly. Economists have no other model whose implications are so
elaborate and so clearly established. Perfect competition is therefore a
powerful tool for use in positive economic analysis, but it also appears
to many as an extremely attractive goal for economic policy.

THE ROLE OF PRICES

Prices play a key role in the achievement of an optimum under perfect competition. In fact, perfect competition is defined as a situation

in which choosers take prices as given. Thus each consumer allocates income among goods on the assumption that the price of each good is given no matter what allocation is made. The producer also chooses output as if that choice will leave both input and output prices unaffected. Every actor on the competitive scene makes a decision by reference to some "going price." The going price summarizes the activities of everyone else in the market and presents that summary in a simple, convenient form that is nevertheless adequate to guide the choice that must be made.

Since prices determine choices, they also determine the quantities bought, produced, and sold, and changes in prices will therefore change those quantities. We have argued in fact that under perfect competition, prices will adjust until each market is brought into equilibrium. Some prices will rise, increasing quantity supplied and reducing quantity demanded until any excess demand is eliminated. Other prices will fall until any excess supply is eliminated. It is one of the theorems of the perfectly competitive model that there exists a set of prices that is consistent with equilibrium in all markets at once. At general equilibrium prices, the choices of all buyers, sellers, and producers will prevent either excess supply or excess demand in any market.

CENTRAL PLANNING AND PRICES

The efficiency with which prices guide an economy toward the optimum under perfect competition has led central planners to consider using prices. If a central planning committee seeks to centralize all choices among alternatives, it quickly finds its information needs overwhelming. Information about individual preference patterns, technological production possibilities, supplies of skills and other resources must be gathered in one place and collated. This is an impossibly large project, but only a first step. The information must then be processed into a set of choices that are consistent with some pattern of preferences. This is another very complex job, and once it is complete then the behavior must be directed in ways consistent with those choices. This presents a management problem that is probably unsolvable.

Faced with such a large and difficult problem, it is obviously tempting to suggest that a central planning commission try to use some equivalent to competitive prices to simplify at least some of these tasks. Such a set of equivalent prices would have to have certain characteristics, which are easily recognized from earlier discussions of maximizing behavior.

The planning commission would have to decree that all inputs and outputs have the same price for all individuals.

Then the given set of prices would have to be consistent with equilibrium in every market. They would have to be general equilibrium prices. This is a most demanding condition unless it is possible for the planning commission to use the same sort of cut-and-try process we used to describe private markets. What is required is that the commission be able to audit exchanges of all goods and raise the price wherever excess demand appears and lower the price wherever excess supply appears.

Moreover, individuals will have to be given incentives to make their choices in the light of this set of prices. For instance, the managers of factories might be required to maximize profits at those prices, and then their own incomes might be tied in some way to their success. Similar incentives would have to be found for all other economic groups.

Needless to say, it is also important that individuals be free to respond to those incentives, that there be no barriers to the mobility of resources in this planned economy.

Even if it is possible to find a set of prices and incentives that meet these requirements, there are obvious economies in knowledge gathering, information processing, and management of a planned economy. These are the economies claimed for a competitive, private market economy, and they derive from its use of prices. They may look very attractive to central planners, however. The planning commission must then accept as its goal the kind of optimum that is achievable under perfect competition. This is essentially a private rather than a group optimum. It depends on individual responses to established prices. It is usually one of the strongest arguments for central planning, however, that it will permit group needs and desires to be ranked ahead of private, essentially selfish needs and desires. The grand utility frontier to which these prices and motives lead is defined by private preference patterns. A central planning commission is likely to find that outcome inconsistent with its basic goals, and even a competitive market economy will find it a severe limitation. It therefore deserves a bit more discussion.

PUBLIC GOODS

The competitive general equilibrium does not include what are called public goods. These goods have two important characteristics. Once a public good is produced, it will add nothing more to its production costs for another person to enjoy it. Moreover, once it is produced, it is impossible to exclude any person from enjoying it. Because of these characteristics, public goods are not likely to be produced and sold in private markets, no matter how important they may be to the well-being of individuals.

Our national parks are a public good with the first of these characteristics. Up to the point where the park gets overcrowded, its use by one person does not reduce its capacity to provide enjoyment to another. Consumption of this good is not rivalrous as it is in the case of a bottle of beer. When one person drinks a bottle of beer, no other person can do so. The person who drinks the beer pays for the right to be the one who gets to drink it. The price rations the supply among demanders. We could charge a person for looking at a waterfall, but this would be inefficient. There is no need for price to ration the view of the waterfall among demanders. The supply of "view" is unlimited (up to the capacity of the national park) relative to the demand simply because a person who consumes the view does not reduce the supply available for someone else to consume as well. Charging a price for the view would reduce the well-being of those individuals who were thereby excluded from the view without making the view any better for those who pay their money and look.

National defense is the most commonly used example of a good with the second characteristic. If our country is adequately defended, then any new citizen will get the benefit of that defense, and within very large limits the addition of new citizens will not increase its costs. No firm can produce and sell national defense simply because they cannot exclude from its benefits anyone who will not pay for it. Nevertheless, the benefits of national defense to each citizen are large. A citizen would presumably be willing to pay for those benefits if private markets could provide the opportunity. Private markets cannot, and so public goods will be underproduced, in the light of their benefits, in a purely private market economy. This is not the only shortcoming of the perfectly competitive optimum. We also need to consider externalities and monopoly.

EXTERNALITIES

By now it should be clear why the externalities discussed in Chapter 14 are so important. Getting onto the grand utility frontier using competitive markets requires that people respond to prices. Those prices must accurately reflect costs and benefits if they are to direct resources into their optimum uses. Wherever an externality exists, however, the market price will fail. The price of steel will not cover the cost of inputs used to clean the smoke-damaged drapes. Steel will appear cheaper relative to other goods than it really is, and consumers will buy more steel than is consistent with an optimum allocation of resources. On the other hand, the price of electricity will have to be high enough to cover all the costs of the hydroelectric dam project. The dam will produce a recreation area as well, and so some of its costs should be covered by the sale of recreation. The sale of such by-products, however, is often impossible or undesirable in a private market economy. Thus electricity will sell at too high a price, and a less-than-optimum amount will be produced. We must therefore note that any claim that the utility frontier under competition maximizes welfare depends on the extent to which externalities can be internalized. The steel company must bear the costs of preventing the smoke or cover the cost of cleaning the drapes. The electric company must be permitted to sell the recreation output of its reservoir. As we argued in Chapter 14, these adjustments are usually very difficult and sometimes impossible.

MONOPOLY

Finally, it is true that the competitive optimum cannot be achieved if some buyers or sellers are monopolists. Monopoly always results in a smaller output and a higher price when compared to the price and output of a competitive industry that is otherwise the same. Thus the quantity of resources used to produce the monopoly good will be less than optimum, and the economy will not reach the grand utility frontier. This problem is especially important because of the existence of natural monopolies. For technological reasons some industries under the regime of competition will become monopolies. No private conspiracy nor government support is needed. No public policy can prevent the situation from arising.

There is an interesting additional problem here. The misallocation of resources caused by monopoly will not occur if all buyers and sellers are monopolists. It can be proved that a world of monopolies will reach the utility frontier. This opens up the possibility that the community woud be worse off if we broke up some but not all monopolies. In fact, it is true that changes that bring the economy closer to meeting the conditions for an optimum, but do not enable it to meet all of those conditions, may in fact make it worse off. This is the conclusion of the "theory of the second best."

THE SECOND BEST

The theory of the second best is concerned with the question of whether we should try to meet some of the conditions for an optimum when we realize that not all of them can be met. Its discouraging conclusion is that we can have no assurance that meeting some but not all optimum conditions will make us better off. This is very unfortunate since most of the things we can do are piecemeal. Some monopolies can be broken up, but it is unlikely that all can be. We may be able to internalize some but not all externalities. We may set up markets for some but not all public goods. It is not certain nor even likely that these partial moves will make us better off.

SUMMARY

Welfare economics is concerned with policies that propose to make the community better off. The economist is concerned with his own capacity to make recommendations about such policies. This chapter has been a very brief summary of the economic analysis of that concern. It is a much more extensive field than these notes can suggest. It must, however, be quite clear that welfare economics is very complicated and very interesting. It is probably fair to say that to date the primary output of study in this field has been an understanding of some limits on the capacity of the economist to recommend policy. This is no small achievement.

Even though the economist has limited power to formulate policy, he has a substantial contribution to make in the implementation of policy. Wherever the policy goal is widely accepted or can be formulated by the government, the economist is well equipped to recommend techniques for its accomplishment, and to analyze its side effects. It is the content of the first eighteen of chapters that equips him for this job. The power of the tools developed in those chapters should not be underrated. Positive economic theory is the most useful model of human behavior ever invented.

SELECTED READINGS

Arrow, Kenneth J. *Social Choice and Individual Values* (New York: John Wiley & Sons, 1951).

Little, I. M. D. *A Critique of Welfare Economics,* 2d ed. (London: Oxford University Press, 1960), chaps. 1–4.

Mishan, E. J. "A Survey of Welfare Economics, 1939–1959," *Economic Journal,* vol. 70 (1960), pp. 197–265.

Index

This book has been set linotype in 10 and 9 point Times Roman, leaded 2 points. Part numbers and titles and chapter numbers and titles are 18 point Broadway. The size of the type page is 26 by 46 picas.